OUTDOOR ACTIVITIES, NEGLIGENCE AND THE LAW

Outdoor Activities, Negligence and the Law

JULIAN FULBROOK
London School of Economics, UK

Published by
Ashgate Publishing Limited
Gower House
Croft Road
Aldershot
Hampshire GU11 3HR
England

Ashgate Publishing Company
Suite 420
101 Cherry Street
Burlington, VT 05401-4405
USA

Ashgate website: http://www.ashgate.com

British Library Cataloguing in Publication Data
Fulbrook, Julian
   Outdoor activities, negligence and the law
   1. Liability for school accidents - Great Britain
   2. Liability for sports accidents - Great Britain
   3. Recreation - Law and legislation - Great Britain
   I. Title
   344.4'1075

Library of Congress Cataloging-in-Publication Data
Fulbrook, Julian.
Outdoor activities, negligence, and the law / by Julian Fulbrook.
     p. cm.
   Includes bibliographical references and index.
   ISBN 0-7546-4235-6
  1. Liability for schools accidents--Great Britain. 2. Liability for sports
accidents--Great Britain. 3. Recreation--Law and legislation--Great Britain.
I. Title.

  KD1994.F85 2005
  344.41'075--dc22

2005017283

ISBN-10: 0 7546 4235 6
ISBN-13: 978-0-7546-4235-0

Reprinted 2007

Printed and bound in Great Britain by Antony Rowe Ltd, Chippenham, Wiltshire.

Contents

Preface

This book aims to set out a concise account of the law on outdoor activities. In particular, it analyses the yardsticks of negligence and statutory liability on which judgements are made in the courts about teachers, volunteers and leaders.

In recent years, perhaps because of a series of high-profile legal cases, there has developed what amounts almost to an irrational terror, particularly in staff rooms, on what the law seeks to do. This has been compounded by the attitude of some teaching unions; for example, after the inquest in 2002 on two teenagers who were swept away at Stainforth Beck in the Yorkshire Dales, Nigel de Gruchy, the General Secretary of the National Association of Schoolmasters Union of Women Teachers (NASUWT), stated that 'We have reluctantly concluded that until society accepts the notion of a genuine accident, it is advisable for members not to go on school trips'. That remains the policy of his union. Unfortunately such an attitude imperils the off-site learning of millions of young people, who lose out on an array of experiences which could do much to enhance their education and develop their maturity.

Mythologies have burgeoned, which appear to suggest that the legal process has a malign intent to undermine any prospect of adventure in the outdoors, or indeed any school trip to undertake field work, or to visit libraries, the theatre, museums, or even the local park. When the Chief Inspector of Schools, David Bell, indicated after his Ofsted report in September 2004, *Outdoor Education: Aspects of Good Practice*, that teachers had 'nothing to fear' if they followed the right guidelines, he was assailed from all sides. Acerbic comments were made on 'parasitical lawyers', 'a culture of litigation', 'professional careers wrecked due to what many would see as an accident', 'paperwork', 'medical forms', 'risk assessments', and the recycling of Mr de Gruchy's comment that the existing guidelines are 'virtually impossible for any normal human being to follow'. Such statements seem to ascribe a deliberate strategy to the legal process, with a purpose designed to denigrate the teaching profession and the voluntary organizations who provide a very high percentage of outdoor activities for young people, and to make life as difficult as possible for local education authorities and other providers.

On the contrary, this book will demonstrate that an analysis of the legal cases shows some very straightforward principles in the law on outdoor activities. While the criminal law is occasionally invoked for serious wrongdoing, most of the cases are civil claims for compensation based on common law principles of tort and on statute. And interestingly, the number of legal claims is going down, contrary to popular misconception. Although the law may appear on occasions to be a mysterious process, there has been a rational development of guidelines in these cases, and it would be helpful if these were more widely known.

In addition, there has been a great deal of research around the world to establish the precise causes of deaths and injuries in the outdoors. Sadly, very few of these instances indicate what Mr de Gruchy terms 'a genuine accident'. What they usually demonstrate is that organizers failed to follow some well-worn pathways of 'good practice'. That is also the basic legal standard that tort law seeks to support. So it is vital that lessons are learned from those occasions when matters go wrong in outdoor activities. While the fatalities on school trips hit the headlines, those in relation to voluntary organizations are not always analysed in such detail, but they are no less illuminating. Similarly, Britain is not alone in sustaining injuries and 'near misses', nor in developing legal principles in relation to them, so it is important to look at comparative experience elsewhere.

Perhaps the best-known case on a school trip disaster is that of the deaths of four teenagers at Lyme Bay in 1993. Its unique features led both to the first successful prosecution for manslaughter of an activity centre and its owner, and also to legislation in the Activity Centres (Young Persons Safety) Act 1995. However, as we shall see, the remit of the Adventure Activities Licensing Authority (AALA) set up under that Act does not cover many school trips in Britain; certainly none of them abroad; nor does it deal with most of the activities of voluntary organizations, either at home or abroad; and there are other quite significant areas of outdoor activities which are wholly outside the legislation. In retrospect it would seem that this Act of Parliament was a 'sledgehammer to crack a nut', drawing up tight regulations from a particularly heinous set of circumstances at Lyme Bay, which now restrict activities which, on the whole, are well-conducted. Nevertheless it is clear that, outside its narrow legislative focus, the AALA licensing authority has had an immensely powerful influence on safety generally in the outdoors in Britain. Not only has the inspection service done much useful work in researching fatalities and injuries but its publications are outstanding, so it has been possible for all those engaged in outdoor and adventurous activities to learn some key lessons. When in response to the latest tragedy the Government of the day invariably considers drawing up yet more 'new guidelines', then a wise response of Parliament and the courts would be to look at what the AALA and others have already discerned to be appropriate responses which could forestall harm.

This book is written as a legal analysis, but hopefully it can prove useful for the general reader, for organizers of outdoor activities, and for those interested in examining the law in its social and historical context. Part One looks in detail at providers and participants, analysing the Lyme Bay case which led to the 1995 legislation, and then at the subsequent fatalities in respect of both schools and the less well-explored area of voluntary youth organizations such as Scouts and Cadets. Part Two of the book examines the legal principles, and particularly that central concept of the Duty of Care which governs cases for civil compensation in the law of tort. Finally, in the third part, there is a drawing together of the law and its practical application to outdoor activities, with the hope that this will lead to further research that will prove helpful in preventative measures against what are clearly risks in the outdoors – but these are by no means risks so overwhelming that they should halt outdoor activities, and certainly not by reason of an irrational fear of litigation.

I owe a great debt to many people and institutions. I would like to thank my colleagues and students at the LSE who have provided great assistance and many useful comments, and in particular: Stuart Andrews; Jesse Elvin; Colleen Etheridge; Carol Harlow; David Person; Tamara Relis; Bob Simpson; Giorgio Monti; and Bill Wedderburn. Richard Lewis at Cardiff University has been a sustaining force over many years. In the world of outdoor activities I would first like to thank my brother Paul, not only for sharing my first expeditions, but many others by land and water. In addition the expert input of Graham Bucknell, Sheila Collins, Ross Faragher, Mark Gittoes, Ray Goodwin, and Jim Raffan has been extremely helpful. Marcus Bailie kindly read through a draft in advance, and while he will not necessarily agree with all the judgments, not least on the AALA, this was invaluable. The library staff of the Institute of Advanced Legal Studies and the British Library of Political and Economic Science in London have been very accommodating, as have the staff at the incomparable Harvard Law School Library on several summer forays. Finally I would like to thank my wife Mary and our three children, not just for enduring some rugged terrain and campsites in the pursuit of 'research', but for being very supportive throughout. Any errors that remain are my own.

Julian Fulbrook
London, April 2005

List of Abbreviations

AALA	Adventure Activities Licensing Authority
APIL	Association of Personal Injury Lawyers
BCU	British Canoe Union
CCF	Combined Cadet Force
CPR	Cardio-pulmonary resuscitation
DfES	Department for Education and Skills
DofE	The Duke of Edinburgh's Award scheme
HASPEV	Good Practice Guide for Health and Safety of Pupils on Educational Visits
HSC	Health and Safety Commission
HSE	Health and Safety Executive
LEA	Local Education Authority
MLTUK	Mountain Leader Training UK
MoD	Ministry of Defence
NASUWT	The National Association of Schoolmasters Union of Women Teachers
Ofsted	Office for Standards in Education
RoSPA	The Royal Society for the Prevention of Accidents
RYA	Royal Yachting Association
UCAS	Universities and Colleges Admissions Service
volenti	*volenti non fit injuria*, a legal defence, which translates from the Latin maxim as 'No injury is done to one who consents'.

Chapter 1

Introduction

When four teenagers on a school trip at a Lyme Bay activity centre died in 1993, it sparked a major public debate on the safety of outdoor pursuits. This kayaking tragedy led to a custodial sentence for the owner on manslaughter charges, to the passing of a private member's bill which became the Activity Centres (Young Persons Safety) Act 1995, and to a raised awareness of safety issues for schools and activity organizations.

But has the balance swung too far? Is there now an aversion to risk, and the threat of legal culpability, which has become counter-productive? Are we in danger of being 'over-lawyered' in the outdoors? Are we losing sight of the considerable advantages that adventurous activities can give to participants, and in particular to the development of young people? And what of the much vaunted 'compensation culture'; is it myth or reality? And even if it is merely a mythical perception, what effect, if any, does this have on outdoor activities?

Criminal charges

In the decade since November 1994, when the Lyme Bay defendants, OLL Ltd and Peter Kite, its managing director, were convicted of manslaughter, there have inevitably been other tragedies leading to the courts. Lyme Bay is unique because it was the first immediate custodial sentence for a company director on a corporate manslaughter charge.[1] One important point in the Lyme Bay case was that it was possible to pinpoint a 'directing mind' in such a small company, whereas in a large business, as with the Zeebrugge disaster in 1987, when 188 people died after the capsize of the ferry *Herald of Free Enterprise*, criminal charges failed because no individual senior personnel were found to be sufficiently at fault. Private prosecutions were also brought after 51 people died on the *Marchioness* when this pleasure cruiser on the Thames sank in 1989, and after the explosion of the offshore oilrig *Piper Alpha* which killed 167 people in 1988; but in both cases these failed for lack of evidence. When the trawler *Pescado* sank in 1991 with the loss of all six crew, the managing agent Joseph O'Connor was acquitted of manslaughter, but was found guilty of gross negligence and was sentenced to three

---

[1] The co-directors of a Lancashire plastics factory were prosecuted after a worker had died falling into a machine in 1988, which was the first work-related manslaughter charge. Norman Holt received a suspended sentence of 12 months' imprisonment. In addition he, his brother David, the managing director, and their company David Holt Plastics Limited, were fined a total of £47,000; 'Director guilty in factory death', *The Independent* (2 December 1989).

years' imprisonment. It can therefore be seen that manslaughter charges are both complicated to bring and very difficult to succeed with.

A very important and unique instance of a teacher being imprisoned, following a school trip, was the case in 2003 of Paul Ellis, who was sentenced to 12 months after Max Palmer, aged ten, drowned in Glenridding Beck while engaged in 'pool plunging'. Mr Ellis, who was head of geography at Fleetwood High School, pleaded guilty to a charge of manslaughter, admitting that his conduct had fallen so far short of a reasonable standard of care that it amounted to 'gross negligence'. Morland J at Manchester Crown Court stated that he had initially considered passing a three year prison sentence, as the teacher had in his view been 'unbelievably foolhardy and negligent', but accepted factors in mitigation.[2] Mr Ellis was a member of Britain's second largest teaching union, the NASUWT, who for several years have urged their members not to lead or participate in school trips. The union refused to comment after the sentence on Mr Ellis, but the general secretary of another union, David Hart of the National Association of Head Teachers, noted that this case 'demonstrates all too clearly the very vulnerable position teachers are in if they act recklessly and without due regard for the safety of pupils in their care'.[3] The current general secretary of the NASUWT, Chris Keates, told the House of Commons select committee on education in 2005 that her members 'faced spurious legal action from parents unable to accept that there was such a thing as a genuine accident' and that there was a 'huge fear of litigation in schools'.[4] The NASUWT claim to have supported twenty members in legal action relating to school trips in the last three years, although only Mr Ellis faced criminal proceedings. This is in the context of a Government estimate that there are around 7 million outdoor school visits each year, although this is probably rather narrowly defined; even so there must be thousands of school trips each week.[5] However, any attempt to make Mr Ellis into a martyr seem doomed to failure; the subsequent Health and Safety Executive's report on Glenridding Beck in 2005 is absolutely damning and the case is clearly an aberration on the normal conduct of school trips. Dr Stephen Garsed, the HSE inspector, concluded that the two main causes of the tragedy were 'the inappropriate actions of the leader' and weaknesses in school management which allowed an 'unsuitable leader to be in charge of a party of schoolchildren in a high-hazard environment'. His investigation showed that the teacher had lied about his leadership qualifications; he failed to make the most basic inquiries about whether the children in his care could swim; he took his group to the hills and to jump into Glenridding Beck with no protective clothing such as wetsuits, waterproofs or buoyancy aids; he allowed the children to 'plunge' when the water temperature was just 8 degrees, the stream was 'raging' after heavy rain, and when he had been starkly warned by teachers in another school group that

[2] 'Teacher is jailed over boy's trip death', *Yorkshire Post* (23 September 2003).
[3] Ibid.
[4] 'Outdoors is great: just about the safest place a child could be is on a school trip', *The Guardian* (15 March 2005).
[5] Department for Education and Skills (DfES), 'Outdoor learning' (Press release 15 February 2005).

the pool was 'too dangerous' in these conditions; and he had no rescue equipment such as a throwbag, nor indeed the knowledge of how to use it.[6] The Glenridding Beck investigation in 2005, and the criminal trial of Paul Ellis in 2003, therefore reveal a hopelessly reckless disregard for safety judged against any guidelines or indeed against even plain common sense. It is indeed a textbook example on most of the obvious issues in how *not* to lead an outdoor trip.

In an earlier case involving drownings, after two schoolgirls had lost their footing in October 2000 and had been swept away in Stainforth Beck, the Crown Prosecution Service decided there was not enough evidence to prosecute teachers, senior school staff or Leeds City Council for manslaughter. This Stainforth Beck case arose out of a 'river walking trip' on an annual adventure week, but there were clear distinctions from Glenridding Beck, as the full hazards of this 'low risk activity' were not clearly understood at the time and the actions of the teachers were not judged by the coroner to have met the standard of 'unlawful killing by gross negligence'. This was a controversial view, contrary to the evidence of several witnesses and the protests of the parents.[7] However, one of the expert witnesses at the inquest was Marcus Bailie, Head of Inspection at the AALA; he actually praised the actions of the teachers, who he said had 'acted in a way which was exemplary and perhaps heroic', after the teenagers had been swept away.[8] Nonetheless he pointed to serious lessons to be learned from this case, such as an underestimation of 'the power of water' and 'inherent practical weaknesses with joint leadership'.[9] The Health and Safety Executive subsequently prosecuted Leeds City Council on lesser charges, for breach of health and safety regulations, leading to a fine of £30,000 plus the costs of the HSE amounting to £50,000.[10]

Other teachers and drivers concerned in school trips abroad have been prosecuted for manslaughter equivalence infractions: for example in 2002 Mark Duckworth, a teacher from Cockburn High School in Leeds won an appeal in a French court against a suspended sentence for six months' imprisonment on involuntary homicide after Gemma Carter drowned at Le Touquet.[11] Several lessons need again to be learned from that case of 'impromptu paddling' at the seaside after an evening meal.

Manslaughter has different aspects, but an important facet of one sort of manslaughter is death through 'gross negligence', and Professor Slapper has shown how 'the offence occupies an indistinct place between, in modern terms, tort and

---

[6] Health and Safety Executive, *Glenridding Beck* (28 February 2002). See also 'Teachers assured over school trips', *Daily Telegraph* (10 March 2005), 'Safety watchdog blames teacher for boy's drowning on school trip', *The Guardian* (10 March 2005).
[7] 'Parents attack "hurtful" inquest verdict', *The Guardian* (9 March 2002).
[8] Ibid.
[9] Marcus Bailie, 'Lessons learned from Stainforth Beck?', *Institute for Outdoor Learning* (20 August 2003).
[10] *The Independent* (28 February 2003).
[11] 'Teacher's sentence quashed on a school trip', *The Times* (17 April 2002).

crime'.[12] As indicated by Lord Mackay of Clashfern LC in the leading case on manslaughter, *R v Adomako*, it is also 'open to a trial judge to use the word "reckless" if it appears appropriate'.[13] Whether the kind of conduct required for a manslaughter charge is portrayed as either 'gross negligence' or 'reckless', this criminal law standard is clearly a level above the civil compensation threshold of 'ordinary negligence'. However, the borderline is inevitably opaque and a 'jury question' to determine on the individual circumstances of each case. Some commentators have called for changes in the law, which would allow for reform of the current manslaughter provisions, and its supplementation by an offence of 'corporate killing', which might set a lower barrier for the culpability of trip leaders and their organizations. A proposal in the Queen's Speech in November 2004 now heralds Parliamentary debate on a draft Bill, which is to be published shortly. Although this measure has been promised for some considerable time and the complexities have been much debated, it is not entirely clear what potential criminal liabilities, if any, might impinge on schools and outdoor organizations in the future. One critic, a partner in the leading solicitors' firm Ince & Co, has suggested that such a 'blame culture satisfies an understandable demand for retribution but drives mistakes underground. This deprives the wider community of the lessons to be learned'.[14]

Civil claims

However, the more important focus of the law on outdoor activities is on civil remedies to obtain compensation for injuries. The last decade since Lyme Bay has seen a small number of high-profile investigations and civil claims, leading to significant alarm in schools, clubs and organizations about their legal liability. The mechanisms for such civil claims is the tort of negligence, which sets yardsticks for a duty of care which may be owed to participants, but there are many mythologies about both the hazards of outdoor pursuits and also the hazards of litigation. To read some commentaries it would appear dangerous in the extreme to organize any outing for youngsters at all. There also seems to have developed in some quarters a repeated mantra about a 'blame culture' which has allegedly been sapping the very fabric of society. For example, Professor Atiyah, the distinguished analyst of tort, has argued that the law is 'too generous' and that he along with 'many members of the public feel uneasy about the increasing spate of claims for damages'.[15] A High Court judge, Rougier J, commented in 1996 that 'It is a truism to say that we live

---

[12] Gary Slapper, *Blood in the Bank: social and legal aspects of death at work* (Aldershot: Ashgate Dartmouth, 1999) 19.

[13] *R v Adomako* [1994] 3 All ER 79 at 89. See *Archbold Criminal Pleading, Evidence and Practice* (London: Sweet & Maxwell, 2004) 19-108 et seq on manslaughter by gross negligence.

[14] Anthony Fitzsimmons, 'Corporate killing bill "politically motivated",' *Lloyd's List* (29 November 2004).

[15] P.S.Atiyah, *The Damages Lottery* (Oxford: Hart, 1997) 138 and 'blame culture' at 139.

in the age of compensation' and that 'There seems to be a growing belief that every misfortune must, in pecuniary terms at any rate, be laid at someone else's door, and after every mishap, every tragedy, the cupped palms are outstretched for the solace of monetary compensation. Claims which would have been unheard of 30 years ago are now being seriously entertained, and public money provided for pursuing them.'[16] The result of such academic and judicial commentary no doubt reinforced Nigel de Gruchy, then the general secretary of NASUWT, to advise his members in 2001 against taking any pupils whatsoever on any school trips, especially abroad.[17] This advice is still the policy of the union, and the current general secretary, Chris Keates, indicated in June 2004 that this was because 'in recent high-profile cases teachers have been heavily penalized. Some have lost [their] jobs as a result of alleged misjudgments.'[18] The NASUWT remain the only teaching union advising its member to boycott school trips, but Ms Keates welcomed an announcement in 2005 by Ruth Kelly, the Secretary of State for Education, which the NASUWT felt 'recognized that the genuine concerns of teachers about the risks involved in participating in educational visits needed to be addressed seriously'.[19] This was a promise of a 'manifesto for education outside the classroom', which the Prime Minister, Tony Blair, indicated (from on board a sailing dinghy in a Worcestershire activity centre during the 2005 General Election campaign) would introduce 'some simple guidelines so if teachers follow those they are not going to be at risk of legal action'.[20]

What is an outdoor activity?

Like many common phrases, the main subject under analysis is not readily definable. The 1995 legislation indicates 'adventurous activities' as its remit, but it deals only with certain outdoor activities. The AALA lists its purview under four main headings – climbing; watersports; trekking and caving – and gives some very helpful advice on definitions that have advanced this debate. North Americans refer to 'experiential education'. Insurance companies often make a demarcation between 'sports' and 'outdoor pursuits', but these are in reality overlapping arenas. An exhaustive categorization of outdoor activities is also not possible because frequently an activity changes its name with geographical location: for example, a distinction is made by some between 'gorge running' and 'ghyll running', although much depends on a north-south language divide in Britain; a description of the latter as 'you wrap up in several layers of clothing, waterproofs and a helmet' before going 'into the water and back downhill following the ghyll's natural

---

[16] Rougier J in *John Munroe (Acrylics) Ltd v London Fire and Civil Defence Authority* [1996] 4 All ER 318 at 332.

[17] *BBC News Online*, 26 July 2001.

[18] 'Teenager killed in cliff fall during college trip', *The Guardian* (16 June 2004).

[19] 'Teachers told not to fear lawyers', *Daily Telegraph* (16 February 2005).

[20] 'Teaching union refuses to call off school trips boycott: Blair offers guidelines to avoid legal action', *Yorkshire Post* (16 February 2005).

course, wading through pools, down waterfalls and even jumping off waterfalls' gives the general idea of both activities.[21] Some of this distinction is no doubt etymological, but when the OED defines a ghyll as a 'deep ravine', a gorge as a 'narrow opening between hills', and a ravine as a 'deep narrow gorge' then pursuit of an ultimate definition for this activity appears somewhat circular. But the hazards relating to variables such as depth and speed of the water and height of the obstructions in such activities need to be assessed for their unique configuration and dealt with accordingly. Indeed, there is a bewildering array of outdoor activities and sports. Youth activities such as those associated with cheerleading and marching bands, which can take place indoors as well as outdoors, would probably not normally be considered, but then a leading case in the Court of Appeal in 2004, *Blake v Galloway*,[22] dealt with the important issue of 'horseplay' during unstructured time in the outdoors at a field study centre in Devon during an interlude in music-making conducted indoors. Just as with sports there are some distinct anomalies; Andrew Faulds, who won the gold medal in Sydney in clay pigeon shooting was accused by his PE teacher at school of 'completely lacking hand-eye co-ordination', because of his inability to excel at sports such as football or cricket,[23] and certainly this clay pigeon shooting does not seem quite on a par with other Olympic events such as the marathon or the decathlon.

Although the anomalies and fringe areas could be endlessly debated, this legal monograph investigates the main outdoor activities and these deal principally with hills and mountains,[24] water,[25] snowsports,[26] air activities,[27] and equestrian sports, many of which, like the last, have a wide spectrum, from ponytrekking through to eventing. No claim is made to be exhaustive, although no doubt even an esoteric activity like 'zorbing' will eventually produce some need for legal analysis – bouncing downhill inside a large inflatable PVC ball, originating in New Zealand, also known as 'sphereing' or 'the human hamster ball', with already two distinct methods emerging, and a safety code for adventure-tour operators and an accreditation scheme in New Zealand.[28] Sadly, even such a seemingly innocent activity as playing with a snowball has its attendant risks; in 2005 Peter Strang,

---

[21] 'Ghyll Scrambling', Newlands Adventure Centre (registered with the Adventure Activities Licensing Authority), the UK's 'longest established' adventure centre near Keswick, celebrating its centenary in 2005.

[22] [2004] 3 All ER 315.

[23] 'Olympic Games: ice-man Faulds keeps cool to shoot gold: psychological training pays dividend for Britain in tense shoot-off', *The Guardian* (21 September 2000).

[24] Abseiling, bouldering, canyoning, caving, climbing, off-road cycling, gorge walking in its various incarnations, ice climbing, orienteering and scrambling.

[25] Canoeing, sailing, kayaking, motorboats of all sorts, rowing, snorkeling and sub-aqua, surfing, swimming and diving, rafting, and windsurfing.

[26] Downhill and cross-country skiing, snowboarding.

[27] Ballooning, flying, gliding, microlighting, parachuting, paragliding, parascending and bungee jumping.

[28] A harness zorb strapped into a padded safety harness, and a hydro zorb where 'a few bucketfuls of water are thrown in, which makes the surface slippery and prevents friction burns'; 'Just call me the... Human Hamster', *Mail on Sunday* (20 February 2005).

aged ten, was playing with his friends near Aberdeen when he was crushed by a snowball, thought to weigh a quarter of a ton. The Grampian police indicated, in words that are so often used in reports on fatalities of all descriptions, that it was 'a freak accident'. However unlikely such an untoward event it has now inevitably to be logged as potentially hazardous, with a warning to others.[29]

Insurance is a key determinant of definitions in outdoor activities, with much dependant on contractual definitions. For most providers a certificate of insurance will be decisive, but different companies have differing perspectives on the 'hazardous sports' they will not cover. For example, some companies exclude a 'wilful exposure to risk', which can embrace matters such as off-piste skiing. As injuries relating to winter sports account for 40 per cent of all injury claims dealt with by a major travel insurance carrier such as American Express, such exclusions are an important consideration. Even policies targeted directly at sports enthusiasts have surprising restrictions. Again, American Express's Accident and Injury Plan, which pays out lump-sum benefits, states that policy-holders are 'covered for most popular sports as an amateur player'. Squash, skiing and cycling are covered, but the small print shows that football and rugby, two of the most popular participation sports in the world, are excluded.

Although 'sport' is a term that covers many pastimes, indoors and outdoors, the emerging area of Sports Law has concentrated on competitive sports, and notably the world's leading game of football. There has been a remarkable surge of interest in that field, and texts on Sports Law now deal with many disparate and related areas such as sports governance, dispute resolution, broadcasting rights, competition law, marketing and sponsorship. However, it is notable that there seems to be a dearth of legal literature on how the tort of negligence is applied to outdoor activities, some of which are sports, but many of which are not. For example in one excellent text on Sports Law there are, comparatively, just a few pages on 'Tort and Sport'.[30] My study therefore analyses complementary issues of civil liability in largely unexplored terrain. The aim is to focus on the legal liability of organizers, schools and 'providers'; to examine critically the rules laid down by cases and legislation; to consider the practical applications; and to suggest further lines of research.

The realistic appraisal of risk

Nothing is of course risk free, but it is very important that the debate on outdoor activities is based on facts rather than mythology. Certainly there are many potential hazards in outdoor pursuits. But these hazards are often well understood: for example, the danger of drowning when engaged in water activities; the danger of falls, whether of the mundane but potentially lethal 'trip and slip' variety, or of tumbling from a height when hillwalking or climbing; and the potentially catastrophic injuries of 'extreme sports' such as a recent craze for snowboarding

[29] 'Boy killed by giant snowball', *The Guardian* (1 March 2005).
[30] Michael J. Beloff, Tim Kerr, Marie Demetriou, *Sports Law* (Oxford: Hart, 1999) 111-125.

down glaciers.[31] In many situations not only are the hazards very much in contemplation by organizers and participants, but extensive preventative measures are in place to deal with them. The research shows that when there are *organized* activities the actual risks are remarkably low. For example, despite a series of high-profile tragedies on school trips, there have actually been only around 50 deaths in the two decades since 1985, and a single coach crash on the M40 in 1993 was responsible for thirteen of these fatalities. In the context that Britain has around 10 million school-age children, all of whom might spend two days or so on out-of-school activities each year, the average of three deaths a year gives a statistically insignificant fatality rate, although of course any death in such activities is an unimaginable loss for those personally affected and it is essential to do everything possible to prevent such tragedies. In 2004, a memorandum from the Health and Safety Executive to the House of Commons select committee on education pointed out that 'fatalities on school trips are very rare', and that in the previous year there had been just one, with the HSE attempting to 'encourage a sensible approach to health and safety – managing risk not trying to eliminate it altogether'.[32] The educational journalist and former teacher, Philip Revell, estimates that 'Children are slightly less likely to be struck by lightning'.[33] Indeed, even staying in the school playground is no complete guarantee that you would escape the very unlikely possibility of being hit by lightning; in a remarkable escape in 2001 Isaiah Blundell was playing football at school in Chadwell Heath when a bolt of lightning struck him, but teachers and the school nurse administered cardiopulmonary resuscitation until an ambulance crew took over, and he subsequently made a recovery.[34]

On the whole, schools, clubs, the national governing bodies of outdoor sports, and the main youth organizations have a very solid and impressive safety record in Britain. The occasional tragedies that occur in these planned activities should not be minimized, but they are rare. There are usually further lessons to be learned, often about the *disorganized* nature of activities that fall below acceptable standards. These occasional failures should certainly not be used to ban participation in outdoor activities, particularly by young people who have so much to gain from them. A study in the *Journal of the Royal Society of Medicine* in 2000 concluded that 'Everything we do has an associated risk... the health risks of

---

[31] 'The ultimate escapade when a Frenchman snowboarded from the summit of Everest ... extreme snowboarding and skiing are very advanced and dangerous pursuits, undertaken down steep, sometimes rocky terrain, where a fall could reap fatal consequences'; 'The 50 Best Adventure Sports', *The Independent* (12 January 2002).

[32] House of Commons Select Committee on Education and Skills, *Written Evidence* (October 2004).

[33] 'Trips that end in tragedy', *The Guardian* (11 March 2002). Actually the rate may be about the same; approximately 30 to 60 people are struck by lightning each year in Britain of whom, on average, three may be killed; see the estimates by Professor Elsom in 'Lightning injuries and fatalities in the United Kingdom', in R. Kithil, (ed.) *Lightning Safety Handbook* (US National Lightning Safety Institute, Louisville, 2002) and by his Tornado and Storm Research Organization, Oxford Brookes University (2003).

[34] 'Boy, 12, struck by lightning in London', *Evening Standard* (14 November 2001).

participating in a well-planned expedition are similar to those encountered at home during normal active life'.[35]

Indeed, what is more clearly a serious danger to modern society is that legends develop about the legal viability of outdoor pursuits. Western societies have chronic levels of obesity and disease caused by inactivity, and this can be much more life threatening than the inherent hazards of outdoor activities. These common pitfalls of the outdoors, noted in the research and in the legal cases, are often well-understood and can generally be dealt with by robust safety features to give very considerable life-enhancing health benefits. As well as fitness, there are also the additional educational benefits of many such pursuits, not least in giving an understanding of risk. Prince Philip, whose Duke of Edinburgh's Award has become a very important national and international yardstick for youth work, has commented that 'not to teach children about risk and responsibility is a failure to provide a rounded education'.[36] An even more ambitious objective for outdoor activities was propounded by Lord Hunt, leader of the Everest expedition, who in 1989 claimed that human survival may depend on cultivating a sense of adventure among the young. A supporter of the theory that adventurous challenge produces better citizens,[37] Lord Hunt and a team of outdoor education specialists theorized that, in the absence of any form of National Service, it was important to develop the potential of young people through outdoor activities: 'They are our most valuable asset and many of them deserve a better chance to enjoy and benefit from leisure time'. This report, *In Search of Adventure*,[38] indicated that there was 'abundant testimony to the view that a taste of adventure enhances self-confidence and initiative, widens perspectives and fosters an attitude of co-operation.'[39] At the time, the *Hunt Report* was the most thorough analysis of adventurous activities undertaken through organizations such as the Duke of Edinburgh's Award Scheme, the Outward Bound Trust, the Scout and Guide movement and the network of outdoor activity centres operated by local education authorities. The study recommended that by 1995, every young person in the United Kingdom should have the chance to take part in adventurous outdoor activity.

More recently, a very strong endorsement for the benefits of outdoor education came in a report from the Office for Standards in Education (Ofsted) in September 2004. David Bell, Her Majesty's Chief Inspector of Schools, indicated that 'the benefits of outdoor education are far too important to forfeit, and by far outweigh

---

[35] Sarah Anderson and Chris Johnson, 'How dangerous is it to be a modern day explorer?', RSM Press Release (2 November 2000). See 'Expedition health and safety: a risk assessment', *Journal of the Royal Society of Medicine* vol 93, (2000) 557-561.

[36] *Times Educational Supplement* (26 October 2001).

[37] See for one of the original proponents, Colin Mortlock, *Adventure Education and Outdoor Pursuits* (self-published, 1973), also his *The Adventure Alternative* (Cumbria: Cicerone Press, 1987) and *Beyond Adventure: An Inner Journey* (Cumbria: Cicerone Press, 2002).

[38] Lord Hunt of Llanfair Waterdine (ed), *In Search of Adventure, a study of opportunities for adventure and challenge for young people* (London: Talbot Adair Press, HMSO and the Royal Geographical Society, 1989).

[39] 'Are the young game for a lesson?', *The Times* (13 November 1989).

the risks of an accident occurring. If teachers follow recognized safety procedures and guidance they have nothing to fear from the law'.[40]

The law also has to deal with *unorganized* and perhaps even illicit activity. For example, the House of Lords in a recent leading case of *Tomlinson v Congleton BC* held that a Bank Holiday weekend visitor to a country park who disobeyed 'No Swimming' notices was immediately transformed into a 'trespasser' when he plunged headlong into a former gravel pit to cool off. His broken neck was held not to give rise to a claim for damages against the local authority. One of the judges, Lord Scott of Foscote, remarked that there is 'some risk of accidents arising out of the *joie de vivre* of the young. But that is no reason for imposing a grey and dull safety regime on everyone'.[41] The local authority in this case had carried out a textbook risk assessment, which indicated the obvious dangers from what is commonly described as 'Macho Male Diving Syndrome'; a majority of judges in the Court of Appeal held Congleton Borough Council to have been negligent when they then failed to carry out their agreed action plan for a relatively inexpensive planting of the beach to inhibit such activity, on the grounds of cost. But that view was overturned on appeal to the House of Lords, with Lord Hoffmann indicating not just traditional legal factors in the law of negligence, such as 'the balance of risk, gravity of injury, cost and social value', but also the philosophical notion of 'free will'.[42] Cost-benefit analysis of activities is not a new factor in the law, but it is interesting to note the underlying financial realities of *Tomlinson*; when the local authority were found not liable, their insurers having fought the case long and hard, the council taxpayers of Congleton still have to pay for the costs of long-term social care for John Tomlinson, along with general taxpayers paying for his health costs. The legal position therefore always needs to be seen in context. And the 'insurance reality' behind much of personal injury litigation can often prove to be a world of mirrors.

International dimensions and their impact

Inevitably there is an international flavour to litigation in this field. When arguments rage in the USA about whether there is a 'torts crisis', there is bound to be a debate elsewhere about civil compensation. While in Britain there is no such thing as a 'runaway jury' in personal injury cases,[43] that does not stop arguments about an alleged 'compensation culture'. Professor Harlow has suggested that, in Britain in 1995, 'We were beginning to see the evolution of a "compensation

---

[40] *Outdoor education, Aspects of good practice* (September 2004), Office for Standards in Education, HMI 2151. Press release from Ofsted on 28 September 2004 quoting the Chief Inspector.

[41] Per Lord Scott of Foscote, *Tomlinson v Congleton Borough Council* [2003] 3 All ER 1122 at 1166.

[42] Headings in Lord Hoffmann's speech, ibid 1150, 1152.

[43] See for the importance of 'procedural posture' in the American litigation, Martin Davies, 'The role of juries in US torts cases', 10 *Torts Law Journal* (2002) 109.

culture" ... the way was opening for an expansive, victim-oriented tort law [and] a risk-averse society was being shaped'.[44] That was a very controversial view then, and now, as the falling number of tort cases in Britain, Europe and North America seems hardly to buttress such a perspective. Lord Steyn in an extra-judicial capacity, while acknowledging the 'perception among many judges, in this respect possibly reflecting public opinion, that the tort system is becoming too expansive and wasteful ... [with] a society bent on litigation', makes a cautionary suggestion on 'hearing further argument' about a so-called 'compensation culture'.[45] Similarly, a senior judge in Australia in examining the suggestion that there is an 'increasingly litigious society' points out 'a dearth of hard evidence to either support or debunk this claim', and suggests that, in any event, the 'perception of the average Australian is not formed by factual information' but what they see on television.[46] The leading proponent of the 'anti-torts' movement in the USA, Professor Peter Huber, asserts that whole areas of the economy and social life are under threat in western countries because of a fear of the tort lawyers. Much of Huber's attack on the 'liability spiral', and those of his colleagues, is based on awards of exemplary damages in the United States: 'Once invited to compensate, juries stayed on to punish',[47] so it is not entirely apposite to transpose the argument to British shores where juries were long ago abolished in all civil claims apart from defamation cases. Indeed, even in the USA the notion of a 'compensation culture' is strongly contested. Countervailing arguments have been raised against the threat of 'capping' and other 'tort reform' legislative measures there, not least that of the veteran campaigner Ralph Nader, who claims that the much-vaunted 'Torts Crisis in America' is just an elaborate hoax by the insurance industry to cover their extortionate increases in premiums.[48]

A related debate in Britain centres on the impact of European regulations, and whether such 'red tape' is strangling initiative and adventure. A 2004 study by the Better Regulation Task Force, an independent body that advises the UK Government, found that the number of personal injury claims registered in 2003/2004 fell by nearly 60,000, and found no evidence to support the idea that compensation claims are rising.[49] David Arkulus, who chairs the Task Force, commented that

---

[44] Carol Harlow, *State Liability: Tort Law and Beyond* (Oxford: OUP, 2004) 4, 5.

[45] Lord Steyn, 'Perspectives of Corrective and Distributive Justice in Tort Law', (Dublin, UCD, 2002) 22.

[46] Peter Underwood, senior puisne judge of the Supreme Court of Tasmania, 'Is Ms Donoghue's snail in mortal peril?', 12 *Torts Law Journal* (2004) 39.

[47] *Liability: The Legal Revolution and its Consequences* (New York: Basic Books, 1988) 18, 127. See also the website http://www.overlawyered.com 'chronicling the high cost of our legal system'.

[48] See generally Ralph Nader and Barbara Ehrenreich, *The Ralph Nader Reader* (New York: Seven Stories Press, 2000). For a sceptical assessment of Nader's first and most famous campaign; Gary Schwartz, 'The Myth of the Ford Pinto Case', 43 *Rutgers Law Review* (1991) 1013-1068.

[49] *Better Routes to Redress* (May 2004).

tabloid tales of people suing one another for vast sums of money for apparently trival reasons have fuelled a commonly-held belief that the UK is heading towards a United States-style "compensation culture". In fact, our report found that registered accident claims actually fell last year and most county court awards were for less than £3,000.[50]

This would appear to be a description of the reality rather than the myth of a British 'blame culture', but will not stop courts and commentators in Britain having their own perceptions or misperceptions in determining liability within the ferment of a wide public debate.

The legal decisions of courts are of course never determined in a vacuum. When Chris Keates, the general secretary of the NASUWT, advises her members to 'think carefully' before taking their pupils on school trips, because they could be sued by 'increasingly litigious' parents even if they had 'followed guidelines', then the perception of what might be an impending legal and professional catastrophe for a teacher has already had an immense effect in schools. That NASUWT viewpoint has been challenged by Colin Ettinger, the President of the Association of Personal Injury Lawyers (APIL), who accused the union of 'misguided scaremongering', claiming that the 'compensation culture' is a myth.[51] Further legislation has also been proposed, particularly a private member's bill in 2004 put forward by Julian Brazier MP, who stated as an 'issue of fact ... that litigation is a real problem rather than a perceived problem'.[52] Several national organizations came to his support, indicating that the principal disincentives to more volunteers were 'fear of blame and threat of litigation over injuries and accidents; increasing bureaucracy around rules and regulations, and health and safety; costs of travel and training; and lack of recognition and support from employers and society.'[53] The aim of Mr Brazier's Promotion of Volunteering Bill was originally to introduce a 'statement of inherent risk', which volunteers or voluntary organizations could ask the users of their services or activities to sign, to ensure that they 'share responsibility for the safe conduct of the activity', rather along the lines of a 'waiver' under North American contract law. The Bill was severely criticized, both on technical and policy grounds. For example, its chief opponent, Andrew Dismore MP, 'talked out' the Bill, and at the end of a three hour speech, the longest in recent Parliamentary history, declared that the Bill would be 'an unlimited charter to injure, kill and maim young children'.[54] It has been estimated by the organization Volunteering England that something like 22 million people a year are involved in volunteering their services, and there is clearly a belief by several

---

[50] Commenting on the Government's response to the report, 11 November 2004, at http://www.brtf.govuk/pressreleases/2004/better_routes.asp

[51] *New Law Journal* (5 November 2004), 1638.

[52] *Hansard*, House of Commons (16 July 2004) 1655.

[53] A letter signed on behalf of a number of organizations, including the Central Council for Physical Recreation, Campaign for Adventure and Girl Guides UK, the largest youth organization in Britain; *The Guardian* (8 March 2004).

[54] House of Commons *Hansard* (16 July 2004) col 1714.

organizations and individuals that this is under threat from an increasingly litigious culture and an excess of red tape. The issue has become part of the political landscape; for example, Lord Falconer, the Lord Chancellor, recently 'dismissed the notion that Britain was in the grip of a US-style compensation culture as a myth, pointing to falling numbers of personal injury claims' but said that 'misleading and harmful' images fostered by claims companies, with mottos such as 'where there's blame there's a claim' were causing activities such as school trips to be cancelled out of a 'fear' of litigation.[55] The Shadow Home Secretary, David Davis MP, set up his own commission in 2004 to 'look at how Britain's compensation culture affects the whole range of employers, from public bodies to private companies', suggesting that the Human Rights Act 1998 has generated too many 'spurious rights' and fuelled a 'compensation culture out of all sense of proportion'.[56] Mr Davis is particularly concerned that volunteering in Britain is in sharp decline with 'risk, fear of blame and litigation' as a cause.[57]

The 'clearing house' for both the actual facts and some informed analysis for much of this wide-ranging and controversial debate on outdoor activities has been the AALA. Set up in 1996 as a result of the Adventure Activities (Young Persons Safety) Act 1995, it has a statutory remit confined to inspecting and licensing outdoor centres that cater for those under 18 years of age. But as we shall see, the work of the AALA has proved very useful for many other organizations dealing with children, such as schools, clubs and volunteer organizations, who plan their own activities both at home and abroad, and who are not formally part of the licensing regime. The lessons that can be learned from the AALA's licensing and investigative work have shaped thinking on many issues. Not only is this 'good practice' fed back to outdoor activity centres through the inspection regime, but it has formed policy and practice for schools through such publications as the Department for Education and Skills *Health and Safety of Pupils on Educational Visits* (HASPEV), first published in 1998, and its later supplements *Standards for LEAs in Overseeing Educational Visits, Standards for Adventure, A Handbook for Group Leaders*, and *Group Safety at Water Margins*.[58] HASPEV has rightly earned a place as the standard reference document on school trips, but also is the model for good practice in much of the voluntary sector. The 'Water Margins' leaflet demonstrates the sort of process that is at work; it takes account the AALA research which showed a significant safety issue on 'river walking' trips in the light of Stainforth Beck, which had previously been thought to be 'low risk', and then co-ordinates experience and feedback from a wide range of voluntary bodies

---

[55] Clare Dyer, 'Ambulance-chasing claims firms get last warning to self-regulate', *The Guardian* (11 November 2004).

[56] Catherine Wheatley, 'Compensation culture wrecking small firms', *Sunday Express* (5 September 2004). See for a rather more informed perspective on the 1998 legislation, Jane Wright, *Tort Law and Human Rights* (Oxford: Hart, 2001).

[57] 'School trips and charities hit by soaring insurance costs: activities for scouts and the disabled among those cancelled by fears of 'compensation culture',' *Sunday Telegraph* (29 August 2004).

[58] All downloadable from http://www.teachernet.govuk/_doc/4557/hspvpdf

to produce a simple and well-informed practical guide. The DfES also worked on that document and others in this list with the Central Council of Physical Recreation, which is the umbrella for the national governing bodies of various outdoor sports, so this is evidence of a serious attempt at 'joined up thinking' on the outdoors.

Civil compensation and criminal cases have other purposes than to inform the public of hazards, but lessons can be learned from these legal cases too, and then fed back into the ongoing search for better standards. An important point to remember here is that the reported decisions of the courts are just the tip of an iceberg of a complex process of investigation, negotiation and legal manoeuvring. Much of the resolution of legal problems goes on behind closed doors, and even cases that get close to the courtroom will perhaps be settled on 'undisclosed terms', so it is not always easy to analyse what has happened. In addition the cases that are fought, and particularly those that go on appeal, are often on finely-balanced points of law, or those that need to be pursued for practical or policy reasons by insurers, and they are therefore sometimes rather 'special' cases with unique circumstances, and not necessarily likely to re-occur. However, decided cases produce legal precedents, and can often be used by analogy in related fields, so they can give guidance as to what may be important in regulating future behaviour.

Similarly, the media reports of fatalities and injuries in the outdoors can produce a pattern that can feed back into thinking through the various possible hazards and then perhaps producing preventative measures to safeguard others. Nothing can of course guarantee safety on all occasions. Even the most seemingly innocuous circumstances can produce disaster, and when no-one could possibly be said to be 'blameworthy', so it is important to have a sense of perspective about what actually is 'risky' and what on an isolated occasion has led to difficulty. For example, in 2004, Asif Bharucha, aged 17 and on a trip with tutors and fellow students from Blackburn College along the Cornish coastal footpath near Lizard Point, fell to his death because, according to the police, he was startled by a friendly dog coming towards him.[59] A newspaper report on the tragedy noted that the Government 'admit that schools are increasingly being deterred from taking children on trips',[60] and yet there would seem no amount of preparation or preventative measures that could have safeguarded this student, other than to ban walkers or dogs on the footpath. And that of course would be a nonsense. Certainly if there was a ban on school or college trips to such locations it would be to 'throw the baby out with the bathwater'. As the Master of the Rolls, Lord Phillips of Worth Matravers, has reminded us in his other capacity, chairing the governing body at his old school, Bryanston, and writing to parents: schools do not 'set out to provide their children with a risk-free education … It's the job of the school to take all reasonable precautions but if you take it to its end, you stop children playing rugger, or canoeing, or climbing trees.'[61] Given his central judicial role in the Court of Appeal, such a statement is noteworthy.

---

[59] 'Boy dies in cliff fall as he flees friendly dog', *The Times* (17 June 2004).

[60] 'Teenager killed in cliff fall during college trip', *The Guardian* (16 June 2004).

[61] 'Judge Risk-it dares you to live on the edge', *Sunday Times* (15 August 2004).

PART I
PROVIDERS AND PARTICIPANTS

Chapter 2

Lyme Bay, the Legislation and Licensing

Kayaking and canoeing are arguably very safe areas of sport and outdoor activities. For example, there has not been one single death in the United Kingdom when individuals have been undergoing training under the auspices of the British Canoe Union (BCU), the national governing body for paddle sports.[1] Some commentators argue that the possible exception is the Lyme Bay incident in 1993, although it is clear that the appropriate British Canoe Union level of instruction was not available there and many BCU guidelines for safe kayaking were flouted. However, as a result of the death of four teenage kayakers at Lyme Bay, a seismic change took place in the regulation of outdoor activities.

The victims – Dean Sayer, 17, and 16-year-olds Simon Dunne, Claire Langley and Rachel Walker – were all from Southway School in Plymouth. Their MP, a former teacher, David Jamieson, subsequently introduced private members' legislation for independent licensing and safety checks, having won a coveted second place in the member's ballot; he noted that he had 'a special opportunity to present a Bill on behalf of my constituents, which is relevant to parents throughout the country'.[2] The passage of what became the Adventure Activities Young Persons Safety Act 1995 was somewhat speedy, and perhaps not entirely thought through. It introduced licensing for adventure activity centres catering for those under 18 years of age. It is particularly noteworthy that only five industries are actually licensed in this way in the UK, as compulsory inspection is a very severe form of regulation. They are the asbestos stripping, the explosives, the nuclear, the offshore oil, and the adventure activity industries. While the extreme hazards of the first four are very readily apparent, many commentators have questioned whether outdoor activities actually require this level of surveillance.

Under the legislation, the Adventure Activities Licensing Authority (AALA), based in Cardiff, was set up in 1996 to inspect outdoor centres and then to license them. Rules and policy formulated by the AALA have become benchmarks, not just for the under 18s, but for the whole outdoor activities sector, for schools and for voluntary organizations, all of which are well beyond the statutory remit of the 1995 legislation. There are now approximately 1,000 activity centres nationwide catering for the under 18s, out of a total estimated in 1994 of 3,000.[3] Since the commencement of licensing, just twenty centres have been refused

---

[1] *Canoeist* (December 2004) 16, chronicling the unique death, seemingly through panic, of a 51-year-old novice in the USA in a sea kayak, who was under instruction from a BCU qualified coach using BCU principles.
[2] House of Commons *Hansard* (27 January 1995), col 590.
[3] 'How safe are activity centres?', *The Times* (12 February 1994).

licences and have been forced to close. However, more than 500 have had to make safety improvements before they could get a licence, and many more have quietly disappeared through takeovers or amalgamations.

It was inevitable that following Lyme Bay there would be many commercial pressures too on the industry. For example a company called Howglen, trading as 'Devon & Dorset Adventure Holidays', had made substantial profits in the three years preceding Lyme Bay. It was not wholly unrelated to the St. Alban's Centre, as its owner Chris Reynard held shares in the parent company there, OLL (Outdoor Learning and Leisure), but the ripples from the Lyme Bay disaster affected the adventure holiday industry as a whole and Howglen in particular. The impact was both by imposing increased costs for safety measures, but even more disastrously through the cancellation and non-renewal of bookings. Commercial pressures were primarily responsible for the company going into receivership in 1996 and then into liquidation in 2001,[4] but unfortunately although Mr Reynard described his Devon & Dorset Adventure Holidays as 'virtually the original multi-activity holiday centre' and he himself had chaired the British Activity Holiday Association, both he and his firm had been the subject of serious allegations about skiing trips, which cannot have helped business.[5] Eventually Mr Registrar Simmonds disqualified Mr Reynard from acting as a director, pursuant to section 6 of the Company Directors Disqualification Act 1986, for 10 years. Having heard his evidence the Registrar found him to be 'a most unsatisfactory witness in that he was disingenuous, equivocal and on some occasions untruthful'. Subsequently, the disqualification was reduced by Blackburne J to five and a half years, and this was affirmed by the Court of Appeal.[6]

It is important to note that there are several exemptions under the 1995 Act; for example, schools and voluntary associations providing activities for their own pupils or members do not require licences. This means that only those providers who offer outdoor activities and who also fall within the narrow definitions of the regulations are legally obliged to apply for a licence. An illustration of the exemption is the Scout Association, the largest youth organization internationally. For example, the Longridge Scout Boating Centre at Marlow is a nationally regarded water activities centre, and caters not just for Scouts but for Guides, schools and youth groups. Longridge is a British Canoe Union approved centre and a Royal Yachting Association recognized teaching establishment, and at the forefront of outdoor activities for young people, but it has no need of an AALA licence because each voluntary group using the Centre has a clearly defined membership and only offers activities to their members. These are known as 'Legitimate Voluntary Outings', and the AALA suggests that many groups such

---

[4] *Reynard v Secretary of State for Trade and Industry*, ChD transcript 22 June 2001.

[5] 'Children's "lives at risk" on trips by travel firm', *The Independent* (4 October 1999), '10-year ban for ski instructor who risked children's lives on the slopes', *The Independent* (25 July 2000).

[6] 'Judge entitled to take account of director's conduct in witness box', *The Independent* (26 April 2002); *Secretary of State for Trade and Industry v Reynard* (2002) Ewca Civ 497.

as independent Duke of Edinburgh's Award units, community associations and church groups are exempt from the legislation.[7] The essential pre-requisite for this exemption is that there must be 'no charge' for the adventure activity leadership or instruction, but there are in reality some very opaque areas here; the AALA give an example of a public-spirited individual who takes children from a housing estate for a sailing outing, hiring the minibus and the dinghies, and purchasing food, and then splitting the costs amongst the youngsters. The AALA believe this mythical 'Uncle Jim' would not be taking part in 'a licensable situation', as this would be a 'legitimate, voluntary outing organized by a group which is not operating in a commercial manner'. They note it would become licensable if there was an attempt to make a profit or any of the participants 'made a living from it', or if this became a 'regular, organized activit[y] e.g. an annual camp or activity holiday open to all'. This point illustrates both the somewhat loose nature of the definitional arrangements under the 1995 Act and the regulations, and the adaptability and plain common sense of the AALA. This 'Legitimate Voluntary Outing' is therefore a useful guidance, which is supportive of public-spirited voluntary effort.

Schools are similarly in an exempt status when they provide adventurous activities for their own pupils. The Consumers Association pressed hard for schools to be included when the legislation was first considered, and stated that 'All children are entitled to the same level of protection... the regulations are not going to do the job that parents expect. People are looking for a guarantee that a minimum standard of safety will be met.'[8] Again there are many anomalies. If a school is hiring a campsite, hiring instructors and hiring boats from a water activities centre they are exempt. But if the Centre is providing the school with an adventurous package then it will be technically licensable. Again the AALA have moved in a sensible way, both to influence the Department for Education and Skills guidelines for schools on trips and outings, particularly HASPEV, and to produce an excellent self-assessment pack for all providers based on the licensing scheme. Essentially the Act and regulations, applicable just to licensing, have been extended in a non-compulsory and non-threatening way to provide a 'common denominator' or 'floor of rights' across all adventurous activities. Nevertheless the distinction remains that there is not necessarily a direct advisory or enforcement regime for schools and voluntary organizations.

How serious a gap is this 'loophole' in the legislation? Or would it be 'overkill' to insist that all adventurous activities come within the licensing regime? In the light of these anomalies some commentators have argued for the inclusion of the whole outdoor activities industry to be within the licensing arrangements, and not just when they offer provision for the under 18s. The legislation specifies that the practice of licensing should be reviewed from time to time, and Marcus Bailie, the head of inspection services at the AALA, has consistently argued for change and believes that parents want 'a single stamp of

---

[7] AALA, Collective Interpretation 2.02 – Legitimate Voluntary Outings.
[8] See generally Phil Revell, 'The taste of adventure must not turn sour', *The Times* (21 March 1997).

approval'. He has proposed a scheme in which licensing would be voluntary but schools would be compelled to use only licensed centres.[9] This would make sense, although it would involve a considerable outlay of expenditure for schools, which many could ill afford. As we have seen, the borderline with voluntary organizations, particularly with 'after-school' activities, is somewhat hazy, and if these too had to use licensed centres then the effect on the main voluntary organizations such as Scouts and Guides would be catastrophic. Given the budgetary infusion from the Ministry of Defence into the Army, Navy and Air Cadets this would perhaps not be so ruinous there, but it would be a very important factor for all other voluntary organizations.

In any event, the AALA has no jurisdiction abroad, and this is inevitably an increasing arena for adventurous activities. School trips for language skills, field and historical studies, and for 'widening horizons', inexorably have a more international dimension in an era of cheap flights and easier access by road to the continent. As we shall see, one of the areas where schools are most in need of support is where children are taken abroad when local standards might not always be at the level that could be expected with an AALA approved centre in the UK. In 2004, a British coroner severely criticized the safety standards of a cable car in South Africa, when Cara Weaver, aged 14, was trapped by the mechanism while sitting on a ledge watching her mother abseil at Table Mountain as part of a locally led climbing group; by contrast, the previous year, a South African coroner had exonerated the company of any blame, judged by local standards on warning signs.[10] One of the criticisms by parents of overseas trips is that schools often represent such trips as 'part of the curriculum', even though they can be very expensive, so that every child is expected to go. This applies even to the many ski trips organized by schools; it is interesting to note that skiing is one of the activities considered hazardous enough to need a licence from the AALA if done in Britain, but the Authority of course has no jurisdiction abroad where the vast majority of school and voluntary organization skiing will take place.

Commentators who argue that the legislation has been effective point out that there have only been seven deaths at licensed centres since the AALA started work, with three of these from natural causes, and even more significantly, no child has died at a licensed centre while engaged in licensed activities. But others suggest that this draconian legislation is 'heavy-handed' and may be stifling outdoor activities. It is interesting to note that the UK is the only European country to have such a licensing body. In addition, Marcus Bailie points out that the lack of control over outdoor centres that cater for adults is 'bizarre', as so many cater for all age groups. Nevertheless he cannot see licensing being extended to them because of the costs involved and indicates that 'Perhaps the best hope of improving standards among adventure providers who are outwith the scope of legislation, including youth organizations, is through voluntary self-

---

[9] 'Real Life: Look Mum No Hands!', *The Observer* (1 June 2003).
[10] 'Cable car firm slammed over 14-year-old's death', *Western Daily Press* (15 July 2004).

assessment'.[11] All of this does underline the 'child-centred' approach of the legislation and inevitably this is because of its genesis in the Lyme Bay disaster.

Lyme Bay was actually not the first occasion for public outcry about safety standards in the outdoors: the first in Britain was in November 1971 when five teenagers and a teacher from Edinburgh died from hypothermia in a blizzard in the Scottish mountains. They had been based at the city's Lagganlia Centre for Outdoor Education near Aviemore. Carol Bertram, Susan Byrne, Corraine Dick, William Kerr and Diane Dudgeon, all aged 14 or 15, and an assistant instructor, Sheila Sunderland, died within 200 yards of a refuge hut which might have ensured their survival, having attempted to build a snow shelter. There were just two survivors, both suffering severe frostbite – Raymond Leslie, aged 15, and the party leader Catherine Davidson, who after two days on the mountain when rescue efforts had been hampered by severe winds, went on her own to make contact with the rescue teams and brought them back to the group location. Strong criticisms were made by Mountain Rescue about the initial decision to take schoolchildren up into the mountains during a weekend of atrocious weather, and subsequently all winter mountaineering courses for Edinburgh schools were cancelled.[12] Sadly the lessons do not always appear to have been learned; in 2004 Mountain Rescue made serious criticisms about a 'near miss', which prompted the highest number of rescuers in any operation conducted in Scotland, when 39 London schoolgirls and their teacher got lost in mist 2,500ft up Meall a' Bhuachaille. Rescue teams rarely pass judgment, so the condemnation that they were 'appalled by the girls' inadequate clothing and footwear, and by the teacher's foolhardiness in undertaking a trek against local advice' is noteworthy.[13] Following the six school deaths in 1971 there had been calls from several Scottish MPs to abandon such winter trips entirely, but no ban was forthcoming, and it was left to the inquest jury to make the self-evident recommendation that 'expeditions should be led by fully qualified and long-experienced instructors in their own field'.[14] The contrasts with Lyme Bay are that, by the time of this major school disaster 22 years later in 1993, not only was there a criminal prosecution of the owners of the outdoor centre, but also the 'historical accident' of the relevant MP having a high place in the ballot to pilot through Parliamentary legislation.

A very important ingredient in the Lyme Bay case was the evidential paper trail which was exhumed to point out the necessary 'gross negligence' required for a manslaughter conviction. Joy Cawthorne, an outdoor activities instructor at the St. Alban's Activity Centre in Lyme Regis, was what has come to be known as a 'whistleblower'. Nine months before the four deaths in Dorset she had written a letter, in June 1992, warning Peter Kite, the managing director of Active Learning and Leisure Ltd, which ran the centre, 'to have a very careful look at

[11] 'How much can we risk?', *The Scotsman* (23 October 1999).
[12] 'Worst disaster claimed lives of children', *The Glasgow Herald* (31 December 1998).
[13] 'Safety first: a parents' guide to exploring the great outdoors', *Daily Telegraph* (10 July 2004).
[14] 'Are outdoor trips worth the risk?', *The Independent* (8 December 1994).

standards of safety. Otherwise you might find yourselves trying to explain why someone's son or daughter will not be coming home'. That letter received no reply, and a subsequent one just a cursory note from Mr Kite, so Ms Cawthorne considered it necessary to resign her job, subsequently finding alternative employment difficult to obtain.[15] This documentary evidence was decisive when in December 1994 Mr Kite was found guilty of manslaughter and sentenced to three years in prison. In passing sentence Ognall J stated that 'what clearly separates this case from any other of its kind is the notice you were given in chillingly clear terms of the risk you were running....[that] forecast became a reality because of your complete failure to heed it.'[16]

The case also made legal history by ruling that the company, OLL Ltd of Cheltenham, which had taken over Active Learning and Leisure Ltd, was guilty of corporate manslaughter. An important factor as we have seen was the size of the company involved, which made it easier for the prosecution to show that the 'mind' of the company was the same as that of the managing director, Mr Kite, who was the 'controlling officer' of the company.[17] This 'size issue' led to acquittal in the Zeebrugge ferry disaster prosecution, because the Crown could not show that a 'controlling mind' had been grossly negligent.[18] That prosecution related to the capsizing of the 'roll on/roll off' ferry *Herald of Free Enterprise* in 1987, and was of eight defendants, including the ferry company Townsend Thorensen and three former directors. Given this 'multi-party' indictment and the complexities of why the ferry was setting to sea with bow doors open, it led to the acquittal in 1990 of all defendants. The size of the company involved, and the difficulty of establishing fault in such an organization, is therefore a key determinant of outcome in a criminal trial.[19] However, there is inevitably a high

---

[15] 'My case is unlikely to inspire people to speak out. I did what I thought was right and look what happened' she commented in later discussion of a statute on whistle blowing; *The Guardian* (27 February 1996). She had resigned with her partner, also an instructor at the Centre: at the trial she stated that 'Our ethics got the better of us'; *The Guardian* (25 November 1994).

[16] *R v Kite* [1996] 2 Cr. App. R. (S.) 295. The sentence was subsequently reduced on appeal to two-and-a-half years.

[17] See the note on *R v Stoddart, Kite and OLL Ltd* in 'Law: Company executives ignore safety issues at their peril', *Lloyd's List* (18 January 1995). For the four-stage test laid down by the House of Lords on involuntary manslaughter by means of a grossly negligent act or omission see *R v Adomako* [1995] 1 AC 171, [1994] 3 All ER 79, a case involving the conviction of an anaesthetist.

[18] See *P & O European Ferries (Dover) Ltd* (1991) 93 Cr App R 72, where Turner J had ruled that a company may be properly indicted for manslaughter, but where the trial ended in acquittal.

[19] See the statement of Lord Denning in *Bolton Engineering v Graham Limited* [1957] 1 QB 159 At 172: 'A company may in many ways be likened to a human body. It has a brain and nerve centre which controls what it does ... directors and managers who represent the directing mind and will of the company and control what it does. The state of mind of these managers is the state of mind of the company.' See generally Barry Hayes, 'Law: Companies and Criminal Law', *Lloyd's List* (1 February 1995).

threshold of evidence to show corporate manslaughter 'by means of gross negligence'.[20] In sentencing both the managing director and the company at the end of the Lyme Bay trial, Ognall J indicated that the evidence showed Mr Kite appeared more 'interested in sales than safety', and that the risks were 'not only serious and obvious, but the directors had full knowledge of them in the letter they were sent'. However, the jury failed to reach a decision on identical charges against Joseph Stoddart, the manager of the St. Alban's Centre, who was actually at the Centre at the time, whereas Mr Kite was in the firm's London headquarters on the day of the tragedy. When the prosecution indicated they would ask for a re-trial of Mr Stoddart, Ognall J indicated that this would be inappropriate, and eventually those charges were dismissed.[21]

A corporate manslaughter charge is therefore very rare in Britain, and indeed many commentators have suggested that the circumstances of the Zeebrugge ferry disaster, when 193 people died, would appear to be more culpable than the position at Lyme Bay. However, manslaughter prosecutions of companies is actually only of relatively recent origin. Professor Gary Slapper, the leading expert,[22] noted that the Lyme Bay verdict was 'symbolic' and he claimed it was 'likely to have a chastening effect on companies'.[23] His researches show that the first such charge was of a welder, Glanville Evans, who fell off a bridge collapsing into the River Wye in 1965, and since then there have been only a small number of attempted prosecutions, and none had succeeded until Lyme Bay. Just the month before Lyme Bay there had been what can perhaps be characterized as a 'near miss' case where a prosecution for corporate manslaughter might have been an option after a death at an outdoor activity centre near Ludlow. Instead, the owner, Vaughan Phillips, and his company were each fined £15,000 in 1994 when Hayley Hadfield, aged 11, died from head injuries in 1992 after hitting a tree while scrambling down a hill on a night hike.[24] In that case the responsible adult failed to call an ambulance for over an hour and a half, the instructor was not qualified and took a 'foolish' short cut down a 55 degree slope, and the camp owner was branded by the Ludlow magistrates as

---

[20] See further the guidelines on corporate manslaughter produced by The Crown Prosecution Service at http://www.cps.govuk/legal/, and their analysis that 'subsequent convictions of companies for the offence of corporate manslaughter have been infrequent'. They give 'three rare examples': *R v Kite and OLL Ltd* (the 'Lyme Bay' case, Winchester Crown Court, 8 December 1994, unreported); *R v Jackson Transport (Ossett) Ltd* (September 1996, unreported); and *R v Roy Bowles Transport Ltd*, (Central Criminal Court 10 December 1999, unreported).

[21] 'Director is jailed for canoe deaths', *The Guardian* (9 December 1994).

[22] See generally Gary Slapper, *Blood in the Bank: Social and Legal Aspects of Death at Work* (Aldershot: Ashgate, 1999).

[23] 'Canoe centre chief and company are found guilty', *The Times* (9 December 1994).

[24] See the comment made by Lady Olga Maitland MP in the debate on Mr Jamieson's Bill, who described how she had spoken to Mr and Mrs Hadfield of Salford after their daughter died in May 1992 at the Manor adventure centre in Shropshire and 'What Mrs. Hadfield told me was hair-raising. It was a story of blinding incompetence on a scale which leaves us speechless'; House of Commons *Hansard* (27 January 1995) col 632.

'guilty of the most callous and reckless disregard' of his responsibilities when he refused to intervene despite being told the child was seriously injured.[25] However, even such appalling circumstances were overshadowed by what took place at Lyme Bay, which is worth close analysis for its lessons as to what comes within a definition of 'gross negligence'.

The facts of Lyme Bay

On 22 March 1993, a party of eight sixth-formers had set off at 10am on what was intended to be a two-hour return trip on the open sea from Lyme Regis to Charmouth. The day before they had engaged in just one hour of basic kayak training. With them was their teacher and two staff members from the outdoor centre, Tony Mann and Karen Gardner; sadly these two individuals could hardly be classed as 'instructors', as they themselves had only recently attended a basic skills course to gain the 'encouragement' award of British Canoe Union One Star: 'A basic assessment of ability at the end of an introductory course. An encouragement award. The test itself should encourage safe practice, regard for the equipment, and fun'.[26] On any analysis this trip was a seriously hazardous enterprise, and it was no surprise that the group got into severe difficulties at sea. Martin Melling, the Regional Coaching Organizer of the British Canoe Union, gave evidence at the Lyme Bay trial that he was 'staggered' that the expedition had been contemplated for beginners. He pointed out that the 'instructors' had been 'totally inappropriate' and that the only safety equipment carried by Ms Gardner, who had joined the St. Alban's centre after previously working for the company as a cleaner, was a whistle.[27] When asked whether a properly qualified BCU senior instructor would have embarked on such a trip, Mr Melling replied: 'Absolutely not'.[28] In answer herself to a question about emergency procedures, Ms Gardner produced the immortal answer that 'I'm not sure I was too familiar with what an emergency was'.[29]

The weather in southern England in March has inevitably to be categorized as 'wintertime'. This was a sea-crossing, calling for sea kayaking skills and specialist sea kayaks, and yet the boats seem to have been standard 'general

---

[25] See the leading article 'When an adventure becomes a disaster', *The Independent* (10 November 1993), and the court report the previous day in *The Independent* (9 November 1993).

[26] The BCU has a classification from One to Five Star for paddling ability; see BCU website at http://www.bcu.org.uk/pdfdocs/. Even the most basic coaching qualification of Level One requires Two Star paddling performance as a preliminary to additional training specific to coaching and first aid skills.

[27] 'Catalogue of mistakes that led to drownings', *The Times* (9 December 1994).

[28] 'Fatal canoe trip left expert "staggered",' *The Guardian* (26 November 1994). A BCU Senior Instructor is a Level Three coach, requiring Four Star paddling ability and many other courses in practical skills and first aid training.

[29] 'Lifejacket error cost lives, canoe trial is told', *The Times* (26 November 1994).

purpose' or slalom kayaks.[30] Wind is a critical factor in canoeing and kayaking, and there was a breeze blowing the participants away from the safety of the shoreline, as well as a tide taking them out to the English Channel. When asked if she had confirmed a weather forecast, Ms Gardner indicated that she had not done so because 'it was not part of my job to check it' and went on to acknowledge that this was her first sea trip.[31]

The clothing worn by the group was minimalistic: the group were wearing lifejackets which were never inflated, as opposed to the buoyancy aids which are routine in paddlesports and which were worn by the two instructors; another witness, Surgeon Commander Edward Oakley, of the Institute of Naval Medicine, said the failure to inflate the lifejackets was 'the single most important factor leading to the children's deaths.'[32] The teenagers were issued with wetsuits, but were not equipped with gloves, footwear or headwear. Neither of the instructors had flares or a two-way radio or even a mobile telephone, all standard items in a paddling expedition in these conditions. Inevitably the group were swept out to sea by wind and tide, and waves then caused capsizes. Two of the party became separated from the rest. Some kayaks sank, indicating insufficient internal buoyancy. There were attempts to swim ashore. A further two of the party became separated. Eventually the entire group were rescued, but from different positions in the bay, and between 5.30 pm and 6.40 pm, when they had spent many hours on or in the water in heavy swell. As well as the four participants who died, the other members of the party suffered severe hypothermia and shock, and indeed it was a testimony to their survival instincts that they did not drown too. Even with a party of fully qualified 'proficiency' paddlers at BCU Four Star level, voluntary organizations such as the Scout Association would recommend consideration of a supporting powerboat,[33] but none was, of course, in attendance. The coastguard had not been notified of any 'float plan', so that neither the St. Alban's Centre nor the coastguards knew precisely where the party ought to have been when the search commenced.

The prosecution produced at trial a full 'dossier' of the causes of this tragedy. It showed a combination of many factors: two wholly inexperienced and untrained 'instructors'; novice kayakers who should not have been on tidal waters; an incorrect weather report giving the wrong wind direction; seriously windy conditions, mounting to wind force three to four on the Beaufort scale,

---

[30] The Dorset County Council tourism website notes that 'the sheltered bays and headlands off the Dorset coast offer exciting sea kayaking [but] this is an open coast and adequate equipment, preparation and training is essential' [note the emphasis on specialist 'sea kayaking']; http://www.atgraph.net/dorsetcc/tourism/things/otwaters.htm

[31] 'My only trip to sea, by canoe tragedy teacher', *Evening Standard* (21 November 1994). When Ms Gardner completed her evidence, she 'wept uncontrollably as she was led from the witness box by an usher'; 'Canoe disaster instructor had only 400 yards sea experience', *Daily Mail* (22 November 1994).

[32] 'Catalogue of mistakes that led to drownings', *The Times* (9 December 1994).

[33] Table of maximum suggested recommendations for a range of BCU competencies when considering Scout association authorizations, Scout Association, *Paddling (Kayaks & Canoes)* FS120604 (May 2000).

when the upper limit for fully-qualified canoeing and kayaking groups would have been force four;[34] the fact that the lifejackets issued were not properly inflated and no instruction was ever given to inflate them fully; no-one was told to wear brightly coloured clothing to assist pick-up; only the instructors and teacher's kayaks had spray decks to keep water out; there was no headgear to conserve warmth; the 'instructors' were not equipped with flares or radio; the coastguards were given no prior details about the trip; Karen Gardner had previously told the teenagers to inflate their lifejackets in an emergency, but when drifting out to sea said nothing; a fishing vessel, the *Spanish Eyes*, reported seeing an empty kayak, but its exact position was not taken; Joseph Stoddart, the centre manager, took three hours to notify coastguards that a kayaking group was missing, although the group had been due back for lunch at 12 noon, and the emergency services were not asked to help until 3.30pm; shipping in the area was not alerted; helicopters arrived at the scene but were directed to look along the coast rather than out to sea; nobody was in overall command of the Maritime Rescue Service Centre at Portland at the time; a serious delay occurred in alerting the helicopter and lifeboats; and twenty minutes was spent investigating reports of kayaks seen returning to Exmouth, further along the coast but which was a wholly unrelated matter.[35]

The sixteen day criminal trial at Winchester Crown Court therefore revealed that the trip and the surrounding circumstances had been a catastrophic catalogue of errors. Perhaps most significant was that neither of the 'instructors' had even the most basic supervisory qualification in kayaking. As we have seen, following the verdict of guilty by the jury, the company behind the St. Alban's Centre was fined £60,000 and its managing director, Peter Kite, sentenced to three years for manslaughter. More importantly perhaps, Ognall J urged a full Government inquiry into the running of activity centres. His view was that where parents and teachers send their children for activity holidays, 'The potential for injury and death is too obvious for safety procedures to be left to the inadequate vagaries of self-regulation'.[36]

The lead in to legislation

Until the trial, despite a storm of suggestions, the Conservative Government of the day had been proposing a voluntary code of practice, which would allow accreditation. An all-party Select Committee on Education recommended that 'a culture of safety' must be entrenched in outdoor activity centres, and there was also a recommendation from the Activity Centre Advisory Committee for compulsory registration. Above all, the demand from Ognall J that 'authoritative

---

[34] Force four on the Beaufort Scale, proposed by Admiral Sir Francis Beaufort in 1806, is a 'moderate breeze', with winds between 13 and 18mph.

[35] See the excellent analysis by Simon Midgley, 'Errors and inexperience cost four young lives', *The Independent* (9 December 1994).

[36] 'Boss is jailed over canoe deaths', *The Independent* (9 December 1994).

control, supervision and . . . intervention is called for' produced a climate of opinion for legislative change. It was entirely fortuitous that the constituency MP was so highly placed in the private members' ballot, but this led to speedy passage of his Bill. Nevertheless, some MPs gave a warning against attempting to eliminate risk altogether; for example, Mark Wolfson MP, chairman of the trustees of the Brathay Hall outdoor activities centre in Cumbria, indicated that 'There is a real possibility that safety could become so dominant an element that the thrill, excitement and the challenge of these activities could actually be squeezed out. Safety standards must be exacting but an acceptable risk is, and ought to remain, a part of this activity.'[37] A key factor in changing the climate of opinion was a study of outdoor centres by the Health and Safety Executive, reported the week before the Second Reading debate on the Bill, estimating that one in ten centres (around 300 of the country's 3,000) still had 'serious and potentially life-threatening flaws'.[38] However, as Anthony Steen MP pointed out, there had actually been over the previous decade 'comparatively few fatalities in activity centres'.[39] He indicated that in his view 'activities such as canoeing on rivers, sailing on the high seas or abseiling are inherently dangerous and one must be extremely careful as to how far one nannies children and prevents them utilizing the activities to develop strength and character and to obtain the skills which the centres aim to develop.'[40]

There was also subsequent civil litigation brought by some of the victims and the parents of the deceased teenagers at Lyme Bay. These actions were settled, principally because proceedings brought by the parents would generally be limited to £7,500 bereavement damages for the death of children. The company were subsequently involved in somewhat unedifying further action against the coastguards, in *OLL Ltd v Secretary of State for Transport*,[41] when they attempted to recoup these sums by alleging a failure to respond promptly. The suggestion was that HM Coastguard had engaged in what was described by counsel for OLL as 'positive miscoordination' of the rescue attempts of others, to the extent that they gave the manager of the St. Alban's Centre misplaced assurance about where the party was likely to be, misdirected the lifeboat to search inshore rather than offshore and in the wrong area, misdirected one Royal Navy helicopter and failed to mobilize another until the late afternoon. The aim was to claim an indemnity against the Secretary of State, or a contribution towards claims settled under the Civil Liability (Contribution) Act 1978 on the basis that the coastguard owed the kayakers a duty of care and that they had

---

[37] 'Activity centre law "must not ban risk"', *The Independent* (28 January 1995). Mr Wolfson was head of the Brathay centre from 1962 to 1966. See for a history of Brathay, Maurice Dybeck, *A Broad River: A History of the Brathay Hall Trust 1946-1996* (Ambleside: Brathay Hall Trust, 1996).

[38] 'Minister's U-turn to stop a new Lyme Bay tragedy', *Daily Mail* (25 January 1995).

[39] House of Commons *Hansard* (27 January 1995) col 618.

[40] Ibid.

[41] [1997] 3 All ER 897. May LJ notes at 899 that the civil claims 'either have been or soon will be settled by the plaintiff'.

conducted the search and rescue operation negligently. The Secretary of State applied to the court for an order that the claim be struck out on the ground that it disclosed no reasonable cause of action, and the Court of Appeal upheld this view. They held that there was no obvious distinction between a fire brigade responding to a fire where lives were at risk and the coastguard responding to an emergency at sea; there was therefore no duty to respond to an emergency call, nor, if they did respond, would they be liable if their response was negligent, unless their negligence amounted to a positive act which directly caused greater injury than would have occurred if they had not intervened at all. The evidence did not show anything like this greater injury. There had been two previous attempts to find coastguards negligent, but both these actions failed too.[42]

The legislation and its enforcement

At the end of the Lyme bay trial Ognall J had essentially demanded Government action. This is a rare and stark example of a judicial pronouncement leading to legislative intervention. He suggested that regulations should deal with 'the authority, control, supervision and, if necessary, intervention, of commercially-run centres ...Nothing else will do'. The judge asked for his remarks to be forwarded to the then Secretary of State for Education, Gillian Shephard, who had just replaced John Patten.[43] Although the facts of the court demonstrated crass misconduct, it was not clear that this activity centre was entirely typical of adventurous activities as a whole. A report by the Local Education Authority, Devon County Council, summarized that 'the immediate cause of the tragedy was, however, the lamentable failure of the St. Alban's Centre to organize and supervise the canoeing activity, to employ suitable staff and to have prepared and operated sensible and pre-determined procedures when difficulties arose'.[44] As other factors had been suggested in respect of the rescue operation mounted, so an additional inquiry was ordered by Brian Mawhinney, the Transport Secretary. Conducted by John Reeder QC, a shipping law expert, this followed an internal investigation by HM Coastguard, which resulted in disciplinary measures against some officers and changes to local rescue procedures. Published in July 1996, the

---

[42] *Skinner v Secretary of State for Transport The Times* (3 January 1995) and *Hardaker v Newcastle Health Authority.* (8 March 1996, unreported QBD), Waterhouse J. The authority on which these two cases, and *OLL*, rest is the consolidated claims in the Court of Appeal of *Capital and Counties plc v Hampshire County Council*; *Digital Equipment Co Ltd v Hampshire County Council*; *John Munroe (Acrylics) Ltd v London Fire and Civil Defence Authority*; *Church of Jesus Christ of Latter Day Saints (Great Britain) v West Yorkshire Fire and Civil Defence Authority* [1997] 2 All ER 865 where it was held that a fire brigade did not enter into a sufficiently proximate relationship with the owner or occupier of premises so as to come under a duty of care merely by attending at the fire ground and fighting the fire. Only where they 'increased the risk of the danger' would they be liable.

[43] 'Director jailed for canoe trip manslaughter', *Daily Telegraph* (9 December 1994).

[44] Quoted by Jan Bradford, Senior Inspector with the AALA and BCU coaching organizer for Devon and Cornwall, 'From Lyme Bay to Licensing', AALA (April 2000).

Reeder report noted that there had been 'some complacency' but completely exonerated the coastguard service. However, the report recommended improvements in radio coverage, the relationship between coastguard and harbour masters and in the coastguard and even in the BCU's advice on sea kayaking, although it added that all of these matters were already being dealt with.[45]

It is important to note that there had already been progress towards a voluntary system, both a national system of registration and codes of practice in the outdoor activity sector, before the Lyme Bay case. There was therefore already an embryonic structure before the licensing system was imposed by the 1995 Act. In addition, the Health and Safety Executive had already commenced visits to outdoor activity centres in 1992 and this was accelerated after the tragedy in March 1993, so the inspection regime under the Act was similarly building on earlier experience. There were and are a number of voluntary codes of practice produced by national governing bodies such as the British Canoe Union and the Royal Yachting Association, along with accreditation under organizations such as the Welsh Tourist Board and the British Activity Holiday Association, which is the trade association for private sector providers of activity holidays and courses in the UK. Another important organization since 1963 has been the Association of Heads of Outdoor Education Centres, originally known as 'The Association of Wardens of Mountain Centres', and speaking for the various centres set up by Local Education Authorities along the model of Outward Bound Schools. This Association is in turn affiliated to the National Association of Head Teachers, but also has representatives on the national governing bodies of the main adventure sports and the key organizations concerned with outdoor education. Outward Bound had started as a short course in 1941, run by the educationalist Kurt Hahn, an exile of Nazi Germany, who was concerned at reports that large numbers of young seamen died with little struggle when forced to abandon ship, whereas older, more experienced sailors were able to survive.[46]

In 1993, the English Tourist Board brought together a group representing all these organizations and most of the voluntary approval bodies and other interested parties, and this was known as the Activity Centres Accreditation Committee (ACAC).[47] The aim was to agree a comprehensive voluntary code of practice, covering issues such as safety, the welfare of participants, management and quality control. However, individual sporting activities would remain to be controlled by the appropriate national governing bodies. In April 1994 the ACAC published a code of practice, which was 'a statement of principles and expectation for the responsible provision of organized outdoor adventure activities' and to remedy any defects in safety, with the Lyme Bay disaster very

---

[45] 'Coastguards exonerated', *The Guardian* (18 July 1996).

[46] See generally Mark Zelinski, *Outward Bound: The Inward Odyssey* volume one (Oregon: Beyond Words Publishing, 1991), volume two (Hamilton, Ontario: From The Heart Publishing, 2002), and Thomas James, 'Kurt Hahn and the Aims of Education', *The Journal of Experiential Education*, vol. 13, No. 1. (May 1990) 39 et seq., updated 2000.

[47] 'How safe are activity centres?', *The Times* (12 February 1994).

much a motivating force in the background.[48] However, this voluntary system was then literally overwhelmed by the statutory licensing scheme under the Activity Centres (Young Persons Safety) Act 1995.

Opinion was indeed very sharply divided in the months after Lyme Bay as to whether there should be national regulation of the outdoor activity industry by statute or whether voluntary self-regulation should remain. The Government view was inclined to the latter perspective, with the then Secretary of State for Education, John Patten, issuing new guidelines to schools on trips, in November 1993, and reminding school governors of their legal duty to ensure the safety of the children in their care. The latter point seemed otiose, as the Southway comprehensive school had most certainly checked out the St. Alban's Centre in advance, following Devon County Council guidelines, both by consulting the brochure and having a teacher do a reconnaissance visit. Unfortunately, the brochure, which had several pages on safety, misled the school into thinking that the instructors on a kayak trip would be properly qualified members of national governing bodies. It was therefore perhaps understandable that parents and the school, in conjunction with their MP, commenced a campaign for statutory regulation. One parent, Carolyn Langley, a legal secretary, insisted that her daughter Claire's death was not an 'unavoidable accident [but] was the result of someone else's carelessness. I have never felt so angry in my life. I was determined to make sure that no other adventure company was allowed to do the same thing again in the future'.[49] The campaign perspective was that many activity centres were sub-standard, and their estimate of possibly 10 per cent was later borne out in the research. With around a million children passing through the centres each year, this suggested that 'tens of thousands are being exposed to cut-price instruction and safety standards'.[50]

Further ammunition was provided in a study of 121 activity centres in Wales, most of them private, carried out by the Swansea Institute of Higher Education, which then called for a compulsory registration scheme to ensure proper standards of staff training. Professor Terry Stevens, one of the authors, warned that 'There would be more tragedies like Lyme Bay unless urgent action was taken'.[51] The report estimated that around nine million adults and children were taking activity courses and holidays at about 3000 centres across Britain in an industry worth an estimated £420m per annum. Inadequate staff training was highlighted as one of the most important concerns, and almost half of the activity centres contacted did not require even basic first aid training from their staff, while more than a quarter of all centres failed to keep any records of accidents. John Patten had also requested the Health and Safety Executive to carry out a random sample of more than 200 centres to see if further regulation was

---

[48] See generally Bradford, op cit.

[49] 'A law unto themselves', *Daily Mirror* (8 August 1998).

[50] Simon Midgley. 'Taking risks with recreation; the adventure industry is divided on how to avoid more tragedies', *The Independent* (9 December 1994).

[51] 'Call for compulsory registration scheme to regulate training', *The Glasgow Herald* (9 December 1994).

necessary, and although their advice was that centres were covered by existing legislation, including the Health and Safety at Work Act 1974, the Department for Education issued a circular in November 1994 entitled *Safety in Outdoor Activity Centres*.[52] It was HSE advice that led to a statement on the very day Ognall J passed sentence on Peter Kite and the company, 8 December 1994, that 'further regulation or statutory accreditation is not necessary'. The DFE spokesman stated that the Government's view 'remains that there is no advantage to be gained from adding to the existing legislation and supports the voluntary accreditation scheme'.[53] However, there was now gathering momentum to support additional controls, particularly when Ognall J issued his *ex cathedra* pronouncement at the conclusion of the criminal trial.

The HSE then published an interim report in January 1995 on their survey of activity centres, which noted that 31 per cent of centres were accredited by an existing voluntary scheme, and that 84 per cent of providers had made a satisfactory assessment of the risks and had adequate control measures in place. Inspectors from the HSE had examined 192 activity centres offering pursuits such as abseiling, rock climbing, sailing and caving. However, the inspectors found that 24 per cent of the centres had no written safety policy, 16 per cent failed to provide even informal training for instructors, and 13 per cent made no risk assessment of activities. Even more worryingly, 8 per cent had no emergency procedures or equipment and no system for recording incidents, while 6 per cent had no system for ensuring equipment was well maintained and safe.[54] This survey was an important additional factor in assisting the passage of the Bill, although the report concluded that while most centres maintained high safety standards, there was 'no room for complacency'. David Jamieson MP ruefully commented that 'If only 84 per cent of airline pilots were competent, that would not give the travelling public much confidence in airlines. Parents feel the same way about outdoor activity centres'.[55] At this point, with Mr Jamieson's private members' Bill gaining support from a wide cross-section of organizations such as the ACAC and the Welsh Tourist Board, the Government suddenly capitulated and decided to support the legislation.

The legislation

In its final form, the Activity Centres (Young Persons Safety) Act 1995 required the Health and Safety Commission to draw up proposals for regulations, and a consultative document was issued in the autumn of 1995 setting out proposals for a statutory scheme for the licensing of adventure activities for young people under 18. In addition there were proposals for a non-statutory scheme to complement the statutory scheme. Following consultation, regulations were

---

[52] DFE circular 22/94.
[53] 'Parents this must not happen again', *Daily Mail* (9 December 1994).
[54] 'Minister's U-Turn To Stop A New Lyme Bay Tragedy', *Daily Mail* (25 January 1995).
[55] 'Activity centres face curbs', *The Guardian* (25 January 1995).

finally issued in March 1996, and took effect from 16 April 1996.[56] However, the definitional ambit of what is captured by 'adventurous activities' has been determined largely the AALA. Operating under the guidance of the Health and Safety Commission, the AALA has been the driving force for subsequent change in the outdoor activities field, with an inspectorate appointed from a range of experienced people. For example, the Head of Inspection Services has been Marcus Bailie, who had previously been Director of The National Adventure Centre for Ireland, and was previously the instructor responsible for British Mountaineering at Plas y Brenin, the National Mountain Centre in North Wales. The author too of one of the standard canoeing and kayaking guides, Mr Bailie has been able to exert an authoritative presence on the inspections.[57] Indeed the AALA under his leadership has been the source of a steady stream of thoughtful and systematic advice to all those involved in outdoor activities. The inspection regime produced an initial group of 875 licence holders, which was about half the original estimate by the ACAC, but this was due to the more restrictive scope of the final regulations. On the whole, the licensing system seems to have worked well, although no doubt some of those refused a licence or withdrawing their applications have perhaps not thought so.[58] The aim throughout has been to provide clear guidance on what is required, and to support good practice; for example, the suggestion in providing a Risk Management Summary was 'to enable licensed providers to meet, in the least bureaucratic form, the ever-increasing demand for written information such as examples of their risk assessments'. By completing the RMS sheet produced by the AALA the licensed provider would then satisfy the requirements both of licensing and those of the Health and Safety of Pupils on Educational visits (HASPEV) which states that 'it is good practice to seek details of their safety management practices'.[59] A triennial review process was envisaged, and the first took place in 1999, with a majority of respondents of the view that the scheme was 'doing its job', and three-quarters indicating that it should continue. That view has continued, and the AALA has consolidated its stance of authoritative yet sensitive expertise on all aspects of outdoor activities.

Activities to which the licensing applies are still perhaps not entirely clear around the edges, and probably never can be, particularly as new disciplines are invented. The criteria originally used to decide the inclusion of activities in the licensing scheme were: whether there was a significant risk of death; whether the competence of the instructors was vital; whether the activity was vulnerable to weather changes; and whether there was a significant risk to the group's safety if

---

[56] Adventure Activities Licensing Regulations 1996 (Statutory Instrument 1996 No 772).

[57] *Canoeing & Kayaking: Techniques, Tactics, Training* (London: Crowood Sports Guides, 1992).

[58] The Adventure Activities (Enforcing Authority and Licensing Amendment) Regulations 1996 (SI 1996 No 1647) allocates enforcement responsibilities for AALA to either the Health and Safety Executive or to local authority inspectors by application of the criteria given in the Health and Safety (Enforcing Authority) Regulations 1989.

[59] Page 14 paragraph 57 of Part 1 of the Supplements to HASPEV.

there was a combination of adverse factors. This statement of policy by the AALA has assisted in the consideration of definitions, but has also enabled them to respond to newly established potential hazards. The classic example is the area of 'combined water and rock activities'. After two girls from a Leeds school were swept to their deaths while 'river walking' at Stainforth Beck in October 2000, urgent attention was given to the hazards in this sort of outdoor activity. Hannah Black, aged 13, and Rochelle Cauvet, aged 14, were in the Yorkshire Dales on a 'walk', which involved scrambling and paddling along the river bed. Marcus Bailie of the AALA appeared as a witness at the inquest in 2002, delayed for at least a year while the prosecuting authorities determined that they did not have the evidence to proceed against the teachers; he pointed out that there had been a previous drowning while riverwalking on a field trip in the Neath Valley the previous year and that there were 'frightening similarities between the two cases' which could perhaps have been prevented if the Stainforth Beck inquest had been able to go ahead.[60] Indeed, the death of Jason Dalton in 2001, while on a 'confidence building' field trip, to which he referred, had been preceded by the death of an experienced outdoor pursuits instructor Kevin Thomas in 1998 at the same location near Neath, Dinas Rock, when he was supervising a party of schoolchildren making a river crossing.[61] These incidents were followed by a similar drowning two miles away of Herve Bola in 2002 on a trip with an outdoor activity centre, although that death appears more due to the fact that he was a non-swimmer.[62] According to the Brecon Beacons National Park Authority there have been five drownings and many near misses in the last decade in this area of limestone scenery, all involving members of led groups, although not all involved in 'river walking'. In response to Stainforth Beck, the Government also issued new guidance clarifying that the legal responsibility for trips rests with the Local Education Authority and also stipulating that every school is required to have a named member of staff to act as educational visits co-ordinator (EVC).[63] Changes also followed in the AALA literature, so that guidelines on gorge walking were added in July 2002, and these were then later subsumed in guidelines for 'Combined Water / Rock Activities' in July 2003.[64] The full range of what may fall within this spectrum of activities is colossal, and many names are used to describe related activities, under what is now developing as an overall label, 'Activities at the Water Margins'.[65]

---

[60] 'The fear factor', *Yorkshire Evening Post* (9 March 2002).
[61] The children from the Hall School, Wimbledon were tied to a safety rope, but when one of the boys got into difficulties Mr Thomas went to his assistance and slipped; *Western Daily Press* (27 June 1998); *Evening Standard* (25 June 1998).
[62] 'Warning: Leisure can cause death', *Western Mail* (8 February 2003).
[63] '"Safety supremos" for school trips', *The Guardian* (6 August 2002).
[64] Collective Interpretation 6.06. These are working documents for inspectors, but are a very helpful list of topics for providers when drawing up their own guidelines.
[65] One of these disciplines, coasteering, was described by an instructor in Woolacombe as 'a mixture of climbing and drowning' and by one of his participants as involving 'most of the things that brought stern looks of disapproval when I tried them as a child'; Matthew Taylor 'Leap of faith', *The Guardian* (9 October 2004).

Section 1(3) of the 1995 Act allows a flexible approach, in that 'facilities for adventure activities' will mean 'facilities, for such sporting, recreational or outdoor activities, as may be prescribed by regulations'. It is therefore very important to look both at the delegated legislation[66] and the licensing practice to establish the full remit. Currently the main outdoor activities are listed by the AALA as:

1. **Caving** (underground exploration in natural caves and mines including pot-holing, cave diving and mine exploration), excluding show caves or tourist mines open to the public, or parts of mines which are still being worked;
2. **Climbing** (climbing, traversing, abseiling and scrambling activities except on purpose-designed climbing walls or abseiling towers);
3. **Trekking** (walking, running, pony trekking, mountain biking, off-piste skiing and related activities when done in moorland, or any terrain over 600m, which is remote, i.e. over 30 minutes travelling time which will be never more than 2.5km from the nearest road or refuge); and
4. **Watersports** (canoeing, rafting, sailing and related activities when done on the sea, tidal waters, or large or non-placid inland waters).

The central aim is still that where instruction or leadership in any of these activities is offered on a commercial basis to young persons under 18, then a provider will need to obtain a licence.[67] The Act came into effect on 28 August 1995.

Exemptions

However, there are significant qualifications to the licensing arrangements, in that the regime does not apply to activities organized by schools, nor to any volunteer organizations. When the regulations were released in draft in 1995 there was considerable criticism of this. However, the AALA guidelines and policies have started to have a significant effect beyond the statutory remit, so that they have become a helpful model for schools and for a number of these voluntary organizations. As these voluntary organizations operate such a large proportion of outdoor activities, the legislative framework has a wide influence. Some of the exclusion for volunteer organizations is because of the law on Crown Immunity; for example, this is an important consideration in cases involving the Army cadet forces. Interestingly a leading case on liability for youth activities, *Harrison v Ministry of Defence*,[68] involved this very organization and indicates that although they are outside the Act they are certainly not immune from cases in the tort of

---

[66] See in particular the Adventure Activities (Licensing) (Designation) Order 1996, SI 1996/771, Adventure Activities Licensing Regulations 1996, SI 1996/772, and the Adventure Activities Licensing Regulations 2004, SI 2004/1309.
[67] Section 1(3)Activity Centre (Young Persons') Act 1995.
[68] 1 December 1997, (1998) CLYB 3929.

negligence. The claimant was undergoing cadet corps training and was told by a Cadet Commander to run up and down a steep embankment at Caldicot Castle in Gwent, in the form of a relay race. The more adventurous ran straight up and down, while others according to Judge Curran at Newport County Court, slid down 'on their backsides'. The claimant ran straight down but tripped over a root and fell, breaking his arm. Their training had been on assault courses and combat trails, but these were inspected carefully and the cadets were shown how to negotiate each of the obstacles during a 'walk through' of the course. By contrast the embankment had not been inspected and no instruction had been given on how to negotiate it, and it was held that these constituted breaches of a duty of care. According to the judge anyone looking at the embankment would have realized that 'it was dangerous and there was a risk of falling and therefore injury'. However, as the victim knew that running up and down the embankment would increase the risk of falling he was found to have been contributorily negligent and damages were reduced by a third.[69]

The AALA has in effect become an independent watchdog on the delivery of outdoor activities, not just for young people but for all participants. Not everything can be foreseen, and inevitably there is going to be development with the benefit of hindsight. Again the classic illustration is the Stainforth Beck case, because river-walking had until then been treated as a 'low risk' activity. Marcus Bailie indicated at the inquest in 2002 that the 'dangers of river walking in apparently gentle streams' had only been recognized as a direct result of these drownings, but 'prior to this tragedy, it had not been foreseen as hazardous by those charged with writing guidelines'.[70] This is a view supported by Peter Cornall, the Head of Water and Leisure Safety for the Royal Society for the Prevention of Accidents, who noted that a ban on 'dangerous trips' would be inappropriate because 'In fact, often it is activities that are NOT perceived to be that dangerous that end in tragedy'.[71] As a result of this realization and following an analysis of accident statistics on school trips, which revealed 'most accidents did not involve activities that one would generally consider to be 'high risk', the AALA revised their *Good Practice in Adventure Activities within the Education Sector* in 2002. This excellent publication, one of a series of 'working documents' for inspectors, illustrates the proactive work of the AALA and was re-published in a second edition in 2002. Along with many other documents it is available on the AALA website.[72] The document points out that 'Individuals at all

---

[69] Challenge courses generally appear to be very safe; an American study investigating 15 deaths found that five were connected with falls from a height, with just one a participant and the others staff members, while the other 10 incidents were classified as sudden cardiac death. Of the falls, four out of five involved a single element, the zip line, where a pulley is attached to a cable for participants to ride down from a high platform; see Thomas R. Welch, MD and Robert Ryan, *Wilderness and Environmental Medicine*, 13, 140 142 (2002).

[70] See generally Martin Wainwright, 'Tragedy highlights perils of river walks: Inquest told of "error of judgment" by teachers', *The Guardian* (5 March 2002).

[71] Commenting on the drowning during a field trip of schoolboy Yunus Moolla who drowned in Gullet Quarry in Worcestershire; 'Perils of the school trip', *Daily Star* (5 July 2001).

[72] http://www.aala.org.uk

levels within the organization, from classroom assistant up to Director of Education, or Chair of Governors have a duty of care. This includes ensuring that the educational potential of out-of-school activities, particularly those loosely described as 'adventurous activities', are realized within acceptable margins of safety.'[73] It then goes on to give a checklist of practical suggestions for safety, as well as dealing with some less tangible matters, such as the 'suitability of activity leaders', and indicates that the aim of all written procedures should be 'positive and enabling, not restrictive or defensive'.[74] Another guidance note issued the following year dealt further with the suitability of activity leaders, reiterating an AALA theme that

> providers should ensure that instructors have the training, experience, *personal qualities* and communication skills appropriate for ensuring the safety of participants... For example, they will need to judge, as best as they can, that the proposed leader is sufficiently mature to make appropriate decisions, possibly whilst under stress.[75]

Marcus Bailie himself has also been active in promoting a philosophy, notably his 'Idiot's Guide approach', which suggests that 'there are only three things that will cause death or disabling injury during an activity session: drowning; impact with something solid (either from above, the side or by falling onto it); and exposure. What we want to know is how do you prevent these from happening during your sessions?'[76] While these basic points might be expanded or redefined, so that for example a draft consultation in 2003 on *National Guidelines for Climbing and Walking Leaders* preferred the term 'hypothermia' rather than 'exposure',[77] they nevertheless encapsulate the essentials from the cases. Mountain Leader Training UK is the coordinating body overseeing training for some six thousand leaders, instructors and guides, and these 2003 guidelines are a very helpful analysis of possible hazards in the outdoors. They are worth quoting in full before we examine in the next two chapters some of the lessons that can be learned from the cases. This MLTUK advice on good practice suggests an apprehension of:

1. **Impact with a solid object**: rocks falling from above; falling onto rock; jumping or falling onto submerged rock; jumping from a height into water; being swept or smashed against something solid;

---

[73] Para 1.4 op cit.

[74] Para 6.9 op cit.

[75] Collective Interpretation 1.16. This is paragraph 18 of *Guidance to the Licensing Authority*, and the AALA point out that employers and providers of activities have a duty to ensure that activity leaders are technically competent under reg 7(1)(b)(i).

[76] 'Risk Assessments, Safety Statements and all that Guff', *The Journal of Adventure Education and Outdoor Leadership and Far Out* Vol. 13, No. 3 (Autumn 1996).

[77] Mountain Leader Training UK, *National Guidelines for Climbing & Walking Leaders*, Advice on Good Practice for anyone with a responsibility for mountain-related activities, encompassing the principles of a safety management system, 2nd Edition (2003) Draft Consultation Document.

2. **Drowning**: entrapment under water; repeated submersion in stopper waves or sea swell; suddenly rising water, e.g. 'freak waves', flash floods, dam releases; slowly rising water, e.g. trapped by rising tides or rising river levels; falling into water and being swept away; sudden immersion (dry/secondary drowning);
3. **Hypothermia**: inadequate personal clothing or equipment during or after the activity; submersion, e.g. being swept out to sea.

Finally, a significant part of the work of the AALA has also been to make appropriate recommendations on health and safety issues that might unduly affect the operation of outdoor centres. For example, in 2004 the new Working at Height Regulations were thought to be incompatible with many common practices in adventure activities. What might have been appropriate in a factory in respect of ladders, additional ropes and safety nets would not necessarily have been appropriate on rock faces while mountaineering. Criticisms were made that the requirement for 'Areas of easily broken or crumbling material' to be signposted or fenced off and an insistence that 'two ropes are to be used at all times' would severely impede the work of Mountain Rescue: 'Perhaps those from Brussels should stop pushing pens for a while and come and join the rescue team for the day to see how it all works at the sharp end?'[78] Following a meeting of the various organizations brokered by the AALA, 'common sense has prevailed' and it was agreed that following the requirements of the national governing bodies, would be sufficient to establish 'good practice' and to satisfy the requirements of licensing.[79] This change was announced by an AALA 'Infolog', a web-based process that provides 'Lessons Learnt From Incidents, Accidents And Near Misses' and is clearly an invaluable service to anyone involved in outdoor activities. The fact that the AALA is involved in general discussions on health and safety outside its remit is necessarily helpful too in providing information gleaned from outdoor activities to the wider safety community, but also sampling 'outside the remit' enables the AALA to satisfy the requirement from the Health and Safety Commission that the licensing authority should look for 'a culture of safety overall'.[80] It is also an example of how the AALA has not only dealt with its remit of ensuring safety standards in adventure centres providing for the under 18s, but has ranged much more widely in endeavouring to protect the public from harm.

---

[78] Alan Crichton, 'Euro safety rules are the height of stupidity', *Aberdeen Evening Express* (26 June 2004).
[79] 'Working at Height Breakthrough', *Infolog* Entry No. 35 (April 2004).
[80] Page 3, paragraph 12 of Guidance to the Licensing Authority (L77) on 'Non-licensable activities'. See generally the AALA *Risk Management Summary* (RMS), in Collective Interpretation 1.17. Examples given of inspection by sampling activities outside the scope of the Regulations in order to verify a culture of safety overall are: climbing walls, ropes courses, walks, off road cycling in lower terrain, quad biking or go-karting, BMX biking, shooting, archery, and canoeing in swimming pools and low-risk bodies of water.

Widening or narrowing the remit?

As we have seen, the AALA's jurisdiction does not cover all organizations by any means, and nor does it cover all outdoor activities. Most equestrian activities are, for example, outside the legislation and regulations, although arguably these are fairly high on the danger scale. Apart from pony trekking when done on moorland or any terrain over 600 metres which is remote, then activities with horses are not licensed. The British Horse Society in its research has found that, unsurprisingly, the main hazard for riders comes in the vicinity of roads, and they have significantly tried to counter the risks over the last twenty years by their own Riding and Road Safety Test. Each year there are more than 3,000 road incidents involving horses, although in 2000 there were fortunately just two fatalities of riders.[81] The BHS safety test is taken by over 7,000 individuals every year, although arguably it is drivers who need more training than the rudimentary parts of the Highway Code about the need to slow down and give horses a wide berth. The BHS also estimate that of the 965,000 horses in the UK, one in five horses are killed in road collisions or are so badly injured that they have to be put down.[82] However, there are very few legal parameters; for example there is no minimum age limit for riding a horse on the road, nor is there any requirement to show a certain standard of proficiency, young riders do not need to be accompanied, and nor do they, or any other riders, need to be insured. The one exceptional requirement is that wearing a helmet is mandatory for anyone under 14 as a result of the Horses (Protective Headgear for Young Riders) Act 1990. As a case study of a fairly hazardous outdoor activity outside the AALA remit, horse-riding must rank fairly high, with on average one rider dying each month and 50,000 people going to hospital every year with a riding-related injury. Horse-riding is estimated to be the most lethal form of transport per mile travelled, and a BHS spokesman has described a horse as 'the only thing on the road capable of doing 0 to 60mph in any direction'. Mythologies abound here too. For example, three-day eventing has been a particular concern for public comment about safety, and after a run of five deaths in 1999 a special committee was set up by the British Horse Trials Association under Lord Hartington to investigate ways of making fences safer, perhaps by changing materials in their construction.[83] Its report after a seven month investigation led to 'frangible fences', consisting of supporting pins that collapse under impact, but these do not include all fences on a cross-country course. After the death of a leading rider, Caroline Pratt, crushed at the Burghley horse trials in 2004, four separate further investigations followed into what was described by the organizers as 'a tragic

---

[81] 'Bringing horse sense to Britain's roads', *Sunday Times* (12 May 2002).

[82] Over one hundred horses are reported as killed on roads every year, or eight each day; BHS *Equestrian Statistics*, based on the BETA National Survey 1999. The BHS also notes a study by J. Nicholl of the University of Sheffield Medical School in 1992 which puts this figure very much higher at 10,658 per year.

[83] 'Equestrian safety drive set in motion after year's fifth horse trials death', *The Guardian* (21 September 1999).

accident'.[84] Again the revealing contrast was that for every one person killed in horse trials, about 10 riders died on the roads. And in considering the full context of statistical risk, a safety spokeswoman for the BHS pointed out that 'the happy hacker who likes going out at weekends and would not dream of going three-day eventing is more likely to be killed.'[85]

As well as bringing in a whole new activity such as horse-riding, there have been other suggestions on individual activities, as the statutory controls cover just a limited range of activities. The AALA list deals with caving, climbing, mountain walking, sailing, skiing, and paddle sports, but there are equally dangerous activities such as indoor climbing, mountain biking, open water sports, archery and shooting, which are engaged in by many young people. Another possibility is to extend the remit of the AALA by continuing to cover the existing areas, but adding in adults too, or even to consider the ultimate oversight of all adventurous activities for any participant of any age in the UK. An extension to overseas activities was much debated after the death of Amy Ransom on a school trip in Vietnam in 2001. However, Charles Rigby, the head of the company, warned that the 'guidelines are already shackling' and 'If we're not careful, we will end up only being able to send students on package holidays not on true expeditions'.[86] Finance would of course be a key factor in any further extensions, as would too the much vaunted 'burden of regulation', which would inevitably increase the paperwork mountains. There is clearly a balance here, and Professor Harlow points out that 'the price paid for a risk-free environment is regulation'.[87]

However, as with many statutes it is the delegated legislation and the way in which those regulations are applied that are of critical importance to analyse the work of the AALA. The *Guidance to the Licensing Authority* was the essential starting point in 1996 when considering practice.[88] The major criticism when those regulations were first produced in draft form in September 1995 by the Health and Safety Commission was that they were 'patchy and illogical', in that they would cover the outdoor activities centre involved in the Lyme Bay disaster, but not many other circumstances involving injury on school trips.[89] However, as time has passed, the work of the AALA has had a major impact by informally determining yardsticks for schools and voluntary organizations well beyond its remit, both by setting standards and also by monitoring generic hazards which can be applied to a range of outdoor activities.

There are of course major debating issues about the AALA as well as the precise legal issues on their remit. The explorer David Hempleman-Adams, whose exploits include reaching the north and south poles and climbing the

---

[84] 'Rider's concerns before fatal fall', *The Guardian* (6 September 2004).

[85] 'Just how safe can we make events?', *Western Daily Press* (9 September 2004).

[86] 'Schools – end of the road for school trips?', *The Independent* (4 April 2002).

[87] Carol Harlow, *State Liability: Tort Law and Beyond* (Oxford: OUP, 2004) 6.

[88] *Guidance to the Licensing Authority on The Adventure Activities Licensing Regulations 1996* (HMSO: HSE Books, 1996).

[89] 'Storm as schools are left out of new rules on outdoor trips', *Evening Standard* (27 September 1995).

highest mountain in each of the seven continents, suggested to the Royal Geographical Society in 1999 that 'We are becoming a nation of softies... surrounding our children in cotton wool... they will not be able to cope with risk when they encounter it as adults'.[90] He was reported in his local newspaper in Bath as being another voice raised against 'red tape, bureaucracy and a growing fear of American-style litigation [which is] discouraging teachers and youth leaders from organising field trips and adventure holidays'. Delegates at the conference had been warned that after Lyme Bay and the AALA regulations 'many teachers no longer dared take pupils on such expeditions, and heard about risk assessments and a blame culture which left schools and youth leaders faced with the permanent threat of lawsuits if there was an accident'.[91] However, commenting on these assertions and some of the school fatalities since Lyme Bay, the educational journalist Philip Revell noted that some of these cases still showed a disquieting disregard of circumstances which 'any competent leader would have avoided'.[92] There are certainly lessons that need still to be learned by schools and voluntary organizations, and in the next two chapters these cases are examined in detail.

---

[90] 'Three cheers for softies', *The Guardian* (3 June 1999).

[91] 'Our nation of softy children', *Bath Chronicle* (1 June 1999).

[92] 'Lest we forget: Look closely at the children pictured here. Every one of them is dead, lost on a school trip', *The Guardian* (17 October 2000).

Chapter 3

Learning the Lessons: Schools

Lyme Bay was a central instance of culpability, but it is sadly not the only occasion of fatalities caused by negligence in the outdoors involving schools. In the decade since the Activity Centres (Young Persons Safety) Act 1995 there have been other fatalities, both within and outside the remit of the Act. It is instructive to look in detail at these instances, and then to make the comparison with voluntary organizations who are invariably operating outside the sphere of the licensing regime. The AALA have drawn up a useful skeletal summary of school fatalities, which has provided useful information in various legal cases and constructively assists the debate on best practice in safety management.[1] It covered as best they could determine the period between May 1985 when four schoolchildren were washed away at Land's End and November 2001 when a 4-year-old autistic girl died after a swimming lesson in Blackpool. Three years later in September 2004 the AALA estimated that between May 1986 and July 2004 at least 51 children and five teachers had died on school trips in Britain and abroad.[2]

Each one of these cases is an agonizing tragedy for the families involved, and many of them speak eloquently of the need to learn lessons to safeguard future generations of children. Although each death has its unique circumstances it is possible to discern some common themes, and it is therefore very important to classify and analyse the sort of hazards that are faced on these school trips. As we have seen, most school activities are actually outside the remit of the AALA, in particular all school trips abroad. In addition, the voluntary organizations are generally also outside the licensing arrangements, so to assemble a complete picture of the pattern of fatalities and injuries in outdoor activities it is important to trawl well beyond the legislative parameters. In addition, all outdoor activities for those above 18 years of age are outside the Act, although again many helpful comparisons on hazards are possible.

Fatalities with no blameworthy cause

Inevitably, with so many children on school trips there will be tragic deaths that have nothing to do with the activity, but have to be ascribed to 'natural causes'. This should often be more accurately described as a genetic defect or disease that had previously been undiagnosed. Fault clearly cannot be ascribed in these

---

[1] 'School Trip Fatal Accident Records Between May 1985 and November 2001', Appendix 2 of the AALA *Good Practice in Adventure Activities within the Education Sector*.
[2] 'Schools urged to curb their fears of the great outdoors', *The Times* (28 September 2004).

instances to schools or activity centres. For example, Charlotte Wright, aged 9 and from Sheerness, collapsed and died during activities on a trapeze at the PGL Centre at Marchant's Hill in 2002. She had been climbing a tree to a small platform, and appeared to faint and fall while secured by a safety harness. With an ambulance summoned she was in hospital in 11 minutes, but sadly to no avail.[3] Another death apparently from 'natural causes' occurred when James Todd, aged 12 and from Washington, was found dead lying on his dormitory bunk at an outdoor activities centre in Northumberland. An inquest was told that he was found to be suffering from cardiac dysrhythmia, which could have struck at any time, and his parents had 'absolutely no inkling' that he had this condition, particularly as he excelled at several sports.[4]

Such conditions are often extremely difficult for the medical profession to diagnose; Danielle Kennedy, aged six had a series of dizzy spells at school and at home and was seen by nine doctors, including five consultants, before she died of what a coroner described as a 'a rare and undiagnosed cardiac dysrhythmia' at Derbyshire Children's Hospital in 1999.[5] A campaigning group, Cardiac Risk in the Young (CRY), point out that there are a whole range of such conditions and believe that up to 400 children may be victims of undiagnosed heart disease each year. They have urged further medical research and screening by electrocardiogram testing in an attempt to define and combat the problem. It is estimated that up to four people under the age of 35 die each week from 'sudden death syndrome', with up to 10,000 unaware that they could be affected.[6] A classic instance of controversy on whether death was due to 'natural causes' or negligence was that of Anna Loyley, a very fit woman aged 26 who collapsed after completing the Bath Half Marathon in 1998 just weeks before she was to be married. Her family sued the St John Ambulance Brigade for incompetent use of an automatic external defibrillator.[7] The case was subsequently settled on the basis that this volunteer organization, launched in 1887 to provide volunteers trained in first aid to attend public events, accepted that 'certain aspects of the resuscitation could have been dealt with better', and the family used the undisclosed damages and other moneys to set up a trust fund for training in such techniques.[8] Ms Loyley was the second person to die in two years at the Bath event, a very well-organized race, but an inquest discovered she had a previously undiagnosed heart condition called Long QT Syndrome. Dr Dan Tunstall Pedoe, the medical officer in charge of the London Marathon, estimates that sudden death worldwide in marathons and half marathons is one death per 100,000 runs,

---

[3] 'Girl, 8, dies climbing adventure centre tree; anguished grandparents tell of family's heartbreak', *South Wales Evening Post* (7 June 2002).

[4] 'We had no inkling of this cardiac problem. James was a very fit and active lad who lived life to the full', *Newcastle Journal* (25 September 2002).

[5] 'Doctors 'missed dying girl's heart problem'', *The Times* (1 August 2001).

[6] 'Sport can be a dangerous game', *Daily Telegraph* (3 August 2000).

[7] 'First aid charity sued over death of runner', *Sunday Telegraph* (8 October 2000).

[8] 'Settlement reached: family halts legal action' *Bath Chronicle*, (20 October 2001).

and over the past decade 70 runners have died in marathons in Britain.[9] It is therefore inevitable that there will be these tragedies in competitive or outdoor events. Indeed the additional exertion may be the trigger to revealing an underlying condition, quite often in otherwise seemingly very fit young people, and in the current state of medical knowledge and poor preventative screening perhaps the only lesson that can be learned is that such 'inexplicable' deaths will occur from time to time.[10]

Then there are fatalities in schools which would appear to have occurred from such a bizarre concatenation of circumstances that they would appear unique. One such death was at the somewhat infamously progressive boarding school Dartington Hall in July 1984. Cathy Pelly, aged 16 and described as a fit, strong swimmer, was found to have drowned in Folly Pool on the River Dart within the school grounds. She and others regularly swam there naked, but as an heiress to part of the Clark's shoes company there seemed to be suspicious circumstances.[11] A team of 60 detectives at first suspected murder but, with just a single bruise on her neck, there was no evidence of this. Eventually suspicion turned to swans nesting nearby. The police persuaded a swan at Paignton Zoo to bite down on some plasticine, and took the result to a Plymouth ontologist, who confirmed it was similar to the mark on the girl's neck. A police diving team then captured two swans, took casts of their beaks and matched the male swan cast to the bite mark on the dead girl. The inquest jury recorded an open verdict, when the coroner was of the view that 'no-one could tell the court whether that mark was caused before death, at death or after death'.[12] When this coroner retired in 2003 after nearly 40 years of service he described this as his most memorable case and as 'quite baffling'.[13] As a result of this death on school premises and certain other lurid revelations this most expensive of British boarding schools closed in 1986.[14] Such an extreme result as a school closure following a fatality seems unlikely elsewhere in the education system, but it does point out the potentially disastrous public relations perspective of such an event.

Road travel the most serious hazard

A key finding in the AALA table is that of the 46 deaths from 1985 to 2001, over one-third, 16, related to road injuries. It is therefore much more dangerous to travel to an outdoor activity than to engage in it. This conclusion bears out the world-wide research that road travel is generally the most hazardous part of any

---

[9] *British Medical Journal* (28 August, 1999).

[10] See 'Jogging tragedy of Steve Cram's brother', *Daily Mail* (26 May 2001).

[11] 'Open verdict on nude swim pupil', *The Guardian* (24 August 1984).

[12] See for the coroner's views on retirement twenty years later, 'Did a swan drown the shoe heiress?', *Western Morning News* (17 February 2004); 'Death of a schoolgirl remains a mystery', *Torquay Herald Express* (5 July 2004).

[13] 'Hamish delivers his final verdict: I'm off', *Torquay Herald Express* (11 December 2003).

[14] 'Dartington to close after scandals and bad publicity', *The Times* (17 April 1986).

trip, outing or expedition. Professor Curtis at Princeton University has developed a model for Outdoor Safety Management which analyses both environmental and human factor hazards. Prominent in his research across a wide range of outdoor activities in the USA is the issue of driving and transportation, with adverse factors such as poor road conditions, overloaded vehicles, darkness, other erratic drivers, rushing to meet a schedule, being overly tired from a long drive, inadequate driving skills and alcohol. This empirical work derives from a 'dynamics of accidents' formula developed at Princeton by Alan Hale in the 1980s, to identify the underlying issues that have precipitated accidents and catastrophic events; the conclusion is that when there are just a few adverse factors they can be overcome, but that when they are several the risk becomes exponential. The aim then is to reduce risk, particularly by adopting strategies, such as defensive driving, to combat adversities on the road. However, the theory has application across a wide range of outdoor activities and is a helpful method in highlighting potential hazards that need risk assessment.[15]

Just one horrendous incident in 1993 accounts for 13 of the 16 road deaths in the AALA summary, and unfortunately this disaster is very instructive too. A minibus returning part of the school orchestra to Hagley Roman Catholic High School in the Midlands, from a visit to the school proms at the Royal Albert Hall in London, collided with the rear of a maintenance lorry on the hard shoulder of the M40, near Warwick. It burst into flames, and the driver, Eleanor Fry, a maths and music teacher, died along with 12 pupils. An inquest was told that she was 'probably exhausted after a 16-hour day of teaching, supervising and driving'.[16] The police accidents investigator indicated that 'feeling sleepy' was the most likely cause of the disaster, with the children dozing in the back, nothing to break the monotony of a long motorway drive at night, no service area then available on the M40 to break the journey, and no one to share the driving. Current advice given to schools is that 'a driver cannot safely drive and supervise children at the same time. Group leaders should ensure that transport by road has seat belts and that the pupils wear them; [and that] there are adequate rest stops for drivers'.[17] In addition, Ms Fry was short-sighted, and a pathologist told the inquest that he found the remains of the frame of the teacher's spectacles clasped between her thumb and forefinger, suggesting she was holding them just before the crash, perhaps to wipe her eyes.[18] The coroner stated that the passengers 'would have

[15] See generally Rick Curtis, *Outdoor Action Guide to Outdoor Safety Management* (1995), based on the earlier work of Alan Hale who administered the *International Outdoor Safety Review* for many years. See too Rick Curtis *Planning a Safe River Trip* (1995), also available on the Princeton University website, and his *The Backpacker's Field Manual* (New York: Three Rivers Press, 1998) illustrating many years of experience with the outdoor education programme at Princeton. See also Rick Curtis and Preston Cline, *Risk Management for Organizations: Keeping the ship afloat* (2002) on the OutdoorEd.com website.

[16] 'Pupils, parents and teachers share grief and confusion', *The Times*, (19 November 1993); 'Families of M40 crash victims seek tougher safety laws', *The Times* (1 July 1994).

[17] *Handbook For Group Leaders*, HASPEV Supplement 3, *Health and Safety of Pupils on Educational Visits: A Good Practice Guide* (2003).

[18] 'M40 driver slept', *Daily Mail* (30 June 1994).

stood a better chance of survival if they had been wearing seatbelts'.[19] He noted the ubiquitous nature of the school minibus. At the time it was estimated that there were 162,000 such vehicles on the road, the majority of them operated by schools, charities, and old people's homes. The law on minibus use was then, and is still, fairly complex, particularly when community, voluntary and other not-for-profit organizations are involved, and the Community Transport Association, representing over 600 organizations operating minibuses in the voluntary and statutory sectors, called for urgent safety legislation, which would include the comprehensive training of drivers and the mandatory fitting of seatbelts.[20] A review of licensing arrangements arising out of the M40 case led to the adoption of new minibus driver rules, and then after 1 October 2001 all minibuses and coaches were required to have forward-facing or rearward-facing seats, and each seat in minibuses has to be fitted with a seat belt. However, the UK still does not conform to an EC directive of 1996, which requires all drivers to obtain a full D1 licence, which involves a medical examination, an additional theory test, and an advanced driving assessment, although this is now a requirement for taking such vehicles on the continent.[21]

The M40 minibus disaster was the worst in Britain, but it was not the only such instance of road deaths en route to activities. The worst abroad was in July 1997, when three British teenagers from St James High School in Bolton died when the coach they were travelling in plunged down a ravine in the French Alps. They were minutes from their destination for a day's climbing as part of a 'curriculum enhancement' visit. Investigators suggested that the British driver, unused to a French left-hand drive vehicle after the original vehicle had broken down, must have had a 'momentary lapse of concentration', and subsequently he was convicted of involuntary manslaughter and fined £1,200.[22] In the same year 39 junior school pupils aged seven to 11 from a school in Belper were taken to hospital after their coach collided with a lorry, then careered across the central reservation of the M1, before crashing into an embankment. They were en route for a week's study visit to Gravelines in France. A police accidents investigator stated that he was 'absolutely astounded' that none of them had been killed, with parents convinced that seatbelts had saved their children's lives.[23]

In 1994, another bad year for deaths in coach crashes involving children, two teenage schoolboys from Biggar died after a collision between their school bus

---

[19] 'Latest chapter in catalogue of school trip disasters', *Glasgow Herald* (8 August 2000).

[20] 'School trip tragedy: M40 deaths renew safety row', *The Guardian* (19 November 1993). See too Community Transport Association, *Minibuses and the Law: Compliance with legislation for non-profit minibus operation* (looseleaf, updated).

[21] Under the Road Vehicles (Construction and Uses) Regulations 2001 drivers aged over 21 who passed their test before 1 January 1997 are automatically entitled to drive a minibus in the UK, while those who took their test after that date can only drive a minibus if they pass the specialist D1 test which requires a medical examination.

[22] *Daily Mirror, The Guardian* (8 July 1997). See an interview with Lesley Boardman who lost her son; 'Who can we trust with our children?', *The Scotsman* (11 July 2001).

[23] 'Children escape injury as coach crashes on M1', *Glasgow Herald* (8 November 1997).

and an articulated lorry on a minor road. Sheriff J Douglas Allan at Lanark Sheriff Court stated that the lorry's speed was a major factor, and also if the lorry had stayed on its side of the road the collision was 'highly unlikely'.[24] The fact that there were no seat belts on this school bus was a hotly disputed issue, as to whether it would have made any difference.[25] In response to these fatalities a Safe School Travel initiative was launched by the Scottish School Boards Association providing a code of behaviour for pupils, parents, and teachers, but also including a video that featured footage shot by hidden cameras on school buses in England; pupils are seen starting a fire in one vehicle, and on another journey, children are attacked by pupils throwing bricks from outside the bus. The Scottish Board indicated that the explicit nature of the film was necessary because travel was 'the most important issue' affecting pupils' safety.[26]

In the vast majority of road collisions world-wide, the literature notes that 'driver error' is the key component. Drivers can become distracted, fatigued and overstressed. The estimate in countless studies is the '90 per cent rule', in that poor driving habits account for 90 per cent of all collisions on the road. Police investigators no longer use the term 'accident' in connection with road offences, because the causes are so familiar and are not 'accidental'. They prefer the word 'collision' or perhaps, 'incident'. It is also clear that 'crashes', another somewhat loaded term, are usually the result of a driver taking a decision to break the criminal law, for example by overtaking at a dangerous place such as at a junction or on the brow of a hill, crossing double lines, speeding, jumping red traffic lights, using a mobile phone while driving, and a catalogue of other road traffic offences. One of the most familiar scenarios is the 'sleepy' driver. The Selby rail disaster, actually the largest claim for *motor negligence* ever, was where Gary Hart was jailed for five years for causing the deaths of ten people on a London-bound express train in 2001, after falling asleep at the wheel. Mackay J told Hart that because of his arrogance in setting off on a long journey without sleep, he had caused 'the worst driving-related accident in the UK in recent years'. He 'had made a choice not to have any sleep in the previous 24 hours. Choosing to set off in such circumstances hauling a two-tonne load made an accident 'almost inevitable'.[27]

Driver and mechanical incompetence combined when, in 1992, eight primary school children and two teachers on a trip to a swimming pool from Benarty Primary School in Ballingry, Fife, were injured. The driver was killed when their minibus rolled over twice and was then involved in a four-vehicle pile-up in thick fog.[28] Visibility was not the major cause, as a subsequent fatal accident inquiry conducted by Sheriff Hamilton in Kirkcaldy was told by a Department of Transport investigator that the driver, who was also the owner and mechanic, had

---

[24] 'Bus horror Mum in fury; no action against lorryman', *Daily Record* (6 September 1994).

[25] 'Investigator plays down lack of seatbelts in Biggar crash', *The Scotsman* (2 July 1994) and 'Bus chief questions safety of passenger seat belts', *The Scotsman* (1September 1994).

[26] 'Safety film shock bid for safety', *Glasgow Herald* (31 August 1995).

[27] 'Selby rail disaster man jailed for 5 years', *The Times* (12 January 2002).

[28] 'School bus driver dies in fog pile-up', *Glasgow Herald* (30 January 1992).

been in the process of preparing the vehicle for its annual MoT test the night before, and 'in effect the front brakes were ineffective'. It was therefore held that death was 'as a result of faulty maintenance'.[29]

When compared with many other forms of transportation, coach travel is actually very safe. Research carried out by the Royal Society in 1992 gave a ranking order for seven different modes of transport on kilometres travelled, which showed coach travel in sixth place with a very low risk; equestrian transportation was not reviewed, although as we have seen it is arguably one of the most risky activities on the roads, but the research showed the followed ranked order: motorcyclist, pedestrian, pedal cyclist, car, rail, coach, airline.[30] If a 'crash' does occur with a coach, then the number of injured can be high because of the passengers carried; in 1990 a double-decker coach carrying American students on a day trip overturned on a slip road from the A40 near Oxford, and as a result two teenagers died and 56 were injured. They had been on their way to an arts festival.[31] Schoolchildren in other countries have also been injured on being transported to activities, and many of the same familiar features apply: speeding, incompetent driving and fatigue. In 2000, eight German children died and 23 were injured when their double-decker coach, bound for a youth camp in Hungary, was involved in a collision in Austria. The police investigation showed that a speeding lorry loaded with paving stones literally 'crashed' head-on into the coach at 4am.[32] Another incident, involving a German tourist coach which killed 33 passengers in Hungary in May 2003, was caused by a driver ignoring warning red lights at a rail crossing; the crossing was unguarded, with no gates or barriers, and his coach had followed a first coach over the line even though a flashing light warned of an oncoming train. An earlier disaster had occurred at the very same crossing in 1980, when 24 Hungarians were killed.[33] Another 'accident', described by Vaclav Klaus, the Czech President, as having 'probably no parallel in our history', killed nineteen skiers in 2003, with another 30 injured, when it ran off the road late at night near Ceske Budejovice, having just crossed over the border from Austria, and although the circumstances are still being investigated it appeared to be yet another illustration of 'driver error'.[34] And when a coach plunged down an embankment near the Austrian city of Salzburg in 2004, killing five Britons, with 20 seriously injured, it appeared that the cause was the driver of a minibus, aged 70, who tried to overtake the coach when a car was coming in the other direction, forcing the coach off the road.[35] A report of that incident catalogued previous cases involving British holidaymakers,

---

[29] 'Driver died on coach with faulty brakes', *Glasgow Herald* (24 September 1992).

[30] N.C. Pidgeon, C. Hood, D. Jones, B. Turner and R. Gibson, *Risk Analysis, Perception and Management* (Royal Society: London, 1992).

[31] 'Latest chapter in catalogue of school trip disasters', *Glasgow Herald* (8 August 2000).

[32] 'Speeding truck kills eight youngsters in tour bus crash', *Birmingham Post* (22 August 2000); *Evening Standard* (21 August 2000).

[33] 'Train kills 33 as tourists' bus cut in two on crossing', *Birmingham Post* (9 May 2003).

[34] 'Czech bus crash kills 19', *The Scotsman* (10 March 2003).

[35] 'Man charged as victims of Austria crash are named', *The Guardian* (13 August 2004).

including a crash in Nevada in September 2000 when 39 British tourists were injured, and were subsequently awarded record compensation in an out-of-court settlement of £14 million, and the worst overseas coach disaster, in September 1999, when 27 elderly British tourists died in South Africa after their bus skidded off a mountain road near Mpumalanga.[36] The driver in the Nevada desert was later convicted of speeding, and the civil case against the American coach company was said by the claimant's solicitors, Irwin Mitchell, to be the highest award for damages ever made to British travellers involved in an accident overseas.[37] The driver in South Africa was sentenced to six years after admitting culpable homicide, but this sentence was later suspended on appeal and he was banned from driving for six years.[38]

Drug misuse, and particularly alcohol, is another straightforward factor in road injuries, estimated to be the cause of nearly 2,000 road deaths in Britain every year. Despite years of public safety campaigns on this issue, an astonishing 8,000 drivers each month are convicted of drink driving, although with increasingly stringent sentencing on drunk drivers.[39] It seems almost unthinkable that a school driver could be under the influence, but this seemed to be the factor involving the death in 2002 of a Scottish pupil Katherine Fish, aged 15 and from Largs. She was killed and several pupils and teachers seriously injured when the coach taking them on a summer trip to Barcelona overturned at 4.30am on a motorway sliproad near Dijon in southern France while speeding. Manslaughter charges were preferred against the driver, Mark Chisholm, who was driving in France for the first time; he was sentenced to a two year suspended sentence after tests showed that he had smoked cannabis six to eight hours before the crash.[40]

Despite this catalogue of cases, travel abroad is actually very much safer by coach than by, for example, a hired car, usually because the driver is professionally trained and working on a regular basis. There are of course some risks with any mode of transportation. World-wide it is estimated that road collisions claim the lives of 500,000 a year, and the International Red Cross have calculated that unless circumstances change, road deaths will be one of the world's biggest killers by 2025. Although there are more than 3,000 road fatalities a year in Britain, the UK has arguably one of the best safety records in Europe. More than 8,000 people a year are killed on the roads of France and Germany, 7,000 in Turkey and Poland, and 42,000 in the US. Some 9,000 people die on South Africa's roads each year, which means that about 140 people died per 100,000 vehicles, compared to 20 in the United States, and 15 in the United Kingdom. Standards of vehicle maintenance in the Middle East, Asia and parts of Africa are often not as high as in Europe, but of course the critical factor in the vast majority of these incidents is plain 'driver error'. As a result, there is

---

[36] 'Holidaymakers killed in bus horror', *The Times* (11 August 2004).

[37] 'Crash victims win claim', *Sunday Telegraph* (9 February 2003).

[38] 'The crash at Long Tom Pass in South Africa', *Birmingham Post* (12 August 2004).

[39] 'Record sentence for 13-pint driver who killed six', *The Times* (8 March 2001).

[40] The driver was also ordered by the French court in Dijon to pay a £3,266 fine and £2,000 compensation and costs to the family; *Daily Record* (4 December 2004).

overwhelming evidence for the view in the Institute of Advanced Motorists' *Minibus Driver's Guide*, that 'driving is probably the most dangerous activity in which any of us participate in each day'.[41]

In summary, the principal lesson to be learned from these transport cases is that this is invariably the most hazardous part of any outdoor activity. Safety considerations, particularly on the road, should therefore take a central role in the planning of any school trip, and transport to and from an activity should not be seen as an afterthought.

The overseas cases

The AALA table of School Trip Fatalities also shows that one-third of deaths took place abroad: 15 out of 46. None of these of course came within their remit, but important lessons can be learned here too. The first deaths recorded abroad by the AALA were of four teenage boys from Altwood school in Maidenhead who fell 300 feet over a precipice on Easter Monday in 1988 at Untersberg in Austria; a coroner found that they were left unsupervised by their teachers after a packed lunch in a restaurant, and were sliding about 'having great fun'. The AALA table records these deaths as occurring while 'sledging' but this would not appear appropriately to describe an activity where, a survivor explained, 'We were sliding down on our bottoms'. Verdicts of death by misadventure were recorded. However, the survivor acknowledged that the teacher in charge had indicated that they should 'be careful and stay on the path as mountains are very dangerous'.[42]

Apart from the three road deaths at Albertville in 1997, where as we have seen the driver had a 'momentary lapse of concentration', and was later convicted of involuntary manslaughter, all the other instances involved a single fatality. Most notorious of all, in 1996 Caroline Dickinson died at a youth hostel in Pleine Fougères, Brittany. The coroner held that 'she was the victim of a vicious sexual assault involving deliberate suffocation to prevent her from crying out for help …It is a nightmare that every parent dreads when they bring up their children'.[43] After intensive investigation, and a number of false trails, a Spanish waiter was sentenced to 30 years for this murder, although he is currently appealing.[44] Under French fire safety laws, the building had to remain unlocked at night, which obviously makes it very difficult to exclude intruders and to give full protection.[45] In a New York case in 2003, when a boy was sexually assaulted by an intruder entering his dormitory room, both the baseball camp being attended and the college where it was located were found to be at fault; the first for negligent

---

[41] *Minibus Driving* (London: IAM, 1995, 2002).
[42] 'Parents not told of all ski trip perils, says coroner', *The Guardian* (7 July 1988).
[43] 'Caroline's family in DNA database plea', *Western Morning News* (6 April 2001).
[44] 'Appeal next summer for Caroline's killer', *Western Morning News* (2 October 2004).
[45] 'Teacher's sentence quashed', *The Times* (24 July 1996).

supervision, and the occupiers for failing to provide adequate security.[46] While the ideal would be a firmly secured door against intruders, with a 'push bar' exit mechanism, this is sometimes said to be difficult given the nature of historic buildings used for youth activities, although the financial outlay is minimal.

Several of the other cases abroad involved drowning. In June 1999 Gemma Carter, aged 13 and from Cockburn High School, Leeds, died while swimming in the sea after dinner on a school trip to Le Touquet in France; her teacher was found guilty of manslaughter by a French judge and was given a six-month sentence suspended for five years, but successfully won an appeal.[47] Although the facts were disputed, a coroner's jury found that her teacher, Mark Duckworth, had not adequately supervised a party of nine pupils when they went to a beach for 'an evening paddle'. Returning a verdict of death by misadventure, the jury foreman in Leeds said 'we feel there was a shortcoming in the supervision of the pupils, specifically in the lack of formal head counts. The group proceeded to the beach activities in a disorganized way and the teacher was unaware of the number of pupils under his control.' A fellow pupil, Jennifer Clagett, gave evidence at the inquest that she warned Mr Duckworth that Gemma could not swim and was 'struggling in the sea', but that he had 'told her not to worry and to go back to the hotel'. Mr Duckworth denied that he had been warned of Gemma's plight and said that when he realized she was not with the group he believed she had gone back to the hotel.[48] His union leader, NUT General Secretary Doug McAvoy, said there should have never been a prosecution as 'Gemma's death occurred tragically in circumstances which could not have been foreseen'[49] and elsewhere he suggested that the post-mortem showed that Gemma died of 'thermal shock – an event no one could have foreseen'.[50] The latter statement seems very questionable, as hypothermia and 'thermal shock' are eminently foreseeable in cold seawater. Indeed, there certainly seemed some evidence for a negligence finding: Gemma's mother claimed she had written in advance of the trip to say that her daughter could not swim and asked for her to be supervised during a planned visit to a swimming pool,[51] although the Headteacher denied seeing this,[52] but in any event for a teacher who was a 'qualified lifesaver' to allow teenagers to go 'paddling' on a steeply shelving beach at night, with warning notices posted about strong currents, would seem very questionable.[53] The French coastguards pointed out that swimming in that location is 'forbidden and treacherous', with warning signs, some in English, and forthrightly noted that

---

[46] *Doe v Athletic Alliance Risk Purchasing Group*, Nassau County Superior Court, No. 29967/99, 11 March 2003.

[47] 'Brittany murder victim had been stalked for days', *The Times* (17 April 2002).

[48] 'Inquest criticizes teacher over death', *The Times* (13 May 2003).

[49] 'Gemma mum blasts delays', *Yorkshire Evening Post* (17 April 2002).

[50] 'Teacher wins trip death appeal', *The Independent* (17 April 2002).

[51] 'I told the head my daughter could not swim; inquest on school trip drowning hears of warning from mother', *Daily Mail* (7 May 2003).

[52] 'Teacher rejects blame for drowning', *The Independent* (9 May 2003).

[53] 'Teacher "ignored" girl's warning on drowning friend', *The Times* (8 May 2003).

'We cannot understand how this girl's teachers could have allowed her to be in such a dangerous place. It just doesn't make sense.'[54]

Another controversial case was that of Bunmi Shagaya, aged 11 and from Brixton, who drowned in Lac de Caniel near Dieppe in July 2001. At first it was not entirely clear whether Bunmi had been abducted or had drowned. This was the Hillmead primary school's first overseas trip, and again the elementary precaution of a head count was not carried out when the school party left the lake to walk to a nearby slide adventure ride. Bunmi's disappearance was only discovered when the school party were about to board their coach for the ride back to the hotel.[55] There was also evidence that another youngster on the school trip was rescued from the lake after apparently getting into difficulties, and no attempt seemed to have been made for 'pairing' or supervisory arrangements on a crowded beach, which contained approximately 300 people overlooked by just two lifeguards.[56]

In the USA, a context such as that of the loss of Bunmi Shagaya would be an immediate trigger for a very substantial award of damages. For example, in a Connecticut case in 1995, Hannah Spruill, aged 5, was attending a summer camp run by the city of Hartford, and was found unconscious by a fellow camper at the bottom of a lake. Despite resuscitation attempts, she died three days later. Her mother sued the director of the city's parks and recreation division and the head lifeguard, on the basis that her daughter was a non-swimmer, and that the defendants should have separated the swimmers from the non-swimmers so they could be properly watched in the water. This would have allowed for practices which have become standard in the USA, such as roping off an area for non-swimmers, prohibiting swimmers and non-swimmers being in the water simultaneously and having the children wearing a distinctive bathing cap indicating their swimming ability. The mother also sued lifeguards for failing to keep a proper lookout and camp counsellors alleging improper supervision; a jury found that this was an 'active' drowning and awarded her $3.5 million.[57] In a similar sort of case in Georgia in the same year a boy aged eight was attending a summer camp run by the army. During a recreational swim with 60 to 80 children, a counsellor discovered him unconscious, and he sustained severe brain damage, having to be hospitalized ever since. The mother sued on the basis that the camp had failed to conduct swimming proficiency tests before allowing children to use the pool, failed to provide life vests for non-swimmers in violation of their own pool rules and representations made to the campers' parents, failed to rope off an area for non-swimmers, failed to employ a 'buddy system' to ensure adequate supervision of a large group of children, and failed to provide adequate staff. There was also a claim that swimming lanes painted on the bottom of the pool were excessively wide and hid a submerged child. On the first day of

---

[54] 'My girl hated the water, so how could she drown?'; *Daily Mail* (11 June 1999).
[55] 'Divers search lake for school trip girl', *The Times* (4 July 2001).
[56] 'Bunmi teachers could face charges', *Daily Mail* (13 July 2001).
[57] *Spruill v Downing*, Conn., Middlesex County Superior Court, No. CV-93-0068193S, 29 March 1995.

the trial the defendants settled for $5 million.[58] While a death in Britain would produce only bereavement damages of £7,500, and a catastrophic brain injury from near-drowning a substantially lesser amount than in the USA, it is arguable that the elementary head-counting techniques of primary teachers on school outings should have been an essential safeguard, particularly when they knew that Bunmi 'could swim only 10 yards'.[59]

Four teachers have been summonsed to appear before a French magistrate in the Bunmi Shagaya case to determine whether they should be charged with 'involuntary homicide', for which they could face suspended jail sentences. Bunmi's parents, Salimata and Hameed Shagaya, have also indicated they will sue Lambeth LEA after the French legal proceedings are completed.[60] However, unions representing teachers reacted with alarm to any threat of criminal and civil action in this case; in evidence to the Select Committee on Education they suggested that not just overseas trips but all outdoor activities could be banned by them. Chris Keates, the general secretary of the NASUWT, noted that

> even in the best ordered of activities things will occasionally go wrong [and that] the union's extensive experience of supporting members who have found themselves the subject of legal action, despite following all available guidance, has led us to conclude that society is increasingly litigious and no longer appears to accept the concept of a genuine accident. It also fails to understand that perfect judgment, total attentiveness and faultless foresight are beyond human capacity.

Her union was particularly concerned at increased risks linked to more adventurous activities and visits to 'exotic locations'.[61] Tim Collins MP, the then Conservative education spokesperson, suggested that 'this shows how the nanny state and compensation culture are now eroding every last part of common sense from Britain' and indicated that his party would urge a 'Teacher Protection Bill' to provide legal immunity for teachers, so that 'going out on a school trip will not see them end up in court'.[62] Such legislation would of course be extremely controversial if it gave teachers immunity from the ordinary standards of negligence liability.

The drowning of Alex Foulkes in July 2003 seemed of a different order from that of Bunmi Shagaya, and self-inflicted. He was aged 17 and a Harrogate Grammar School student who drowned while wading across a river during a trek in the Italian Alps, or possibly as a result of a slip on the riverbank.[63] He was

---

[58] *Hemmingway v United States*, U.S. District Court, S.D. Georgia, No. CV 194-065, 13 December 1995.

[59] 'Ministers accused over swimming promise after drowning of Bunmi', *Sunday Telegraph* (8 July 2001).

[60] 'Teachers to face drowning inquiry', *The Times* (8 December 2003).

[61] 'End of school trips; teachers tell MPs: we're so frightened of being sued that we dare not take children out of class', *Daily Express* (1 November 2004).

[62] Ibid.

[63] Schools wary of "blame culture",' *Yorkshire Post* (28 September 2004).

certainly looking for a short cut, while walking ahead of the rest of his group with two friends, and they had ignored a bridge to contemplate wading across a 15 metre stretch of water. One possibility was that he may have suffered a heart attack through 'thermal shock' brought on by the bitterly cold water, as the river fed directly from a glacier. However, the Italian authorities considered a prosecution for negligence, on the basis that the three teenagers had been separated from the staff in charge and also on whether the party had been sufficiently warned about the dangers of the river near their base at a mountain refuge.[64] This seemed somewhat tenuous in the light of a police source quoted by *The Times* who indicated that the teenager 'took a short cut across the river to arrive at the lodge first'.[65] This trip had been organized by Exodus Travel, founded in 1974, and describing itself as the UK's 'leading adventure tour operator'. An inquest jury in 2005 returned a verdict of 'accidental death', with the coroner stating that the trip was well-organized and that he was satisfied party leaders had done everything possible to ensure the safety of the pupils.[66]

Slipping cases are sometimes quite difficult to diagnose. Tell-tale marks on the riverbank were investigated in the death of Alex Foulkes, as there were no immediate witnesses when he entered the water. One somewhat extraordinary case involving the death of a teacher 'slipping' on a mountain had several witnesses. But many years later they have changed their story. Howard Keeley was a student teacher who fell to his death in 1962 from Ben Nevis. Pupils interviewed at the time claimed that he had slipped over the edge while retrieving an ice axe. 41 years later police re-opened their inquiry when a former pupil at this school for children with behavioural problems came forward to implicate classmates who, he alleged, had kicked the teacher in the face and pushed him over. They have not yet concluded their inquiries.[67]

Winter sports have also taken their toll, although in the context both of the numbers involved in school skiing trips and the potential for injury, it is perhaps remarkable that only three deaths have resulted. This suggests excellent preparation on British school ski trips and high standards of leadership in what is clearly a 'high risk' activity, whereas fatalities have actually been occurring on what are often perceived as 'low risk' activities where there is perhaps not so much attention to detail. In January 2000 there was a ski fatality in Heavenly Valley, Nevada, when Rachel Williams, aged 15 and from Hayle, lost control and careered off the marked slope into a tree. She was not wearing a helmet despite the resort's recommendation that skiers should do so.[68] It was at this very resort where Sonny Bono, the US Congressman and former husband of the singer Cher, had died in 1998 in similar circumstances.[69] The teacher in charge of the school

---

[64] 'Fatal short cut of pupil drowned on trip to Alps', *Daily Mail* (17 July 2003).

[65] 'School in mourning after pupil's body found in river', *The Times* (17 July 2003).

[66] 'Pupil's death accidental', *The Times Educational* Supplement (8 April 2005).

[67] 'Teacher's climbing death "no accident",' *The Times* (24 February 2003).

[68] 'Real life: Look Mum No Hands!', *The Observer* (1 June 2003).

[69] Described as an 'avid and competent skier' the congressman was last seen leaving an intermediate run to detour through 'a gladed area of trees' ahead of his family; 'Sonny Bono

trip had been skiing for 30 years and had organized over 20 school ski trips; everyone agreed that his instructions were clear: 'Stay within your comfort zone; remember what was said about control; don't overtake each other.'[70] Although it is not clear that a helmet would have prevented this tragedy, there is an increasing usage on ski slopes, and the Ski Club of Great Britain recommends that 'all children should wear them but for adults it is a matter of personal choice... it may just be a matter of time before they become an accepted part of skiing'.[71] The lack of a helmet was certainly a factor in the second British school snowsports fatality, when a tobogganist was killed in February 2001; Nasreen Jamalzadeh, aged 15 and from London, was thrown off a sled in Fusch, Austria, and hit her head on rock. Opinions vary as to whether Nasreen Jamalzadeh and her fellow students should have been wearing helmets. Trevor Hamer, the British operator of the toboggan run, which took place under floodlights on a disused road at 10.30pm, insisted that 'Helmets are not required anywhere'. However, the Ski Club of Great Britain stated that 'It should be mandatory for children to wear helmets in these sleds, which can travel at great speed'.[72] Collision with a hard object is inevitably going to be a hazard in such sports, and unfortunately it does not have to be a very large object, as exemplified in the third British case when a teacher was killed in April 2001; Joanne Tanner collided with her pupils and then into a padded piste marker at the French ski resort of Valloire.[73]

In an era of cheaper air travel, school trips are also extending their range. Inevitably there may be difficulties in harsher terrain, and perhaps also in countries where there are not quite the same safety standards as in the UK. Buckinghamshire County Council issued new guidelines after an inquiry when Amy Ransom, aged 17 and from Wycombe High School, died in Vietnam. She fell 500 feet down a ravine after losing her grip on a tree as she descended backwards down a muddy slope on Mount Fansipan in July 2001. She had been on a school trip organized by World Challenge Expeditions, who objected to the inquiry report and suggested Government action 'because sixth-formers who want to go on challenging, character-building expeditions should be allowed to

---

killed in skiing accident', *The Times* (7 January 1998). There are divergent legal cases on fatalities caused by skiing into trees; in *Bouchard v Johnson*, 555 N.W. 2d 81 (North Dakota 1996) it was held that it was impossible to eliminate all skiing dangers because of the sport's 'inherent risks', but in the particular circumstances of a 'large, unmarked patch of ice' operators in *Hansen v Sunday River Skiway Corporation*, Maine, Oxford County Superior Court, No. CV-95-07, 7 November 1997, were held liable for a 'failure to warn' by appropriate marking, such as bamboo poles, and a jury awarded $600,000 as this was no longer an 'inherent risk' but a failure to mark a trail hazard.

[70] 'Skier's death "accidental"', *The West Briton* (20 April 2000). See also Phil Revell, 'On slippery ground: as thousands of schoolchildren head for the ski slopes, asks why Britain still allows its teachers to lead school parties after only one week's specialist training', *The Guardian* (6 February 2001).

[71] 'Staying safe on the slopes', *Birmingham Post* (22 January 2000).

[72] 'Why no helmet? father of sledge tragedy girl asks', *The Times* (21 February 2001).

[73] 'Mistake on ski slope led to death of teacher', *This is Wiltshire* (22 August 2001).

do so'.[74] Bucks LEA concluded that had the party known the nature of the route in advance, they would never have attempted this mountain trek, and although World Challenge disputed this, its own inquiry into the accident recommended that this particular path should not be used by future school groups. However, somewhat paradoxically, Charles Rigby, the chief executive of World Challenge Expeditions, then called for tighter regulation of overseas expeditions, which he estimated involved 15,000 young people a year, and his suggestion was for a 'national watchdog body to regulate expeditions abroad by schools and young people', which would be an 'overseas counterpart' of the AALA.[75] Mr Rigby's organization has taken many parties to the most extreme of locations around the world, but he claimed this was always with 'extremely well-trained, well-qualified and experienced' guides, as with the 'jungle-trained' leader on this trip.[76] Raleigh International, which sends more than 1,000 young people abroad each year, has suffered just three deaths since it was established in 1984; the death of David Shaverin when an Argentinean bus overturned;[77] the murder of Amy Lightfoot in Belize;[78] and the road death of Siobhan Shannon in Namibia.[79] This is another very enviable record for an organization operating in some very hostile terrains. Indeed, a survey of self-organized 'gap year' travels inevitably reveals some tragedies, with several murders in Australia, and other deaths in Thailand, Chile, Colombia, Costa Rica, and Ecuador, although the Foreign Office stresses that most of the thousands of backpackers who set off on adventures each year 'enjoy a trouble-free trip'.[80]

In the light of Amy Ransom's death, another teaching union, the Association of Teachers and Lecturers' annual conference called for yet more reform of school guidelines, because of the 'culture of regulation, bureaucracy, blame and litigation', and suggested that the AALA should extend its powers to cover schools, overseas trips and 'voluntary associations, such as the Scouts'.[81] Peter

---

[74] 'Schools – end of the road for school trips' ('rules have been tightened after a series of fatalities on school trips, but should pupils be denied any challenge?'), *The Independent* (4 April 2004).

[75] 'Calls made for tighter regulation of trips abroad', *The Guardian* (2 August 2001). In 2004 WCE organized expeditions for 40,000 young people in the 9 to 18 age group; written evidence to the House of Commons Select Committee on Education and Skills (October 2004).

[76] 'Schoolgirl dies on Vietnam trip', BBC News (2 August 2001). Mr Rigby noted that 'there are many cases of fully-grown adults walking in Wales and Scotland who slip on paths and fall'.

[77] 'Teenager dies in bus smash', *Sunday Mercury* (20 April 2003).

[78] 'Cornish woman's killer shot by police', *Western Morning News* (8 November 2002).

[79] 'Irishwoman dies in Africa crash', *Irish News* (3 December 2001).

[80] 'Unlucky few who don't return home', *Birmingham Post* (16 October 2004). Judge Thomas A. Dickerson has looked in detail at package tours designed for US students, particularly Spring Breaks, and suggests that 'tragedies can be avoided if parents understand just how dangerous student tours can be'; see his article in *The International Travel Law Journal* (1996) updated on http://www.classactionlitigation.com/library/studtour.htm

[81] 'Blame culture "could end trips",' *The Guardian* (2 August 2001).

Smith, their general secretary, but supported by other teaching unions, then wrote to Estelle Morris, the Secretary of State for Education, urging reform of the guidelines introduced in 1998 and stating that 'the future of valuable school trips is at stake'.[82]

However this stridency does not equate easily with the research on overseas trips; for example it was established by the Royal Society of Medicine in 2000 that the health risks of taking part in a well-planned overseas expedition were lower than going to a rock festival.[83] No doubt safety could be improved both at rock festivals and on trips abroad, but it is important to have a sense of perspective. This was certainly shown by Ward LJ, the father of Amelia Ward, who died in August 2001 when she was struck on the head by a falling rock in South Africa on a Duke of Edinburgh's Award trip with City of London School. The coroner described the case as a 'terrible tragedy' arising from a 'misunderstanding' where there was 'no place for retribution', and the verdict of a 'freak abseiling accident' was accepted by her father. However, the case again raised an issue as to why participants and bystanders were not wearing protective helmets; the research of the Mountain Rescue Council shows that the evidence is 'very clear' and 'the chance of receiving significant head injuries is three times greater when not wearing a helmet than when wearing one'.[84] In South Africa a climbing helmet is not a mandatory requirement, but the coroner was told that the trip leader insisted on helmets being worn 'during abseiling'. However, due to the 'misunderstanding', permission was given to one of the students who was wearing a helmet to inspect the height of the climb from the bottom of the face, and when Amelia Ward went too, although she was not at that moment part of the abseiling party, she was struck by a stone dislodged by one of the abseilers, which bounced off the rock face; her lack of a helmet was said to be 'because she was not thought to be in danger'.[85] Although this death was described as 'freakish' it would seem that someone standing without a helmet below abseilers, for whatever reason, is decidedly at risk of serious injury.

None of these overseas incidents comes within the statutory remit of the AALA, but it is extremely helpful to have their analysis because of the obvious commonalities with fatalities in the UK. Indeed, Marcus Bailie has pointed out that the AALA already advises many LEAs and schools and 'we would be happy to advise or to be part of an inquiry team'. He also notes that 'a common knee-jerk reaction to accidents is to simply ban further activities. Some activities will always involve a certain level of risk, but a proper inquiry system would allow

---

[82] 'Teachers' unions want new code on risky school trips', *Western Mail* (3 August 2001).

[83] Sarah Anderson and Chris Johnson, 'Expedition health and safety: a risk assessment', *Journal of the Royal Society of Medicine*, vol 93, (2000) 557-561, which surveyed expeditions from 1995 to 1997, during which they found only two deaths – Indonesian members of an expedition, who were kidnapped and murdered by Papuan independence fighters. The conclusion was that 'more medical incidents per person per day occur at rock festivals than on the expeditions'.

[84] Mountain Rescue Council, *Incident Report 1999* (2000) 1.

[85] 'Judge's family "still utterly bereft" after girl's death', *The Independent* (14 March 2002).

lessons to be learned'.[86] While each of these tragedies has unique circumstances, some common patterns emerge: poor supervision, lack of head count, and the fact that 'low risk' activities such as wading and hillwalking seem to lead to fatalities in as many cases as 'high risk' activities, perhaps because safeguards are more likely to be in place to deal with the latter.

The home cases

The UK casualties on the AALA list starts with the loss of four schoolboys from Stoke Poges in Buckinghamshire, who were swept to their deaths by a big wave off a beach near Land's End in May 1985. An inquest was told that there were no warnings on information brochures or on posted notices about this hazard at a private activity centre running the adventure holiday.[87] A jury returned a verdict of misadventure and the parents of the dead boys then held a press conference to announce that they were suing Buckinghamshire County Council for compensation, on the basis that the headteacher had been responsible, as he had seen the children clambering on the rocks but had 'not thought it was dangerous'.[88] The coroner made recommendations to Buckinghamshire for improving the supervision of school parties, including full briefings for parent-helpers about the scope of their responsibilities and a suggestion that a teacher should act as advance guard to carry out safety checks whenever a group encounters a potentially dangerous area. A subsequent inquiry by the chief education officer concluded that the headteacher 'failed to plan the trip adequately, failed to organize sufficient supervision and failed to act when he saw the children in danger'.[89] The Land's End case is very significant, because it led in 1989 to national guidelines for school trips, *Safety in Outdoor Education*, which indicated clearly that teachers must 'exercise control and discipline on school journeys'.[90] This 'booklet on safety in outdoor pursuits' stated that 'Challenge and adventure are never free of risk... However, there must always be

---

[86] 'Education: on slippery ground', *The Guardian* (6 February 2001).
[87] 'No warnings given on dangers, Land's End inquest told', *The Times* (18 July 1985). Subsequently notices were erected stating that 'The cliffs and sea are natural hazards and a potential danger. Please be careful', *The Times* (29 July 1985).
[88] 'Head's job fear after verdict on drownings: inquest into death of boys who drowned at Land's End', *The Times* (20 July 1985). Their solicitor at the inquest was Roger Pannone. A subsequent offer of £3,500 for each child was described by a parent as an 'insult; *The Guardian* (9 September 1985). The parents were eventually responsible for fundraising towards a new lifeboat at Sennen Cove, which was named *The Four Boys* in their memory; *Lloyd's List* (30 March 1992).
[89] 'Head censured over drownings', *The Times* (12 November 1985).
[90] 'Safety guide puts onus on teachers', *The Independent* (6 July 1989).

an acceptable framework of safety. It is indefensible to expose young people to dangerous conditions and unnecessary risks.'[91]

The Land's End case is unfortunately also fairly typical of school trip fatalities, in that 19 of the 46 listed by AALA are deaths due to drowning. Apart from the multiple drownings at Land's End, Lyme Bay and Stainforth Beck the others are single instances, but cover common themes. For example, many of the cases on the list and incidents after 2001 are in what would be regarded as 'low risk' environments. In May 1995, a school secretary from Nottingham, Joan Whitehall, was helping to supervise an educational trip when she fell into the Grand Union Canal in Birmingham, while reversing a narrowboat through a tunnel. She was holding the tiller when the craft apparently hit the bank, she slipped, and was then trapped under the vessel. The narrowboat was said to be of 'traditional design' and had no safety rail at the rear.[92] Wing Commander Gordon Sinclair, the President of RoSPA, commenting on the death of Joan Whitehall, stated that 'One is appalled every time a new quirk of accident arises', and his organization is of course another very important 'clearinghouse' of information, and this case led to more safety rails being fitted to narrowboats and other small craft. If in RoSPA's analysis Ms Whitehall's death was a 'new quirk', then many of the school cases show a complete degree of predictability on well-established themes. For example, in July 1997 Adil Naseem, aged 11 and from Hounslow, drowned at an activity centre in Buckinghamshire. Hounslow Council pleaded guilty and were fined £25,000 for health and safety failures that led to his drowning, because Adil and 46 other children from Feltham Hill Junior school in Hounslow were allowed to use the swimming pool without any lifeguards present.[93]

Other cases show very clear negligence too: in September 1999 Elizabeth Bee, aged nine and from Hampshire, drowned when she became trapped under a boat on a school trip in Portsmouth harbour. Nine pupils had been taken out in a motorboat from the Royal Navy's sailing centre at Whale Island, all wearing lifejackets, after a determination that winds gusting up to Force 6 conditions were far too difficult for sailing. However, the school motorboat had a ring missing from the bow, allowing water to rush in, and the engines repeatedly cut out; the craft then tipped over when the pupils rushed to one side to see a jellyfish. After the capsize the teacher failed to carry out an elementary head count, asking instead if 'everyone was OK', and an inquest heard evidence that it was not until Elizabeth's twin sister noticed that she was missing that the teacher began to realize there was a problem. The coroner noted that the teacher was not trained to the standard expected by the AALA and nor was the private school bound by guidelines that called for another adult to be on board the boat. The inquest jury

---

[91] Department for Education and Science, *Safety in Outdoor Education* (HMSO, 1989), and echoed in many publications; e.g. HSC and Glasgow City Council, *Safety In Educational Outdoor Activities – A Code Of Practice* (Circular 33, 1988).
[92] 'School secretary killed under barge propellers', *The Times* (15 May 1995).
[93] 'Schools: perils down a legal loophole', *The Guardian* (17 March 1998).

returned a verdict of accidental death contributed to by neglect.[94] Following a criminal prosecution for health and safety offences at Portsmouth Crown Court, to which he pleaded guilty, the teacher, Paul Dove, was fined £2,000, and Boundary Oaks Preparatory School in Fareham was fined £25,000. The court heard that the school had not conducted a risk assessment nor did it have a safety policy, and no records were kept of any maintenance on its boats. Mr Dove was originally arrested on manslaughter charges, and was perhaps very fortunate that these were not pursued.[95] Judge MacKean suggested that the heavy fine 'might encourage other schools to keep the highest possible standards to reduce the risk of further accidents'.[96]

Several cases involve the rock/water interface, which can sometimes be categorized as fatalities either from drowning or from hitting the head on a hard object. In 1996, the British Safety Council called for tougher rules on outdoor activities involving children after Richard Barber, a 13-year-old boy died during a school trip to the Yorkshire Dales in June that year. He had been traversing a waterfall at Buckden Ghyll.[97] One account suggests that he was 'drowned in pool at an education centre' which perhaps suggests an indoor pool, but the AALA listing shows death caused by a fall from a height in an adventure activity.[98] In this environment even an experienced instructor can slip, as we have seen happened with Kevin Thomas at Dinas Rock in the Neath Valley in 1998; he was assisting a school party from the Hall School in Wimbledon, who were tied to a safety rope. However, when one of the boys got into difficulties Mr Thomas went to his assistance and slipped on the wet rocks himself.[99] This very same area saw another drowning when Jason Dalton was swept away after jumping into the river in an attempt to rescue his college lecturer and a friend. This case did not originally appear on the AALA list of 'school trip fatal accident records', although it was a 'school trip' somewhat haphazardly 'organized' by Ystrad Mynach College near Caerphilly, a 16 to 18 Further Education College, where Jason Dalton was a student aged 17. Marcus Bailie made the very important connection on this category of case and tellingly referred to Jason Dalton's death at the Stainforth Beck inquest, indicating that 'There are frightening similarities between the two cases and perhaps if the findings of the Stainforth incident had been made available sooner, Jason's life could have been saved'.[100] His death had sparked yet another call for such a 'college adventure trip' to be brought under the direct remit of the AALA, and also for certification of leaders and equipment. This ill-judged venture was described as a field trip for 'confidence building' and an inquest in 2002 heard evidence that it had been led by someone who was both unqualified and ill-equipped. When the Health and Safety Executive and the

---

[94] 'Teacher blamed for girl's death', *The Times* (8 June 2001).
[95] 'Teacher arrested over child's sailing death', *Evening Standard* (19 October 1999).
[96] 'Teacher fined over death of pupil', *The Times* (29 October 2002).
[97] 'Waterfall death', *Glasgow Herald* (29 June 1996).
[98] 'Other school trips which have ended in tragedy', *The Scotsman* (28 June 2002).
[99] 'River hero praise', *South Wales Evening Post* (29 June 1998).
[100] 'The fear factor', *Yorkshire Evening Post* (9 March 2002).

parents stated they were contemplating further legal action, Caerphilly County Borough Council as the LEA distanced itself by insisting that the college was a corporate body responsible for its own affairs.[101] Sadly the lecturer, Alun Davies, had received no safety training, he did not have relevant experience or qualifications – 'I didn't think I needed them' – and stated at the inquest that he had not seen a copy of safety procedures before taking six students on the trip. He indicated to the coroner at Merthyr Tydfil that 'The only safety equipment we had was the 22 foot length of blue nylon rope ... borrowed from the college caretaker'.[102] Mr Davies noted that he had taken his four sons to this location five weeks earlier and they had jumped into the pool safely as there were no signs saying it was dangerous. Contemporaneous reporting shows that clearly the conditions had changed dramatically since that reconnaissance; it so happened that a reporter from the leading Welsh national newspaper was with the Wales Air Ambulance service that day and so gives a graphic story of the disarray on the riverbank 'as the River Sychryd boiled angrily below us, swollen with the sudden rains'.[103] A jury returned a verdict of accidental death in this case, and called for local authorities to ensure that they used qualified supervisors on such trips. The Glamorgan coroner endorsed their recommendation, stating that this death was a 'salutary lesson' for anyone organising school or college trips'. However, the Crown Prosecution Service ruled out a criminal prosecution, although the HSE are considering further legal action, and the parents are pursuing legal action against the college and Caerphilly Council. Jason's mother stated at the inquest that 'this accident was wholly avoidable if necessary precautions had been taken by the college and the teacher'.[104]

Unfortunately, yet another fatality took place in the Neath Valley when Herve Bola from Essex, drowned while on an outdoor activities course with members of the Woodford Youth Club in August 2002. He was a non-swimmer, a fact that was allegedly on a form filled in prior to the trip. Aged 16 and from Woodford Green, he was taking part in an outdoor activities course based at the Glasbury Outdoor Centre in Herefordshire, owned and operated by the London Borough of Redbridge. During the activity it appears that some individuals opted to jump into the pool at the Scwd y Gladys Falls. When Herve disappeared a local teenager, Kerion Williams, plunged into what was described as 'deep muddy water' to attempt a rescue, but it was too late.[105] Herve Bola had originally come from Zaire two years before, and his parents had sent him to live with his grandmother in the hope of a better education; when the parents arrived from Africa they were accompanied to the location by their lawyer, Georgette Djaba, who described it as

---

[101] 'Calls for licensing system sparked by Jason's death; certification of leaders and equipment sought', *Western Mail* (23 August 2002).

[102] 'Activity leader not trained to help drowning pupil', *The Independent* (22 August 2002).

[103] 'Airborne team who can make a difference', *Western Mail* (20 October 2001). An extended version was published in *OneWales*, the national magazine for Wales (October/November 2001) to fundraise for the Wales Air Ambulance Service.

[104] 'Girl saw sweetheart swept away by river', *South Wales Evening Post* (22 August 2002).

[105] 'Inquest into waterfall death', *Western Mail* (1 August 2002).

'fraught with danger because of a lack of warning signs' and suggested that the family would be asking the 'obvious' question "Why was Herve allowed to jump into the water if it was known he could not swim?"[106] However, there then ensued a number of procedural hurdles in this case, which is still not concluded; the inquest was delayed to allow the family to claim legal aid and to insist that Redbridge pay the family's expenses to travel to Wales and to have a translator, and the Council suggested they did not have 'the power to fund' these.[107] A further attempt to have expenses paid by the coroner in South Wales led to a High Court application by the mother, Muzinga Bokwa, for judicial review, citing the Human Rights Act 1998, and this has yet to be fully determined.[108] Eventually an inquest took place in 2005, with the rare verdict on an outdoor activity trip of 'unlawful killing', although this was by a majority and was hotly contested. The National Union of Teachers, representing Daniel Brown, a part-time youth worker, labelled the finding as 'disturbing and perverse', indicating they would be considering an application for judicial review. There had been a direct clash of evidence between the teenage members of the group who testified that Mr Brown had called to Herve to jump into the pool, a claim he denied, and which other staff members all testified they had never heard. The coroner indicated to the jury the 'high level of proof necessary to bring in a verdict of unlawful killing', and noted that they had to consider whether 'anyone present had a duty of care to Herve and if so, whether they failed in or breached that duty of care'. Following the decision the family called for the prosecuting authorities to re-open the case, and civil proceedings continue for compensation, with a strong likelihood of a judicial review application by the NUT.[109]

In the meantime, several changes have been made in the Neath Valley at this location as a result of these legal cases, following a meeting between the police, the Brecon Beacons National Park authority and representatives from safety organizations. From this a Waterfalls Safety Advisory Group was established, a mock-up rescue operation took place at the falls, extra warning signs have been put up, and thousands of leaflets explaining the potential dangers of the waterfalls have been distributed to visitors. A spokeswoman for the Brecon Beacons National Park, said in 2004: 'it seems to be working. In the past two years there have been no serious incidents in the area'.[110]

The classic case on this rock/water interface was of course that at Stainforth Beck in 2000. Rochelle Cauvet, aged 14, and Hannah Black, aged 13, were swept away and drowned when they and other children from Royds Comprehensive School in Leeds, were 'river walking' in this tributary of the River Ribble, in the Yorkshire Dales. The beck was swollen with floodwater after 48 hours of rainfall.

---

[106] 'Drowning victim's family visits death trap falls; Vale of Neath: lawyer questions lack of warning signs', *Western Mail* (16 August 2002).

[107] 'Teen death family wants compensation', *This is Local London* (18 October 2003).

[108] 'Mum fights for inquest cash', *Western Mail* (11 September 2004).

[109] 'Somebody should have taken action to ensure a non-swimmer did not swim', *Western Mail* (21 April 2005).

[110] 'Safety is stepped up at the falls', *South Wales Evening Post* (2 August 2004).

Following three weeks of evidence an inquest jury returned a verdict of accidental death, and the coroner called for higher safety standards on school outings and a review of 'river walking', which had previously been thought to be a 'low risk' activity.[111]

Inevitably the definitional boundaries in the various disciplines attaching to this sort of rock/water activity are questions of degree. At the riskier end of the spectrum is 'canyoning', where participants deliberately engage in 'rappelling' down steep gorges and body-surf down mountain rapids and waterfalls. Such an 'extreme' sport claimed the life of Vikram Reddy, a trainee Scottish solicitor on an adventure holiday in France in 2002, even though he was wearing a helmet and a wet suit when he went on to the River Loup.[112] The same discipline disabled Carolyn Jones, a former international rower, when she was trapped underwater in an endurance event in the Via Mala gorge in 2001.[113] Canyoning also killed 21 people – including three Britons near Interlaken in 1999, when they were caught in a flash flood. The sport was famously described then as 'white-water rafting without the raft'.[114] Subsequently, six staff members from a Swiss adventure sports company were given suspended prison sentences for this incident, after being convicted of manslaughter, with Judge Zbinden commenting that the company's safety guidelines were 'not sufficient', as 'the guides were not trained properly, particularly in terms of the weather. They admitted themselves they rushed the groups through in the midst of a storm when really they should have followed the simple rule – suggested by mountain rescue services – not to go out'.[115] 'Impromptu canyoning' was the description by Mountain Rescue after the death of a young woman in 2000, who was sliding down a waterfall 'without appropriate safety equipment such as ropes, safety helmets and buoyancy aids', although it was indicated that this 'sport may include hiking beside a gentle stream, swimming across clear rockpools and abseiling down waterfalls'. This victim had either been trapped by the current and drowned or had banged her head. The River Llugwy at this waterfall, known as Pont Cyfyng, was very low at the time, much too low for canoeists who would normally be there, and it was

---

[111] 'Parents condemn river walk accident verdict', *The Times* (9 March 2002).

[112] 'Lawyer dies in gorge fall', *The Scotsman*, 15 June 2002.

[113] 'Adventure sport woman "critical" after river ordeal', *Daily Telegraph* (6 September 2001). It appeared that she was uninsured for such an activity and rowing colleagues set up a trust fund to deal with unpaid bills for the evacuation and her long-term care; 'Rowers dip in to help injured pal', *Edinburgh Evening News* (18 September 2002).

[114] '18 die in adventure holiday disaster', *The Times* (28 July 1999).

[115] 'Suspended sentences for canyon tragedy bosses', *The Scotsman* (12 December 2001). This analysis was vigorously disputed by Georg Hoedle, one of the owners of Adventure World, the company that had organized the trip, who said 'Something absolutely extraordinary, incomprehensible and unforeseeable must have happened, because our guides know every centimetre of the river'. However, this 'unforeseeable' matter turned out in the judge's view, based on expert evidence, to be an ordinary summer storm producing a flash flood.

thought that she had hit her head or been entrapped even with very benign conditions.[116]

Conditions at Stainforth Beck were normally quite benign too, and nothing so extreme as the 'normal' canyoning conditions, but several witnesses commented on the particular conditions the day the Royds School party went for their 'walk'. For example, a river bailiff told the inquest 'it was foolhardy in the extreme', and a cave rescue organizer with 30 years' experience as an outdoor activities instructor, said the trip 'should not have been allowed. To me, it's a commonsense decision. I don't think you need a qualification. I don't think you need any form of education to understand that, when it rains, rivers and streams rise. I would not have gone near the place.'[117] Two teachers, Andy Miller and Liz Schofield, had taken the party of 15 teenagers into the beck, which was described as 'shin-deep'. Mr Miller's only qualification in outdoor activities was a Leeds City Council-administered certificate in fell walking, and he told the inquest he did not enjoy going on river walks but he took part in this trip because the original teacher who co-ordinated the event had pulled out with a heavy cold. Neither teacher had seen LEA or government guidelines on school trips, no formal risk assessment had been carried out on river walks by the teachers, and they had not checked the weather conditions prior to the activity.[118] They were also unaware of the local knowledge that 'another boy had been washed away and rescued on the same beck the same morning', all of which understandably led to some bitterness and anguish from the parents of the two teenagers.[119]

Following the refusal by the coroner to consider a higher verdict of unlawful killing by gross negligence because he judged the cases 'did not meet the criteria', the parents regarded the actual verdict of accidental death as 'hurtful, disappointing and inadequate after three weeks of evidence about lack of preparation and ignorance of river-walking's dangers',[120] pointing out their view that their children had been killed in 'treacherous conditions without proper supervision and with minimal safety equipment'.[121] The Cauvets, parents of Rochelle who drowned at Stainforth Beck and who now live in France, were endeavouring to take the inquest case to the European Court of Human Rights, on the grounds that their daughter's right to life was violated. They came to a view in 2005 'after much soul-searching' that the case was having a deleterious impact

---

[116] 'Woman dies in Snowdonia on canyoning trip', *The Times* (1 May 2000). In 1999 a British schoolgirl, Siobhan Halls, aged 17, drowned in the Blue Mountains near Sydney, where she was on holiday. Her father confirmed she had not been wearing a helmet and 'was not a strong swimmer but had been taking lessons'; 'Teenage girl dies in new danger sport', *The Times* (8 April 1999).

[117] 'Tragedy highlights perils of river walks: inquest told of "error of judgment" by teachers', *The Guardian* (5 March 2002).

[118] 'We'll never forgive, say parents of river victim', *Yorkshire Post* (9 March 2002).

[119] 'My daughter drowned because of the arrogance of her teachers and I expected them to show remorse', *Mail on Sunday* (10 March 2002).

[120] 'Parents attack "hurtful" inquest verdict', *The Guardian* (9 March 2002).

[121] 'Parents condemn river walk accident verdict', *The Times* (9 March 2002).

on their family and particularly their son, and abandoned the claim.[122] Unfortunately even a 'riverside walk' along the bank can have its complications in certain conditions; in 1998 a newly-married couple, Lynn and Barry Collett, on their second day of honeymoon set out for a walk from Appletreewick in the Yorkshire Dales, heading for the ruins of Bolton Abbey along the banks of the River Wharfe. When a body was seen floating in the river it was traced to their rented cottage with 'scores of cards, presents and a tier of wedding cake'. The safety guide at their planned destination, Bolton Abbey, contains a cautionary saying that 'Where the Aire drowns one, the Wharfe drowns five'.[123] The evidence at the inquest was that the river level 'rose by up to five feet in less than a minute' due to heavy overnight rain.[124]

A somewhat different perspective from the parents on the Stainforth Beck case came from the indefatigable Nigel de Gruchy, the General Secretary of the NASUWT who said that 'no amount of guidance can prevent tragedies', that 'teachers often have the finger of blame pointed at them before the facts of the incident have been examined', and that 'the NASUWT has reluctantly concluded that until society accepts the notion of a genuine accident it is advisable for members not to go on school trips'.[125] The most significant evidence, however, had been given in this case by Marcus Bailie from the AALA. Noting that the scrambling and paddling involved in river walking might 'seem utterly absurd' to an adult, but that children 'loved it', he stated that 'the power of moving water could deceive even experienced mountain walkers' and that 'rule books had not caught up with this': 'Tragically, as a result of this very case, it is now recognized widely that this activity can be fatal'. In a very significant passage, indicating the developing nature of a legal 'state of knowledge', Mr Bailie said that 'Now that it has happened it is manifestly foreseeable. But prior to this tragedy, it had not been foreseen as hazardous by those charged with writing guidelines'. On another occasion he had examined Stainforth Beck and found it to be 'completely benign and low risk', and river walking had been 'traditionally' categorized as low-risk.[126] As we have seen, Mr Bailie also praised the teachers for their 'heroic'

---

[122] 'Tragic girl's family ends legal fight', *Yorkshire Post* (1 March 2005).

[123] 'Honeymoon couple are feared drowned', *The Guardian* (21 August 1998).

[124] 'Honeymoon couple killed by a deluge; drowned while out for a walk', *Birmingham Evening Mail* (20 November 1998).

[125] 'No mass of guidance can avert tragedies, says teachers' leader', *Yorkshire Post* (9 March 2002).

[126] Subsequently the AALA Collective Interpretation 6.06 on 'Combined Water/Rock Activities' (2003) drew up some helpful delineations in a 'working document' to attempt definitions on these activities, which necessarily cover a spectrum of related themes: 'sea level traversing (to most people is primarily a dry rock-climbing activity); gorge walks or scrambles (can be wet or dry or alternating the two, involving the ascent or descent of a water course); ghyll scrambles (another name for gorge walks or scrambles); river walks (usually non-technical in nature); adventure walks or scrambles (covers a multitude of variations); canyoning, (usually wet. It traditionally involves the descent of a steep water course and sometimes involves technical ropework); adventure swimming (another name for coasteering or a non-technical variation of canyoning); river running (deliberately swimming down white

actions after the incident, but indicated that 'Whether they should have entered is another matter, and I believe it was an error of judgment'.[127] Ultimately Leeds City Council, the LEA, were fined £30,000 over these deaths, when they admitted a charge under the Health and Safety at Work Act 1974 of failing to ensure pupils were not put at risk. They were also ordered to pay £50,000 costs. Pitchers J indicated that the fine would have been more if he had been dealing with a commercial company, but a large fine would be 'counter productive and would only hit council services'. The Crown Prosecution Service announced that no teacher, other individual or organization would be prosecuted over the deaths, although civil compensation was paid to the families.[128]

Extensive information was also given out about the dangers of a water/rock environment, when in July 2001, Yunus Ismail Moola, aged 17, was drowned in Gullet Quarry near Malvern. He was at an end-of-term barbecue with fellow students from Gloucestershire Central Technology College accompanied by their Head of Sixth Form; when a student got into difficulties while swimming their teacher instructed them to return to the minibus. An inquest heard how Yunus then left the mini-bus and said that he wanted to clean his trainers, but was then seen by the teacher swimming across the lake and also getting into difficulties. Despite the rescue efforts of the teacher and another swimmer, the teenager drowned. Following advice from the coroner that he need not feel compelled to give oral evidence if he felt it could in any way incriminate him, the teacher exercised his right not to reply to certain questions. Shabir Bahm, adviser for the Muslim community who was representing the Moolla family, told the inquest there was a lot of 'conflicting evidence from the family's point of view' and that 'The line that has been adopted' almost means that the teacher 'has been given amnesty'.[129] West Mercia police commented that people often swam in the lake despite warnings not to do so.[130] There had been an earlier death at the same quarry in July 1995 when Clifford James drowned while swimming during a celebration of his 25th birthday,[131] but the death in September 2002 of Andrew Pedlingham, aged 17, was probably caused by plunging off a cliff into the quarry, which has also claimed other lives in the past.[132] The water here seems particularly cold, as the quarry is situated on the north side of a hill and rarely gets sunshine, so that even divers in wet suits have had problems; of those who have drowned in such outdoor locations, RoSPA warn that 'many have been good

---

water rapids); coasteering (usually a wet activity often involving swimming and/or jumping from a height into water as an integral part); and coastal exploration (anything from a beach ramble to coasteering).

[127] 'Tragedy highlights perils of river walks: inquest told of "error of judgment" by teachers', *The Guardian* (5 March 2002).

[128] '£30,000 fine over river-walk deaths', *Yorkshire Post* (28 February 2003).

[129] 'School trip death: "accident" verdict', *The Gloucester Citizen* (21 March 2003).

[130] 'Teenager drowns at college barbecue', *The Times* (5 July 2001).

[131] 'RoSPA: parents told to be vigilant at all times', *This is Worcestershire* (17 August 2004).

[132] 'Thrill-seekers are climbing over a two-metre high fence and barbed wire to jump off a cliff into a lake where three people have drowned in recent years', *This is Worcestershire* (27 June 2003).

swimmers who have often disappeared without a struggle'.[133] Quarries notoriously harbour unseen hazards, and to deal with the difficulties the Quarry Products Association have produced a resource pack entitled *Play Safe Stay Safe* and the organization also hosts organized school parties to quarries rather than have informal, unofficial or even illicit visits.

A controversial case on swimming, which led to legal action, is that of Laura Zielinski, aged ten, who drowned in 1997 at Shell Island near Barmouth on a school trip. An inquest recorded a verdict of misadventure on hearing that Laura, who was with fellow pupils from Christ Church Junior School in Oldbury, had drifted with the tide into a rocky area of turbulent water while bathing near the shore. The coroner said that teachers had not appreciated the dangers of rocky outcrops when the children were allowed to go bathing. Solicitors acting for the parents Lynne and Pat Zielinski brought a negligence action against Sandwell Council.[134] The allegations suggested that no teacher with the group had lifesaving qualifications, they had not sought local advice which would have revealed that Shell Island's owners warned against swimming at this location, and indeed on that day an activity centre nearby had cancelled swimming altogether because of a safety inspection which suggested that the sea was too rough. An initial offer of £3,500 was turned down, and then another of £9,000; Mrs Zielinski stated that this sum was still nowhere near enough to compensate for the death of Laura, and she believed 'the full story of what happened that day should be heard in court.'[135] An interview in their local newspaper shows just how harrowing an experience this had been for the parents, who had not changed their daughter's room since her death. Mrs Zeilinski refuses to refer to this death as an 'accident': 'it was not an accident, because accidents are preventable and cannot be foreseen. This incident was preventable and could have been foreseen. Someone will pay for Laura's death. We want justice'.[136]

Even with much older children the sea can be a hostile environment. A 'near miss' in July 2003 amply demonstrated this, when 12 teenagers and a teacher almost drowned after getting into difficulties at Druridge Bay in Northumberland. They were all from Walker Technology College in Newcastle, and needed hospital treatment after being rescued by helicopter. This was a week before an initiative announced by the Royal Society for the Prevention of Accidents (RoSPA) and the Health and Safety Executive (HSE) for a pilot scheme to assist trainee teachers in how to spot dangers. Juliet Brown, the RoSPA head of education, indicated that 'A number of high-profile accidents, some on school trips, have focused attention on the need for teachers to understand more about risk education and risk management.'[137] The incident in Northumberland was the

---

[133] Becky Kirkwood, the development officer of the Society's water safety division, 'Hidden hazards of cooling-off swim', *The Times* (4 August 1990).

[134] 'Tragic Laura legal battle; parents' action after girl drowned on school trip, *Birmingham Evening Mail* (27 January 1999).

[135] 'Drowning cash offer snubbed', *Birmingham Evening Mail* (4 August 1999).

[136] 'Our living nightmare over Laura's death', *Sunday Mercury* (20 September 1998).

[137] 'Teachers trained to spot trip dangers', *Northern Echo* (23 July 2003).

subject of an LEA inquiry. It had started with an end-of-term barbecue on the beach, despite wind and rain. The 31 students were aged between 13 and 17, with two teachers. Two girls went a swim in shorts and T-shirts and ended up on a sand bank 100 metres offshore, with waves washing over them. One of the party leaders then waded in to try and help while a human chain was formed with other students, but then they in turn got into difficulties and the emergency services were called. A spokesman for Newbiggin Coastguards commented that 'in this case, these youngsters have been very, very lucky – we do not like to go out on too many of these potentially tragic situations. The sea was rough and there was lots of surf on the shore. Conditions were worsened by low visibility…. I would like to advise people to take more care and respect the sea.'[138]

The only higher number than the 16 road fatalities on the AALA table is the figure of 19 from drowning. It is notable that very few of those drowning deaths relate to swimming pools, although school visits to such premises are routine. This paucity reflects the fact that, generally, life-guarding standards and supervision at swimming pools in Britain are very high. An exceptional case was a drowning in Blackpool in 2001, when Emma Farrar, aged four and with autism, went for a weekly swim with her school, which specialized in special needs children. Emma had not yet learned to communicate using language and had complex care needs because she was 'entirely without fear'. Swimming lessons were held at a neighbouring special needs school with its own small pool, but Emma drowned after 'being left in the pool unnoticed for more than 15 minutes' after staff and 10 other pupils went into the changing rooms after the lesson. A prosecution was eventually dropped against Pauline Mills, the swimming instructor, who had been charged with manslaughter. She was also cleared of failing to take reasonable care for the health and safety of others, along with Keith Berry, the Headteacher. However, the case against Blackpool Council, who had always admitted liability, continued on three counts of breaching health and safety regulations, and the council was fined £120,000 plus costs of £11,000.[139] Douglas Brown J criticized the school's decision to allow teaching assistants to help supervise classes: 'There can be no doubt there was a serious failing of those charged with looking after the safety of children in that pool. It is quite remarkable that her absence was not noted until a quarter of an hour from when she was missing.' The judge also criticized the police, the Crown Prosecution Service, and the Health and Safety Executive for delay in bringing the Council to court. As Emma's mother pointed out 'None of the adults in charge of the children that day knew them personally or much about their special needs … The swimming teacher had not been told that Emma had no sense of danger, yet at the end of the lesson the children were told to remove their armbands to play in the water … No one counted the children out of the pool, or they would have known

---

[138] 'School trip pupils saved from the sea', *Northern Echo* (18 July 2003).
[139] '£120,000 fine over pool death', *The Guardian* (22 October 2004).

she was missing. I am disgusted and outraged, and can't believe that no one has been found responsible for the loss of my little girl.'[140]

The low point of open air drowning cases, and indeed one of the most important cases on outdoor activities, was in May 2002, when Max Palmer, aged 10 and from Lancashire, was swept away by floodwaters on a school trip in the Lake District. Geography teacher Paul Ellis pleaded guilty to a charge of manslaughter and was sentenced to 12 months at Manchester Crown Court. Max was not a pupil at the Fleetwood High School, but had accompanied his mother Patricia, an education support assistant, and she watched as her son threw himself off rocks into a pool in Glenridding Beck.[141] This is the very first case where a teacher has admitted manslaughter of a child on a school trip, but there may have been additional reasons for this. Morland J indicated he was considering a three-year term for this 'unbelievably foolhardy and negligent' outing, so the last-minute switch to a guilty plea was very helpful for the defendant. However, in addition to this tactical plea to reduce the length of sentence, several newspapers indicated that the boy's mother had been conducting a clandestine affair with the teacher, and therefore he pleaded guilty 'to save Mrs Palmer the trauma of giving evidence [and] … it also ensured no mention was made in court of the affair.'[142] The prosecution evidence of gross negligence was also damning; as Mrs Palmer herself indicated, she had lost 'our most precious child who had so much to give this world. A rope or a lifebelt would have saved him, yet neither was taken on the trip.'[143] Manchester Crown Court heard that the teacher had once attended a mountain leadership course, but had not completed it. He claimed to have led many similar trips but on this occasion had left his rescue rope in the boot of his car: he told police: 'In my experience if you take a rope it scares the kids and they think straight away there is something dangerous about it.'[144]

Increased attention has been paid to drowning issues, particularly among young people, with the first National Water Safety Conference in Blackpool in September 2001. Drownings have been running at the level of around 500 a year in the UK, and all but a handful occur in open water, so it is inevitable that there are risks to be countered when engaged in many water-related outdoor activities. Some of these are 'unofficial' activities, sometimes loosely allied to fishing, but often individuals are deliberately 'plunging' or falling into water, and this may be

---

[140140] 'My darling Emma died on a school trip doing what she loved most. But still no one can tell me why', *Daily Express* (5 November 2004). The court was told that Park School's physical education policy states that during swimming lessons a qualified teacher must be in charge: on the day Emma died, Ms Mills was being assisted by three nursery nurses and a classroom assistant, none of whom had any special training or lifesaving qualifications. Five weeks earlier, the qualified teacher who normally accompanied the swimming party had been put on other duties by the headmaster.

[141] 'Teacher jailed for pupil's death on Lakes trip', *Lakeland Echo* (1 October 2003).

[142] 'Jailed Sir and drowned boy's Mum were lovers; Exclusive: husband didn't know of affair', *Sunday Mirror* (28 September 2003).

[143] Ibid.

[144] Ibid.

much colder than expected. Many of these locations are repeatedly the scene of tragedies; for example a quarry near Rugby where six people have drowned in the past 30 years, including two boys, aged 10 and six, who fell into the water while playing on their bicycles in 1990. That incident led to the quarry being turned into a country park with warning signs and fences.[145] Another obvious hazard is the risk of entanglement in weeds or other detritus; Liam Robinson, aged 12, drowned after he became entangled in a discarded fishing line after he was swept away on the River Wear near Durham City in 2003. He had tried to swim across the river while fishing with friends in the May half term holiday. The coroner said 'Children cannot be watched seven days a week, 24 hours a day. My only hope is that when parents read the report of what happened to Liam that they will redouble their efforts to warn their children of the dangers of rivers and ponds'.[146] A central lesson to be learned from all these drowning cases is that the ability to swim is an essential life skill. The contrast with drowning in open water is the record of just half a dozen deaths out of 300 million public swimming pool swims a year, which is an excellent safety record.[147] The 2001 conference brought together all those involved in providing aquatic facilities, with a particular focus on men between the ages of 15 and 30, because these are the most likely to drown. Another perspective centres on differing standards abroad; Ralph Riley, the chief executive of the Institute of Sport and Recreation Management, pointed out that four British children had died in swimming pools in Spain in the month following the drowning of Bunmi Shagaya while on a school trip to France 2001, and yet her case alone had received massive public interest.[148] Following the conference, several projects were launched, including the National Ocean Awareness Scheme, which provides kits for teachers and children's group leaders.

Conclusion on schools analysis

The schools fatality cases, tragic as they all are for the individual families, demonstrate that on the whole school trips in Britain are extremely safe. Nevertheless some important conclusions need to be drawn from these isolated instances of disaster, which will further inform local education authorities, teachers and school governors. What is clear is that there are very few 'freak accidents', although this is often the term used at inquests and in explaining calamities; in general there are straightforward causes, and many of these follow familiar patterns. The key themes that need examination are: a prior assessment of medical background to raise awareness of the potential for 'sudden death'; the much more hazardous environment of road travel to and from an activity,

---

[145] 'Don't be tempted to cool off here', *Coventry Evening Telegraph* (11July 2003).

[146] 'Boy, 12, drowned caught in fish line' *Newcastle Journal* (29 October 2003).

[147] Andrew Ebben of the Royal Life Saving Society, 'Swimming keeps you fit but also saves lives', *The Times* (11 August 2001).

[148] Ibid.

particularly by minibus drivers over-stretched by other commitments; the dangers of unsupervised and impromptu play in a hazardous environment rather than the organized outdoor activities themselves; the need for serious leadership training and supervisory skills; guarding against failures to take such basic precautions as headcounts, local advice or weather forecasts; and the perspective that seemingly 'low risk' activities, such as wading in water or hillwalking, actually need to be treated with far greater care, particularly when rivers are in spate and when 'trip and slip' problems on wet rocks or on steep terrain can lead to disaster.

These school trip cases inevitably attract an enormous amount of attention, and invariably a huge public debate after each heartbreaking death. Perhaps understandably these fatalities can then lead to suggestions that all school trips should be banned because they are too dangerous; that there should be legal immunity for teachers; and that the AALA licensing regime should be extended to school trips both at home and abroad. But these are hasty responses. A careful analysis suggests that none of these draconian reactions would be appropriate.

First, the enormous educational, social and health benefits to schoolchildren of trips, expeditions and outings vastly outweigh the risks. Furthermore there are conclusions that can be drawn from these past disasters which can assist in future safety. It is clear that some hazardous circumstances are repeated, so further dissemination of constructive advice and information is vital. Secondly, and as we shall see in detail in Part Two of the book, dealing with the legal parameters of negligence liability, teachers should feel able to follow some well-established principles of tort law, so that they can feel confident they have acted 'reasonably' and will not be prosecuted or sued vexatiously. Thirdly, both schools and voluntary organizations, which we examine next, are outside the licensing remit, and it is often suggested that the AALA regime should be extended to cover all activities for those aged under 18. The historical creation of the AALA after the Lyme Bay disaster was understandable in the light of those extraordinary circumstances, and in the context of suspicions that such laxity might apply in other outdoor activity centres, but to extend licensing to all school activities would be unnecessarily burdensome. More importantly, the advisory effect of the AALA, based on their inspection experience, has already proved to be a powerful force for informing schools practice and DfES documentation, and that is very much more useful, and low cost, than a tight regulatory regime, that might be seen as yet another obstacle which would prevent school trips. Part Three of the book combines these practical applications with the legal principles covered in Part Two, to give serious guidance as to the standards required in outdoor activities.

Chapter 4

Learning the Lessons:
the Voluntary Sector

As we have seen, the licensing regime under the 1995 Act does not cover the volunteer organizations who provide the bulk of outdoor activities for those under 18. Iain Peter, the chief executive of the Plas y Brenin Mountain Centre in North Wales has the view that 'the stupid thing is that there has hardly been a death in a pursuit centre since the legislation. The danger areas are schools, Scouting and voluntary organizations. But the government refuses to extend the legislation to cover those hazard areas'.[1] The Scout Association is the largest youth organization in the world, with over 25 million members in 216 countries. Along with Girlguiding UK, the Boys' Brigade, the Army Cadet Force Association, the Sea Cadet Association and similar uniformed organizations, these volunteer bodies run a huge range of outdoor and camping activities which provide the main opportunities for adventurous activities for young people in the UK. They rely in very large part on adult volunteer effort. It has been suggested for some time that the level of community volunteering has been in decline, and the assertion of David Davis, the Shadow Home Secretary, is that 'the fear of litigation is leading to teachers declining to take children on trips, doctors practising "defensive medicine" to avoid being sued and a downturn in the number of people working as volunteers'. Mr Davis is therefore considering 'ways of preventing frivolous claims' in an effort at 'cutting the cancer of litigation' out of the voluntary sector.[2] Actually the numbers in voluntary organizations in the UK has been declining over several decades, along with individuals taking a role in political parties, civic and amenity groups, tenants associations, churches and religious organizations, trade unions, mutual aid associations and friendly societies, and charities generally. A report in 1996 underlined 'the alarming extent to which our neighbourhood life and civil society have disintegrated'.[3] So although 'fear of litigation' may indeed be a factor in the declining numbers of volunteers, it is clearly not the only one.

It is actually quite difficult to obtain a complete breakdown of numbers, as the voluntary sector is so disparate, and many adventurous activities are organized on an ad hoc basis. The National Council for Voluntary Youth Services has been co-ordinating such activity since 1936 and lists over 160 national voluntary organizations working with young people. These vary considerably in size, activities and ethos; for example, the Woodcraft Folk have a 'co-operative outlook encouraging young people to learn the value of co-operation through

---

[1] 'Peak season brings school trip fears', BBC News (5 July, 2002).
[2] 'Tories plan to reverse "claims culture",' *The Times* (20 August 2004).
[3] 'Civic responsibility: self-help citizenship', *The Guardian* (30 October 1996).

games, play and adventure activities', whereas the aim of the Church Lads' and Church Girls' Brigade is to provide 'fun, faith and fellowship ... through sports and adventurous pursuits'.[4] The common denominator in most of these youth organizations is therefore 'adventurous activities'. This voluntary and community sector is not only a major provider of services to children, young people and their families, but the Government's White Paper *Every Child Matters: Change for Children*, arising from the Children Act 2004, recognizes 'that they have significant expertise to offer in developing strategy and planning provision'.[5] Safety issues are invariably described by the various youth organizations as 'paramount', and in 2003 the NCVYS launched a programme 'Sound Systems', based on their own document *Keeping it Safe: A young person-centred approach to safety and child protection*, which was an attempt at a 'comprehensive guide' to all aspects of youthwork policy and practice, including the provision of 'safe activities'. This was endorsed by the DfES.

Given the actual numbers involved in their adventurous activities, these organizations have an extraordinarily good safety record. However, as with school trips, a number of lessons can be learned from the few cases where things go tragically wrong.

Road injuries

What is true of school fatalities on the road is inevitably the position too with voluntary organizations. As well as travelling to and from camps and activities, there is just the everyday toll of road deaths, including to and from weekly meetings. In 2003, Gemma Ford, aged 12 and from Erith, died as her stepfather was driving her to Guides, when the driver of a stolen white van collided with them. The van driver fled the scene.[6] An earlier case involved Jacalyn Nisbet, who was a mother picking up her daughter from Guides in Edinburgh in 1995, when a 17 year old driver ploughed into her, travelling at 75mph in a 30mph zone; Edinburgh Sheriff Court heard that the driver had 'just passed his test when the horror happened', and he was sentenced to what would appear to be the fairly lenient sentence for dangerous driving of 240 hours' community service, a ban for five years and a requirement to resit the driving test.[7] In 2004, a boy aged 13 who had just been picked up from a weekly meeting of Army Cadets died in a road collision in Hastings, which brought the deaths on what was described as the town's 'fastest road up to eight in just five years'.[8] Inevitably too there have been fatalities through the use of minibuses and coaches taking youngsters to and from adventurous activities, along similar lines to those with schools. Sometimes the

---

[4] National members' list, *The NCVYS Directory of Youth Services*.
[5] DfES, *Working with voluntary and community organizations to deliver change for children and young people* (DfES/1123/2004).
[6] 'Learning to live with the death of grandchildren', *This is Local London* (24 June 2003).
[7] 'Shame of car killer', *Daily Record* (27 September 1995).
[8] 'Three die and four injured in horror crash', *Hastings Observer* (10 September 2004).

vehicle is carrying both schoolchildren and those from voluntary organizations; for example in August 2000 Craig Norsworthy, aged 15 and from Edinburgh, was killed when a coach carrying a party of Boys' Brigade members from Edinburgh and schoolchildren from the Chadwell Heath Foundation School in Essex, ploughed off the road near Vierzon in France.[9] This case was noteworthy in that it distinguished 'sleepiness' on the part of a driver, which was culpable, from 'microsleep' which allowed this coach driver to escape from manslaughter charges. Both the Boys' Brigade and the school were on their way to a week-long adventure holiday of canoeing, abseiling and whitewater rafting organized by PGL, the largest British holiday adventure firm for young people; 15 of them were seriously injured.[10] The investigation showed that the driver, Adrian McDonald, was on his first trip abroad and fell asleep at the wheel, ten minutes after taking over from another driver at 6.15am. He was charged with involuntary manslaughter but it was later reduced to dangerous driving, and he was fined £200 by French magistrates and given a three-month suspended sentence.[11] His lawyers argued that he suffered from an episode called a 'microsleep', categorized as 'a short period of inattention where the sufferer momentarily loses concentration, effectively falling asleep for several seconds at a time'.[12] Professor Jim Horne, of Loughborough University, who has researched 'microsleep', has indicated that about half the people who have accidents after falling asleep at the wheel are men under 30, but that drivers falling asleep for any reason cause one in five of all deaths on the road, more than drunk drivers.[13] His own research suggests that, fairly prosaically, drivers experience fatigue as a result of the length of a journey, from monotonous driving situations and from the time of the day.[14]

One factor in the voluntary sector cases is that minibus drivers are usually 'amateur' rather than being engaged everyday in driving such vehicles. In the past they have received very little training for this demanding role, and many are also combining driving duties with other leadership or instructional responsibilities when the group reaches the activity. In 1994, two eight-year-old Cub Scouts, Andrew Lyle and Richard Olsson, and their Cub Leader, Anthony Milburn, were killed when their minibus was in collision with a coach carrying Army Cadets, during driving rain on the A59 at Hopperton in Yorkshire. Over 30 people were

---

[9] 'Other school trips which have ended in tragedy', *The Scotsman* (28 June 2002).

[10] 'Tragic toll of holidays abroad', *Glasgow Evening Times* (27 June 2002).

[11] 'Horror on school hol', *Daily Record* (28 June 2002).

[12] 'Suspended sentence for driver in fatal coach crash', *The Scotsman* (29 March 2002). The official report into the 1997 Southall rail disaster accepted that the train driver may have suffered 'microsleeps', leading him to ignore warning signals. Seven people died and more than 150 were injured when a Great Western express ploughed into a freight train. The driver was acquitted at the Old Bailey in 1999 of seven counts of manslaughter and one health and safety offence.

[13] 'Fatal crash driver will not face prison; French prosecutors decide on reduced charge after "microsleep" ruling', *Daily Mail* (11 July 2001).

[14] See J. A. Horne and L. A. Reyner, 'Sleep related vehicle accidents', *British Medical Journal* (1995) 565-567 and 'Driver sleepiness', *Journal of Sleep Research* (1995) 23-29.

injured in the crash, and an inquest found that 'an inexperienced minibus driver' with a hired vehicle was to blame for the head-on collision. The coroner indicated too that 'even if the minibus passengers had been wearing seatbelts, they would not have been saved', but he was in no doubt that the principal cause was that the minibus driver 'drove the vehicle once or twice a year for cub scout outings' and, when braking, his minibus spun out of control across the road, into the path of the oncoming coach; the police accident investigator stated that the rear wheels had locked and 'The reason for this can only be due to inattention or misjudgment on the part of the driver'.[15] Subsequently the Scout Leader who was the driver, and who had survived the collision, admitted driving without due care and attention and was fined £200.[16]

Driver error was also to blame for the worst road case involving a uniformed organization, when in September 1994 three Guides and two Leaders died after their double-decker bus went under a low bridge in Glasgow on their way home from an outing to Ayr. Fifteen Guides were injured, six of them seriously. Subsequently, and controversially, the driver, Campbell Devlin, was found not guilty of dangerous driving at Glasgow Sheriff Court, but was convicted of the lesser charge of careless driving. The court was told that there had been 37 'bridge bashing' incidents in the previous four years with this overhead rail bridge. It appeared that the driver had been unsure of the route and was following a Guide Leader in her car, but in a civil case brought against her by the parents of Catherine McKnight, aged ten, Lady Cosgrove in the Edinburgh Court of Session ruled that the action against the Guider was 'fundamentally irrelevant' as there was no reason for her to have known the bridge was too low for the bus.[17] On the other hand the bus driver should have been on the alert, although he had only been driving buses since April the previous year, and overlooked the warning signs of a low bridge: 'I was following the car and did not see any signs. My mind was on other things.'[18] 'Other things' might have included the fact that 18 days before this incident the same bus driver had been involved in a collision which killed a man of nineteen, although he was subsequently cleared of careless driving on that matter, when Sheriff Charles McFarlane upheld a defence submission that there was no case to answer because of 'insufficient corroborative evidence'. In respect of the Guides' case the driver was subsequently dismissed by his employers for gross misconduct, was fined £750 for careless driving, and was given nine penalty points on his licence.[19] On both occasions the court in Glasgow had to be cleared because of the anger of the families involved.[20] The civil case against the bus company, Glasgow City Council, as responsible for warning signs, and Railtrack, who owned the bridge, continued to an undisclosed settlement with the insurers. The mother of Catherine

---

[15] 'Cubs' driver blamed for death crash', *The Guardian* (9 November 1994).

[16] 'Cub trip horror', *Daily Record* (31 March 1995).

[17] 'Guide leader cleared over bus death', *Daily Record* (24 December 1998).

[18] 'Anger as driver cleared of causing bus crash deaths', *The Scotsman* (22 March 1995).

[19] '£40,000 memorial to bridge-crash Guides', *Glasgow Herald* (15 May 1995).

[20] 'Anger as bus driver cleared over death crash', *The Scotsman* (8 February 1996).

McKnight was said to be 'so guilt-ridden about giving her daughter cash for the trip that she attempted suicide', but fortunately recovered and organized fundraising for a memorial garden at her daughter's primary school.[21] Reflective strips and improved information on the height of the bridge were also installed after this disaster; the signage cost £5,000.[22]

Seat belts are not usually worn on chartered buses, but in minibuses they are now mandatory, and the research suggests that they are an important factor. When a community minibus overturned on the M6 the year after the M40 school minibus disaster, one teenager was killed, but the other teenagers in a dance group survived; a spokesman for Staffordshire Ambulance Service, said: 'There is no doubt whatsoever that the children were saved because they were wearing their seatbelts. Without them, they would have been killed, or at the least very badly injured or maimed.'[23] Police said the minibus had appeared to 'flip' and no other vehicle was involved. In another case on the M6 in 1988 road layout and design were factors when seven members of a Halifax ramblers' club died. An inquest heard that driving conditions were poor because of spray after heavy rain, and an articulated lorry jack-knifed when overtaking a slower vehicle. The lorry driver was subsequently charged with careless driving, and the inquest heard a statement from him that 'many vehicles were travelling too fast in the conditions and [were] too close behind each other'. An inquest jury returned verdicts of misadventure.[24]

Not all such disasters can be blamed on driver error; sometimes the minibus, particularly if hired, can be wholly defective. This appeared subsequently to be the position with a minibus hired by football supporters in Liverpool, on their return from a Glasgow Rangers match. The driver was convicted of careless driving, but an inquest heard that the minibus, hired from a firm in Ormskirk, had faulty steering, a broken front seatbelt, a leaking fuel filter and no current MoT test certificate. It appeared that diesel seeped on to the tyres, causing the minibus to skid, spin out of control, and hit the central reservation. The driver, Donny Sutherland, indicated how he had had 'to live through a two-year nightmare... I had been told by a court that I was responsible for the deaths of two of my closest friends and, even though I knew I was innocent, I couldn't help but question myself'. He had been fined £850 and banned from driving for a year, but this was quashed on appeal.[25] After a complaint from a Guider in 2001 about a hired vehicle used to transport her Guides, trading standards officers in Birmingham hired a similar van from the company and had it tested by an independent engineer who reported that it had defective steering, lighting, bodywork and exhaust emission. The firm pleaded guilty to offences under the Road Traffic Act,

---

[21] 'Guide leader cleared over bus death', *Daily Record* (24 December 1998); 'Blossoming of a memorial garden', *Glasgow Herald* (24 June 1999).

[22] 'Court has caught the tiddlers, but let the big fish go free', *The Scotsman* (23 March 1995).

[23] 'Crash kills dancer; friends are saved by seatbelts in minibus tragedy', *Daily Mail* (30 August 1994).

[24] 'Contraflows faulted at M6 inquest', *The Guardian* (13 February 1988).

[25] 'Death crash fan to launch an appeal', *Liverpool Daily Post* (26 October 2002).

Business Names Act and Consumer Protection Act, and were fined £2,250 plus costs of £750 at Birmingham Magistrates' Court.[26]

However, even where the injury in these minibus and coach cases seems unique, the circumstances are often foreseeable. For example, when Stephen Adair, aged 18 and an Army Cadet on a trip organized by the Army Schools Liaison office, climbed up to peer through the roof skylight of a coach travelling along a motorway near Gorinchem in the Netherlands and returning from a British Army base at Osnabruck in Germany, no-one appeared to stop him. The coach went under a low viaduct and he was decapitated.[27] Up until the inquest this had been described as a 'freak accident',[28] but the East Yorkshire coroner heard that the Cadets had been drinking and that some had been sticking their heads out of the skylight for fresh air. It seemed rather disingenuous for the suggestion by a colleague that 'Nobody warned us about the roof hatches and there were no signs near the hatch'.[29] Alcohol was also a factor when an Army Cadet commander, Neil Fairman, aged 29, took his seat belt off and stood up in an open top car in a surfing posture. He had been seen to do this 'car surfing stunt' before at a training camp, but on this occasion fell and died of head fractures. His alcohol level was equal to the drink/drive limit. The coroner commented that 'in your 20s you have a great sense of adventure. You think you're fireproof and bad things happen to other people. But this leads to tragedy and loss of life. This is devastating for family and friends'.[30]

Transport hazards need not of course always be on the roads. A party of nineteen Girl Guides and their five Leaders were involved in a head-on train collision in the Swiss Alps in 2003. Eleven were taken to hospital for minor injuries and then discharged.[31] In 1991 five Sea Cadets were aboard a BP tanker *British Trent* when she was hit amidships by a Panamanian-registered bulk carrier *The Western Winner* in the English Channel. They were fortunately some of the survivors, having to jump overboard, as fire swept along the ship's gangways, making escape by lifeboat impossible. A Sea Cadet, Joanne Waddy, aged 19 and from Hull, who was on her maiden voyage, told *The Times* how she was trying to get into a lifeboat 'when a fireball came down the gangway', engulfing the lifeboat in flames.[32] An inquest in 1993 recorded verdicts of unlawful killing on four Britons who died, on the basis that the master of *The Western Winner* had committed 'virtually every navigational sin in the book', and was strongly criticized by the British Marine Accident Investigation Branch for travelling too fast and not making proper use of radar.[33]

---

[26] 'Too many hire cars potential death traps', *Birmingham Post* (16 June 2001).

[27] 'Coach trip Cadet, 18 dies after his head hits bridge', *Daily Record* (27 July 1998).

[28] 'Tributes paid to coach accident victim', *Hull Daily Mail* (28 July 1998).

[29] 'Student died in coach horror', *Hull Daily Mail* (10 December 1998).

[30] 'Fatal fall after "surfing" on car', *This is Local London* (17 December 2002).

[31] 'Girl guides in Alps rail crash', *The Express* (9 August 2003).

[32] 'Tanker crew tell of escape in blazing Channel', *The Times* (4 June 1993).

[33] 'Channel victims unlawfully killed', *The Guardian* (13 May 1995).

Is self-regulation enough for Scouting?

The essential question for voluntary organizations is whether self-regulation outside the licensing regime of the 1995 Act is enough to deal with the hazards of adventurous activities. The main youth organization engaged in adventurous activities and outside the remit is the Scout Association, so they are a useful case study. At the outset it can be noted that Scouting has very strong Parliamentary support, so it is most unlikely that the 1995 Act would be extended to cover them, however much some critics would like this, although that no doubt has to be premised on the basis that Scouting does not suffer a calamity of Lyme Bay proportions. Indeed, in the debate on Mr Jamieson's private members Bill in 1995, Jacques Arnold MP, then the secretary of the all-party parliamentary Scout Association group, estimated that about one-third of MPs had been Scouts. With increasing numbers of female MPs the tendency is probably for an even higher percentage to have been Scouts or Guides, as more than half of Britain's female population have, at some stage in their lives, been members.[34] Mr Arnold supported the legislation, particularly against 'cowboy operations', but warned the House 'to be extremely careful about what it brings to the statute book because it is only too easy to throw out the baby with the bath water.'[35] He extolled the work of the voluntary organizations, as did other MPs, but pointed out that 'It is a sad fact that bad accidents can lead to bad law.'[36]

However, the Scout Association has not been wholly insulated from injury or fatalities, although on the whole it has an excellent safety record. In particular, on boating activities, where the Scout Association follows the national guidelines of organizations such as the BCU and the RYA to assess water authorizations for its leaders and instructors, there has been an impeccable record. By contrast, the position on mountain activities has not been nearly so reassuring. Has there been a pattern to these disasters? Or are the fatalities in Scouting just 'accidents' that no lessons can be learned from? Commentators such as Phil Revell have suggested that 'it is significant that many of the incidents in the last five years involve activities organized and run by schools and youth groups such as the Scouts'.[37] One family in particular suffered grievous loss on two occasions: first when one son, David Weaver, died when an overhanging rock face suddenly fell on him and a friend as they sat around a camp fire at a Scout camp at Cleobury Mortimer in 1997; and then when his brother, John Weaver, slipped to his death on wet grass at Tal y Bont in 2000, walking back down the mountain.[38] The first death was judged to be 'an accident which could not have been predicted' by the South Shropshire coroner. Two Scout Leaders, David Weaver, aged 21, and

---

[34] 'As Britain's biggest voluntary Movement faces a dire shortage of Pack Leaders; where are our Guiding lights?', *The Express* (30 December 2003).

[35] House of Commons *Hansard* (27 January 1995), col 625.

[36] Ibid.

[37] 'Education: training, not tinkering', *The Guardian* (18 September 2001).

[38] 'Second son is killed in plunge; new tragedy hits family', *Birmingham Evening Mail* (4 October 2000); *Kidderminster Evening Mail* (11 October 2000).

Stuart Perkins, aged 20, died instantly when a huge sandstone escarpment fell on them shortly after midnight on an Easter weekend camp. Initially it was conjectured that 'the camp fire had dried out the sandstone rock causing it to collapse,'[39] but a geotechnical engineer commissioned by West Mercia police stated that there was no evidence that a fire started by the Scouts had contributed to the tragedy. Indeed, it is often suggested, as in the American Federation of Mineralogical Societies *Safety Manual* giving advice on field trips, that 'an overhanging rock is the best reflector' for a campfire.[40] This campsite had been in regular use by Scouts for many years, generally with a campfire lit under the escarpment, and the Leaders were sitting around the fire at the end of the day, the Scouts having gone to their tents after their own singing and storytelling session there. The only warning was when a piece of soil fell one or two seconds before the collapse.[41] The other family death, that of John Weaver slipping on wet grass in 2000, is obviously rather more of a recognisable hazard in hillwalking. For example, a study of Scottish mountain deaths the previous year recorded how two very experienced climbers had fallen after slipping on wet grass, at a spot on a narrow ridge which had claimed several lives; the team leader of Dundonnell Mountain Rescue noted that 'a simple slip can often have fatal consequences'.[42] In the decade to 1998 the Scottish mountains had claimed 398 lives and 'the most common accident is a simple slip'.[43] John Weaver was described by his mother as 'a very experienced climber. He would never take any risks', and was in his third year as a student of environmental biology at Bangor, so had much hillwalking experience in North Wales. He had also spent a summer as a climbing instructor at the Kandersteg International Scout Centre in Switzerland.[44] He fell while walking on what was described at the inquest as an 'easy' section of a mountain climb at Craig yr Ysfa, moving from one grassy ledge to another, and the North Wales coroner, Dewi Pritchard Jones, recorded a verdict of misadventure.[45]

However, the most notorious Scout death was in a very different category. In returning a verdict of accidental death, the same North Wales coroner indicated that in this case the lack of supervision by a Leader amounted to negligence; he stated that he had been 'close to delivering a verdict of unlawful killing because of gross negligence'.[46] Jonathan Attwell, aged 10 and from Bristol, fell 600 feet to his death on Snowdon in October 1999. He was with a party of eleven other boys, and the principal allegation from the outset was that his Scout Leader had failed to provide adequate supervision. The coroner told the inquest in Caernarfon that the climb was 'entirely unsuitable' for such a group. The boy was the youngest, having just come up from Cubs, and had no previous experience of

---

[39] 'Fall kills Scout leaders', *The Guardian* (1 April 1997).
[40] Chapter Four, 'What to do if you are lost', AFMS *Safety Manual* (2004).
[41] 'Scout deaths "accidental",' *The Guardian* (23 May 1997).
[42] 'Climbing Accidents 1999: Fatal', *Aberdeen Evening Express* (17 May 1999).
[43] 'How death stalks the mountains in winter', *Daily Mail* (31 December 1998).
[44] 'Family mourns second son after 200ft fall', *Birmingham Post* (4 October 2000).
[45] 'Inquest on climb fall', *Birmingham Evening Mail* (1 December 2000).
[46] 'Snowdon boy's 600ft death fall', *The Times* (18 February 2000).

either mountaineering or hillwalking. He was somehow allowed to walk at the back of the group down the East Ridge route, about which the Snowdonia Park mountain warden said bluntly 'I would not take a group down that ridge'. The inquest heard too that this Leader, Peter Finlay, had at first been positioned in the correct place for a walking descent, at the back of the group, but later allowed Jonathan and another boy to fall behind and become isolated. Mr Finlay, who turned out not even to be in possession of current mountain authorization for Scouting, as he had allowed this to lapse because of a failure to renew a first aid certificate, had also by his own admission 'done no planning for the trip', and, contrary to Scout rules, left no route card.[47] The Crown Prosecution Service then brought criminal proceedings for manslaughter against Mr Finlay, prosecuting counsel alleging that the Scout had been 'left to pick his way down' one of Britain's highest mountains 'alone and totally unsupervised...No boy of 10 could be expected to tackle such a descent safely on his own'. Although the evidence in this case was damning, and indeed soon after the inquest, the Scout Association expelled both Mr Finlay and his deputy who was with him on Snowdon at the time, one factor that mitigated against the higher level of gross negligence was that Mr Finlay was a volunteer 'trying to do his best'. Lord Elwyn-Jones, the former Lord Chancellor, once noted that although Welsh juries are 'against sin, they are not dogmatic about it',[48] and a factor that must have weighed in the balance on finding a volunteer guilty of manslaughter was whether anyone else would be found to take on such responsibilities voluntarily in the future. The jury in Caernavon therefore acquitted Mr Finlay of manslaughter, although the family continued with a civil action against The Scout Association.[49] The case appears to be the nearest a volunteer leader in Britain has come to a conviction for manslaughter.

Another death in 2000, not far away at Cader Idris, was of a Scout Leader, Christopher Oliver, who was judged by the coroner, again Dewi Pritchard Jones, to be 'oblivious to the danger' of a treacherous cliff face. Mr Oliver had taken one of his Scouts, Gareth Cole, aged 14 and from Devizes, up a steep gully without ropes or other specialist climbing equipment. Mr Oliver fell to his death and his Scout was eventually rescued after two hours when another climber heard his cries for help. They had left a larger, well-organized party to attempt this 'scramble'. The coroner said the pair were 'simply following their noses', and Mr Oliver had no climbing qualifications and no specialist equipment. The coroner pointed out that climbing guide books described this gully as 'loose and dangerous', and indicated that by the time they went up wholly unprepared it was 'very wet'. He recorded a verdict of death by misadventure,[50] and the death of the Scout Leader himself inevitably precluded any further civil or criminal proceedings in respect of him.

---

[47] 'Focus: tragedy in Snowdonia', *The Observer* (13 January 2002).
[48] See Elwyn Jones, *In My Time* (London: Weidenfeld & Nicolson, 1983).
[49] 'Scout chief cleared over death of boy on Snowdon', *Daily Telegraph* (17 October 2001).
[50] 'Scout blind to cliff peril', *Daily Mirror* (9 February 2000).

Choosing the right kind of location was also an issue when Jamie Chambers, in a small party of Scouts from Birkenhead, was hit by two very large boulders on Little Tryfan, a spur of Snowdon in the same year. An inquest recorded a verdict of death by misadventure; however, the coroner, Dewi Pritchard Jones, noted that the incident had occurred in a place that was regularly used by mountaineering teams and there appeared to be nothing that could have prevented it. The Scout Association too indicated that 'it looks as though this was a tragic accident that was totally unpredictable and unforeseeable'.[51] But a contrary view was taken by Iain Peter of the Plas y Brenin National Mountain Centre, who stated that the group could have been better equipped, because one of the climbing ropes was not recognized mountaineering equipment, and that the death was preventable because there were safer areas close by where the Scouts could have climbed: 'It's hard to understand exactly why that venue was chosen, there are better venues very close by.[52]

An over-sized party of walkers and a lack of clear directions seemed to be the problem when 18 months earlier, in 1998, Scott Fanning fell 60 feet down a ravine at Ashworth Valley, near Heywood, during a Scout camp. An untrained adult helper took a dozen boys for a walk, and there appeared to have been no 'risk assessment' or prior reconnaissance for this activity. It was clear that the group was too large for one adult to manage on this terrain, and the coroner in Rochdale called for better-defined qualifications and training for Scout Leaders; for ratios to be made clear; and for walks of this nature to be checked first for safety. Peter McPhillips, the helper, told the inquest that he had missed a turning as he led the group onto an unofficial path on the side of the gorge, some 30 yards below the recognized public footpath. The coroner said many of the problems could have been foreseen with 'more planning and foresight'.[53] Sadly, Scott Fanning's father never recovered from losing his son and two years later was found dead in a fume-filled car; he had been a Cub Scout Leader and at that inquest the coroner again called on the Scouting movement to review its procedures on supervised adventure activities.[54] Mrs Fanning received bereavement damages of £7,500 for her son's death from the Scout Association, which is the statutory maximum,[55] but considered suing for the death of her husband.[56] However, the medical evidence showed that Mr Fanning's mental difficulties arose before the death of his son, and partly as a result of the

---

[51] 'Climber, 15, crushed to death by one-ton rock', *The Sun* (23 October 2000).

[52] 'Boy killed by rocks', *South Wales Echo* (26 July 2001). 'Misadventure ruling on Scout's death; Inquest: "Accident could not have been averted",' *Western Mail* (26 July 2001). Mr Peter was also an expert witness in *Chaplain v Scout Association* (CA transcript 22 November 1996) where he stated his view that all the climbers, including the leader, were inexperienced, and expressed surprise that the leader had been cleared to supervise groups of Scout novice climbers on routes of a very difficult standard.

[53] 'Inquest told of Scout tragedy', *The Independent* (5 August 1998).

[54] 'Grieving father dies in car', *Birmingham Post* (22 April 2000).

[55] Section 1A Fatal Accidents Act 1976, added by section 3 Administration of Justice Act 1982.

[56] '£7,500 for son's death an insult', *Manchester Evening News* (19 January 2002).

breakdown of his marriage, so the case was discontinued. Unfortunately this particular ravine had seen many other falls, over a dozen since Scott Fanning's death, and one of the difficulties for Rochdale Council in dealing with the safety issues was to discover the owner of this spot, known locally as 'Dead Man's Drop'.[57]

In 1999 there was severe condemnation for Scout leaders from the Austrian police when Roy Thornton, aged 15 and from Wembley, died in the Alps. He slipped after his Scout group became lost in thick cloud. Inspector Michael Fritz criticized them for being inadequately dressed, alleging 'they were wearing short trousers and plimsolls when climbing in relatively steep terrain with the weather closing in'. As well as the wholly inappropriate attire he commented on timing, weather and navigational skills as 'they set out in mid-afternoon – far too late in the day for an Alpine climb. There was thick cloud and a light rain came down, and they lost their way.'[58] The Scout party had ascended a section of a 12,000 foot high mountain in the Tyrolean Lech valley by cable car, and they had then strayed from a footpath on their way down, when the Scout slipped on a grassy verge. The local representative of Jeka Holidays, which organizes many Scout trips, stated that 'the weather was not good enough. ... they were not supposed to go in that weather with bad shoes.'[59] The Scout Association vigorously contested allegations on preparations and equipment, showing photographs of the party with appropriate footwear, waterproofs and woolly hats, but admitted that there had been errors in failing to consult a map, which was also of an inappropriate scale, a failure to read the contours properly, a deviation from the marked route, and that the party were late setting off, which had caused hurried decisions and even an argument between leaders. There was therefore an admission that the party leader had failed to 'observe procedure' and indeed Paul Beardmore was found guilty of culpable homicide 'through inadequate preparation of a walking tour and as a result of the fact that he left the marked path during the descent [leading] the group of young people into a steep, unmarked, rain-soaked area of grass without a footpath'. He was sentenced in Austria to two months imprisonment, suspended for three years. Somewhat at variance with this finding the coroner in London in 2000 recorded a verdict of accidental death.[60]

Another Scout party, well-equipped in the Alps, perhaps just made a classic mountaineering mistake. Andrew Hindley, aged 23, and in a party of four Venture Scouts from Marlow, fell 2,000 feet down the Jungfrau. The group had set off at 3am to make the best of early hard ice, but at 10,000 feet, they rested for an hour before attempting the last push to the summit. Mr Hindley commenced to free-climb – without using a rope – but the snow was already melting and had lost its stability. Another Scout, Andrew Pascall, went after him and fell too, sustaining a broken wrist, a skull fracture and knees that later required operations;

---

[57] 'Family's plea over Dead Man's Drop', *Manchester Evening News* (8 August 2000).

[58] 'Scout in death plunge; Alpine police condemn walking party leaders', *Daily Mail* (24 August 1999).

[59] 'Scout, 15, in Tyrol death plunge', *The Times* (24 August 1999).

[60] Information from Scout Insurance Services.

as he slid down the mountain he was fortunately able to brake to a halt on an ice field, and then spent over 10 hours crawling to safety. The other two Scouts lashed themselves to a fixed rope and were rescued by helicopter.[61]

Perhaps the very worst Scouting case was a caving death when Lee Craddock, aged 11 and from Blackpool, fell in North Yorkshire in 1995 at Gaping Ghyll, which at 1,300 feet is Britain's deepest pothole. The facts were disputed, but it was claimed that he was the first of a party of Scouts to crawl into the narrow Jib Tunnel, leading off the main cave, and in the pitch dark he failed to see a 360 feet drop; in the British caving literature this is described as 'the most spectacular free hanging abseil in the country'.[62] His mother, Pat Craddock, commenced proceedings against the Scout Association and Judge Appleton made scathing comments in court about the 'woeful ignorance' of the Scout Leader, commenting in particular that the equipment and the supervision was inadequate. He awarded damages of £50,000, well above bereavement damages of £7,500, and perhaps indicating that the boy's father had been present, allegedly standing 'helpless' outside the tunnel, but also reflecting what the judge thought were the heinous circumstances.[63] The Scout Association in defence of their leaders had first blamed the landowner for not placing adequate signs to warn of the hazards, but the judge held that there was appropriate signage in the nearby car park about dangerous pot holes near the country's most famous caving system, and that the real reason for the tragedy was that the party leader, Martin Bailey, 'lost control' and 'bathed in the sun' while the Scouts went into the tunnel. The British Cave Rescue Council report on this incident records that Lee 'was a member of a Scout *walking* group' [my emphasis].[64] In a caustic passage, the judge stated that 'as Mr Bailey was lazing on the grass at Gaping Ghyll, reflecting on how more agreeable the area was than Blackpool, Lee was taking a fatal journey into Jib Tunnel. There was no evidence he had consulted an Ordnance Survey map and he had no sense of the dangers, therefore was in no position to warn anyone. If you take a group of urban 11-year-olds to dangerous countryside you must exercise reasonable care for their safety. Mr Bailey utterly failed in this responsibility.'[65] The court heard independent testimony from a teacher walking nearby how these Scouts had 'behaved in an inappropriate manner', for example in filming a Scout waving his arms about on the very brink of Gaping Ghyll. The Assistant Leaders admitted to the court that they were unaware of Scouting Association rules that walking expeditions in this terrain should not be in groups of more than seven.[66] However, several points were vigorously contested; for example, it was suggested that Lee's father, who was present as a parent helper, had out of the earshot of the leaders, agreed to his son exploring, supplied him with a cigarette lighter for

---

[61] 'My best friend plunged past me to his death', *Daily Mail* (1 July 1993).

[62] Russell Myers, *The Craven Pothole Club Record*, Number 36, October 1994.

[63] '£50,000 for Scout death', *The Sun* (20 April 2001), 'Family of death plunge Scout agree settlement', *Daily Mail* (20 April 2001).

[64] BCRC, *Incident Report 1995* (1996) 2.

[65] 'Scout chief blamed for boy's cave death fall', *Daily Mail* (18 November 2000).

[66] 'Landowner cleared of blame in death fall', *This is Bradford* (30 November 2000).

illumination, and followed him in with just one other Scout. The evidence of the teacher was also disputed, particularly when he claimed that he knew these were Scouts by their uniforms, when on this outing uniforms were not worn. The best person to sort this matter out, particularly on the claim that he had refused permission to go caving but had been overruled without his knowledge by the father, was the party leader; unfortunately Mr Bailey 'collapsed and died' at home earlier in 2000,[67] with the view of his colleagues that his death had been hastened by the stress of this 'travesty' of a case. Nonetheless, given the judge's comments in the civil case it seems highly likely that if it had not been for that death, criminal proceedings might have been taken further, as on the judge's view of the facts it would certainly appear to have fallen into the 'gross negligence' category which might have buttressed a manslaughter prosecution. The Scout Association initially indicated that it was considering an appeal on civil liability, but subsequently decided to forego this, principally because it was an issue of fact for which there would not have been a right of appeal. The other slight mystery was that this incident was reported in some media outlets as a 'a school pot-holing trip'[68], but the truth is that it was unfortunately a Scouting expedition of the very worst kind.

Mrs Craddock claimed in 2001 that in the years since her son had died in 1995 there had been eight deaths in Scouting, although a spokesman for the Scout Association stated that six of these 'were either unavoidable accidents or incidents where boys, who happened to be Scouts, were on private trips'.[69] That spokesman, John Fogg, their long-serving director of communications, had of necessity to make several statements to the media in difficult circumstances over the years. Sometimes he had been able to be reassuring; for example in 2004 when announcing an inquiry into how some Southport Scouts had been assisted by Mountain Rescue in Cumbria he was able to indicate that their route to an overnight in a cave in the fells 'was well known to them'; that they had appropriate emergency equipment 'including GPS navigation systems'; that this party of five Scouts and two Leaders 'may have abandoned their expedition' when two 'civilian' walkers were picked up and 'began to struggle, even though they were in sight of their destination'; that they had ample supplies of clothing, food and water; that they had 'carried out a complex risk assessment before they set off, including checking the weather, and decided it was well within their capabilities'; and that the 'leaders are very experienced and have their Form Ms, a mountaineering qualification which is very rigorous'. Mr Fogg added that, with the addition of the two 'civilians', the Scout party themselves 'took the decision to stop and call for help. It is far better that they recognized a change in the

---

[67] 'Scouts blamed for Lee's death', *This is Lancashire* (30 November 2000).

[68] 'Pot-holing tragedy', *The Independent* (26 July 1995).

[69] 'Scout Association involved in legal cases where children died', *Western Mail* (18 October 2001). The 'private expedition' defence was also developed in *Chaplain v The Scout Association* (CA transcript 22 November 1996), a procedural tangle about expert evidence following injuries sustained in rock climbing.

situation than continued and tried to be heroes'.[70] On several occasions Mr Fogg resorted to humour – 'the rubbing together of sticks is no longer required for fire-lighting, as the Scout movement has recognized the existence of the match.'[71] On occasion he praised bravery in the face of insuperable odds – 'the Marlow Venture Group is the finest of its type in the world and the courage of Andrew Pascall is what you'd expect from a Queen's Scout'.[72] And occasionally Mr Fogg showed justified fury, as when explaining that Thomas Hamilton had been expelled from Scouting 'in disgrace' as an Assistant Scout Leader in 1974 after two weekend camps in which boys in his charge had 'got extremely wet and cold' on outdoor activities, long before 1981 when Mr Hamilton was also driven out of a leadership position with the Boys' Brigade, and 22 years before he went on a rampage and murdered 16 children and their teacher in Dunblane.[73] However, Mr Fogg in the *Attwell* case had to change from the initial Scouting line that 'nothing appears to have emerged which would suggest that they were doing something they shouldn't have been doing'[74] to the announcement after the damning verdict of the inquest that there would be a 'major review of procedures' to reduce 'to an absolute minimum' risks associated 'with the conduct of adventurous activities'.[75]

Scout campsites have also had problems, and one in particular. After a death at Broadstone Warren Scout Campsite in 1999 there was a criminal prosecution. There was another too in respect of an earlier death in 1997. The 1999 death was of Jack Sudds, aged 8 and from Eltham, who drowned in an unattended outdoor swimming pool. He had been a non-swimmer, one of 28 children at the camp with Middle Park Play Scheme, a charity group on a London council estate. The East Sussex Scout Council was fined £15,000 and ordered to pay £10,995 costs. That prosecution followed a verdict of death by misadventure when an inquest heard that the boy entered the outdoor pool alone when his friends had returned to their camp site and a lifeguard failed to lock the doors to the boys' changing rooms.[76] The inquest jury was also told that a hole in the fence that surrounded the pool had not been repaired and that an alarm used in emergencies did not work when activated after the boy's body was found.[77] The prosecution brought by Wealden District Council indicated what were described as 'multiple and continuing breaches of health and safety', and the justices found that the Scout Council had neglected to follow their own guidelines and had ignored the concerns of their own lifeguard. There had also been an earlier prosecution in 1997 at the site, after a Scout, Michelle Stanley, aged 16 and from Ashford, died

---

[70] 'Scouts rescue probe', *Liverpool Daily Post* (9 February 2004).
[71] 'Scouting prepares for girls', *The Times* (9 February 1990).
[72] 'British Scout plunges to his death in Alpine climb', *Evening Standard* (29 June 1993).
[73] 'Guns put in the hands of a human timebomb', *The Scotsman* (15 March 1996).
[74] 'Scout killed in 600ft fall from Snowdon peak', *The Times* (18 October 1999).
[75] 'Jonathan should never have been on Snowdon… he was just 10 years old; family's fury at Scout leaders over disaster trip', *Western Daily Press* (18 February 2000).
[76] 'Scouts in crisis after boy's pool death fine', *Birmingham Post* (15 September 2000).
[77] 'Cub Scout drowned as pool door left unlocked', *The Independent* (19 February 2000).

when she had been standing on a tractor, slipped and fell under the trailer wheels.[78] An inquest recorded a misadventure verdict and the coroner was informed that the volunteer driver had never driven a tractor before.[79] Subsequently at a criminal trial it was found that the site warden had given the driver a 'wholly inadequate' ten minutes of driving instruction, and the Scout Council admitted failings in the management, administration, control and supervision of activities at the campsite; it was fined £5,000 and ordered to pay £7,000 costs.[80] Perhaps needless to say these two criminal fines were very considerable sums for a voluntary and charitable body, which would have been better used for youth activities.[81]

Inevitably with such a very large organization engaged in outdoor pursuits there are going to be some injuries. In the same way as we have seen with AALA licensed premises there may be the possibility of sudden death, perhaps through natural causes. A climbing instructor, Jim Wilson, died in 1999 at Kibblestone Scout campsite, and the coroner recorded an open verdict. Mr Wilson had gone to the aid of a Scout who had landed badly while abseiling and then he himself landed heavily and died. It appeared that he suffered a brain haemorrhage and died ten days afterwards. Pathologists were unable to pinpoint whether Mr Wilson had suffered the haemorrhage before the fall or because of it.[82] By contrast, death by misadventure was the verdict of Dewi Pritchard Jones on Barbara Pearson, a Cub Scout Leader from Smethwick who was using a 'rubber ring' in the sea '40 to 50 metres off the shore' near Pwllheli in 2004; his conclusion was that 'at the end of April the cold sea would have led to hypothermia and brought on disorientation', so that she was 'unable to do anything' when a fellow Leader paddled out and 'got a rope to her'. The coroner also indicated that 'inflatable rings were unsafe in the sea'.[83] Opinions varied as to whether this Leader was a 'strong swimmer' (her family)[84] or could not swim at all (the coastguard),[85] but however strong a swimmer this type of 'cold water drowning' was a foreseeable hazard in the sea at that time of year, and particularly when not wearing a buoyancy aid.

---

[78] 'Scout killed at camp', *The Times* (24 November 1997).
[79] 'Scout death', *The Times* (8 July 1998).
[80] 'Scouts fined over tractor girl's death', *Daily Mail* (16 February 1999).
[81] Scout Council crisis over pool tragedy fine', *Birmingham Evening Mail* (15 September 2000).
[82] 'Walk tribute to Scout leader', *Stoke Sentinel* (3 June 1999).
[83] 'I tried to rescue drowning Scout Leader', *Birmingham Evening Mail* (17 September 2004). 'Drowning horror on sunny day', *Daily Post* (17 September 2004).
[84] Her sister and her police officer son confirmed that she was 'a very strong swimmer' who swam frequently in indoor pools and at this camping location; 'Mystery of Scouting sea death; mother "a good swimmer",' *Birmingham Evening Mail* (28 April 2003).
[85] 'Sea-trip Scouts leader drowns', *Mail on Sunday* (27 April 2003), 'Cub Leader is drowned', *Sunday Mirror* (27 April 2003), 'Drowning horror on sunny day', *Daily Post* (17 September 2004), and the advice of the coastguards that 'people who can't swim should not use inflatables'.

However, in response to some of these incidents, and in particular the *Attwell* case, the Scout Association ordered a full internal inquiry. They had been under a bombardment of criticism, especially from Alan Pugh, the Welsh Assembly Member for Clwyd West, a qualified mountain leader, and the Welsh Deputy Minister for Education and Lifelong Learning. Mr Pugh claimed that the high-profile prosecution of the former Scout Leader Mr Finlay had 'not improved safety for children in the Welsh mountains'. He asserted that 'poorly equipped groups of youngsters were still being taken into the Welsh mountains every weekend by volunteers who were not up to the task'.[86] In the Welsh Assembly Mr Pugh initiated a debate in which he pointed out that the Assembly had the power through secondary legislation to close what he described as a 'loophole' which left the voluntary organizations outside the 1995 licensing regime. He suggested that 'Even the threat to do this may persuade the handful of voluntary organizations that organize a large percentage of outdoor activities for children in Wales to improve their safety record', and claimed that he had 'seen too many ill-equipped and abysmally-led children's groups on our summits in driving rain or with ice underfoot, to be complacent about the current set-up', and he was very dismissive that the Scout Association had refused to meet the AALA to discuss mountain safety and that they had insisted on 'using internal checks, rather than the UK leadership qualifications framework'.[87] The Royal Society for the Prevention of Accidents (RoSPA) has also campaigned to close what they describe as 'such a glaring loophole...for Scouts and Guides' and believes that there should be 'full safety training for all who look after young people on such expeditions'.[88]

The Scout internal report in February 2000 reported a finding of an old-fashioned 'cavalier attitude' towards safety rules. It stated that some Scout Leaders were steeped in a '1960s-1970s attitude to adventure and risk that is not acceptable to society in 2000'. The inquiry team most interestingly included Iain Peter, from the National Mountain Centre at Plas y Brenin, who had been an earlier critic, and who even subsequently indicated that 'Where I disagree most with the Scouts is they bring in more rules and regulations, but unless they change their whole culture, the rules do not make any difference'.[89] This 'culture' perspective was in fact evident in the report, which stated that in certain activities and areas there had been a culture 'geared to leader wants rather than young persons' needs, and leaders who went out to climb the highest peak regardless of party ability'.[90] The report led to a wholesale revision of Scout expedition and outdoor activity procedures, with a series of meetings to notify all those with authorizations for mountain and water activities. A letter sent out to Scout

---

[86] 'Jonathan had been entrusted into the care of others for only a few days and was expected to return home safely', *Western Mail* (17 October 2001).
[87] Welsh Assembly Record of Proceedings (8 February 2001); The Short Debate: Death in the Mountains; Improving Mountain Safety in Wales.
[88] Christa Ackroyd, *Sunday Express* (15 October 2000).
[89] 'Mountain safety tests "vital",' *BBC News Online* (26 January 2002).
[90] 'Scouts criticized for "cavalier" attitude to safety', *The Guardian* (16 February 2000).

Leaders by John Bevan, the Chairman of the Committee of Council and former National Commissioner for Activities, outlined the new rules and made clear that those who failed to follow them would not be supported by the Association. An important factor he noted was that 'if we do not take immediate action to change the attitude and culture of some of our leaders, the Committee of the Council believes that we are in grave risk of an outside body imposing regulatory restrictions upon us'.[91] One of the revamped 'fact sheets' in the new mountaineering authorization scheme, introduced in February 2001, was actually entitled 'Mountaineering with Scouts – The Vital Culture'. However, Iain Peter commented that 'the challenge that the scouts face is that it's not just about having rigorous and robust rules – it's in making people stick to them.'[92]

Unfortunately these Scout cases and the conclusions of their own report do not entirely square with the assertion by Jacques Arnold MP in the 1995 debate that 'the Lyme bay tragedy could not have happened at a Scout Centre [because] the requirements imposed by the Scout Association about the qualifications of the personnel involved, the standard of equipment and the weather conditions would have prevented that expedition.'[93] Such over-confidence is perhaps never entirely justified, but it seems very odd too that the Scout Association, according to Marcus Bailie, have 'twice refused advice' from the AALA. One offer to give advice came in the same month that Jonathan Attwell died on Snowdon, and two letters were sent to the Scout Association by the AALA offering assistance in improving its safety standards on mountains. John Fogg on behalf of the Scout Association indicated that they 'were in talks with a number of mountaineering governing bodies and it is possible that we felt that we had all the expert advice at that time'.[94] Clearly some of those experts were not at all happy with the new Scout arrangements in 2001. Several indicated that 'although the Scouts have made changes in regulations governing adventure trips, they do not go far enough' and that 'the Scout Association appears not to be listening to well-intentioned advice'.[95] And Marcus Bailie noted that 'although the Scouting movement had been involved in talks since Jonathan's death with the British Mountaineering Association and the Mountain Leader Training Board, it did not appear to have applied the advice … [Scout regulations] allow exactly the same inappropriate leaders leading groups of people on the hills as before'. Mr Bailie suggested that the Scout Association seemed to be afraid of being brought within the remit of the AALA, which they felt 'would almost certainly make it impossible for it to function as a voluntary organizer of adventure events', but what the AALA 'and other industry leaders want is for the scouts to apply their

---

[91] Quoted by Philip Revell, 'Scouts criticized for "cavalier" attitude to safety', *The Guardian* (16 February 2000).
[92] Ibid.
[93] House of Commons *Hansard* (27 January 1995), col 626.
[94] 'Scouts "turned down offers of help with mountain safety"', *Western Mail* (18 October 2001).
[95] 'Adventure experts fear another Scouts mountain tragedy', *Western Mail* (18 October 2001).

standards while remaining outside the legal framework of the AALA'.[96] John Cousins of the Mountain Leader Training Board indicated that they and other mountain groups had met the Scout Association a few weeks before, but 'We are a long way from being happy with their leadership criteria'.[97] John Fogg countered with the point that the Scout mountain rules had been 'fully revised'. Iain Peter, who as we have seen was part of that revision, nevertheless felt that 'the single most important thing the Scouts could have done to prevent Jonathan's death was to ensure the competence of the leaders, that the trip was properly planned and organized and appropriate to the skills and experience of the participants' and that 'It would be good for voluntary organizations to meet the industry standards, but they should not have to be licensed'.[98] John Bevan for the Scout Association, himself a hillwalker for over 50 years and a national expert on the health and safety of adventurous activities, concurs with the view that statutory regulation would be unworkable: 'If you take a large organization like us, then we could probably adjust our procedures to make allowance for licensing. But if you extend it to all children, what does the local curate do when he wants to take his Sunday school out for a walk?'[99]

However, there is perhaps a cautionary tale in the hubris of the former Education Secretary, John Patten, who at the time of the Lyme Bay saga claimed that it was an 'isolated incident'.[100] In 2004 a further consultation was launched in Scouting, in order to revamp the authorization rules. The proposals of this *Authorization Review* were that the authorization scheme be replaced by a 'permit' scheme', that attendance at a national governing body approved course will be recommended as 'best practice', and that each activity will have a recommended text 'typically a book or manual approved by a National Governing Body'.[101] The outcome is likely to be that Scouting standards are equal to and possibly in some instances superior to the recommended AALA standards for activity centres.[102] Calls for an extension to the 1995 Act to cover voluntary organizations are likely to continue unless the Scout Association take account of changing circumstances, and only if their internal rules are fully enforced within Scouting. Currently these calls have become less strident, and it would appear that Scouting has learned many of the lessons from inside and outside their Movement. Nevertheless, as with schools, there will continue to be a close scrutiny. Indeed from the outset in 1995 it was education officials who called for

---

[96] Ibid.

[97] Ibid.

[98] 'Changes needed to culture that took Jonathan to his death, warns expert', *Western Mail* (17 October 2001).

[99] 'Focus: tragedy in Snowdonia', *The Observer* (13 January 2002).

[100] 'How safe are activity centres?', *The Times* (12 February 1994).

[101] *Review of the Scout Association's Authorization Scheme for Adventurous Activities* (October 2004).

[102] See Scout Association *Commercially Led Activities Index Fact Sheet* FS120086 September 2003 Edition no 2, which lists requirements in the AALA sector, and the analogous *Scout Led Activities Index Fact Sheet* FS120084 September 2003 Edition no 3, which together with various other Fact Sheets gives the full picture for Scouting activities.

the licensing system to cover voluntary organizations, and one such call from the Durham LEA made the estimate that there were perhaps 50,000 voluntary organizations providing adventurous activities in the UK.[103] To include all these which would be a licensing regime of a wholly different magnitude. Nevertheless that suggestion was echoed by one adventure-holiday operator, Superchoice, who considered the rules to be 'too vague' and required the inclusion of the whole adventurous activities sector, commercial and voluntary.[104] There would certainly be likely to be a renewal of such demands if Scouting suffered further tragedies of the Jonathan Attwell and Lee Craddock variety.

Army Cadets and crown immunity

Army Cadets have also suffered fatalities, but as well as being a youth organization outside the remit of the 1995 legislation they are also in a special arena of the law as possessing crown immunity. If anything their safety record has been much more problematic than that of Scouting. It is important to make a distinction between armed forces training in the combined cadet forces (CCF), where it is a uniformed youth organization sponsored by the Ministry of Defence engaging in outdoor activities, and military training for professionals which will include battle preparations of the most extreme variety. Military training therefore spreads across a continuum, and it may be that some of the difficulties lie in not making clear delineations between the 'leisure' and the 'full-time soldiering' aspects. The term 'cadet' can cover both the volunteer youth service and also the early part of training for operations, which perhaps adds to the confusion, compounded as we shall see by some secretive processes attached to crown immunity, as well as a cultural reluctance to discuss any difficulties openly. The CCF is of course a very important recruiting ground to display aspects of military life, and a 'taster' of full military training is helpful, but further analysis suggests that the full rigour of common civilian standards should apply, and there is therefore a direct comparison with other uniformed organizations. Although training for war cannot possibly be an excuse for seriously injuring or killing young soldiers, it is inevitable that risk is higher in that sector, and although a different context applies, this should not negate a need for full risk assessment. It is clear that fatalities occur when training for 'special duties' and covert operations, where live ammunition would be needed to prepare soldiers, for example in anti-ambush drills. Although after every live firing exercise all ammunition is purportedly checked and certified, there have clearly been lapses and there is no excuse for that. Courts martial and boards of inquiries are subject to closure for periods up to one hundred years in the National Archives, so it is rather difficult to assess the contemporary position of safety in armed forces training. From the cases that do emerge into the public domain it is clear that

---

[103] See the comments of the Durham LEA in 'New rules on outdoor activities attacked', *Northern Echo* (28 December 1995).
[104] 'Safety rules "too slack",' *Sunday Times* (12 November 1995).

there are some serious problems across a whole range of issues, but the analysis here will concentrate on outdoor activities.

Many of the fatalities have been vehicle-related, but as well as the road deaths that we have considered, there have also been a number of incidents occurring 'off road' during training. For example, in 1998, Clare Shore, aged 15 and a member of the Staffordshire and West Midlands Army Cadet Force, was on a summer course when an Army vehicle crushed her as she crawled through grass during a night-time exercise.[105] HSE inspectors considered issuing a Crown Censure against the Ministry of Defence, which is the military equivalent of a Crown Court prosecution, and the most serious admonishment the MoD can face for breaches of health and safety rules. After an inquest verdict her mother, Jackie Shore, accused the Army Cadet organizers of gross negligence: 'Justice has not been done and it's clear that the individuals responsible made many serious mistakes that cost my only daughter's life…you send your children to the Army Cadets and you expect them to be safe'.[106]

Figures show that since the Second World War more soldiers have been killed in vehicle accidents than by enemy fire. Indeed, just since 1990 there have been at least 1,748 deaths of members of the Armed Forces in and around their barracks, many more than have died in action, leading some campaigners such as Kevin McNamara MP to demand 'a complete culture change within the Armed Forces'.[107] Not much seemed to have been learned from the death of Clare Shore, because in 2000 Christopher France, aged 18 and in the Parachute Regiment, was run over by an ambulance while he lay in grass after he was ordered to be a 'casualty' during instruction. It took three years for the MoD to admit liability, although his parents claimed there were still 'unanswered questions over the vehicle's condition and how fast it was travelling', as an HSE investigation found that the brakes were not properly maintained.[108]

Another vehicle-related training incident was when a coroner recorded a verdict of misadventure on two Army Cadets, Karen Buttershaw and Rebecca Norris, who were members of the Oxford University Training Corps. Their Land Rover rolled backwards down a steep hill, somersaulted and burst into flames during an exercise on Salisbury Plain in 1995. The cause appeared to be a faulty cap on the fuel tank, but the coroner recommended the Army to investigate the circumstances under which an unqualified driver would be permitted to drive an army vehicle without a supervising instructor present, the type of fire extinguisher carried, the provision of communication equipment in the event of an emergency, and whether diesel fuel vehicles should be used in such

---

[105] 'How many more of our soldiers must die in training?', *Daily Express* (17 April 2000).

[106] '"No Justice" says Mother after verdict on Army Cadet's death', *Birmingham Post* (21 May 1999).

[107] 'Are these men and women casualties of a huge cover-up?', *Western Daily Press* (19 June 2003).

[108] 'Dead Para's parents still seek answers', *The Northern Echo* (12 April 2003).

exercises.[109] Another death through fire was that of Stephanie Gibbins, a member of the Southampton University Officer Training Corps, who was trapped in a house where she was posing as a terrorist during a training exercise at Longmoor camp in Hampshire. She died from smoke inhalation after a smoke grenade set fire to a settee, and an inquest jury returned a verdict of accidental death.[110] An army board of enquiry was set up to investigate the death, but Lieutenant Colonel Briggs, the camp commandant, stated that 'For security purposes I cannot say anything about the type of training that takes place inside Longmoor Camp'.[111] This total refusal to discuss the circumstances behind the death of a university student engaged in an extra-curricular 'leisure' activity is hardly conducive to finding ways to prevent further such tragedies. No details were ever released of the findings of this inquiry, and a constant criticism of the MoD is, according to John Cooper, a barrister specializing in this area of law, that 'in dealing with the MoD one is coming up against an organization that is bred on a culture of secrecy and makes litigation involving the military a war of attrition'.[112]

A verdict of misadventure was also recorded on the death of Gordon Daniel, aged 17 and in the Eton College Combined Army Cadet Force. Technically, as this was literally on the playing fields of Eton and during school time, it should properly be recorded on the AALA list of school fatalities. It was thought that the cadet fell 40 feet to his death while parascending because he may have accidentally released his parachute before take-off and then held on for two minutes before losing his grip. The inquest heard how the cadets received just fifteen minutes instruction before making their first ascents, and the dead cadet was on his second run when the disaster happened. His father called for better training and equipment checks, saying 'I think the procedures should be re-examined.' The HSE investigation suggested that the cadet may have been gripping a clip on his harness so tightly that he involuntarily pressed the release bar. The British Hangliders Association recommended that the cadets should have had more instruction: 'the ground preparation was not good'.[113]

Army Cadet instructors have also died, and two deaths in 1993 were particularly noteworthy when cadets were engaged in 'river walking'. This was long before the Stainforth Beck inquest in 2002 recognized this activity as no longer 'low risk'. Indeed, as we have seen, Marcus Bailie indicated then that Jason Dalton's death in 2001 might have been preventable if the Stainforth Beck inquest had not been so delayed, so arguably lessons could have been learned long before about the potentially hazardous nature of this activity when rivers are in spate. Captain Michael Veal and Sergeant Jeremy Lander, both volunteer leaders, were swept to their deaths in the Yorkshire Dales near Pateley Bridge.

---

[109] 'Coroner says fuel leak led to deaths of Cadets', *The Times* (4 May 1995). 'Cadets verdict', *The Independent* (4 May 1995).

[110] 'Fire death of Cadet accidental', *The Independent* (1 November 1991).

[111] 'Woman dies in fire during army exercise', *The Times* (31 July 1991).

[112] 'Lawyers find the MoD a formidable adversary', *The Times* (11 January 2005).

[113] 'Death mystery of Eton parascender who lost his grip 40ft in the air', *Daily Mail* (4 March 1994).

An inquest heard how the instructors from the Cambridgeshire Army Cadet Force, were 'gorge running'. Another sergeant, Simon Nolan, explained that both leaders 'were extremely safety-conscious' and Captain Veal 'had done the gorge run on other occasions. The river was very high but nobody raised any doubts about going in'. Other witnesses described the river as a 'raging torrent', but the coroner, in recording verdicts of accidental death, stated somewhat contradictorily that 'Nobody could have anticipated quite how horrendous the water conditions were'.[114]

Army training is necessarily gruelling, but the suggestion has been made that the Army can occasionally push their Cadets too hard. Here we cross over from the distinctly 'leisure' side' to battle training where a different standard needs to apply, but where it is suggested that 'gross negligence' or recklessness would be an applicable yardstick to protect young recruits. In 1998 three Sandhurst Cadets collapsed at the end of a seven mile endurance march at the military academy. Graham Holmes subsequently died of multiple organ failure due to heat stroke, a state beyond hyperthermia and heat exhaustion, and another cadet, Adrian Muir, was in intensive care but made a recovery.[115] The cadets were dressed in a double layer of battle-fatigue clothing, wearing boots and carrying a water bottle, webbing, pack, rifle, and a heavy helmet. Dr Alan Porter, a specialist on heat exhaustion who has studied marathon runners, but increasingly turned his attention to the many Army Cadets collapsing under the weight of 40lb loads, suggested in *The Lancet* that he hoped that 'good sense will prevail in the end, if junior commanders can be persuaded that the training exercise responsible for heat illness is not only irrelevant but also foolhardy and irresponsible'. The MoD rejected Dr Porter's claims as 'ridiculous', suggesting that they had well-established 'protocols' for dealing with cadets who suffered heat-related injuries. However, Dr Porter has continued to assert that 'this sort of training should be stopped. It is quite unnecessary'.[116] Four weeks after the inquest on Cadet Holmes a similar training run at Sandhurst saw four Army Cadets taken to hospital with heat exhaustion and a further sixteen reported as unwell. An Army spokesman described this as 'a pretty light exercise', while an ambulance service spokesman stated that 'we are concerned that the cadets were made to run in full kit in such extreme heat'.[117]

'Heart attack' might be an appellation due to 'natural causes' or, as with some Army Cadets, due to heat exhaustion or over-exertion, so it is not entirely clear what happened when in 1998 Marine Cadet David Vallance died of a heart attack while jogging to a firing range near Exeter, and when in 1996 Nigel Foster died after suffering a 'heart attack' during a swimming exercise, also in Devon.[118] In young and fit recruits a heart attack sounds very unlikely, although as we have seen 'sudden death syndrome' might explain some cases.

---

[114] 'Instructors killed in gorge torrent', *Glasgow Herald* (15 January 1994).
[115] 'Heat exhaustion killed Scottish Army Cadet', *The Scotsman* (17 July 1998).
[116] 'Cadet's death prompts review call', *The Scotsman* (11 February 2000).
[117] '"Too hot" soldiers collapse', *News of the World* (18 July 1999).
[118] 'Roll call of deaths during military exercises', *The Guardian* (1 April 2000).

A full list of the deaths of young army recruits as well as cadets makes for grim reading. Some, such as the death in 1997 of Andrew Charnock on Dartmoor are due again to heat exhaustion. Some are due to drowning while 'wading', such as the death in 1998 of Nathaniel Burton, aged 16, and also on Dartmoor. Junior Recruit Burton was into the eleventh week of his training course as a Marine and had swum just over half of the 120-foot wide Crazywell Pool with a kit bag and rifle when he disappeared under the surface; this pool at Dousland is 70 feet deep, so it is difficult to categorize as 'wading', and his body was eventually recovered by police frogmen.[119] Far more obviously culpable was the death of Pierre Bolangi, aged 17, and a member of Charlton Athletic's youth academy who was undergoing 'army leadership training' at Aldershot in 2000; his squad were 'asked to cross a muddy lake wearing full football kit underneath an army boiler suit', and none had been 'asked if they could swim'. Lieutenant Colonel Robin Hodges confirmed that the boys had not been asked if they could swim because 'it wasn't thought to be necessary'! An army instructor allegedly told the Charlton youth team members that the water was 'chest height... just over your waist', although Pierre Bolangi, who was 5 foot 8 inches tall, was recovered from water over 6 foot deep.[120] This would appear to have been *prima facie* a reckless instruction, suggesting shoddy preparation, wilful absence of a swim check against the obvious hazard of drowning, no prior reconnaissance to check the depth of the water, and a complete disregard for the safety of someone clearly engaged on a 'leisure' activity.

Another particularly notable Army drowning occurred on a caving expedition in the Porth yr Ogof cave complex in the Brecon Beacons in 2002; Kevin Sharman, aged 17 and a non-swimmer, got into difficulties in the Resurgence Pool which has claimed the lives of eight cavers over the years, including two other young Army recruits.[121] The HSE censured the Ministry of Defence following a special hearing to deal with the case, in the procedure reserved for bodies with crown immunity from prosecution.[122] However, after a rare criminal prosecution in 2004 against the instructor, Matthew Doubtfire, a civilian caving instructor working for the MoD, he was acquitted of manslaughter after a seven week trial at Swansea Crown Court, when the jury was unable to reach a verdict. Mr Doubtfire's defence was that he had never been in the caves before, 'went into the complex through the wrong entrance and became disorientated'.[123] An army expert called as a witness for the prosecution, Lieutenant Colonel Adams, agreed that, as a known non-swimmer, Kevin Sharman was taken beyond his capabilities: 'none of the students were qualified or experienced or mature, therefore they were totally

---

[119] 'Marine death probe will look at water safety', *Western Morning News* (20 October 1998).

[120] 'Army blunders blamed for footballer's death in lake', *Sunday Times* (13 August 2000).

[121] See the listing at http://www.ukcaves.co.uk/, which describes Porth yr Ogof as: 'an open access cave with several entrances and a very bad reputation for deaths. The cave is very much overused by adventure groups ... The resurgence pool at the water exit is the area that has claimed so many lives being deep and cold with strong under-currents'.

[122] 'Military "Guilty" in teen cave tragedy', *Birmingham Post* (19 January 2005).

[123] 'Wife backs up instructor's pool defence', *Western Mail* (26 February 2004).

dependent on their instructor to guide them safely through the cave system'. In the course of his evidence Lt Col Adams revealed in the public domain that he personally had dealt with sixteen Army drownings in the previous seven years – this contrasts with nineteen on the AALA schools list over a much longer period of 16 years, with half of those drownings of course being accounted for in three cases at Lyme Bay, Land's End and Stainforth Beck.[124] A civil claim for compensation inevitably followed the death of Kevin Sharman, although this is likely to be settled for bereavement damages.[125] The two earlier Army deaths at this location were, in 1973, of Graham Alston, aged 15, and then, in 1992, of Amanda Stead; Lance-Corporal Stead, aged 26, was said to be a 'weak swimmer' who drowned in what the coroner described as a 'hopelessly under-equipped' exercise.[126]

Somewhat ironically it was a piece of Army incompetence in 1965 that led to John Stevens achieving what is acknowledged as 'the longest free dive in caving history'. Aged 16 and repeatedly ordered by an army instructor to dive into a pothole near Buxton, and swim to an open cavern, Mr Stevens was told he 'was not trying hard enough' when he reported that the passage was flooded. Finally he just kept swimming, until 90 feet along an underwater shaft he reached a tiny air pocket; 13 hours later a cave rescue team reached him. Mr Stevens commented on a return visit 36 years later: 'You forget the arrogance of the people who controlled us. The guy had to be off his trolley to send a 16-year-old boy down there. I had been in three times. I kept coming back to say it was flooded and he said it couldn't be and to get back in there.'[127]

Then there are injuries that are rather specific to army training and which appear due to negligence with live ammunition; for example, the death of Richard King in 1998, who was accidentally shot dead when live bullets were wrongly mixed with blanks on a night-time training exercise in Powys, and whose family was initially told that he had 'collapsed and died in a trench';[128] the death in 1992 of Lance Corporal Mark Richards who died during a live firing exercise in Belize; and the deaths in 1994 of two corporals, Robert Hawksley and Martin Bailey, who were killed by 'friendly fire' during an exercise in Canada, and whose deaths were described in an inquest as the 'result of mistakes and inaccuracies by those in charge'. In 2005 the Army received another Crown Censure when an 'ammunition mix-up' led to the death of Wayne Richards, aged 17 and on a Royal Marines Commando night-time exercise, who was shot in the head; although the literature advertising this elite force suggests that training is very rigorous, and that 'ninety-nine per cent need not apply', that incompetence

---

[124] 'Caving death could have been avoided, military expert tells court', *Western Mail* (30 January 2004).

[125] 'Recruit's family set to sue MoD', *Derby Evening Telegraph* (11 March 2004).

[126] 'Killer caves victim; Cadet is latest to die', *Daily Mirror* (24 July 2002), 'Instructor died trying to save boy from cave pool', *Glasgow Herald* (28 November 1992).

[127] 'Reunited after 36 years', *Daily Mail* (5 September 2001).

[128] 'How many more of our soldiers must die in training?', *Daily Express* (17 April 2000).

was clearly reckless.[129] In 1994 during a 'mock battle' in Kenya Captain Chris Kelly was killed by colleagues when he accidentally manoeuvred his platoon into the line of troops firing live ammunition and, despite contacting headquarters three times by radio to inform them of his mistake, he was shot dead. An army inquiry recommended no action be taken against commanding officers.

As well as fatalities, there has also been concern expressed about the level of injuries on army training, particularly to those under 18. Statistics are very difficult to obtain, but a letter from the MoD to Amnesty International, who were investigating risk for younger soldiers and Army Cadets, revealed that in the four years from 1996 to 1999, 407 injury incidents involving those under 18 were recorded.[130] Amnesty also indicated that in their view there is a 'disturbing unofficial side to training, which has given Amnesty International serious reason for concern: there are many allegations of ill-treatment and bullying of recruits'. In December 2004 the House of Commons Defence Select Committee started an investigation into such matters, particularly the mysterious circumstances at Deepcut Barracks in Surrey where four young soldiers have died. One of these, Geoff Gray, aged 17, allegedly committed suicide, but this seems rather unlikely, as he was found shot, twice, in the top of his head, and had also allegedly fired four rounds after this; a report by an independent ballistics expert stated that it would be 'highly unlikely' that any of the four young soldiers took their own lives.[131] Currently there are 173 allegations about conduct at Deepcut arising out of a report by Surrey police, including gang rape, bullying and sexual harassment. A report on Deepcut by the House of Commons Select Committee in 2005, appropriately entitled *Duty of Care*, recommended the creation of an independent military complaints commission to deal with concerns about bullying or intimidation.[132] This is only the latest in a series of reports; commenting on an earlier set of recommendations in 2003, Lieutenant-General Anthony Palmer said that the Army had to 'ram home to NCOs that bullying, whether it's physical or mental, is completely out', but then controversially advanced the theory in 2005 that army suicides were at a much higher level because 'there is statistically a predisposition to self-harm and suicide among the less intelligent and by and large the Royal Air Force and Royal Navy recruit at a higher level of educational attainment than the Army'.[133] Unfortunately there are many allegations other than at Deepcut, particularly at Catterick, Britain's largest army camp, where racist

---

[129] 'Army censured after gun death', *Liverpool Daily Post* (20 January 2005).

[130] MoD letter to Amnesty International of 10 May 2000, cited in their report *U-18s: Child Soldiers at risk* (2000) 10.

[131] 'Deepcut: proof soldiers could not have killed themselves', *Mail on Sunday* (3 August 2003).

[132] 'Filling the ranks', *The Times* (15 March 2005). See also the report of the Adult Learning Inspectorate investigation, which among many other matters found a 'laxity in safely storing weapons and accounting for ammunition [which] poses an unnecessary risk to the safety of recruits' and called for a 'broad cultural change'; 'Bully beef', *The Guardian* (12 April 2005).

[133] 'Army chief's insult to suicide victims; Deepcut father attacks "less intelligent" jibe', *Liverpool Daily Post* (22 March 2005).

taunting, unexplained injuries and unlikely suicides have also been the subject of inquiries.[134] One death, that of a young black recruit, William Beckley-Lines, who was on a 'routine' two-mile training march, was allegedly caused by 'exhaustion' and a 'heart attack'. The subsequent evidence was that he was repeatedly bullied and had lost six stones in weight in his time at Catterick. A verdict of natural causes was recorded on the basis that death might have been from sudden death syndrome, although a second post-mortem examination carried out at the insistence of the family found that 'there were cuts under his testicles and bruising – a fact not revealed in the first post-mortem'.[135]

Other uniformed organizations and legal matters

Scouting and Army Cadets are not of course the only voluntary organizations to suffer problems, but as Scouting is the largest dealing in adventurous activities and the Army has some of the most hazardous activities involving vehicles and ammunition, it is perhaps inevitable that they should be so much the focus. However, criticisms were also made of the Prince's Trust, founded by the Prince of Wales to boost the self-esteem of unemployed young people, particularly after two volunteers were killed in a trench on the Orkney island of North Ronaldsay in 1997. Neither Garry Leaburn, aged 25, nor Derek Taylor, aged 19, had been trained to carry out what was described as a major structural engineering operation on a seawall, when a five-tonne slab fell on them. There were no supports or props holding the weight of the wall, and the foundation was unsupported. The procurator-fiscal indicated that 'Risk assessment is not a one-off but a continuing responsibility' and that these deaths were 'entirely foreseeable'. Following a prosecution for health and safety violations, the Prince's Trust was fined £10,000, and two other defendants, Adult Community Training in Dundee and Angus College were fined £5,000 and £2,500 respectively at Kirkwall Sheriff Court. Sheriff Colin Scott Mackenzie said: 'It must be thought that the Prince's Trust is where the buck stops'.[136] These fines might be thought to be swingeing on charitable organizations, until one recalls that a trench death in Newport in 2001 saw a fine imposed of £30,000 on a leisure company,[137] and when two men were crushed in a trench on a building site in 1998 Judge Groake fined the developer £40,000, his firm £200,000 and gave the sub-contractor an 18-month suspended sentence for reckless endangerment, along with a £7,000 fine for breaching the health and safety regulations infringed by the Prince's Trust.[138]

---

[134] 'Army embattled by claims of widespread bullying', *This is The NorthEast* (24 May 2003).

[135] 'Fit soldier's unexplained death on run', *The Northern Echo* (24 May 2003); 'Mystery of a 'bullied' soldier's death run', *Daily Mail* (15 April 1999).

[136] '£10,000 fine for Prince's Trust over work deaths', *The Scotsman*, 25 November 1998).

[137] 'Death trench firm fined £30,000', *Western Mail* (28 April 2001).

[138] 'It's too lenient; sister's agony at £250k fine for death of builders', *Daily Mirror* (22 November 2001).

Other Prince's Trust cases, but in Wales, include Laura Turner, aged 15 and a Pembrokeshire College student, who slipped and was trapped in the Llygad Llwchwr caves in 2002. This matter received wide press coverage, suggesting that she had 'sustained spinal injuries', but the West Brecon Cave Rescue Team were able to confirm that this cave was suitable for novices, the group had been properly equipped and well led, and the conditions underground were dry: 'Nobody did anything wrong and no safety advice was ignored – it was just one of those things'.[139] A spokesman for the Prince's Trust confidently stated that 'All of our projects are fully risk-assessed and all of our instructors are fully qualified'.[140] Earlier in the year an unnamed student aged 17 from Warwickshire had fallen more than 200 feet at St. Brides's Bay from the Pembrokeshire Coastal Path; it appeared that she had suffered a blackout while on a Prince's Trust trip. Fortunately she was discharged from hospital within days.[141] More tragically, Julia Tatley, aged 18 and from Slough, died in 1999 after being trapped under the hull of an Explorer dinghy near Pembroke Dock. Marine investigators considered that she may have been entangled in the rigging, but she was wearing a buoyancy aid when the capsize took place in calm seas, and an instructor on board, Squadron Leader Alan Coy, righted the boat and attracted immediate attention by using a flare.[142] An inquest was informed that the unemployed teenager who was on the course to 'kick start her life' had 'suffered from a weak heart and had a low tolerance to exercise', but the verdict was of accidental death due to drowning. The Director for the Prince's Trust Volunteers in Wales indicated that 'It's important that we learn every possible lesson from this terrible tragedy'.[143] Subsequently Martin Grain, who was working as an outdoor pursuits instructor for the Prince's Trust, was given an award by the Royal Humane Society for his part in the attempted resuscitation, having been nominated by Dyfed and Powys Police.[144] Another fatality for a Prince's Trust volunteer in 1999 occurred when Christopher King, aged 22 and from Liverpool, accepted a bet of £5 that he could run around Llyn Idwal lake in Snowdonia within ten minutes; he drowned when he took a short cut through the water, and an inquest recorded a verdict of misadventure.[145]

A Boys' Brigade outing from Liverpool was to see the football semi-finals at Hillsborough on 15 April 1989, with the dreadful consequence that one of the stadium fatalities was that of Phil Hammond, aged 14 and on a BB trip. 96 people lost their lives that day. His father, also named Phil Hammond, has described how

---

[139] 'Hopefully I'll do a lot more caving, but I'll take it easy now for a few days'; *Western Mail* (18 October 2002).

[140] 'Girl in cave rescue drama', *Western Mail* (16 October 2002).

[141] 'Prince's Trust woman "comfortable" after 200ft cliffs fall', *Western Mail* (14 March 2002), 'Rucksack saves girl in 200ft cliff fall', *Coventry Evening Telegraph* (15 March 2002).

[142] 'Prince's sorrow at death of Trust girl', *Daily Mirror* (5 February 1999).

[143] 'Prince's charity not to blame for sailing death', *Daily Mirror* (28 May 1999).

[144] 'Boat tragedy hero given high honour', *Coventry Evening Telegraph* (5 November 1999).

[145] 'Prince is "Distressed"; Charles's tribute to drowned student', *Daily Mirror* (22 July 1999), 'Rescuers give up hope for sea tragedy boy', *Daily Mirror* (29 October 1999).

in panic at the developing news on television he telephoned the coach company that had taken the Boys' Brigade outing to the ground, and was relieved to be told that all the boys were coming home on the coach. Subsequently this was found to be false.[146] Like the other victims at Hillsborough he too had been crushed and asphyxiated because the police decided to relieve crowd pressure by opening gates. Mr Hammond senior was subsequently one of the most prominent campaigners for the Hillsborough Families Support Group, seeking compensation for the victims, but also for a full investigation and a quashing of the inquest findings of accidental death 'as that would at least acknowledge that the deaths of our loved ones were not an accident'.[147] The inquest in 1990 recorded verdicts of accidental death, but an inquiry by Lord Taylor CJ placed most of the blame on South Yorkshire police, and this was the view of a further inquiry by Stuart-Smith LJ.[148]

Girlguiding UK, as the inventors of the First Response course, have a formidable reputation for first aid and safety procedures. Although perhaps not best known for adventurous activities they certainly engage in them, and have an excellent record. When Jane Booth, a teacher and Guide Leader for over 30 years in Northumberland died in what was described as a 'freak accident', crushed under a 'young and flighty' horse, an inquest was told that 'her appetite for adventure took her across the globe and saw her cliff-jump and paraglide with her Guides and Rangers'.[149] Legal actions against the Association seem to have centred on being singed while cooking sausages. In 1995 a Guide aged eleven attended her first camp and burnt her leg while cooking sausages. She claimed on the basis that the first aid treatment was inadequate and that there were insufficient levels of instruction and supervision. The first point was always perhaps unlikely; it was abandoned when Judge Vincent congratulated Guiders on their prompt first aid treatment of the victim, and he found that the instruction had been adequate too. On supervision, having regard to the claimant's age, her previous experience and the instruction she had received, the action was dismissed. The judge added that 'a Guide Camp should be an enjoyable experience for all, and was also to teach, and inform the young and to encourage a level of responsibility in the young'. There was 'good supervision throughout' and 'A stifling supervision would have had the effect of discouraging all initiative'.[150] Recently David Davis MP has drawn attention to an unreported settlement where the parents of a Guide received £3,500 after singeing her fingers while cooking sausages; it was claimed that the proposed Promotion of Volunteering Bill was 'intended to prevent cases such as a writ for damages issued against Girlguiding UK after one girl complained about spitting fat from sausages'.[151] As with many organizations, most injuries occur in the confines of

---

[146] 'A grief which refuses to die', *Glasgow Herald* (19 July 1997).

[147] 'Hillsborough appeal', *The Independent* (15 February 1998).

[148] 'Straw sets up review of football tragedy', *The Independent* (27 June 1997).

[149] 'Guide leader died in horse accident', *Newcastle Journal* (11 November 2004).

[150] *Leonard v Girl Guide Association* Truro County Court (25 May 1995) CLYB 1995 3662.

[151] 'Three hour speech to wreck Bill', *Daily Mail* (17 July 2004).

the weekly meeting indoors, and most are of a minor nature; an exception was the seemingly innocent fall suffered by Lynsey Calderwood one evening at a Guides meeting, when she fell off a chair and banged her head. When her parents were summoned she was unable to recognize them as she sustained total amnesia, and she was admitted to a psychiatric unit at Gartnavel Hospital, Glasgow, where she was labelled 'arrogant and difficult'. As a result, she became depressed and developed an eating disorder, but eventually struggled through her disabilities to become a writer.[152] Camping is generally benign, but again may have its safety hazards: a near miss for a potentially deadly assault was when the man convicted of the murder in 1996 of Caroline Dickinson on a school trip at a youth hostel in Brittany was considered by the South Wales police to have been involved in the attempted rape of a 13-year-old Guide from Hull on the Gower Peninsula in 1993. The victim escaped when others heard her screams. Two years earlier and nearby, a French Guide aged 15 narrowly escaped a similar attack. And the same suspect was implicated in a previous attempted rape in the same area in 1989.[153] In discussion of legal issues on children giving evidence in delayed trails it was indicated by Professor Spencer of Cambridge University that he was aware of a case where a Guide aged 11 was dragged from her tent at camp and raped at knife-point; it was 17 months before the case was tried.[154]

All such organizations have their occasional unexplained tragedy. 'Natural causes' or the undiagnosed medical problem may be a factor. Christopher Sammu, aged 14, came home from his Sea Cadets' meeting in Stockport and went to bed; he was discovered to have died in the night. The previous week he had been mugged on his way to the Sea Cadets, but this did not appear to be a factor. His death was a mystery, as a minor asthma problem was considered similarly unrelated and a toxicological report ruled out any relationship to drugs or chemicals. The coroner stated his death was therefore 'unascertained', although there was some possibility that the death might have been due to the condition known as Adult Respiratory Distress Syndrome, which affects teenagers and shows characteristics in common with 'cot death'.[155]

It is not just the mainstream uniformed youth organizations that have their difficulties, as many others not so centred on robust outdoor activities will still engage in activities that have some risk. Even in the relatively risk-free environment of supervised swimming in an indoor pool, with many lifeguards and adults in the vicinity, there can be tragedy; for example in 2001 a non-swimmer, Helen McCulloch, aged eight, drowned while playing in the water of a swimming pool at the Whithaugh Park Holiday Centre near Newcastleton, run by the Barnabas Trust, which was formed in 1922 to provide holidays for disadvantaged children from inner-city areas. She was part of a Christian youth

---

[152] 'An innocent life lost', *Sunday Express* (14 March 2004). See Ms Calderwood's autobiography, *Cracked: Recovering after Traumatic Brain Injury* (London: Jessica Kingsley Publishing, 2003).
[153] 'Police seek to interview Montes over attacks in UK', *The Independent* (16 June 2004).
[154] John Spencer, 'Law: the value of children's stories', *The Independent* (21 July 1989).
[155] 'Death riddle of boy, 14', *Manchester Evening News* (24 March 2000).

group, the Campaigners, who are a uniformed evangelical youth organization where 'Safety is a priority'.[156] They were staying for a week-long activity holiday, and six adults and a lifeguard were supervising 25 children in the pool.[157] The lifeguard spotted the girl struggling, dived in to rescue her, resuscitation was commenced immediately, an ambulance was there within four minutes and a doctor soon after, but to no avail.[158] Following the deaths of two teenage boys on a 'Splash' activity scheme run by Barnet Council in 2002 at the Metropolitan police training centre in Hendon, a police lifeguard, PC Danny Phillips, faces counts of manslaughter and contravention of health and safety regulations. The full facts are not yet known, but the committal proceedings suggested that Gameli Akuklu, aged 14, and William Kadama, aged 15, drowned when they were with 35 other youngsters and six youth workers at the police swimming pool. It was suggested that the police officer was giving first aid treatment to another boy who had gashed his knee when the victims were seen lying at the bottom of the pool.[159]

Conclusion on the voluntary sector

The fatalities in voluntary organizations have until now remained far less open to examination than the school cases. In particular the Army Cadet cases have been cloaked in secrecy, and yet they deserve the closest analysis, because on any cursory inspection this is one of the most dangerous sectors in outdoor activities. The shocking information revealed by a witness during the trial of Matthew Doubtfire, that there had been sixteen such Army drownings in the previous seven years, should give serious cause for public concern. In addition, the harrowing and as yet not fully explained circumstances of the Deepcut Barracks 'suicides', the catalogue of bullying allegations there and at Catterick, along with a sizeable number of other 'training' cases, suggests a deep-seated culture of recklessness that is wholly inappropriate. The argument that legal immunity should be granted to teachers and volunteer leaders is hardly tenable when an examination is made of the continuing hazardous treatment of young recruits and cadets, where there is a significant operation of Crown immunity to prevent investigation and transparency. The evidence that surfaces intermittently from below this cloak of secrecy demonstrates repeated errors on wading in deep water, allegedly 'freak accidents' with live ammunition, and a reckless disregard of safety issues with off-road vehicles which cannot give public confidence that the current armed forces system is drawing appropriate conclusions from these fatalities and taking action to prevent future harm. The repeated assurances that there will be a further upgrade of the internal 'protocols' are not sufficient, given the circumstances of these fatalities. There would now appear to be an

---

[156] http://www.campaigners.org.uk/how_do_campaigners_work.htm
[157] 'Pool death of girl who couldn't swim', *Daily Record* 31 July 2001).
[158] 'Desperate bid to save pool girl, 8', *Daily Mail* (31 July 2001).
[159] 'Courts: Met officer summons in pool deaths', *The Guardian* (24 March 2005).

unanswerable case for the most searching investigation of risk in armed forces training by an independent body such as the AALA. While no-one would deny the benefits of a tough regime of such training for recruits to the armed forces, this cannot excuse the sometimes senseless expenditure of young lives that is apparent in the cases.

A useful comparison can be made with Scouting, the largest youth organization engaged in adventurous activities, which was in the past also very seriously criticized for several cases of death and injury. However, that organization appears to have made a 'cultural' change after the death of Jonathan Attwell. Similarly, other uniformed youth organizations have taken account of the AALA and DfES literature and the need to have risk assessments of their activities which learn from experience. Interestingly it was the Scouts who attracted most calls for being brought within the licensing regime, but that may be because their difficulties were in the public domain. As a result they made the necessary changes.

There would therefore seem to be a public interest in maintaining negligence liability on all activity organizations, because this broad mechanism of social change is likely to lead to modifications, possibly through insurance pressures, but also through the avoidance of adverse effects on image and public relations. With blanket immunity cloaking both the nature and the circumstances of death and injury in the armed forces, a vital engine of modifying practice is absent, and indeed the secrecy of the Crown Censure proceedings means it is also not possible for the wider outdoors community to draw conclusions that might inform their own practices and guidelines. It follows that one straightforward proposal would be for the Government to lift Crown immunity on outdoor activities when part of armed forces training, and to have exposure to the Common Law principles of negligence and, where appropriate, prosecutions for manslaughter. Such legal possibilities would no doubt produce a cathartic change in army 'protocols', and would very likely be resisted by the MoD, but such a change would undoubtedly save lives. In Professor Felix Frankfurter's famous dictum, 'sunlight is the best disinfectant', and this gloomy corner of outdoor activities needs some searching examination.

PART II
THE LEGAL PRINCIPLES

Chapter 5

The All-important Duty of Care

Almost every day there is a media story or two about the supposed impossibility of doing anything in the outdoors without serious legal liability. Many of these are just rural or urban myths which make the headlines before fading into some common sense settlement or solution well away from newspaper coverage. Where there is a consideration of negligent as opposed to intentional acts, then liability in these cases is anchored in the concept of a 'duty of care', and this is the first hurdle to consider in any civil claim for personal injuries. When is this duty owed? If a legal precedent exists, then that statement of the legal duty will be the primary focus. Where none exists, then argument will be on the basis of analogy from similar or comparable cases. An illustration of whether a duty of care exists can be seen in the recent American case of *Stroumbakis v The Town of Greenwich*, and it suggests that some of the 'reality' of litigation is the very fear of litigation itself. That anxiety can lead to a defensive mindset which can have a dampening effect on all sorts of activities, as it leads potential defendants to take draconian action to avoid what they perceive as potential liability by abandoning them altogether. As a result of this case in 2004, the township of Greenwich, Connecticut, one of the very wealthiest communities in the USA, announced that they were considering banning winter sledding on the slopes of the appropriately named Sleigh Hill, which had been used for many years for just such an outdoor activity. Dr Nicholas Stroumbakis, and his son aged four were going for 'one last run' in January 2000, when their sledge struck a drainage ditch at the base of the hill. The doctor suffered multiple fractures of his back and leg that put him in hospital for twelve days, including five in intensive care. It was seven months before he could return full-time to his medical practice. He sued for negligence, claiming the local Council had created a public nuisance by failing to maintain the ditch. A jury agreed, awarding him damages of $6.3 million, one of the largest negligence awards against a municipality in the USA, especially in a case in which nobody died.[1] The case is currently on appeal, but the town's selectmen were immediately considering a ban on 'not just sledding, but ice-skating and things like that that are done on town property'.[2]

Many issues in the current debate on legal liability can be illustrated by this case. First, the reality is that the Council would only be paying $500,000 of the

---

[1] *Greenwich Times* (25 April 2005), quoting an attorney James Tallberg who was of the view that 'Greenwich is Gold Coast Fairfield County, and I think juries think there are deep pockets there. Generally, you don't see numbers that high simply because there aren't pockets deep enough to pay an award that big.'

[2] 'Stung by suit, Greenwich weighs ban on sledding', *New York Times* (26 April 2004). See also 'In Depth: after lawsuit, City considers ban on sledding' in *Common Good* (26 April 2004): "What are kids going to do instead – smoke crack?" one exasperated resident asked.'

award, just eight per cent of the total, with the remainder covered by the insurance company Genesis. Secondly, the jury were clearly convinced of the straightforward need to warn of the ditch in an environment where the very name of the hill suggested a winter pastime. Thirdly, Dr Stroumbakis was clearly incapacitated, and as a leading cancer and urology specialist was unavailable for his patients.[3] One irony is that Dr Stroumbakis is one of many doctors in the USA who have been campaigning for a cap on jury awards in medical malpractice cases, and his photograph even appeared in local newspapers showing him marching with other doctors to the state capitol in protest at the level of awards against doctors.[4] Another irony was that he himself had requested an award of $500,000, but the Town Hall refused to accept this settlement offer and fought the case, neatly illustrating the 'forensic lottery' of tort cases. Another factor is that Dr Stroumbakis's attorney would have been operating under contingency fee arrangements, normally about 33 per cent, but sometimes running to 50 per cent, and would therefore have an incentive as well as a duty to get the highest possible award. Next, part of the defence was to suggest that Dr Stroumbakis 'contributed' to his injuries, as his plastic toboggan could not be steered, the part of the hill that ended in the drainage culvert was the steepest and not usually used by other sledders, and although Sleigh Hill had been used for sledding for many years, it was not 'officially sanctioned' for such use. Indeed, the jury lowered the award because of these factors. However, as with all legal cases, the evidence was crucial to establish liability. Documents from the Parks and Recreation Department showed a site inspection which recommended filling in the 'hole', and that the culvert was covered by a piece of plywood held down by rocks, concealed by snow at the time and unmarked. This was in conspicuous contrast to the Council's main defence that the sledding field was 'undisturbed natural land' without a 'man-made feature' and that any maintenance was a 'discretionary act' entitling them to qualified immunity.[5] Probably compounding the air of civic incompetence was the fact that no written report or photographs had been taken by a police officer, employed by Greenwich, as part of a required procedure at the scene of any accident on town property. The local newspaper suggests that one lesson to be drawn by 'municipalities, particularly affluent ones like Greenwich' is that the town needs 'better risk management in order to avoid liability suits'.[6]

---

[3] See his practice details at http://www.greenwichurology.com/stroumbakis.html indicating that he had recently been awarded an 'America's Top Physicians for 2003' honour from the Consumers Research Council of America.

[4] 'Doctor who won $6M wants malpractice caps', *Greenwich Times* (25 April 2004).

[5] See for a useful legal analysis of the trial, complete with diagrams of the screws, pins and rods in Dr Stroumbakis's right leg, Thomas B. Scheffey, 'Greenwich Doc a $6 Million Man: sledding case hinged on town immunity', *The Connecticut Law Tribune* (April 2004).

[6] 'Dr Stroumbakis vs. The Town of Greenwich', *Greenwich Magazine* (June 2004).

The key concept

As the leading practitioners' commentary states, the historical development of the tort of negligence has been through 'the progressive recognition of various kinds of harm'.[7] The critical first hurdle has been whether a 'duty of care' was owed to the victim. Rather than questioning on each occasion as to whom such a duty might theoretically be owed, the Common Law has established precedents for relationships that often give rise to personal injury, such as employer/employee, doctor/patient and motorist/other road user. Where there is an established legal precedent then the courts will generally follow that prior determination as to whether a duty of care exists, but establishing this legal duty in unusual circumstances where there is no precedent is essentially a question of judicial or legislative policy. For when courts consider a potentially 'novel' duty, then as Lord Denning indicated in *Dutton v Bognor Regis UDC*[8] they now openly ask the question 'What is the best policy for the law to adopt?' although he added that this has often 'been concealed behind such questions as: Was the defendant under any duty to the plaintiff? Was the relationship between them sufficiently proximate? Was the injury direct or indirect? Was it foreseeable, or not? Was it too remote? And so forth. Nowadays we direct ourselves to considerations of policy.' It might be thought that Lord Denning was perhaps somewhat optimistic that his views would be followed by all judges, as labels are still used to obscure policy matters.

In the swirl of cases looking for concepts and definitions on duty of care, the current law has rested on a three stage test: foreseeability, proximity, and whether it would be 'fair, just and reasonable' to impose a duty of care.[9] 'Foreseeability' is essentially risk analysis, and in the words of Aneurin Bevan it is not necessary to 'gaze in the crystal ball if you can read the book'. Scientific understanding of risk and particularly the gathering of information about hazards is therefore essential in gaining experience that will produce 'foreseeability'. Once a danger has been appreciated, then it will become theoretically 'foreseeable' on another similar occasion. Much of course depends on whether 'notice' is taken, and sometimes knowledge becomes buried or obscured. However, 'foreseeability' has been an enduring theme through the various attempts at finding a general principle. 'Proximity' as a concept is linked to who might be affected, and Hobhouse LJ has suggested that it is about 'control over and responsibility for a situation which, if dangerous, will be liable to injure the plaintiff, [and] the defendant is liable if as a result of his unreasonable lack of care he causes a situation to exist which does in fact cause the plaintiff injury'.[10] Finally there will be the judgment of whether it would be 'fair, just and reasonable' to impose a duty, and this is inevitably a matter of judicial policy to be weighed in the balance

---

[7] See generally *Clerk & Lindsell on Torts*, Chapter One on 'Principles of Liability in Torts', (ed. Anthony Dugdale, 18th edition, London: Sweet & Maxwell, 2001).
[8] [1972] 1 QB 373 at 397.
[9] Per Lord Bridge of Harwich in *Caparo v Dickman* [1990] 1 All ER 568.
[10] *Perrett v Collins* [1998] 2 Lloyd's Rep 255.

of competing interests, particularly the imposition of unreasonable burdens of cost or where insurance is not practicable because of potentially unlimited liability. The House of Lords in *The Nicholas H* indicated that it would be unduly burdensome to impose liability on a small classification society concerned with the protection of lives at sea when a bulk ore carrier foundered and the cargo was lost; the owners were protected by a cap on damages relating to the tonnage of the vessel and it was held that it would be 'unreasonable' to impose the balance on the classification society for the alleged mistake of allowing the vessel to sail across the Atlantic when there were temporary welds on cracks in the hull.[11]

The theoretical underpinnings of negligence are still disputed terrain, but one of the enduring concepts has been that of 'reasonableness' in the sense of proportionality when considering the balance of interests between a perpetrator and a victim of harm. The *American Restatement of Torts* suggests that 'Negligence is conduct falling below the standard demanded for the protection of others against unreasonable risk of harm.'[12] That standard in many fields of tort will be to inquire what is 'good practice' or hopefully what amounts to the same, that of 'standard practice'. When defendants follow 'good practice' this will not always absolve them of liability, as the courts have a right to overrule this to set out new standards, but the likelihood is very high that it will. The next consideration is the evidential issue of whether defendants can show they follow good practice, and 'evidencing' in writing is always preferable; it is likely to be of very considerable probative value, well beyond that achieved by the oral testimony of witnesses. That is why a 'paper trail' can be so important, as it is likely to demonstrate the evidence of good practice. However, beyond the paperwork there needs to be, in addition of course, a practical manifestation that good intentions on paper have been actually put into effect.

Various judicial attempts have been made at an over-arching conceptual framework for the law of negligence, none more famous than that of Lord Atkin's 'neighbour principle' in which he attempted to rationalize and develop the law, commenting that it was 'remarkable how difficult it is to find in the English authorities statements of general application defining the relations between parties that give rise to the duty.' His suggestion was of a rule of law that 'you must take reasonable care to avoid acts or omissions which you can reasonably foresee would be likely to injure your neighbour' and he further defined neighbours as 'persons who are so closely and directly affected by my act that I ought reasonably to have them in contemplation as being so affected when I am directing my mind to the acts or omissions which are called in question.'[13] The Atkin formulation was excoriated in its early years, but by 1970 Lord Reid in *Home Office v Dorset Yacht Co. Ltd* stated that it was a 'milestone' and that 'the time has come when we can and should say that it ought to apply unless there is some justification or valid explanation for its exclusion'.[14] The 'outdoor

---

[11] *Marc Rich & Co AG v Bishop Rock Marine Co Ltd, The Nicholas H* [1995] 3 All ER 307.

[12] 2d 282.

[13] *Donoghue v Stevenson* [1932] All ER Rep 1.

[14] *Home Office v Dorset Yacht Co. Ltd.* [1970] 2 All ER 294 at 297.

activities' in the *Dorset Yacht* case were the illicit extra-curricular maraudings of seven borstal trainees. They were from a group of ten who were working at Brownsea Island in Poole Harbour as part of their rehabilitation, in the custody of three officers, who 'simply went to bed leaving the trainees to their own devices'. Following their breakout the trainees boarded a yacht, set it in motion, where it collided with the respondent's yacht, which they then boarded and vandalized. All the absconding trainees had criminal records and five of them had a record of previous escapes, so it was not difficult to see that escape was 'foreseeable' and indeed with numerous vessels moored in the harbour for the courts to consider that it was a 'likely consequence' that a yacht would suffer damage. The case turned on a preliminary issue as to whether the Home Office owed a duty of care to the yacht owner, and they argued strenuously against this. Their first point was that it would be a new departure to establish liability of this kind, but Lord Reid indicated that there was now a 'steady trend' and 'when a new point emerges, one should not ask whether it is covered by authority but whether recognized principles apply to it'[15] and these were now the Atkin 'neighbour' principles. Secondly, it was suggested that there should only be liability for employees under the principles of vicarious liability, but Lord Reid pointed out that this was a case not of liability for the vandals but on supervision by the officers, whose 'carelessness would probably result in the trainees causing damage of this kind'.[16] Thirdly, the defence was that on grounds of public policy there should be immunity for such officers. However, no statutory immunity was available, and despite the invocation of an American precedent against liability in these circumstances, because to 'hold otherwise would impose a heavy responsibility upon the State, or dissuade wardens ... from continued experimentation with "minimum security" work details', Lord Reid rejected such an argument because of a belief that 'Her Majesty's servants are made of sterner stuff'.[17] Statutory immunity does exist in various contexts in Britain, and increasingly in the USA,[18] but without such an express formulation then general principles will apply, and liability might follow.

Intentional conduct

In practice, the initial search is for a legal precedent. If none exists, then the attempt is made to extend by using analogy from a related area. Only when a uniquely 'novel' position is disclosed will there be an argument from 'first principles'. However, the quantity of cases on a point is usually in inverse proportion to whether the law is settled. For example, where conduct is

---

[15] At 297.

[16] At 298.

[17] At 302, commenting on *Williams v New York State* (1955) 127 NE (2d) 545 at 550.

[18] See for a view on 'a preference for quasi-immunity' in Australia, Kumaralingam Amirthalingam, 'Negligence and public authorities: a pearl in the oyster of another Greek tragedy?', 11 *Torts Law Journal* (2003) 197, at 207.

intentional, then the law was often formulated at a fairly early stage of development, usually under the law of trespass to the person. For example, the law on assault and battery is of ancient vintage, and rarely gives rise to litigation because it is generally straightforward, so there are actually very few recent cases. If intentional conduct is proved, then liability is hard to resist. Even where conduct causes psychiatric injury, which is often a problematic matter for the courts in negligence, then if the conduct is *intentional*, for example by way of a practical joke, liability is usually uncomplicated. The leading case is *Wilkinson v Downton*, where Lavinia Wilkinson was subjected to the hoax that her husband 'had had a smash up' and she was to go immediately in a cab to a public house where her husband was 'lying with both legs broken' so that she could fetch him home. The evidence showed that this caused her hair to turn white and she became so ill it was thought her life was in danger, inducing 'shock', vomiting and other consequences 'threatening her reason and entailing weeks of suffering and incapacity'. Wright J and a jury found liability for Mrs Wilkinson in the sum of £100, plus the two shillings expended in rail fares for those she had sent to bring her husband home.[19] In *Janvier v Sweeney*,[20] the Court of Appeal approved that decision and confirmed a similar judgment at first instance, this time for £250 by a jury directed by Avory J. A private investigator represented that he was a detective inspector from Scotland Yard who wanted to question Mlle Janvier, who lived as a paid companion in a house in Mayfair and corresponded with a German who was interned as an enemy alien on the Isle of Man; this was represented to her as 'corresponding with a German spy'. The victim said she had been 'extremely frightened' and 'suffered from a severe nervous shock', and there was also an element of an attempt at blackmail in the exchange, which made it perhaps even more reprehensible than *Wilkinson v Downton*. In the USA this behaviour is classified as the 'tort of outrage', defined as where 'extreme and outrageous conduct intentionally or recklessly causes severe emotional distress to another.'[21] For example, where a wedding was called off in Utah just hours before the ceremony, and later it was revealed that the groom was already married, the victim recovered for actions which were 'outrageous and intolerable in that they offend generally accepted standards of decency and morality'.[22] A further illustration was where the Kentucky Supreme Court held that a priest, who had an affair with a woman while providing her marriage counselling, could be liable to the husband for the tort of outrage.[23]

Reality TV and ritual game show humiliations are sometimes a target for such legal actions; for example, MTV is currently defending a $10 million lawsuit from a couple who found a fake corpse in their hotel room in Las Vegas on a Reality TV show entitled 'Harassment', and were filmed as they tried to flee before the way was

---

[19] *Wilkinson v Downton* [1895-99] All ER Rep 267.
[20] [1918-19] All ER Rep 1056.
[21] Proposed in *Restatement (Second) of Torts* Section 46 (1948), and adopted by most states.
[22] *Jackson v Brown*, 904 P. 2d 685 (Utah 1995).
[23] *Osborne v Payne* (Kentucky, 22 November 2000).

blocked by two actors posing as security guards.[24] This show, described as a 'guerilla-style *Candid Camera*', is likely to land MTV in further legal trouble, as they are still in litigation over the taping of a programme called 'Dude, This Sucks' when two 13-year-old girls in California sued the network after they were sprayed with human excrement in April 2001.[25] MTV apologized for that incident and promised never to air footage of it, and like many such cases it is likely to be settled discreetly. Nevertheless these cases illustrate that in the USA if, in activities of any sort, there is an element of bullying, harassment or humiliation, then there is likely to be straightforward liability if injury occurs. Some instructors in outdoor activities, particularly as we have seen in several of the Army cases, have strayed into this terrain. The position in Britain is not yet as clear; for example, Lord Hoffmann indicated he would 'wish ... to reserve my opinion' when individuals 'say things with the intention of causing distress and humiliation to others', on the basis that this 'shows lack of consideration and appalling manners but I am not sure that the right way to deal with it is always by litigation'.[26] Despite this reluctance on the part of Lord Hoffmann, it is suggested that, even if well-intentioned, a deliberate intention to 'shock' participants, or recklessly to endanger their well-being, may well land up in the courts for assault and battery, or lead to a speedy settlement of a legitimate claim.

One example of a purposeful attempt in Britain to shock teenagers involved police and the relatives of suspected 'joyriders'. Although it did not appear to give rise to litigation, it could easily have done so. Ten boys were targeted as potential offenders by police at Merthyr Tydfil, and on their way by minibus to an outdoor activity centre, they came upon an 'accident' in the Brecon Beacons, where they saw police, fire and ambulance crews battling to save their own relatives from the twisted wreckage. The scene was 'so dreadful' that the teenagers, aged 14 to 17, 'needed counselling on the spot'. Senior police officers stated that 'it was the first time in Britain that police have staged a fake road accident to frighten youngsters away from joyriding'. The parents of the children signed consent forms before the mock crash. However, the National Association for the Care and Rehabilitation of Offenders condemned the strategy as 'risky and potentially dangerous', and exposing youngsters to 'such a traumatic incident', even with the presence of trained counsellors and prior parental notification, seems legally hazardous.[27] As we have seen in the Army cases, and in child protection matters generally, if

---

[24] 'Murder? Just our little joke', *The Times* (28 June 2002).

[25] 'Reality it stinks', *Daily Star* (11 April 2003). Monique Garcia and Kelli Sloat, both aged 16. Other reality 'victims' in the USA pursuing lawsuits include Darin Goka who says an underwater stunt on NBC's 'Dog Eat Dog' left him brain damaged; Patrick Finnegan who sued Comedy Central's 'The Man Show' for airing footage of him on the beach being harassed by a teenager using lewd language; and in Britain Latania Mitchell claims she was 'traumatized' on Guy Ritchie's show 'Swag' when she answered an advertisement for a job only to find herself 'held' in a dark basement by 'burly thugs'; *New York Daily News* (10 April 2003).

[26] *Wainwright v Home Office* [2003] 4 All ER 969 at 982.

[27] 'Shock tactics that forced tearaways to face the bloody reality of joyriding', *The Express* (10 March 2000).

intentional conduct can be shown to have caused serious harm, then civil liability is near-automatic.

A further head of liability in Britain is the impact of Human Rights legislation, although as yet the optimism of commentators on a wide extension of tort has not been apparent. In *Wainwright v Home Office*[28] the House of Lords in 2003 had to consider a strip search of a family member visiting his bother, who was a prisoner suspected of dealing in drugs. Alan Wainwright, who had physical and learning difficulties, claimed psychiatric damage under the 1998 Act, but it was held that there were no damages for 'mere distress' and the officers had not intended to cause harm. Lord Hoffmann indicated that there was no breach of Article 3 of the European Convention on Human Rights, as prison rules allowed such a search to prevent contraband, and what had taken place was nowhere near the degree of humiliation held by the European Court of Human Rights to be degrading treatment.

Obeying the rules of the sport or pastime

The duty of care is therefore a flexible concept, but has been particularized with a series of precedents relating to specific activities. Where there are rules of a sport or pastime, and a participant flouts these, then there will be a presumption that they breached their legal duty of care. In a classic case on football, *Condon v Basi*, the Court of Appeal considered a foul tackle on James Condon playing in a Sunday local league in Warwick. Sir John Donaldson MR indicated that in 1985 there was 'no authority as to what is the standard of care which governs the conduct of players in competitive sports generally', which he found surprising. However, he was able to analyse judgments from the High Court of Australia, *Rootes v Shelton*, in a case involving three water skiers being towed behind a motorboat with lines of varying lengths; the skipper passed close to a stationary vessel and the middle skier crossing over the wake and, temporarily unsighted by spray, collided with it. Barwick CJ indicated that 'by engaging in a sport or pastime the participants may be held to have accepted risks which are inherent in that sport or pastime …but this does not eliminate all duty of care of the one participant to another' and when considering the circumstances 'the rules of the sport or game may constitute one of those circumstances'.[29] Kitto J, whose view was preferred by the British Court of Appeal, concentrated on whether the defendant acted reasonably, and he might be doing this 'even though he infringed the "rules of the game"'; the Master of the Rolls indicated that in practice these differing views would perhaps not make the 'slightest difference'. Sir John indicated in any event that 'none of these sophistications' arose in *Condon* because there had been a blatant foul in breach of the rules of the game which was clearly 'unreasonable'. Judge Wooton at first instance had found negligence and awarded £4,900, having heard evidence from the very experienced Class I referee who had officiated: 'The slide tackle came late, and was made in a

---

[28] [2003] 4 All ER 969.
[29] *Rootes v Shelton* [1968] ALR 33, at 34.

reckless and dangerous manner, by lunging with his boot studs showing about a foot to 18 inches from the ground... In my opinion, the tackle constituted serious foul play and I sent [the defendant] from the field of play.'[30] With clear rules in a sport, the showing of the 'red card' to the player was a very potent piece of evidence to support breach, and this case has become the principal yardstick in judging other outdoor games and activities in Britain. However, note that the case involved an intentional battery.[31] The 'least touching of another in anger' is a battery, which is a tort of trespass to the person. Assault is the 'threat' of a battery. Although football, like many contact sports involves quite an amount of assault and battery, in most circumstances other players 'consent' to this at an appropriate level. This could be analysed either as 'no duty of care' or as 'assumption of risk' under the defence of *volenti non fit injuria*. There is also the potential in such matters for criminal prosecution; in *R v Barnes* the Court of Appeal allowed an appeal on the basis that a conviction would be unsafe on what was characterized by the prosecution as a 'crushing tackle, which was late, unnecessary, reckless and high up the legs', although that case discusses criminal liability for what conduct is outside 'legitimate sport', and no doubt there will be further developments in the criminal law.[32]

An issue therefore arises in many such cases as to whether there was a valid consent. And if so, consent to what level of risk? Kitto J indicated in *Rootes v Shelton* that 'unless the activity partakes of the nature of a war or of something else in which all is notoriously fair'[33] then there has to be a threshold level. However, the difficulties with the concept of qualified consent are legion in criminal law,[34] and are no less difficult in the civil sphere in torts. For example, the American Restatement only appears to analyse sports injuries in the context of intentional torts, and in the context of apparent consent to an intentional invasion. The commentary describes the 'touching' to which a player willingly submits by taking part in a game as 'a willingness to submit to such bodily contacts or restrictions of liberty as are permitted by its rules or usages. Participating in such a game does not manifest consent to contacts which are prohibited by rules and usages of the game if such rules and usages are designed to protect the participants and not merely to secure the better playing of the game as a test of skill. This is true although the player knows that those with or against whom he is

---

[30] [1985] 2 All ER 453. Contrast this with 'a late and no doubt clumsy tackle ... It was a foul but I am not satisfied it was more. It was an error of judgment in the context of a fast moving game', and therefore no claim in *Pitcher v Huddersfield Town Football Club* (QBD transcript 17 July 2001).

[31] See for a review of 'on-ice and on-field violence' in North America, Jeffrey A. Citron and Mark Ableman, 'Civil Liability in the arena of professional sports', 194 *University of British Columbia Law Review* vol 36: 'the prevailing view in the US appears to be that recklessness is the appropriate minimum standard of liability in the context of sports injury litigation'.

[32] [2005] 2 All ER 113.

[33] Ibid, at 37.

[34] Law Commission Consultation Paper No. 134, *Consent and Offences against the Person* (1994).

playing are habitual violators of such rules'.[35] Although this was not mentioned in *Condon v Basi,* it fits very well.

Even where the 'rules' have been punctiliously observed, that will not necessarily stop someone being sued. This is sometimes a very hard issue to confront with individuals and organizations who have so patently being doing their very best to avoid harm to others. But it is an essential plank of a free and democratic society that litigation can rarely be 'censored'. As we have seen, unmeritorious actions can be struck out at an early stage or unceremoniously dispatched at trial, but the 'safety valve' aspect of unfettered litigation means that some decidedly odd cases come through to the courts, and there are occasionally financial and other implications in defending any such unworthy claims. If an action has been wholly misconceived, then it is possible to apply not just for strike out of the claim but also for costs on the basis of the action being 'vexatious and frivolous'. The High Court also has the power to stay proceedings where a litigant 'habitually and persistently and without reasonable cause' brings an action.[36] But this is an extreme instance of an 'abuse of process', and very few cases fall into that category. Generally, the potential award of costs against the unsuccessful party acts as a considerable deterrent to bringing unlikely claims, and without wide possibilities of legal aid, solicitors have a financial disincentive against making speculative civil claims as they will have to bear the costs to a large extent.[37] Nevertheless there can still be cases which fail, which possibly never should have been brought, and yet still cost defendants time and money. It is important to separate out myth from reality here, as successful defendants will often protest that a claim should never have been brought when considered from their perspective. But nevertheless it is clear that some organizations can attract exploratory litigation with a view to seeking a settlement, and that organizations and their advisers can and do settle such cases for 'nuisance value'. As the Scout Association has found in the past it can sometimes be unhelpful in the long term to be seen as an 'easy target' for settlements, and a more robust defensive posture can be cost-effective. This 'hard line' attitude will not minimize the short-term costs; in 2005 an action against a Chorley Scout Group for an injury to a Beaver Scout at an outdoor activity was successfully defended on the basis that 'leaders followed their scouting training to the letter'. But by the nature of the legal system the Scout Association still had to pay £1,000 in costs of their own which were irrecoverable, the leaders were put through a great deal of stress, and seven volunteers were lost as a result of the court action, with more now being needed to replace them. Fortunately the action could be defended on the basis that the leaders in question had been through several years of training in matters such as

---

[35] *(Second) of Torts* (1965), section 50.

[36] Section 42 Supreme Court Act 1981.

[37] The decreasing level of accident claims in tort in the last few years is partly due to the collapse of claims 'farming' organizations, but also to the withdrawal of legal aid and the substitution of conditional fees which has 'made solicitors more reluctant to pursue such cases'; see Richard Lewis, 'Insurers and personal injury litigation', *Journal of Personal Injuries Law* [2005] 1/05 2.

'first aid, health and safety, risk assessments and ensuring members benefit from creative learning', or the downside costs could have been much worse.[38]

Assuming an 'inherent risk'?

In the USA, sports participants are generally not liable to other players for injuries arising simply from negligence; this is known as the 'contact sports exception'. The legal analysis is *either* that no duty of care is owed because of an 'inherent risk' *or* because the defence of 'assumption of risk' or *volenti non fit injuria* negates tortious conduct. Conceptually it is the first analysis that is to be preferred, although the result is likely to be similar. Lord Denning's famous difficulty on categorizing economic loss in *Spartan Steel v Martin* is a similar dichotomy, when he stated that 'the more I think about these cases, the more difficult I find it to put each into its proper pigeon-hole. Sometimes I say: "There was no duty." In others I say: "The damage was too remote." So much so that I think the time has come to discard those tests which have proved so elusive'.[39] One reason for adhering to the 'absence of duty' concept is to avoid some very difficult points on waiver of liability through the auspices of contract, as in many jurisdictions in the USA,[40] or of entering too speedily into the quagmire of consent, actual, implied or constructive, and then on into issues of 'informed consent'. It can be seen that in key outdoor activities such as mountaineering, skiing and water sports there are plenty of 'inherent risks', but at what level does acknowledgement of these absolve an organizer from liability? The preliminary legal hurdle therefore is to consider whether a duty of care can exist in the sport or pastime, and here a clear division has developed between 'contact sports' and other sporting or outdoor activities.

In the leading American case in 1997 on contact sports, *Jaworski v Kiernan*,[41] a woman was injured in an amateur football match when she was 'tripped from behind', and the Supreme Court of Connecticut held that participants must refrain from reckless or intentional conduct, but are not liable for injuries as a result of negligence. A jury here had found against a claim that the defendant had been 'wanton and reckless', but stated that it was negligent conduct and gave rise to liability. However, the appeal court stated that physical contact was 'inherent in a

---

[38] 'Court case could close Scout group', *Chorley Guardian* (17 March 2005).

[39] *Spartan Steel & Alloys Ltd v Martin & Co (Contractors) Ltd* [1972] 3 All ER 557 at 562.

[40] Although this is being increasingly contested, as in *Brunner v Different Strokes Expeditions, Inc.*, Washington, King County Superior Court, No. 95-2-21383-1, 6 June 1996, where a church-sponsored rafting trip ended up wrapped around a bridge pillar; one of the boys and a father were trapped when their legs became entangled in a so-called 'suicide line' running down the centre of the raft and drowned. It was alleged that the raft was overloaded, that the 'suicide line' was dangerous and outdated, that the guides were inadequately trained and equipped to effect a whitewater rescue, and that all this amounted to 'gross negligence' which was a liability that could not be waived by a contractual exclusion. The parties eventually settled for $3.5 million to each estate.

[41] 696 A. 2d 332 No. SC 15562, 1997 WL 324394 (Connecticut, 17 June 1997).

competitive game' and therefore there was always an assumption of risk. The court added that if 'simple negligence were adopted as the standard of care, every punter with whom contact is made, every midfielder highsticked, every basketball player fouled, every batter struck by a pitch, and every hockey player tripped would have the ingredients for a lawsuit if injury resulted.'[42]

The majority of states in the USA have followed this line of reasoning that liability requires at least recklessness.[43] The kinds of sporting endeavour have stayed mainly with field sports, such as football,[44] baseball and its junior partner softball,[45] hockey,[46] and basketball,[47] but have also included warming-up in ice hockey[48] and an injury sustained in a doubles tennis match.[49] This 'contact sports exception' principally applies to injuries in amateur conditions, and particularly of sports in a 'pickup' or non-competitive environment; for example, in *Crawn v Campo* in New Jersey where the standard adopted was that of a 'reckless disregard for the safety of others' in a game of 'pickup' softball.[50] However, the test has been adopted too in professional activities, such as in *Turcotte v Fell*,[51] where the 'reckless or intentional standard' was applied in a case involving a professional jockey injured during a horse race. Indeed, the concept of 'contact sport' would not necessarily be thought to apply to the conduct of jockeys, but this test is obviously gaining wider currency in the USA. For example, in *Marchetti v Kalish*[52] it was applied in dealing with a child who was playing the 'informal sport' of 'kick the can', and in *Hathaway v Tascosa Country Club, Inc.*[53] to a recreational game of golf.

What really is a 'contact sport' where the presumption might be that a participant 'assumes a risk', inherent or otherwise? Will it apply to 'horseplay' or outdoor activities generally? What is meant by contact? The position in the USA is as yet very unclear. Some states have therefore explicitly indicated that this higher standard of 'recklessness or intentional misconduct' is explicitly limited to

---

[42] *Jaworski v Kiernan*, 696 A.2d 332, 337 (Conn. 1997), at 338.

[43] The language varies, but states adopting a 'reckless or intentional conduct' or a 'wilful and wanton or intentional misconduct' include California, Connecticut, Illinois, Kentucky, Louisiana, Massachusetts, Michigan, Missouri, Nebraska, New Jersey, New Mexico, New York, Ohio, and Texas.

[44] *Knight v Jewett*, 834 P.2d 696, 711 (California 1992), football. *Kabella v Bouschelle*, 672 P.2d 290, 293 (N.M. Ct. App. 1983), an informal game of tackle football.

[45] *Picou v Hartford Ins. Co.*, 558 So. 2d 787, 790 (La. Ct. App. 1990), softball.

[46] *Gauvin v Clark*, 537 N.E.2d 94, 96 (Mass. 1989), a college hockey game.

[47] *Dotzler v Tuttle*, 449 N.W.2d 774, 779 (Neb. 1990), a 'pickup' basketball game.

[48] *Savino v Robertson*, 625 N.E.2d 1240 (Illinois App. 1995), injured in the eye by a puck in a 'warm up'.

[49] *Hoke v Cullinan*, 914 S.W.2d 335, 339 (Kentucky 1995).

[50] 643 A.2d. 600, 601 (New Jersey 1994).

[51] 502 N.E.2d 964, 968 (New York 1986).

[52] 559 N.E.2d 699, 703 (Ohio 1990).

[53] 846 S.W.2d 614, 616 (Tex. App. 1993).

contact sports. For example, in the Illinois case of *Pfister v Shusta*[54] it was held that participants who voluntarily engage in contact sports cannot recover for injuries resulting from the negligence of other players and, instead, must establish wilful and wanton or intentional misconduct. The 'contact sport' in question was a somewhat unusual one: 'two college students spontaneously began to kick a crushed soda can in the lobby of a college dormitory'. After allegedly being pushed, Pfister attempted to break his fall and put his left arm through the glass door of a fire extinguisher case on the wall. In stark contrast the same appeals court in Illinois found that the state's standard for golf is negligence.[55] Another serious difficulty is to determine quite what is meant by 'wanton or reckless conduct'. 'Wanton' translates as intentional conduct, as in *Greer v Davis*, an unreported Texas appeal in 1996, where the allegation was that the defendant recklessly and intentionally collided with the plaintiff when he was running the bases in a municipal softball game. Testimony showed that the defendant barged over his victim and on returning to the dugout indicated to his team-mates 'I was aiming right at the son of a bitch.' Months earlier, the pair were in a church league basketball game, and after a physical skirmish the defendant had deliberately thrown the ball at his rival.[56] By contrast in *Novak v Lamar Insurance Co.*, where the defendant struck the plaintiff in the face while running to first base, this conduct was held not to be negligence, let alone recklessness, and certainly not 'unsportsmanlike', so that it was merely a collision in a 'game played competitively with maximum diligence'.[57] In such cases the evidence is all-important, as it will delineate between 'accidental' contact, as opposed to intentional or reckless injury. An example of 'wilful or reckless disregard' in equestrian sports was the case of *Sieber v Wigdahl*: the plaintiff was killed in a game of polo, when the defendant violated one of the sport's safety rules by deliberately riding into him with the intention of knocking over his horse.[58]

'Reckless' needs to be judged in the 'heat of the game' or the 'heat of the moment', and in many outdoor activities it is easy to envisage the split second needed to make decisions that can, with hindsight, prove to be less than ideal. In the USA, as would be expected, the national game of baseball (and its junior partner softball) provides many cases of where juries and appeal courts draw the line. The 'no collision' rule at the bases has led to fashioning a duty of care on the basis of 'a reasonably prudent baserunner'. For example, the Louisiana Court of Appeal in *Picou v Hartford Insurance Co* judged that a broken ankle, caused by a collision between two women at second base, was not a violation of this

---

[54] 657 N.E.2d 1013, 1017 (Illinois App. Ct. 1995). See also *Ross v Clouser*, 637 S.W.2d 11, 14 (Mo. 1982), adopting a recklessness standard for contact sports in Missouri.
[55] *Zurla v Hydel* 681 N.E.2d 148, 152 (Ill. App. Ct. 1997). See also in Missouri where *Gamble v Bost* 901 S.W.2d 182, 186 (Mo. Ct. App. 1995) held that a negligence standard is appropriate in bowling, as it was non-contact sport.
[56] 'Contact sport exception allows for participant negligence', Parks & Recreation, *NRPA Law Review* (May 1998).
[57] 488 So.2d 739 (Louisiana 1986).
[58] 704 F.Supp. 1519 (N.D.Illinois, 1989).

theoretical standard, and found instead that the defendant was an 'enthusiastic participant, not unreasonable or unsportsmanlike'.[59] An American commentator has pointed out that the US courts have been using 'inconsistent formulas', some using the definition set out in the *American Restatement of Torts* from 1965,[60] and others inventing *ad hoc*.[61] So there is here a conceptual problem in both defining recklessness and what is a contact sport, and then considering public policy as to whether to categorize an activity. In *Crawn v Campo* the New Jersey Supreme Court pointed out that in their view there would be something 'terribly wrong with a society in which the most commonly-accepted aspects of play – a traditional source of a community's conviviality and cohesion – spurs litigation'.[62] They therefore adopted a 'heightened recklessness standard', proposing this as a 'commonsense distinction between excessively harmful conduct and the more routine rough-and-tumble of sports that should occur freely on the playing field and should not be second-guessed in courtrooms'.[63]

It is important to note here the 'playing field' connation, and in moving to outdoor fields of 'play' the US courts have perhaps had more difficulty in considering the public policy aspects. For example, in skiing and skating there has been a divergence. In *Ritchie-Gamester v City of Berkley*[64] it was held that 'co-participants' owe each other a duty not to engage in reckless misconduct in a case involving a collision between two recreational skaters. Is this a distinction between players and co-participants or between types of recreational activities? In *Novak v Virene*[65] the Illinois appeals courts had concluded that negligence is the appropriate standard between skiers, whereas as we have seen in *Pfister* it was a higher standard in contact sports. So far in Britain there has been little litigation on these 'contact' points, although a single judge of the Court of Appeal in

---

[59] 558 So.2d 787 (1990). See a similar 'non-deliberate' decision in Louisiana in *Ginsberg v Hontas*, 545 So.2d 1154 (1989), sliding head first into second base in recreational softball. See for a case where the YMCA was held not to owe a duty of care when a catcher sustained a broken arm in collision with a runner was trying to reach home base, *Vaillancourt v Vaheem Latifi*, AC 23942 (Court of Appeals of Connecticut 16 February 2004).

[60] 'The actor's conduct is in reckless disregard of the safety of another if he does an act or intentionally fails to do an act which it is his duty to the other to do, knowing or having reason to know of facts which would lead a reasonable man to realize, not only that his conduct creates an unreasonable risk of physical harm to another, but also that such risk is substantially greater than that which is necessary to make his conduct negligent'; *Restatement (Second) of Torts* 500 at 587 (1965).

[61] See generally Ian M. Burnstein, 'Liability for Injuries suffered in the course of Recreational Sports: Application of the Negligence Standard', 71 *University of Detroit Mercy Law Review* 993, 1014 (1994). For example the Louisiana Court of Appeals in Bourque, 331 So. 2d at 43, defined recklessness 'in terms of consequences to the victim', whereas the Illinois Court of Appeals in *Nabozny v Barnhill*, 334 N.E.2d 258, 261 (Ill. App. Ct. 1975), defined it in terms of the 'actor's "reckless disregard" for the safety of other players'.

[62] 643 A.2d at 600.

[63] Ibid.

[64] 597 N.W.2d 517, 518 (Michigan 1999).

[65] 586 N.E.2d 578, 579 (Ill. App. Ct. 1991).

Halling v Scout Association had to consider a 'wide game' between adults on a leader training course, which had led to a 'soft tissue injury'. Judge Simmons in the Luton County Court struck out the claim, having come to the conclusion 'that the collision was nothing more than an accident', and Brooke LJ refused leave to appeal against that order, indicating that the judge had had an opportunity to hear testimony from witnesses and the Court of Appeal would be most unlikely to interfere with findings of fact.[66]

Triathlon in none of its three disciplines of swimming, cycling and running would normally be regarded as a 'contact' sport, although 'bumping' occurs frequently in the swimming leg of such events. In 2001 the Indiana Court of Appeals had to consider an injury caused in the cycling section when a competitor negligently 'cut up' another competitor and caused her to fall. It was held in *Mark v Moser* that although disqualification ensued, there would be no liability, as the higher 'recklessness' standard would be applied.[67]

Boxing and most martial arts are certainly in the 'contact sports' arena; as Daniel Lazaroff has pointed out it is 'inconceivable that professional boxing or full contact karate matches could be conducted without some injury to one or both participants [as] [c]ausing bodily harm is the very essence of the match'.[68] However, injury through legitimate punching is again in a different vicinity from biting, gouging and low punches, which are unsavoury elements well outside the Queensberry rules but are occasionally features of boxing even at the highest level. Boxing has also led to an important negligence standard case in Britain, *Watson v British Boxing Board of Control*, where the allegation was the absence of serious ringside medical care when Michael Watson was treated amid chaotic scenes in a crowded ring after collapsing following a knock down in a title fight in 1991. He was in a coma for 40 days and it was feared he could be paralysed for life, but he has made a remarkable recovery and is now able to speak coherently and walk unaided. Safety regulations were radically overhauled in boxing as a result of this case, with all fighters licensed in Britain undertaking annual scans, although the litigation nearly bankrupted the British Board of Boxing Control. They subsequently lost their appeal, obtained leave to appeal to the House of Lords, but then settled the case.[69] In common understanding football, wrestling and rugby would also be delineated as contact sports. But in others, such as basketball, illegal contact is characterized as a foul, for which a sanction is imposed, although in reality much more contact is permitted than a 'reading of

---

[66] CA transcript 24 August 1999.

[67] No. 29A02-0010-CV-623.

[68] 'Torts & Sports: Participant Liability to Co-participants for Injuries Sustained During Competition', 7 *University of Miami Entertainment & Sports Law Review* 191, 194 (1990).

[69] *Watson v British Boxing Board of Control* (*The Times*, 12 October 1999). See also on the subsequent settlement by agreement in the High Court, *Daily Telegraph*, 9 October 2001). See also for an article by one of the doctors who saved Mr Watson's life, Peter Hamlyn, *Daily Telegraph* (24 September 2001).

the rules would indicate'.[70] The Supreme Court of Iowa has adjudged paintball to be a contact sport, although it would not appear that participants collide with each other when attempting to fire gelatine capsules filled with coloured vegetable oil at each other. Nevertheless the court ruled that the 'contact sports exception' to the general rule of negligence applied, so that Eric Leonard, aged 15, had to prove recklessness when he was hit in the eye. Each participant had been provided with a slingshot and goggles, and during the game the plaintiff's eye protectors had fogged up and he had placed them over his head, when he was shot in the eye. The court indicated that it needed to balance 'on one side the interest in promoting vigorous athletic and sporting competition and the interest in protecting those who participate in those events on the other', and concluded that there was no evidence to support a claim of recklessness to be put to a jury.[71]

Can the 'contact sports exception' apply to spectators? In ice hockey spectators are occasionally involved as skirmishes from the rink spill over into the stands. But in a 2004 case involving a foul ball at the Boston Red Sox stadium in Fenway Park, the courts reaffirmed the principle that such an incident gave no rise to liability, because the spectator assumed a risk by attending. Jane Costa had to undergo reconstructive surgery that installed eight plates in her face when she was hit by a ball estimated to be travelling at about 90 mph when it struck her about 141 feet from home plate. The owners were held to be under no duty to warn of the 'obvious danger of a foul ball being hit into the stands'.[72] On the field of play a 'bystander' was 'struck out' both in court and during the game; this was a Little League baseball player who was injured by a wild pitch, and the Californian appeals court held that this was because of the 'inherent risks' of the game.[73]

Skiing is probably one of the more dangerous outdoor activities. Is it a contact sport? Certainly not in terms of downhill and slalom racing, where competitors go one at a time or even in mogul jumping, where pairs of racers are widely spaced apart. However, here the cases in the USA are very inconsistent. For example, in *Cheong v Antablin* in California the 'assumption of risk' element was not used as a defence, but the appellate court confirmed the trial court's view that assumption of risk barred a claim altogether: 'coparticipants do not owe a duty of care in an active sport unless they act so recklessly that they are outside the bounds of the sport activity'.[74] Both parties were skiing down a slope when they collided, causing the plaintiff to suffer leg fractures and sue on the basis that the defendant had allegedly been skiing too fast. Part of this sport's allure, the court reasoned, includes the camaraderie and socialising in riding up the lifts and skiing down the slopes in mutual enjoyment of the sport, so collisions with other skiers are

---

[70] 'Contact sport exception allows for participant negligence', Parks & Recreation, *NRPA Law Review* (May 1998).

[71] *Leonard v Behrens*, No. 180 / 97-2191 (13 October 1999).

[72] *The Boston Globe* (10 June 2004). According to Red Sox officials, three to four dozen patrons each season are injured by foul balls.

[73] *Balthazar v Little League Baseball, Inc.*, 72 Ca. Rptr. 2d 337 (Ct. App. 1998).

[74] 57 Cal. Rptr. 2d 581 (Ct. App. 1996).

therefore an inherent risk of skiing. Since the defendant did not act intentionally or recklessly, his actions were within the bounds of the activity. But in 2004 the Connecticut Supreme Court distinguished skiing from their earlier football decision in *Jaworski v Kiernan* when they indicated in *Jagger v Mohawk Mountain* that a negligent collision can be grounds for suit. In addition, a ski area operator could be liable for a collision, if caused by an employee, despite state legislation that states skiers assume the risk of 'collision with any other person by any skier while skiing'. The majority of the court held that this did not apply when a ski instructor caused the collision. Mary Ann Jagger was skiing on an intermediate slope when she collided with a ski instructor, allegedly due to his negligence. In considering the nature of 'contact sports' the court compared skiing to golf, running and bicycling, where physical contact is unusual, as opposed to football, hockey and basketball, where contact is expected. In a very illuminating judgment they traced the evolution of the assumption of risk doctrine in skiing to a 1951 Vermont federal case, *Wright v Mt. Mansfield Lift*, denying recovery to a woman who hit a snow-covered stump, hidden on a marked trail. That decision was emphatic that anyone taking part in a sport accepts its 'inherent dangers'.[75]

However, in 1978, the Vermont Supreme Court in *Sunday v Stratton Corp.*[76] produced a seismic change, and a legislative backlash, when they held that a skier could recover $1.5 million after becoming entangled in a snow-covered clump of brush just off the ski trail. The court there held that skiers assume the risk of 'the hazards inherent in skiing' but not a failure to clear brush, which had been caused by the negligent operation of the ski area. Following this case, Connecticut, along with many other snow belt states, provided legislative immunity to ski operators for inherent risks. However, in *Jagger v Mohawk Mountain* in 2003 Norcott J and the majority of the Connecticut Supreme Court held that this 'assumed risk' did not apply to collisions between skiers when caused by the negligent operation of the ski operator. As an illustration of the knife-edge debate in such cases, a strong dissent by Borden J in *Jagger* adopted the language of Norcott J's earlier dissent in *Hyson v White Water Mountain*, a case the previous year which argued that sports enthusiasts should be able to assume the risks, through a signed release, of injury from dangers inherent in snow tubing, including any negligence on the part of an operator. If this was not possible, then Norcott J had warned of 'grievous consequences' for recreation in Connecticut: sport is voluntary, and was used by individuals for 'exercise, to experience a rush of adrenaline, and to engage their competitive nature'. It was therefore 'a matter of public policy... that exculpatory clauses are appropriate in the context of recreational activities'.[77] Francesca Hyson had been injured while snowtubing when she went over a cliff at the bottom of the hill. Clearly the precise language of the Connecticut statute is

---

[75] *Jagger v Mohawk Mountain*, 269 Conn. 672 (2004), *Wright v Mt. Mansfield Lift, Inc.*, 96F Supp. 786 (D. Vt. 1951).
[76] 135 Vt. 293, 390 A2d 398 (1978).
[77] *Hyson v White Water Mountain Resorts of Connecticut*, 829 A.2d 827 (Connecticut Supreme Court 2 September 2003).

decisive, and another key factor is the procedural issue of overturning a trial court's decision, so the distinctions are not just about whether the victim is skiing or snowtubing, but nevertheless these cases illustrate the considerable difficulties in determining what is the appropriate response of negligence law to such outdoor activities.[78]

Spectators and bystanders

In certain circumstances a duty of care may be owed to those who are not active participants. In ball games spectators are hit on occasion, and are usually held to have assumed a risk and therefore no legal duty of care is owed. Alternatively they can be found *volenti* to the risk, with a valid defence raised against them. In *Wooldridge v Sumner* a film cameraman, who was inexperienced with equestrian events, was originally awarded £6,000 for injuries sustained when struck by a horse ridden at the 1959 Horse of the Year Show. He had been taking little interest in the proceedings and 'took fright' at the approach of the galloping horse and 'stumbled back into its path'. However, this decision was overturned by the Court of Appeal who said that by getting close to the arena the plaintiff had implicitly agreed to 'careless' riding. They further said that both the competitor, who was very experienced, and the horse itself (later adjudged supreme champion in its class at the Show), were not negligent but had made 'an error of judgment'.[79] Such a finding of no blame attaching to a horse is rather rare! They held that the rule should be that a spectator attending a game or competition 'takes the risk of any damage caused to him' by any act of a participant of adequate skill and competence, notwithstanding that such act may involve an error of judgment or a lapse of skill. Liability would be founded only where there was conduct such as 'to evince a reckless disregard of the spectator's safety'. Diplock LJ, a considerable riding enthusiast who obviously enjoyed dealing with this matter, opined that 'it is a remarkable thing that, in a nation where, during the present century, so many have spent so much of their leisure in watching other people take part in sports and pastimes, there is an almost complete dearth of judicial authority as to the duty of care owed by the actual participants to the spectators'. However, he indicated that 'if, in the course of a game or competition at a moment when he really has not time to think, a participant by mistake takes a wrong measure, he is not to be held guilty of any negligence'.[80]

---

[78] See generally Thomas B. Sheffey, 'Ski Area Negligence: a Slippery Slope', *The Connecticut Law Tribune* (6 July 2004).

[79] [1962] 2 All ER 978.

[80] At 989. Diplock LJ also pointed out that a 'reasonable spectator' would recognize that a 'reasonable participant will concentrate his attention on winning, and if the game or competition is a fast-moving one will have to exercise his judgment and attempt to exert his skill in what, in the analogous context of contributory negligence, is sometimes called "the agony of the moment".'

The leading bystander case in sports is *Bolton v Stone*[81] where the House of Lords had to consider an injury caused to Miss Stone by a cricket ball, hit for six from the Cheetham Cricket Club on to the adjoining highway. The ball was hit out of the ground at a point at which there was a protective fence rising to seventeen feet above the cricket pitch and the distance from the striker to the victim was about one hundred yards. The evidence showed that on some six occasions in a period of over thirty years a ball had been hit into the highway, but no one had been injured. It was held that for an act to be negligent there must be, not only a reasonable possibility of its happening, but also of injury being caused, and here the risk of injury to someone on the highway was so small that the probability of such an injury could not be anticipated by a reasonable person. Lord Oaksey pointed out that 'The standard of care in the law of negligence is the standard of an ordinarily careful man, but, in my opinion, an ordinarily careful man does not take precautions against every foreseeable risk. He can, of course, foresee the possibility of many risks, but life would be almost impossible if he were to attempt to take precautions against every risk which he can foresee. He takes precautions against risks which are reasonably likely to happen.'

The contrast with that case is *Miller v Jackson* in the Court of Appeal, when a new housing estate was built close to a cricket ground at Lintz,[82] and the evidence showed that several cricket balls landed in the plaintiffs' garden and four balls hit the house, damaging brickwork and tiles. Geoffrey Lane and Cumming-Bruce LJJ held that the club were liable in negligence for a foreseeable risk of injury to the plaintiffs and their property, but Lord Denning dissented passionately, on the basis that in considering the balance of competing interests, he would 'give priority to the right of the cricket club to continue playing cricket on the ground, as they have done for the last 70 years. It takes precedence over the right of the newcomer to sit in his garden undisturbed'.

Omissions

Tort law has found it difficult to impose duties on 'omissions', or a passive failure to act, as opposed to active negligence. For example, in the classic American case of *Osterlind v Hill*,[83] the defendant hired out a canoe to individuals who he knew to be intoxicated. The canoe capsized within yards, and after hanging on for half an hour and 'making loud calls for assistance, which calls the defendant heard and utterly ignored' the luckless learner canoeist drowned. Dean Prosser commented on this 'reluctance to countenance "nonfeasance" as a basis of liability... some of the decisions have been shocking in the extreme.'[84] But even after the Atkin 'neighbour principle' was laid down as a general principle in *Donoghue v Stevenson*, Lord Atkin himself had to admit of

---

[81] [1951] AC 850, [1951] 1 All ER 1078.
[82] [1977] 3 All ER 338.
[83] 1928, 263 Mass. 73, 160 NE 301.
[84] Prosser & Keaton, *Torts* 375.

an exception in *East Suffolk Rivers Catchment Board v Kent*[85] where flooding could have been prevented by re-building a sea wall. The defendant Board were adjudged to have delayed beyond reason, but nonetheless were possessed of a 'mere power' rather than being under a duty to rebuild. Where human life is at risk, rather than property and possessions, the balance in the modern era would appear to be tilting towards a more proactive response. This trend can perhaps first be seen in the American case of *Zelenko v Gimbel Bros.*[86] where a customer in the store was taken ill, so was escorted to an appropriate room but was then left unattended for many hours and died. It was held that emergency services should have been summoned or some basic first aid given. This thread was followed through in the British case of *Barrett v Ministry of Defence*,[87] where the claimant was the widow of a naval airman on a training base in Northern Norway where the facilities were described as 'uninviting', and drinking in three bars provided the main 'recreation'. The deceased had celebrated both his 30th birthday and promotion to leading hand; he asphyxiated on his own vomit, having been placed in his bunk where he was only cursorily overseen. Queen's Regulations, with the benefit of many years of experience in the Royal Navy, suggested a close watch in such circumstances, and indeed the senior naval officer was later found guilty of failing to discourage drunkenness on the base. Contributory negligence was increased by the Court of Appeal to two-thirds, from a finding of 25 per cent, but nevertheless there was a finding of liability in failing to protect the deceased from obvious harm.

Statutory liability

Parliament can also fix a duty of care. A classic illustration is in the Occupiers' Liability Act 1957, where there are standards set out to deal with lawful visitors to property, and in the Occupiers' Liability Act 1984, where there are standards to deal with trespassers. The Common Law position was far from satisfactory and so was codified in these two pivotal statutes, but inevitably there have been subsequent cases to refine what is meant by the Parliamentary language. An obituary in *The Times* noted that Sir John Fiennes, the First Parliamentary Counsel who wrote the 1957 Act, was 'unquestionably the ablest legislative draftsman of this century' and that the four-page Occupiers Liability Act 1957 was 'widely regarded as a model of drafting in plain English'.[88] A critical first question is to determine who is the lawful occupier of premises, and sometimes these can be in 'multi-occupation' or an owner can be difficult to determine when dealing with, for example, footpaths on open

---

[85] *East Suffolk Rivers Catchment Board v Kent* [1940] 4 All ER 527.
[86] 287 N.Y.S. 134 (1935).
[87] [1995] 3 All ER 87.
[88] *The Times* (23 April 1996).

land.[89] Children are a very important focus, as under the 1957 Act 'An occupier must be prepared for children to be less careful than adults. If the occupier allows a child to enter the premises then the premises must be reasonably safe for children of that age'.[90] Age is nonetheless a fairly arbitrary matter and the law has great difficulty on the borderlines on what is meant by a 'child', and particularly when learning disabilities may be involved; as we have seen the Activity Centres (Young Persons Safety) Act 1995 relates solely to those under 18. However, much depends in the application of the law on a sliding continuum to do with the facts and circumstances of the case, and the mental age of the child. Devlin J in *Phipps v Rochester Corporation* had to consider the circumstances of Yvonne Phipps aged seven and her brother Ian aged five who had entered building land in search of blackberries on an unofficial expedition. Ian fell into a trench nine foot deep and broke his leg. Children were known to play on the site, so they were implied visitors in law, rather than being trespassers and perhaps at the time owed no legal duty at all. But even as 'visitors' Devlin J held that the local authority were not liable, and he indicated that in addition to the law recognizing a distinction between adults and children, 'there might well, I think, be an equally well-marked distinction between "big children" and "little children".' In broad terms the judge suggested that big children 'know what they are about' whereas little children should be accompanied by a responsible adult – 'the responsibility for the safety of little children must rest primarily upon their parents … It would not be socially desirable if parents were, as a matter of course, able to shift the burden of looking after their children from their own shoulders to those of persons who happen to have accessible bits of land.'[91] Another attempt to shift a parental duty to a local authority occurred in *Simkiss v Rhondda Borough Council* where Catherine Simkiss, aged seven, and her friend of the same age were having a picnic on the grass outside her parents' flat. Afterwards they walked up the mountain and slid down on a blanket as a makeshift toboggan, until they fell thirty feet over a natural bluff and were injured. However, the defendants were held not liable, because they were entitled to assume that parents would have warned their children of the dangers. The standard applicable to the occupier was that of a reasonably prudent parent, and the Rhondda Council could not be expected to fence off every natural hazard which would provide an opportunity for children to injure themselves.[92] These are key cases, because the parental duty can shift to an organization such as a school or voluntary body when they are acting *in loco parentis*, although liability only follows when they are held to be in breach of a duty of care.

The school environment is familiar territory for analysing the responsibility of those *in loco parentis*. An aphorism of Cave J in the 1890s was that 'The duty of a schoolmaster is to take such care of his boys as a careful father would take of

---

[89] See for the definition of an occupier *Wheat v Lacon* [1966] 1 All ER 582, the Countryside and Right to Roam Act 2000, and for footpaths, *McGeown v Northern Ireland Housing Executive* [1994] 3 All ER 53.

[90] Section 2(3)(a) OLA 1957.

[91] [1955] 1 All ER 129.

[92] (1982) 81 LGR 460.

his sons'.[93] That standard yardstick for teachers can then be extrapolated by analogy to many other circumstances where someone is a guardian, a corporate parent, a foster parent, or an instructor or a volunteer in a youth organization. Many such cases will occur actually on school premises, but again the duty of care when 'offsite' can be compared and occasionally contrasted. The classic case of an injury at school is *Martin v Middlesbrough Corporation*[94] where Janet Martin, a schoolgirl aged 11, slipped on an icy surface in the playground and was injured on broken glass. At the time glass was a common feature of playgrounds, because it came from the free milk bottles provided by local education authorities until a change of government policy in 1971. MacKenna J at first instance was satisfied that the arrangements for disposing of empty one-third pint bottles were satisfactory, but the Court of Appeal held that the defendants were liable in negligence, for the risk of an accident was a reasonably foreseeable risk against which they could and should have guarded by making better arrangements. In their view the existing arrangements would not have commended themselves to any reasonable parent, and that was the appropriate standard. Willmer LJ indicated that the test for a school was 'would be expected of a prudent parent in relation to his own children', and the evidence unfortunately showed that there was 'abundant opportunity for the occasional breakage of a milk bottle' and that glass was swept up a couple of times a week by the school caretaker.[95] Salmon LJ added that he was 'unable to accept the finding of the Judge that there was no serious risk. I think that there was a very serious risk of serious injury to the children; indeed, it was perhaps a miracle that an accident of this nature had not happened before'.[96] The litter in school playgrounds has perhaps become even more lethal in certain areas, with several reported cases of hypodermic needles giving rise to anxiety and HIV testing.[97] The reality may also be that not all of this drugs paraphernalia is deposited from over the fence; a survey in Scotland in 1994 led to guidelines which included sweeping up used needles from school playgrounds, and found that a small number of drug users had started injecting at the age of 12.[98] It is therefore becoming a commonplace for headteachers and caretakers of schools in certain locations to be vigilant for 'sharps' and to clear these so as to prevent injury and infection to children.

'Foreseeability' is a key concept in fixing a duty of care, and although the striving is for an objective test, it is clear that there are often differing viewpoints.

---

[93] Quoted in David Palfreyman, 'Suffer little children: the evolution of the standard reasonably expected in the duty of care to prevent physical injury on school premises', *Education and the Law* vol 13, No 3 (2001).

[94] (1965) 63 LGR 385.

[95] At 386 and 387.

[96] At 395.

[97] See for example 'Aids fear for boy', *The Times* (6 November 1997), where a boy of four was stabbed with a drug addict's used hypodermic needle in a school playground in Derby, by another boy aged eight who had found the syringe.

[98] 'English pupils to learn from Scotland in drug-danger education', *The Scotsman* (9 November 1994).

The overriding need is for a response that is 'reasonable' in the circumstances. Cost-benefit analysis is a constant theme in the cases, so that a balance must be struck between the requirement for safety and the need for 'prudence' in managing scarce resources.[99] In *Latimer v AEC*[100] the House of Lords had to consider the circumstances of a large factory of fifteen acres flooded by an unusually heavy rainstorm. River water mixed with oil left a film making the floor very slippery, and three tons of sawdust, all that was available, was laid down, with forty men set to clean up. Pilcher J found that the employers 'took every step which could reasonably have been taken to deal with the conditions', but the plaintiff on the night shift, given a warning, slipped on the floor, and a barrel he was placing on a trolley rolled on to and injured his ankle. At first instance the plaintiff secured a judgment, but this was overturned in both the Court of Appeal and the House of Lords. Lord Tucker asked rhetorically: 'Has it been proved that the floor was so slippery that, remedial steps not being possible, a reasonably prudent employer would have closed down the factory rather than allow his employees to run the risks involved in continuing work?'

In *Gough v Upshire Primary School*[101] a boy aged eight toppled over a banister and sustained serious head injuries. Matthew Gough, it was conjectured, was attempting to slide down. However, this stairway had been in place since 1936, it complied with building regulations which require schools to have banisters of a height difficult to climb for a child of five or under, and there had never been a previous incident of sliding. Subsequently, the school fitted studs to the banister to prevent a re-occurrence, but Judge Grenfell came to a view that, in the circumstances, it had not been negligent in failing to guard against a possibility, which although theoretically 'foreseeable', was considered no more likely than many other risks which might befall children at the school. Having set out the duty of care required, the judge indicated in a helpful phrase that 'a reasonably careful parent, although he or she may not realize, is continually involved in risk assessment in the sense of balancing risk against actions to be taken or not taken'.[102]

Another recent case also demonstrated the need for supervision and control, particularly on informal 'playing around'. In *Kearn-Price v Kent County Council*[103] the Court of Appeal had to consider in 2002 the duty of care owed by a school for pupils on school premises before 'normal' school hours. Standing in the playground at Tunbridge Wells Boys Grammar School, before the start of school one morning, Daryl Kearn-Price suffered a serious injury when he was struck by a full size leather football. He lost all useful vision in his left eye. The judge found that the injury had occurred during formal school time, which included 'lining up', and that the use of such footballs had been banned by the

---

[99] Guido Calabresi, *The Cost of Accidents: A Legal and Economic Analysis* (Hartford, Conn: Yale, 1970).
[100] [1953] 2 All ER 449.
[101] [2002] ELR 169.
[102] At para 6.
[103] [2002] All ER (D) 440.

school, although the rules had been flouted daily. He held that there had been a lack of any positive action on the part of the school staff to enforce the ban, particularly during the pre-school period, although to have required the school to make spot checks during that time, shortly before registration started, would not have been unduly onerous. At this time there would have been between 30 and 40 teachers in the staff room preparing for school, but there was no patrolling of the playgrounds. The Headteacher claimed that none of the schools he had worked at previously provided supervision of the playground in the morning before school started. However, having reviewed the evidence, the judge, Mr Recorder Gerrey, found that the defendants had not taken reasonable steps to discharge their duty of care in enforcing the ban on leather footballs in order to avoid the risk of obvious and foreseeable injury: 'no flying visits to check what was happening, no attempt as the boys filed into school with their full-sized balls in plastic carrier bags to check the size. There was the occasional confiscation of a ball from the playground during break-times, but nothing further. Therefore on the evidence before me, it really seems that apart from imposing the ban and repeating the ban, there is no evidence whatsoever as to any positive steps taken by any members of the staff to ensure that the ban was complied with.'[104] Dyson LJ expressly approved the statement in *Clerk & Lindsell on Torts* that 'it is the duty of the teacher to supervise children in the playground but supervision before school or as the children leave school may not be required',[105] but upheld the award on the basis that these facts had required such supervision.

In an earlier case of *Ward v Hertfordshire CC*,[106] a pupil aged eight was running a race up and down the school playground just before the start of school, when she stumbled and hit her head against a wall and suffered injuries. The children, who began to arrive at school from 8.15 am onwards, were not supervised until classes began at 8.55 am, and although the claim in negligence succeeded at first instance, the defendant's appeal was allowed. Lord Denning MR commented that the wall was not dangerous, there was no duty to supervise, the staff were indoors preparing for the day's work and could not be expected to be in the playground as well; and even if staff had been in the playground they could not have prevented the accident. However, Salmon LJ noted that if the injury had been caused by the children fighting or indulging in 'some particularly dangerous game which a master should have stopped if he had been there, the fact that there was no supervision at the time might have afforded anyone who was injured in that way a good cause of action'.[107] Having considered that case in detail, Dyson LJ in *Kearn-Price* stated that he 'would unhesitatingly reject the proposition that, as a matter of law, no duty to supervise can be owed by a school to its pupils who are on school premises before or after school hours. As I have explained, *Ward* is not authority for such a proposition.' The Headmaster 'conceded' in cross-examination that he emphasized the leather football ban in

---

[104] Ibid.
[105] Paragraph 7-230 of (18th edition).
[106] [1970] 1 All ER 535.
[107] At 538.

assembly because he thought it was something 'important ... because he had carried out a risk assessment'.[108] But even though the ban had been indicated in school publications and in assemblies, no action had been taken to enforce it in this pre-school period, and liability therefore was upheld. In *Staley v Suffolk County Council and Dean Mason* a mid-day break in a school was supervised by 'dinner-ladies', one of whom was injured by a tennis ball hurled inside a classroom by a boy aged 12, who had intended to hit another boy. Both the County Council and the boy were held liable, the latter on the standard of care to be expected from a child of that age.[109]

Off-site duty of care by schools

The Court of Appeal held in *Bradford-Smart v West Sussex County Council* in 2002 that schools are not generally liable for bullying outside their premises unless it happens on a school trip.[110] Clearly there would be a duty to prevent such behaviour if it occurred on the school premises. There might also be circumstances just outside the school perimeter. Judge LJ indicated that 'one can think of circumstances where it might go beyond that, for example if it were reasonable for a teacher to intervene when he saw one pupil attacking another immediately outside the school gates. It will clearly extend further afield if the pupils are on a school trip, educational, recreational or sporting. But the school cannot owe a general duty to its pupils, or anyone else, to police their activities once they have left its charge'.[111] Garland J found that Leah Bradford-Smart had not been bullied at the Ifield Middle School, but that she had been bullied on the way to and from school on the bus and on the estate where she lived. He said that he regarded the duty as going no further than to prevent the bullying actually happening inside the school. This can be contrasted with *R v Newham London Borough Council, ex parte X* where Brooke J had to deal with an incident of 'hazing' which led to the permanent exclusion of a student; he had, according to certain versions of events 'received insults from another, slightly younger, boy and, in response, he took the boy's trousers and, possibly, his underpants and his socks and shoes off and humiliated him'. After making inquiries the Headteacher used her powers to make the exclusion. Brooke J rejected the argument that a

---

[108] At 27.

[109] *Clerk & Lindsell on Torts* para 10-60.

[110] See an earlier decision of *Cotton v Trafford Borough Council* in the Manchester County Court, referred to by Garland J at first instance in *Bradford-Smart v West Sussex County Council* (*The Times* 8 November 2000). In *Cotton*, a case involving homophobic name-calling and taunting for the most part at the school, Judge Holman excluded a serious indecent assault on a school trip to France, on the basis that it was unforeseeable. However, that was a critical point, as the learned judge found that the conduct of the teachers had fallen short of the school's own procedures and strategies.

[111] *Bradford-Smart v West Sussex County Council* [2002] LGR 489. See also *The Times* (29 January 2002). See Jesse Elvin, 'The duty of schools to prevent bullying', 11 *Tort Law Review* 168.

school could not use their disciplinary powers for incidents outside school, but the case was determined on procedural grounds under the Education (No 2) Act 1986 as to whether there had been a failure to give the parent an opportunity to make representations.[112]

Many of the cases here are about special educational needs, and whether an LEA or school should have exercised discretion to assist such pupils, so they are not directly relevant to mainstream activities. However, in one such case Auld LJ helpfully indicated in *Gower v London Borough of Bromley* that 'teachers have a duty to take such care of pupils in their charge as a careful parent would have in like circumstances, including a duty to take positive steps to protect their well-being … a duty to exercise the reasonable skills of their calling in teaching'.[113] This approach was upheld when that case, and others, reached the House of Lords in *Phelps v London Borough of Hillingdon*, although Lord Slynn warned that 'the difficulties of the tasks involved and of the circumstances under which people have to work in this area must also be borne fully in mind. The professionalism, dedication and standards of those engaged in the provision of educational services are such that cases of liability for negligence will be exceptional'.[114]

Generally, in outdoor activities, the children involved will be those who are *in loco parentis*, but there can also be occasions when children are just lawful visitors and may also be engaged in 'mischief'. The leading case is *Jolley v Sutton LBC* where the House of Lords had to consider the balance of competing interests when personal injury occurs to a teenager. Justin Jolley was a boy of 14, who was severely injured when the abandoned cabin cruiser he was repairing, as opposed to vandalising, fell on top of him. Lord Woolf in the Court of Appeal noted that he planned to take the boat from North Cheam to Cornwall because 'that was where pirates were to be found', so maturity is perhaps not always related to physical age. A warning notice placed on the derelict boat by the defendant local authority, who had been asked by neighbouring council tenants to remove the boat, was the scarcely apt 'Danger. Do Not touch this vehicle unless you are the owner'. Lord Woolf described *Jolley* as a 'novel' case, and although he held that the boat was both an allurement and a trap, the cause of the paraplegia had been the jacking up of the boat to work underneath it: 'even making full allowance for the unpredictability of children's behaviour, I am driven to conclude that it was not reasonably foreseeable that an accident could occur as a result of the boys deciding to work under a propped up boat'. By contrast, the House of Lords reinstated the 'wise decision' of the judge at first instance. Lord Steyn regarded the comment by the judge that 'meddling' with the boat was reasonably foreseeable and that 'play can take the form of mimicking adult behaviour' as 'perceptive'. He found the reasons given in the Court of Appeal 'less than satisfactory'.[115] And Lord Hoffman added that in cases about

---

[112] *R v London Borough of Newham and another ex parte X* [1995] ELR 303.
[113] [1999] ELR 356 at 359.
[114] *Phelps v London Borough of Hillingdon, Anderton v Clwyd CC, Jarvis v Hampshire CC* [2000] 4 All ER 504 at 519.
[115] [2000] 3 All ER 409, at 415.

children it has been repeatedly said 'that their ingenuity in finding unexpected ways of doing mischief to themselves and others should never be underestimated'.[116]

And yet when does a 14-year-old 'child' become an 18-year-old 'adult'? Such age borderlines are inevitably very arbitrary. The Children's Legal Centre leaflet entitled *At What Age Can I?* shows a veritable legal maze,[117] but in any event each individual must be treated uniquely in the light of their special circumstances and not just on age. As well as their mental and physical attributes, which may amount to special needs, it appears that their religious allegiance may even have to be taken into account to protect them from harm. In 2004, a Muslim teenager, Asif Bharucha, aged 17 and on a field trip with his college, fell to his death from the Cornish coastal footpath near the Lizard. The Principal of Blackburn College indicated that he was running away from an overly-friendly black retriever because 'it is my understanding [that] Muslims view dogs as dirty and not something they want to touch'.[118] At the inquest in 2005 a fellow student confirmed that because of his religious belief Asif had regarded dogs as 'unclean', but also avoided contact with them for fear of being bitten. One of the two tutors accompanying the four students, Dawn Norse, in a textbook reconnaissance, had run along the proposed route earlier in the day to make sure it was suitable for her students. But such an unexpected reaction by an individual student would have been difficult to foresee unless there had been prior knowledge or experience with this particular individual of his aversion to dogs.[119] Only with such information about special circumstances and needs would a duty of care have been established, and the College Principal suggested that this activity 'was considered low-risk because the path was mainly flat' and 'obviously you cannot foresee a dog leaping up or barking'.[120] With respect, dogs on a coastal footpath certainly are foreseeable, and this tragedy is now a salutary lesson of an unusual hazard, particularly when something was characterized as a 'phobia' in that individual or where a religious context may be important. The practical way to deal with this matter is in the 'personal and medical details form' required from families in advance of an activity, where vital information ranging much more widely than the standard 'swimmer or non-swimmer' status needs to be classified. Clearly Blackburn College were not at fault on this occasion, but no doubt an AALA *Infolog* will be forthcoming in due course on the topic to warn others of a potential risk.

---

[116] Ibid 420.

[117] Carolyn Hamilton and Alison Fiddy, *At What Age Can I: A Guide to Age-Based Legislation* (Essex: CLC) annual publication.

[118] 'Teenager in cliff fall was scared by dog', *Western Morning News* (17 June 2004).

[119] 'Cliff death teenager frightened by dog', *Western Morning News* (27 January 2005).

[120] 'Dog phobia boy chased over cliff by labrador', *Daily Mirror* (17 June 2004).

Chapter 6

The Breach of Standards of Care

Although there are generalized duties of care on issues such as supervision, each discipline may also have its own unique standard for the duty of care. But the critical next step in negligence liability is to determine, based on the practicalities of evidence, whether there has been a breach of that specific legal standard. This is a question based partly on the law but also on the facts in the particular case, and therefore depends greatly on the evidence, which principally consists of documents but could mean witness testimony if a case goes to trial. The standard of care applied may be seen in Britain to focus on the 'state of knowledge' of hazards in the activity, which can be developing generally but also moves in response to legal cases. Some common themes occur in litigation on outdoor activities across the world, particularly as to whether – a key set of phrases in the American cases – there are 'inherent risks' or dangers that are 'open and obvious', and what the balance of responsibility might be between organizers and participants. Although hazards may vary in jurisdictions, and there are sometimes different legal solutions, commonalities are certainly emerging; in the Alabama case of *Lilya v The Greater Gulf State Fair*[1] where injury was caused while being thrown off a 'mechanical bull', the rider had signed an 'express assumption of the risks and release of liability' and the Appeals Court found that even if this was not a 'waiver' or 'immunity' in contract law, then there was nevertheless an assumption of 'open and obvious' risks. In Britain, although the mechanical bull might be improbable at present, the legal result would be the same, although expressed in different language: no exclusion of liability in contact, but *volenti* in tort law through voluntarily assuming a risk.

The leading case in Britain on breach in outdoor activities involves mountaineering, where the precise standard of care was held to be that 'of a reasonably careful and competent alpine mountain guide'. The inquiry then had to centre on whether that standard was breached by the defendant. This case, *Woodroffe-Hedley v Cuthbertson*,[2] was brought by the infant son of a mountaineer who had been dragged off and killed on the north face of the Tour Ronde, one of the peaks of the Mont Blanc Massif. This is an area that has the 'highest body count' in the world, with an annual death toll of over a hundred climbers, probably due to ease of access for many European climbers, not all of expert standard.[3] The defendant, David Cuthbertson, was an experienced alpine climber on rock and ice, who was being paid £500 by his friend, Gerry Hedley, to act as a guide. Both were roped up on an ice climb, taking turns to lead, and at the

---

[1] 855 So. 2d 1049 (Ala. Sup. Ct., February 2003).
[2] QBD transcript 20 June 1997.
[3] 'Come home alive', *Sunday Times* (12 September 2004).

end of each pitch the leader would cut a ledge for inserting two ice screws, so as to set up a belay or anchor. Each belay was at an interval of about 40 metres, and about half-way there would be an intermediate or running belay, effected by hammering one ice screw into the ice. The function of this was to reduce the 'fall factor' in the event that the leader became detached. The defendant decided to work towards one side of the ice face because of melting caused by the sun and the potential for rock and ice falls. However, at the critical belay he hammered in just one ice screw, as all three of his remaining screws were blocked with ice. When Gerry Hedley climbed up to him, a matter of ten to fifteen minutes, David Cuthbertson neglected to ask for one of the ice screws hanging on his friend's belt, but instead moved off swiftly towards the rocks to his left, having clipped Mr Hedley on to the single screw belay. The judge indicated that he had therefore ignored the 'elementary and fundamental' practice of making a safe belay. In evidence the defendant stated that he made 'a deliberate decision not to lose time by hammering in a second screw', although this would have taken about thirty seconds to affix, and another minute or so to unscrew in due course. Shortly afterwards, when Mr Cuthbertson had climbed about 20 or 30 metres up the slope, and had also not created a running belay, he fell, probably because a large sheet of ice broke away from under his feet. The shock of the fall wrenched out the single ice screw, and in the resultant fall, Mr Hedley was killed and Mr Cuthbertson suffered a fractured knee. The plaintiff's case 'in a nutshell' was that the use of two screw belays was the acknowledged, safe and appropriate standard for creating ice belays. Dyson J came to 'the clear conclusion that, in deciding to dispense with the second screw, Mr Cuthbertson fell below the standard to be expected of a reasonably competent and careful alpine guide. He was also negligent when he compounded that error by his decision not to use a running belay.'

The commentary on this case is illuminating of divergent viewpoints. Andy MacNae of the British Mountaineering Council, believed that the ramifications should not be underestimated: 'It is potentially very serious. Anyone who is involved in climbing takes risks. Having a guide may minimize those risks but it will never eliminate them. It could mean that a guide would not feel confident at a given moment to do what they think is right. It could actually make some routes, where snap judgements are needed, difficult to climb.' On the other hand, the widow, Lynda Woodroffe, believed that her husband had been 'killed by machismo' in skimping on safety to beat the time indicated in the guidebook for the climb.[4] Further criticism of the judge came from Roger Payne, the general secretary of the British Mountaineering Council, who said that the reaction from the climbing world was one of 'utter disbelief', adding that it was a 'grotesque decision'. His view was that 'it brought the law into disrepute. In all hazardous sports while there are general principles for safety that can be followed, they

---

[4] 'Go tell it on the mountain', *The Guardian* (21 June 1997).

cannot be governed by hard and fast rules and regulations.'[5] Another climber, Charles Arthur, suggested that 'the bizarre spectacle of a High Court judge making pronouncements about conditions prevailing on the side of a mountain six years ago to which there are no independent witnesses, [and] the prospect of widows (or, for that matter, widowers) suing over unpredictable accidents in risk sports is deeply worrying.'[6] However, as was pointed out by the successful litigant's solicitor, John Gillman, the judge had based his decisions on the views of eminent mountaineering experts, including the opinion of Allen Fyffe, 'a formidable mountaineer with many years' experience' who stated that 'the guide's failure to set up a belay which could hold a leader fall was a gross error of judgement'.[7]

What was specific about *Woodroffe-Hedley v Cuthbertson* was the breach of a common practice yardstick. It is clear that no-one can guarantee safety on mountains, and there will indeed be many circumstances where no fault could possibly be ascribed. An excellent contrast is the incident in 1998 that was described as Scotland's 'worst avalanche accident'. Three climbers survived for 16 hours trapped under tons of snow in sub-zero temperatures after four of their party died; they were Scout Leaders who had been on a winter skills training course near Ben Nevis. The leader of the Lochaber mountain rescue team said that it was the first time in 35 years of rescue work that he had seen anyone escape alive from an avalanche.[8] The very experienced leader, Roger Wild, himself a member of the mountain rescue service, was completely exonerated of any negligence in a subsequent public inquiry conducted by Sheriff Kenneth Forbes: 'From the evidence I heard, I find Mr Wild to be a proficient, experienced, careful and well-respected mountain guide. The steps he took on this particular day were in accordance with his usual practices and, according to the evidence I heard, in accordance with the practices of other guides operating in Scotland'.[9] The sheriff concluded that the tragedy was, on the evidence, 'not foreseeable'.[10] Avalanches are perhaps the most unpredictable hazard to be faced in winter conditions by climbers and skiers, so there is a significant risk in many locations. In 1990 an avalanche at Peak Lenin on the border between Tajikistan and Kyrgyztan killed 43 climbers when an avalanche obliterated a base camp, and

---

[5] 'Top climbers clear Scot of blame in fatal fall', *The Scotsman* (7 October 1997), following the decision of the British Mountain Guides' professional standards committee that David Cuthbertson could continue work as a guide.

[6] 'Warning: the thrill of living is at risk; Courts should not try to second-guess decisions made on mountains', *The Independent* (21 June 1997).

[7] *The Guardian* (25 June 1997). Mr Fyffe is the secretary of the Scottish Mountain Leadership Training Board, and an author with Iain Peter of *The Handbook of Climbing* (London: Pelham, 1998).

[8] 'Escape from avalanche a miracle', *The Scotsman* (31 December 1998).

[9] 'Climbing guide cleared of blame', *Glasgow Herald* (15 December 2000).

[10] 'Mountain guide is not to blame for deaths', *Aberdeen Press and Journal* (15 December 2000). See also 'Avalanche deaths were unavoidable', *This is Local London: Bexley* (18 December 2000).

this did not appear foreseeable.[11] During Canadian winters, school and voluntary organization trips often centre on snowsports, and skiing and snowboarding represent over 40 per cent of the injuries reported on school field trips; in 2003 seven pupils from the Strathcona-Tweedsmuir School in Alberta on an annual cross-country ski trip in British Columbia were killed in an avalanche.[12] However, a subsequent independent report found that there had been an inadequate consideration of the risks involved in this backcountry trip by this private school, including a misreading of the snow conditions and a failure to heed warnings posted in an avalanche bulletin, so it is likely that civil compensation will follow.[13]

Preventative measures of testing snow conditions, of weather analysis, and of using explosives to clear potential avalanche dangers have all been shown to be helpful, but they are by no means wholly sufficient to guard against disaster. Personal protective devices such as radio beacons and air rucsacs may also have some use, but the main difficulty is that most avalanche victims die from asphyxia; the research suggests 68 per cent, followed by trauma at 13 per cent.[14] There have been several cases of remarkable recovery from asphyxia and hypothermia, including that of Dr Anna Bagenholm, who when skiing became wedged under ice in Norway and was submerged in freezing water for 40 minutes. She made a full recovery, but this is a unique case.[15] Another very experienced mountaineer, Cameron McNeish, editor of *Great Outdoors* magazine and President of the Ramblers' Association in Scotland, almost lost his entire team of eight climbers in the Cairngorms twenty years before Roger Wild's case. He too had been instructing his group on ice-axe skills when he was avalanched, but was fortunately flung clear and then managed to dig out his fellow climbers. His comment on the *Wild* case was that : 'The horrible irony is Roger Wild's clients were killed learning their skills. These people were doing everything right...Sometimes, even when you do everything right, you come a cropper...death is always a part of mountaineering'.[16]

---

[11] 'Come home alive', *Sunday Times* (12 September 2004).

[12] 'Avalanche kills seven high school students', *The Independent* (3 February 2003).

[13] Genny Na, 'Avalanche Tragedy Report Released: Managing the Risks of Outdoor School Excursions', *Canadian Association for the Practical Study of Law in Education Newsletter*, September 2003, vol. 13, No. 1.

[14] M. Rostrup, M. Gilbert, 'Avalanche accidents', *Tidsskr Nor Laegeforen*, (30 March 1993) vol. 113(9), 1100-2.

[15] M. Gilbert, R. Busund, A. Skagseth, P.A. Nilsen and J.P Solbo, 'Resuscitation from accidental hypothermia of 13.7 degrees C with circulatory arrest', *The Lancet*, (29 January 2000) vol 355(9201), 375-6.

[16] 'You can do everything right but still end up battling for survival', *Daily Record* (31 December 1998). Roger Wild was appointed the Scottish Mountain Safety Adviser in 2002 by the Mountaineering Council of Scotland; *The Scottish Mountaineer*, issue 12 (May 2002).

Supervision

A key component in assessing whether breach has occurred in the outdoor activities cases will be a failure to provide adequate supervision, particularly where children are involved. The level of control required depends greatly on the age of the child. As we have seen, the courts have often been called on to adjudicate on responsibilities towards children, and the duty of care for teachers, instructors and youth workers is that generally they are required to act as in a 'reasonably prudent' parental capacity. But the yardstick of *in loco parentis* is very much easier to state theoretically than to apply, and evidence to show breach or to deny breach may not always be straightforward. There is also a philosophical dimension to this sliding scale of supervision, particularly with young people and their need to mature and make their own judgments. Eric Langmuir, the author of *Mountaincraft and Leadership*, the official handbook of the UK Mountain Leader Training Boards, indicates the need for a balance between ensuring safety and providing young people with an opportunity to benefit from adventure activity: 'It is important as far as possible to provide a real experience for youngsters. Sometimes there is a tendency for adults to take over and try to make everything too safe. Judgement will only develop if they are involved in every stage of the adventure.'[17]

In a leading case on teachers and local authorities, *Carmarthenshire CC v Lewis*,[18] the supervision in question was about two very young children at a nursery school in Ammanford, who were readied for a walk. Their teacher left them for a moment to visit the toilet herself and then to give first aid to a boy who had fallen and cut his leg. Meanwhile, David Morgan, aged 4, determinedly striking out on his own, was able to go out through an unlocked gate and, wandering on to the main road, caused the death of a lorry driver who swerved to avoid him. The House of Lords exculpated the teacher, who had many other supervisory concerns to deal with, but Lord Reid deftly pointed out that 'it was not impracticable for the appellants to have their gate so made or fastened that a young child could not open it and, in my opinion, that was a proper and reasonable precaution for them to take'. The duty of care was the 'standard which an ordinarily prudent man or woman would observe in all the circumstances of the case' and the County Council had breached this. No doubt the county councillors in Carmarthen were perplexed when held to be 'personally' liable for this unlocked gate, but a blizzard of nursery handles and bolts above the level of small hands was the practical result of this case. It would now be unthinkable not to have such protection installed as a routine part of any 'risk assessment' of nursery premises; for example in the *Sure Start* arrangements there is the obvious listing for security issues that 'the premises and any outside play area are secure

---

[17] Interview by Felicity Martin in The Scotsman 'How much can we risk?' (23 October 1999).
[18] [1955] 1 All ER 565.

and children are not able to leave them unsupervised'.[19] However, it is important to note that the *Lewis* case fell under what is now the statutory remit of the Occupiers' Liability Act 1957, which is the central legislation statute on premises, and establishes a specific statutory duty of care. It famously requires that 'An occupier must be prepared for children to be less careful than adults'.[20] In pursuance of such a duty to a small boy, where verbal advice or a written notice or even an admonition after previous misconduct might be ineffective to guard against serious danger on the roads, the physical restraint of the lockable gate would become the appropriate preventative measure. Another concept, that of 'magnitude of risk', is also factored in to consider the consequences of breach. In *Paris v Stepney Borough Council* in 1951, still in an era where safety goggles were not mandatory in the workplace even if eye injuries were in prospect, the defendants were nonetheless held liable to a one-eyed garage hand who lost his other eye through their failure to provide eye protection.[21] The 'gravity' of the situation had to be taken into account in assessing the conduct of the defendants. Similarly, a prudent parent would need to do rather more to safeguard a child from harm on an open fire than merely to give an oral warning; a guard, a fence or a physical barrier would inevitably be rather more important. Again, any special needs of participants have to be considered and are likely to raise a heightened duty of care, although as ever the facts are critical; in 1998 a canal boat sank at a lock in Gargrave on the Leeds-Liverpool canal, and despite heroic efforts from other boaters who pulled out three disabled holidaymakers, four drowned as they were from a centre for adults with learning disabilities in Cumbria and could not save themselves. The coroner found that a rope fender at the bow had caught in a 'uniquely tragic mishap', tilting the boat as the lock emptied so that water flooded over the stern; the chief safety engineer for British Waterways indicated this was 'a unique combination of events' and exonerated the carers from blame.[22]

The courts have also developed another heightened duty of responsibility to children when there are special dangers, and again the circumstances and the evidence are decisive in showing breach. This is the doctrine of 'allurement' or 'trap', which is applied to objects that are particularly attractive to childhood curiosity. In *Glasgow Corporation v Taylor*[23] a boy aged seven died as a result of eating the berries of a poisonous shrub in the botanical gardens. This was

---

[19] Para 6.4 *Sure Start*, 'National standards for under 8s day care and childminding', developed from the Day Care and Childminding (National Standards) (England) Regulations 2003 No.1996, under the Children Act 1989.

[20] Section 2(3)(a) OLA 1957. Following his death in 1996, *The Times* obituary described Sir John Fiennes as 'unquestionably the ablest legislative draftsman of this century', and stated that 'the four-page Occupiers' Liability Act 1957 [was] widely regarded as a model of drafting in plain English'. It was indicated that Sir John 'leaves two sons and a daughter': *The Times* (23 April 1996).

[21] *Paris v Stepney Borough Council* [1951] 1 All ER 42.

[22] 'Teenager dived in vain to save four on sinking barge', *The Guardian* (4 June 1999), 'Four died in "unique" canal lock accident', *The Times* (4 June 1999).

[23] [1922] 1 AC 44.

belladonna or 'deadly nightshade', whose fruit is intensely sweet. The apothecary John Gerard had noted as long ago as 1597 several cases of children being poisoned by eating the berries, and exhorted everyone to 'banish therefore these pernicious plants out of your gardens and all places neare to your houses where children do resort'.[24] In the light of that knowledge of deadly risk it was clearly unreasonable to have these plants unprotected in Glasgow in the twentieth century where children were likely to be playing. In a Connecticut case, *Bresnan v Pachaug Marina & Campground Assn Inc.*, two small boys, aged two and three, wandered away from their family to a brightly coloured portable playground at a campsite; it was eight yards away from a pond, and there was no barrier, fence or gate between. The court found that there was negligence in 'placing attractive playground equipment near a water hazard without taking any precautions concerning the foreseeable risk of a child falling into the pond' and a jury made an award for the 'wrongful death' of $2.2 million.[25] Another American case got very close to establishing a duty of care on having appropriate training to supervise a 'backyard pool' where the neighbour's children had been invited round; in *Sober v Goldberg*[26] a boy aged 11 drowned and his parents sued for 'inadequate supervision', suggesting that the neighbours should have been continuously monitoring the children and that Mr Goldberg should not have left his wife in charge, 'knowing that she did not have lifeguard and first aid training' and would be unable to 'mount an effective rescue effort'. The parties eventually settled for $800,000.

Most cases on allurement involve 'unofficial visitors', such as the long line of railway cases; the first in the House of Lords was one of the last appeals from Ireland before the declaration of the Irish Republic, *Cooke v Great Western Railway of Ireland*,[27] where children habitually played on a railway turntable in sidings, leading to injury, and no-one had done anything to warn them off. They were just about in the category of 'visitors', although unwanted. A lesser duty is owed to trespassers, and in a more recent case on youths 'surfing' trains, *Scott v Associated British Ports*, Simon Brown LJ dealt with the issue of physical barriers where warnings and exhortations had failed. Two children from the very same family, both truanting from school, had lost limbs when attempting to ride moving trains at the Hull Docks. The startling point was that, although these railway incidents occurred in the same location, the injuries were in fact four years apart. The teenagers were described by Rafferty J as 'foolhardy to attempt the stunt',[28] and Simon Brown LJ in considering a point that security fences had been allowed to fall into disrepair indicated that, in the circumstances of incessant 'surfing' even secure fences 'would have been wholly effective in eliminating this practice'.[29]

---

[24] John Gerrard, *The Herball, or Generall Historie of Plantes* (1597).

[25] Conn, New London County Jud. Dist. Ct., No. CV-99-0551308S, 13 June 2001.

[26] Md., Baltimore County Circuit Court, No. 95/257/94 CV10173, 9 October 1995.

[27] [1909] AC 229. Professor Heuston, formerly editor of *Salmond on Torts* noted that, on a motoring holiday, he had seen children playing on the turntable some 50 years after the case.

[28] *Daily Mail* (23 November 2000).

[29] [2000] All ER (D) 1937 [20].

The level of supervision or control that was given in advance of an injury, and the preventative measures taken if advice or admonition is likely to be ineffective, will therefore be a primary focus in any subsequent litigation. What may be appropriate for someone aged four in a nursery class will not be appropriate for a sixthformer on an expedition or for an argumentative adult on an outdoor activities course. A sliding scale of command and control will need to be applied, which will be specific to the age, maturity and skill of the participant, as well as judging the 'magnitude of risk' in the context of the potential hazards. In 2004 Judge Bullock at Newcastle County Court rejected a claim by Ula Heywood, subsequently a medical student, when she was diagnosed with Achilles tendonitis after a Duke of Edinburgh's Gold Award expedition. He noted that she was a sixthformer aged 18 and 'an adult' at the time that she had 'decided to go for the Gold award without having participated in the lower awards and in retrospect this was probably not a particularly good decision. The claimant bit off more than she could chew'. The allegation was that the expedition supervisor, Phil Murray, had allowed her 'to continue in pain' with a heavy pack when he owed her a duty of care, even as a 'remote' supervisor with the obligation just to visit once daily; however, his factual evidence was that 'complaints about feet hurting are not uncommon on these types of expedition' and he had given her the option to stop, which she did on the third day of the four-day expedition.[30] The claim was unceremoniously thrown out as lacking any substance, and clearly the suggestion that this was negligent supervision was without merit.

Breach of an 'accepted' standard

The failure to adhere to recommended rules or standards has become an increasingly more likely trigger for liability, and particularly if there are adventurous activity or sporting standards which are commonly accepted. Some of these evolve into 'rules', particularly of games. A classic example is rugby football, which has just about the most complex rulebook of any sport, and which has produced some very important cases which have wide application. Indeed the rugby rules are noteworthy too because they have evolved to deal with some of the hazards of the game as revealed in the medical literature. There can now be discerned a clear trend, both in the courts and on the pitch, towards enforcing the rugby rulebook, and indeed to find liability against referees who have failed to supervise games or implement the rules in accordance with a strict interpretation.

In *Van Oppen v Clerk to the Bedford Charity Trustees*[31] Boreham J had to consider the inextricably intertwined issues of a duty of care in rugby and whether that had been breached by a school on the facts of the case. This very important decision therefore raises many of the issues under discussion in sports

---

[30] 'Suing for damages, the girl who got sore feet trekking towards a Duke of Edinburgh's award', *Daily Mail* (19 October 2004); 'Footsore student's case is kicked out', *Newcastle Journal* (19 October 2004).

[31] [1989] 1 All ER 273.

and outdoor activities. Simon Van Oppen, aged 16, severely injured his spine in an inter-house rugby match. As well as alleging negligent coaching, it was argued too that the school was under a duty to insure against such injuries or at least under a duty to advise parents to take out their own insurance. On the rugby claim, the judge held that the claim would be dismissed, because on the facts the school had not failed in its coaching of proper tackling techniques. After analysis it appeared that the other schoolboy being tackled suddenly checked his stride, with the result that the tackler's head collided with the thigh rather than going behind his hip; in the judge's opinion it was 'no more and no less than a tragic accident'.[32] Boreham J said he was 'satisfied that the defendants, through the staff "taking" rugby, were well aware of the inherent risks in playing rugby football and of the need for the application of correct techniques and the correction of potentially dangerous errors and lapses. I am also satisfied that the standard of supervision was high, that the refereeing was vigilant and strict and that, as one of the plaintiff's contemporaries put it, there was at the school an emphasis on discipline, which meant playing the game correctly. There is therefore no substance in the allegations of negligence'.[33] This is a key passage which indicates the general legal requirements in supervision and control, and this perspective was endorsed by the Court of Appeal. It is of course widely applicable to many other outdoor activities.

On the insurance claims, the school had the year before received a report from the school medical officers' association recommending that schools take out rugby personal accident cover, but at the time of the injury they were still considering the implications. These insurance aspects were described as novel, and formed the main basis of an appeal.[34] Balcombe LJ reviewed the history in the 1970s of a growing awareness by medical and rugby officials of the hazards in tackling and in collapsed scrums. Such an overview is another key element in the decided cases on sports and outdoor injuries, as this survey of the literature may establish breach against a 'state of knowledge' of hazards, perhaps fixing a date when the danger would be apparent; for example, in employers' liability cases it is often possible to point to a particular statute or a change in the regulations or the judicial fixing of a significant year in a review of the medical literature, and this is then fixed as a 'date of knowledge'.[35] Dr John Silver, a consultant at the National Spinal Injuries Centre in Stoke Mandeville, gave evidence in the *Van Oppen* trial that he 'had been horrified at seeing so many boys left paralysed by rugby injuries', and although he himself was 'passionately

---

[32] At 276.

[33] At 277.

[34] *Van Oppen v Clerk to the Bedford Charity Trustees* [1989] 3 All ER 389.

[35] For example, see the banning of blue asbestos in 1931 and white asbestos in 2002 (*Control of Asbestos at Work Regulations 2002*) or the fixing of a 'date of knowledge' by Mustill J for industrial deafness as '1963', when protective ear devices should have been used, although it was only in 1974 that a *Code of Practice for reducing the exposure of employed persons to noise* was issued and that they became mandatory; *Thompson v Smiths Shiprepairers (North Shields) Ltd.* [1984] 1 All ER 881.

fond of the game', he 'would regard rugby as the most dangerous sport or activity taking place in schools'.[36] Indeed, Dr Silver's work in the field of sporting injuries led both to changes in the rules of rugby and also to the introduction of insurance cover by the Rugby Union for all players, including many school children.[37] Approximately half of spinal injuries at the time in school rugby came from games against adults in 'old boys' matches, and after one such incident at Christ's Hospital School in 1978 a meeting was convened in January 1979 at St Thomas's Hospital of the medical officers of schools association. It was their subsequent report that stated that 'schools *must* take out accident insurance for all their rugby players before the beginning of the 1979-1980 season', pointing out that English schoolboys 'are seldom insured against sports injuries' although all rugby club players were compelled to carry insurance cover.[38] At Bedford School the master in charge of rugby was pressing for insurance cover, while the bursar was considering the various options, pointing out to the Headmaster that no other comparable private school had such insurance. In the midst of this internal debate at the school the injury occurred to Simon Van Oppen in November 1980. Having considered all the evidence the Court of Appeal held the judge had been correct in declaring that there was no general duty requiring the school to insure its pupils against accidental injury or to advise a parent of the dangers of rugby football or of the need for personal accident insurance, just as a parent was under no legal duty to insure. The judge had found a 'criticism of stagnation to be unjustified... The most I think that could be said is that it would have been prudent and careful so to advise the parents.'[39] On appeal this was broadened to an issue of 'proximity' in that it would not be 'just or reasonable' to impose such a duty on a school at that time, although the medical officers' report had 'initiated a debate on what ought to be done'.[40] That is perhaps the critical point about the changing nature of 'good practice', adapting to circumstances. Rugby insurance was most certainly on the school agenda at the time, although the details had not been finalized, and indeed as a result of this case it became universal in schools playing rugby. If a *Van Oppen* case re-occurred now, and the school did not have insurance, then given the 'state of knowledge' on spinal injuries in rugby it would be likely that a school without insurance would be found negligent. The 'state of knowledge' about rugby has therefore moved on. In the same way, knowledge develops in outdoor and sporting activities generally; the classic illustration has been the 'rock/water interface' following the Stainforth Beck case, when, at the inquest in 2002, Marcus Bailie of the AALA noted that there were 'frightening

---

[36] 'Rugby "the most dangerous sport",' *The Times* (22 March 1988).

[37] See the report of a conference at Stoke Mandeville, 'Safety lesson the parents must learn', *The Times* (30 July 1990). See some of Dr Silver's research: J.R. Silver, 'Injuries of the spine sustained during rugby', *British Journal of Sports Medicine*, (1992) vol 26, No. 4 253-258; J.R. Silver, D. Stewart, 'The prevention of spinal injuries in rugby football', *Paraplegia* (1994) vol 32 No. 7 442-453; J.R. Silver, 'The need to make rugby safer', *BMJ* (1988) 296:429.

[38] Noted by Balcombe LJ at 393.

[39] Boreham J at 293, to which Balcombe LJ expresses his 'complete agreement' at 412.

[40] Croom-Johnson LJ at 415.

similarities' between several cases. It would now be difficult to think of circumstances after the *Van Oppen* case where a school or voluntary body would not routinely take out personal accident cover to deal with injuries arising out of sporting or adventurous activities. Indeed, such cover would be strongly advisable for any adult engaged in such activities, and one of the very considerable advantages of being a member of a national governing body is that this will invariably offer protection for a relatively modest amount.

Other rugby cases have involved referees, and these are particularly important in defining the duty of care, and the sort of conduct that will amount to breach of that duty, when someone is engaged in instructing or controlling an outdoor activity. In *Smoldon v Whitworth*[41] the Court of Appeal upheld a claim against a referee for failing to supervise a game. Lord Bingham of Cornhill CJ pointed out that while there had been previous cases between participants in sports, there appeared to be 'no previous case in which a rugby football player has sued a referee in negligence'.[42] Ben Smoldon, aged 17, was playing in his usual position as hooker for Sutton Coldfield Colts when the scrum collapsed, and he suffered a broken neck. The case against an opposing player was dismissed, but that against the referee, Michael Nolan, continued. Lord Bingham noted that the case was 'of obvious importance to the plaintiff, whose capacity for active and independent life has been blighted in the flower of his youth', but that it was also of concern to many who feared that such a judgment 'will emasculate and enmesh in unwelcome legal toils a game which gives pleasure to millions'.[43] The relevant rule in the rugby *Laws of the Game*[44] was that in scrimmaging there should be a sequence described as 'Crouch – Touch – Pause – Engage' (CTPE). Curtis J at first instance was satisfied by the evidence which he heard that, throughout the match, the scrums were repeatedly coming together in a rushed way and with excessive force, that there were roughly three or four times the 'normal' number of six or so collapsed scrums in this game, and that the referee had 'fallen below the standard of a reasonably competent referee'. A counter-claim of *volenti* was dismissed, as although the plaintiff would consent to the risk of some injury in rugby, he could not be held to have consented to the breach of the rules by the referee. The Court of Appeal indicated that the level of care required of a referee was that which was 'appropriate in all the circumstances', and the circumstances were of crucial importance: 'Full account must be taken of the factual context in which a referee exercises his functions, and he could not be properly held liable for errors of judgment, oversights or lapses of which any referee might be guilty in the context of a fast-moving and vigorous contest. The threshold of liability is a high one. It will not easily be crossed'.[45] There could be no doubt that the

---

[41] [1997] ELR 249. See for the first instance judgment *The Times* (18 December 1996), [1997] PIQR 133.
[42] At 250.
[43] Loc cit.
[44] Issued by the International Rugby Football Board. Vernon Pugh QC was the IRB's first independent Chairman, so the rules have passed serious legal scrutiny at many levels.
[45] Loc cit.

relevant rules were designed to minimize the risk of spinal injuries caused in collapsing scrums, so this was clearly a 'foreseeable' risk, of which those managing or coaching rugby teams or refereeing or playing in matches were by October 1991 well aware. This 'state of knowledge' of hazards was therefore fully established. The Court of Appeal also indicated *per curiam* in a sort of 'postscript' that, in the words of Lord Bingham, it was 'caused to wonder whether it would not be beneficial if all players were, as a matter of general practice, to be insured not against negligence but against the risk of catastrophic injury, but that is no doubt a matter to which those responsible for the administration of rugby football have given anxious attention'. Such a strong hint would obviously be a very potent factor in the settlement process and in any future litigation.[46]

The *Smoldon* case inevitably attracted a flurry of adverse comment, such as that from Simon Jenkins, the former editor of *The Times*, who said it was 'a sad day for rugby and for personal liberty', suggesting that 'most reasonable people will have been left gasping' that an 'honest man giving up an afternoon to help boys to enjoy their sport is found guilty of culpable negligence for not stopping a scrum collapsing ... I find all this obscene. The courts have now thrown open their doors to players in any game to treat a referee's decision as vulnerable to judicial review'.[47] 'Any game' is a correct analysis, as the courts are entitled to adjudicate on any matter involving the protection of a citizen through negligently inflicted harm. And *Smoldon* is certainly a very important precedent on all referees and others exercising supervision in the outdoor arena. But on the general issues which Mr Jenkins finds 'obscene', one important corrective came from Michael Napier, the President of the Association of Personal Injury Lawyers, who pointed out that the case was decided on its facts, which clearly showed a breach of the rules, and was not necessarily 'the opening of a floodgate of litigation against referees'.[48] The redoubtable Dr John Silver, now consultant emeritus at Stoke Mandeville, also answered Mr Jenkins, noting that he had seen 82 patients who had injured their spinal cords in a similar manner when a scrum collapsed. As a result of his research showing that injuries occurred as a result of the head being driven down to the ground, and then his representations to the rugby authorities, new laws have been introduced to keep the head above the level of the shoulders: 'If the laws are kept to, these accidents can and should be prevented'. His critique of Simon Jenkins' statement that 'individuals should be left with some responsibility for their actions', was damning: 'As four fifths of rugby players are schoolboys, they have little choice in this matter as they are put under compulsion by their peers, schools and parents to play the game and they have no knowledge of the risks involved'.[49] Dr Silver also mentioned in passing another legal case in 1988 in which he had given evidence, where a schoolboy

---

[46] Mr Smoldon ultimately received £1.9 million in settlement of his claim, continues to manage the Sutton Colts rugby team, and recently married; *Sunday Mercury* (14 November 2004).

[47] 'Kicking accidents into touch', *The Times* (20 April 1996).

[48] *The Times* (27 April 1996).

[49] 'Responsibility for ensuring safety in schoolboys' sport', *The Times* (23 April 1996).

hooker, Brian Quinn, alleged that Alun Rees, his coach, had taught him inherently dangerous playing techniques at Exeter College. After several days in court in front of Ognall J, Devon County Council settled that claim for an undisclosed amount.[50] Mr Rees had maintained that the 'injuries were the result of a freak accident' and that although he had 'a tremendous amount of sympathy for Brian... it has not changed my opinion of the game or the way I teach it.'[51] In Australia a case against a school, involving a hooker yet again, was successful on the basis that if the team coach had been made aware of a pack entitled *Don't Stick Your Neck Out*, and distributed in a lacklustre way by the Ministry of Education, he would never have placed the plaintiff at the front of the scrum as he 'had a long neck'.[52] Inevitably there will be cases on which there is a divergence of evidence about whether a breach occurred, but if a contravention of sporting rules can be shown, or even clear guidance in the game designed to prevent injury, then this is prima facie evidence that negligence took place.

Vicarious liability

An important loss-shifting principle in the law is that an employer is liable for the torts of an employee. This principle extends in other relationships such as parent and child or guardian and ward, but the principal occasion for shifting a suit to the 'longer pocket' is where an employment relationship exists. Vicarious liability is of extremely ancient origin, but inevitably it requires a 'supervising' role, generally by an employer. Although vicarious liability has been stretched in recent cases to deal with 'self-employment' when it was under a situation of 'control' by another company,[53] or in circumstances of workers travelling to and from work locations,[54] until recently vicarious liability did not apply to amateur volunteers. However, in a further very important rugby refereeing case, *Evans v Vowles*,[55] the Court of Appeal in 2003 extended vicarious liability to cover the role of unpaid volunteers. This was another leading case, considering several factors of a duty of care and the evidence needed to prove breach. Liability was found not just against David Evans, the first case in any sport involving an amateur referee in an adult amateur game, but vicarious liability against the Welsh Rugby Union. The case involved the very serious injury of Richard Vowles, playing at hooker. He was a very fit young man, having been a former

---

[50] 'Settlement in rugby injury case', *The Times* (29 October 1988). See also 'Schoolboy rugby star sues over crippling injury', *The Guardian* (25 October 1988).

[51] 'Rugby player's injury damages claim settled out of court', *The Guardian* (29 October 1988).

[52] *Watson v Haines* (1987); the New South Wales Supreme Court confirmed an award of $2,187,460 for this exposure 'to an unreasonable risk of spinal injury'.

[53] *McDermid v Nash Dredging and Reclamation Co.Ltd.* [1987] 2 All ER 878.

[54] *Smith v Stages* [1989] 1 All ER 833. See also for a recent statement on vicarious liability *Lister v Hesley Hall* [2001] 2 All ER 769.

[55] [2003] EWCA Civ 318, [2003] PIQR P544, [2003] 1 WLR 1607.

Commonwealth Games featherweight boxer, but he also played a lot of rugby and on this day was in the front row for Llanharan 2nd XV in a 'local Derby' against Tondu. There had been much rain before the game and the pitch was described as 'boggy', so that Lord Phillips of Worth Matravers MR indicated that 'In consequence it was a forwards' game and there were a large number of set scrums.' Additionally, as a result of injuries, there had been several changes in the front row, so that ultimately the referee was then told that Llanharan did not have a replacement front row forward on the bench. He told their captain that they could provide a replacement from within the scrum or that they could, if they wished, opt for 'non-contestable scrummages'; in answer to a question he indicated that if the latter option was chosen the team would not be entitled to points in the League competition. Llanharan opted to play on, moving a flanker to the front row where he said he would 'give it a go'; unfortunately just before the final whistle there was yet another scrum collapse, caused by this inexperienced prop, and Mr Vowles broke his neck.

The focus for the courts was again to look in detail at the rugby *Laws of the Game*, including the point that a team 'must have four players who can play in front row position' and whether replacements are 'suitably trained/experienced'. And if that was not possible, then when 'no other front row forward available due to a sequence of players ordered off or injured or both, then the game will (*sic*) continue with non contestable scrummages'. Before Morland J, as well as in the Court of Appeal, the *Caparo v Dickman* suggestion was made that it would not be 'fair, just and reasonable' to impose on an amateur referee a duty of care.[56] However, the defendants had conceded the other *Caparo* tests, that the relationship between player and referee was sufficiently 'proximate' and that it was 'reasonably foreseeable' that injury might result when there was a breach of the rules. The defendants' principal assertion was that such an imposition of a duty of care upon an amateur referee would discourage participation in rugby by amateur referees, officials and players. Morland J rejected this view, indicating that he did not 'consider it logical to draw a distinction between amateur and professional rugby' and 'when rugby is funded not only by gate receipts but also by lucrative television contracts I can see no reason why the Welsh Rugby Union should not insure itself and its referees against claims and the risk of a finding of a breach of duty of care by a referee' where 'the threshold of liability is a high one which will not easily be crossed'. Lord Phillips took judicial notice that 'rugby football is an inherently dangerous sport' but pointed out that 'some of the rules are specifically designed to minimize the inherent dangers' and that 'players are dependent for their safety on the due enforcement of the rules. The role of the referee is to enforce the rules. Where a referee undertakes to perform that role, it seems to us manifestly fair, just and reasonable that the players should be entitled to rely upon the referee to exercise reasonable care in so doing'. Turning to the precise circumstances, Lord Phillips indicated that the referee had himself regularly played rugby until he retired and had then taken up refereeing. His

---

[56] One of the key considerations in the test of the House of Lords in *Caparo Plc. v Dickman* [1990] 1 All ER 568.

refereeing qualifications were appropriate for the game, and as 'a solicitor employed by the National Union of Teachers who specializes in personal injury claims' he had some skill in these issues, but the judge at first instance had found that he had 'effectively abdicated his responsibility' under the rules, making no inquiries as to whether the replacement was 'suitably trained and experienced. He clearly was not'. Rather than deciding to impose non-contested scrums, the referee essentially left the choice up to the Llanharan captain 'to elect whether to proceed with non-contestable scrummages or to try out his flanker as a front row prop. On no reading of the Law was it proper to offer him that option', and this constituted a breach of his duty of care.[57]

Interestingly this case too had its own 'postscript', on the issue raised by the defendants that 'if we upheld the Judge's finding that an amateur referee owed a duty of care to the players under his charge, volunteers would no longer be prepared to serve as referees'. Lords Phillips indicated that the Court of Appeal did not believe this result would follow, as

> Liability has been established in this case because the injury resulted from a failure to implement a Law designed to minimize the risk of just the kind of accident which subsequently occurred. We believe that such a failure is itself likely to be very rare. Much rarer will be the case where there are grounds for alleging that it has caused a serious injury. Serious injuries are happily rare, but they are an inherent risk of the game. That risk is one which those who play rugby believe is worth taking, having regard to the satisfaction that they get from the game. We would not expect the much more remote risk of facing a claim in negligence to discourage those who take their pleasure in the game by acting as referees.

A direct result of the *Vowles* case was a much closer adherence to the rules; for example, the Irish RFU reacted to the Court of Appeal ruling by ordering mandatory 'passive scrums' whenever a shortage of specialist front-row forwards occurs, stating that the front row replacements must be named and advised to the referee prior to the match.[58] Richard Vowles, who has not yet been paid compensation beyond £91,000 which was the maximum payment under the insurance cover provided by the WRU, commented that 'The WRU are going to have a kick up the backside to make sure the rules of the game look after the players'.[59] The referee, in response to the refusal by the House of Lords to take up a further appeal, vowed that he would 'never pick up a whistle again'.[60] Once again media commentators suggested that such a judgment 'could lead to a flood

---

[57] At 37.

[58] 'Rugby Union: passive scrums order of the day in Ireland', *Western Mail* (14 March 2003).

[59] 'I'd give all that money back to play sport again', *Wales on Sunday* (10 August 2003). In the USA a case involving injury to a hooker whose head was driven into the ground led to a settlement of $2 million. It was alleged to have been negligent to have 'inserted a tired newcomer into that most difficult of positions'; *Simmons v Brigham Young University*, US District Court., D. Color, No. 93-S-2199, 10 March 1995.

[60] 'Vowles Official: 'I'll never referee again', *Western Mail* (1 August 2003).

of litigation, with hundreds of thousands of weekend sportsmen and women across the UK in other sports as well as rugby all now potential litigants should something go awry on the field of play'.[61] However, the more reasonable approach was that of Nigel Hook, senior technical officer of the Central Council of Physical Recreation, which represents all the national governing bodies, who stated that 'This is a landmark case which will cause all our members to look very closely at their regulations and insurance policies.'[62]

Under health and safety legislation it is always the employer who is responsible for vicarious liability claims, so in the case of school pupils and voluntary organizations it is important to consider the 'duty holder'. Even though individual schools may appoint their teachers, it is the legal entity which employs that is important. It may be the local education authority as with most state schools, but in foundation or private schools it is likely to be the school's governing body. The employer's responsibility will certainly extend to the actions of their employees, such as teachers, classroom assistants and administrative staff, but will also include volunteers such as parents. Anyone affected by the actions of employees and volunteers will be a potential litigant, and the prime focus will of course include pupils and participants. A similar legal position of vicarious liability will exist for all providers, including, it is suggested, all voluntary organizations. Who is a defendant is usually a fairly obvious target, such as an LEA, governing body or committee. They will have the 'longer pocket', particularly if they are insured; Professor Lewis has pointed out that 'insurers are the paymasters of the tort system', being responsible for 94 per cent of tort compensation for personal injury.[63] In rare circumstances, individuals in a voluntary organization may agree to be 'each responsible for their own safety', as appeared to be the position when Dean Brittain, who was an experienced open canoeist, drowned by entrapment on the River Barle in 1998 while canoeing with fellow members of the Blackwater Valley Canoe Club; he was pinned against a tree when the river was in spate. A report by the BCU showed that intense questioning by the police seemed aimed at establishing 'whether there was any question of payment to a leader' before determining that 'the club and the trip are non-profitmaking and entirely voluntary'.[64]

---

[61] 'Court victory changes face of sport forever', *Western Mail* (14 December 2002).

[62] 'Officials held liable for rugby player's paralysing injury', *The Times* (14 December 2002).

[63] Richard Lewis, 'Insurers and Personal Injury Litigation', *Journal of Personal Injury Litigation* [2005] 1/05 3, citing the Pearson *Report of the Royal Commission on Civil Liability and Compensation for Personal Injury* (1978) Cmnd. 7054, vol 2, para 509.

[64] Adam Box, 'River Barle Fatality', BCU *CoDe* issue 88, 6–7. A related report deals with the entrapment of a kayaker on the River Dart that same day, a member of the Basingstoke Canal Canoe Club, James Bilson, who was pinned nose down against a fence post which would normally have been out of the water. The coroner recorded deaths of accidental death for both tragedies, although Mr Box suggests lessons should be learned from the Barle incident, as the open canoe did not have whitewater buoyancy and after some capsizes there would have been 'no shame in quitting while you can'.

A 'range of reasonable responses'

One very important protective device against 'opening the floodgates' to litigation is that the courts should not 'second guess' a decision when it was within a range of reasonable responses. For a successful claim the focus will be on whether that decision was negligent, blameworthy or careless, and the defendant must be shown to be 'at fault'. Many decisions, with the considerable benefit of hindsight, are perhaps not seen to be ideal, but they may be 'mere errors of judgment', and that is not necessarily enough reason to impugn them. In the classic *Bolam* test in medical negligence it was sufficient to exonerate a doctor if it could be shown that 'he exercises the ordinary skill of an ordinary competent man exercising that particular art'.[65] The 'highest skill' is not required, and where there are competing viewpoints among experts, Lord Scarman warned that a 'judge's "preference" for one body of distinguished professionals to another also professionally distinguished is not sufficient to establish negligence in a practitioner whose actions have received the seal of approval of those whose opinions, truthfully expressed, honestly held, were not preferred'.[66]

Such a perspective has been applied to other professionals, and most importantly to a teacher on a school skiing trip in *Woodbridge School v Chittock*[67] in 2002. The headnote in this very important case reads that 'Where there are a number of options for a teacher as to the manner in which he might discharge that duty, he is not negligent if he chooses one which, exercising the *Bolam* test, would be within a reasonable range of options for a reasonable teacher exercising that duty of care in the circumstances'.[68] Although as we have seen there have been some injuries and fatalities on school trips in Britain, very few cases have actually reached the courts in a reported civil action, so this is a very important precedent. Most such claims for compensation have been quietly settled by the insurers, often on an undisclosed basis. This was therefore an exception, having been fought out to the Court of Appeal, so it is a vital yardstick in dealing with the vast majority of cases which are settled. The case also seems to have been widely misunderstood, or perhaps not fully digested, by some of the teachers' unions.

Simon Chittock, aged 17, had been reprimanded three times on a skiing trip in 1996 for inappropriate behaviour, twice by skiing off-piste, but then subsequently lost control when he was skiing on-piste. He slid off the edge, fracturing his spine. At first instance Leveson J found that the student had acted recklessly, but held that the school was 50 per cent liable for the injuries he suffered, because the teacher had not confiscated his ski pass or in not arranging for him to ski under

---

[65] A first instance jury direction by McNair J in *Bolam v Friern Barnet Hospital* [1957] 2 All ER 118, at 121. See the endorsement by the House of Lords in *Bolitho v City and Hackney Health Authority* [1997] 4 All ER 771.

[66] *Maynard v West Midlands Regional Health Authority* [1985] 1 All E.R. 635, at 638-639.

[67] [2002] EWCA Civ 915, [2002] ELR 735.

[68] Headnote in the Court of Appeal in *Woodbridge School v Chittock*, supported by reference to *X (Minors) v Bedfordshire County Council* [1995] 2 AC 633.

close supervision after the earlier poor behaviour. The judge declared that if the teacher had taken either of those steps the injuries would not have occurred and that his negligence was allegedly therefore a cause of it. Straight after this first instance judgment, the NASUWT said that it was advising its members not to organize any school trips because the risks of legal action and consequent threats to their jobs were now too great.[69] This skiing holiday to Kuhtai in Austria had been organized by Woodbridge School for forty pupils, of whom three were sixth formers, including Simon Chittock, who had been on three previous trips; by agreement with their parents these three 'seniors' were to be permitted to ski 'unsupervised' on all the slopes.[70] The Court of Appeal, in reviewing the judge's determination of what was the appropriate duty of care, particularly with regard to supervision, expressly approved the formulation: 'teachers *in loco parentis* should provide a level of supervision appropriate to the age, skiing experience, ability and behaviour of the pupils in their charge'.[71]

There were five teachers on the trip, one of whom, Andrew Jackson, was in charge. On handing over their three ski passes to the seniors he instructed them to 'take it easy and not to be stupid', and they were then observed to be skiing sensibly on the first day. However, on the second day Mr Jackson had reason to admonish the three sixth-formers, when he found them smoking in their bedroom with some of the junior girls, and they were punished by the removal of their ski passes for two hours on the following day. A second incident, also early in the trip, involved this trio skiing off-piste, although when Mr Jackson required an explanation they explained that they 'had lost their way because of bad weather – a "white out" – higher up the mountain', and he accepted this, although reminding them that they should not ski off-piste, as it was not covered by the school's insurance. Thirdly, towards the end of the week, the claimant and another sixth-former skied off-piste one kilometre to the hotel, following the day's skiing, instead of joining the others on a coach. Mr Jackson vehemently denied that he gave permission for this and stated that he had reprimanded the boys severely. He said that he had threatened to confiscate their ski passes, but had decided not to do so because he was trying to treat them as adults and they assured him that they would not ski off-piste again. It was put to him in cross-examination that this incident had been 'sheer stupidity and very dangerous' and that 'the boys could not be trusted to behave properly in other circumstances on the slope'. Mr Jackson's reply has the voice of authoritative experience: 'I am not sure I agree with you. I think in a situation like that with teenagers, if you were to take the attitude that once they had put their foot wrong once they were then to be wholly untrustworthy for however long it was, I think you would be in a very difficult situation. If they apologize and assure you that they are not going to do

---

[69] 'School blamed for ski boy who crippled himself', *The Times* (26 July 2001).

[70] The parents signed a consent form which affirmed *inter alia* that 'We are happy that our son... should be allowed to ski with [the names of the other two senior boys] whilst unsupervised by staff during the Junior Ski Trip. He has our permission to go out unsupervised in the evening and to consume moderate amounts of alcoholic drink.'

[71] Para (v).

the same thing again, you have to give them the opportunity to have learned by their mistakes.'[72]

The next day the claimant was skiing on a red intermediate piste, well within his capabilities, and in overtaking he lost control and skied off the edge of the piste, leaving him permanently paralysed from the waist down. An Austrian investigation concluded that the accident occurred 'presumably because he was travelling too fast'. Leveson J found the claimant's carelessness to be the primary cause, but as we have seen, apportioned damages 50:50 in a 'Solomon's judgment', and the school appealed. Auld LJ in the Court of Appeal indicated that the precise duty of care applicable in such a case was that which 'would have been exercised by a reasonably careful parent credited with experience of skiing and its hazards and of running school ski trips, but also taking into account Simon's known level of skiing competence and experience, the nature and conditions of the particular resort and the teachers' responsibilities for the school group as a whole.'[73] This might, in appropriate circumstances, include a duty 'to take positive steps by way of supervision or otherwise [to] protect Simon from doing himself harm'. However, the duty owed was not to ensure safety against injury from skiing mishaps such as those that might arise from his own misjudgement or inadvertence when skiing unsupervised on-piste. In particular Auld LJ noted that 'The accident the next day had nothing to do with skiing off-piste or with deliberately irresponsible behaviour of that sort. It had to do with carelessness.'[74] Most importantly, the Court of Appeal overturned the judge's finding that Mr Jackson's decision was not within a range of reasonable responses for a teacher in his position. Mr Jackson's reaction in giving the boys a severe reprimand and accepting their assurances not to ski off-piste again was not, in the court's view, outside the range of reasonable responses in the circumstances.[75]

Interestingly the commentary on the successful appeal in *Chittock* seems rather sparse and subdued, by contrast to the considerable amount of coverage on the first instance judgment. One legal commentator, Michelle Iles, suggested in 2002 before the appeal, that 'As legal actions over duty of care mount, some teachers are considering an end to trips'. Indicating the stance of the NASUWT, she suggested that *Chittock* was 'The most significant case to have reached the courts in recent years [and] illustrates the union's concerns'.[76] However, in an earlier analysis in 2001, Michael Whincup noted that although *Chittock* was controversial, it was being appealed, and suggested that 'Legal liability for schools is based on common sense', balancing the view that 'judges know the standard of care must not be too demanding' with the point that 'at the same time, parents must be assured that their children will be cared for as best they can in the

---

[72] Answer given in cross-examination and reproduced *verbatim* by Auld LJ at para 9.
[73] At 18.
[74] At 11.
[75] At 27.
[76] Michelle Iles, 'Why school outings could soon disappear', *The Times* (2 April 2002).

circumstances.'[77] Unfortunately the NASUWT seems not to have noted the overturning of *Chittock*; straight after the judgment at first instance Chris Keates, then the deputy general secretary, indicated that 'Our advice is stark. These trips are so fraught with difficulty that we advise our members that it is not in their interests to go on them.'[78] And following the successful appeal in *Chittock*, Ms Keates, now the General Secretary of the NASUWT, seems merely to have repeated her position; in a statement in 2004 she insisted that 'teachers should stop supervising trips to avoid the danger of being sued should anything go wrong' and an itemization of cases which 'have been blamed by NASUWT for leaving teachers vulnerable to further claims' still included *Chittock*, although the newspaper article noted that 'The school later won an appeal against the ruling'.[79] Despite its convoluted gestation, the Court of Appeal decision in *Chittock v Woodbridge School* looks eminently balanced and reasonable, and it is the current statement of the law on school trips. Although an appeal was contemplated, David Wilby QC for the family stated that they were now 'without funds' to pursue a final appeal to the House of Lords, so this appears to be where the law rests currently.[80]

The impact of warnings

Warnings of danger cannot always exonerate an instructor, teacher or organizer of activities from liability, but they are an important factor to be considered. Warnings operate in several different ways: they can suggest that there may no longer be any duty of care owed, or that evidentially there was no breach of a duty, or that defences of *volenti* or contributory negligence operate in these circumstances. The overriding test on notices is reasonableness. For example, the duty owed to lawful visitors under the Occupiers' Liability Act 1957 is that 'Where damage is caused to a visitor by a danger of which he has been warned by the occupier, the warning is not to be treated without more as absolving the occupier from liability, unless in all the circumstances it was enough to enable the visitor to be reasonably safe.'[81] However, the Act makes clear that the defence of *volenti* is still available: 'The common duty of care does not impose upon an occupier any obligation willingly accepted as his by the visitor.'[82] Scrutton LJ in *The Calgarth* famously stated that 'When you invite a person into your house to use the staircase, you do not invite him to slide down the banisters.'[83] In Britain a critical change was made in contract law in 1977 by the

---

[77] Michael Whincup, 'Teachers need not fear their duty', *The Times* (28 August 2001).

[78] 'School blamed for ski boy who crippled himself', *The Times* (26 July 2001).

[79] 'End of school trips; teachers tell MPs: we're so frightened of being sued that we dare not take children out of class', *Daily Express* (1 November 2004).

[80] 'School ski trip victim denied payout as teacher is cleared', *Evening Standard* (26 June 2002).

[81] Section 2(4) OLA 1957.

[82] Section 2(5) OLA 1957.

[83] [1927] P 93, 110.

Unfair Contract Terms Act, and it is no longer possible to use a contractual waiver to exclude business liability for death or personal injuries 'howsoever caused'.[84] This does not stop companies trying, particularly if a foreign location is involved; for example, when Lucy Wicker, a London civil servant died after her inflatable dinghy capsized and she was entrapped by a tree on the Tana River in Kenya in 1993, the owner of the Nairobi-based company Wilderness Safaris pointed out that she had 'signed a disclaimer absolving him and his company ... from any blame should an accident happen', although her family indicated that 'As a complete beginner, Lucy put her trust in the wisdom of a decision made by people she presumed knew the river sufficiently well'.[85] Even in North America, with a great deal of litigation on these 'ticket cases', so named because exclusion clauses are a very familiar part of entry and travel ticket documentation, it is by no means certain that they are effective in all situations. A great deal depends on 'knowledge' of the risks before a party can be taken to 'agree' to exclusionary terms; for example, the British Columbia Supreme Court ruled in 1994 that Judith Greeven, a British tourist injured while skiing in 1991, could sue the ski facility because ticket warnings 'were not good enough for newcomers'.[86] But 'waivers', 'releases' and 'exemption clauses' are still a common feature in outdoor activities, because of their potential effect in tort. For example, in a bungee jump fatality, raising money for a hospital in Swansea, the participants had all been required 'to sign a legal waiver saying they would not claim against the organizers in case of an accident'.[87] The ankle harnesses appeared to have come loose as a teacher, Christopher Thomas, aged 22 and weighing 18 stone, plunged to the ground from a crane 180 feet above the ground in front of his parents and a crowd of several hundred. Mr Thomas was uninsured and died in the hospital for which he was raising money. The coroner recorded a verdict of accidental death and called for a review of all bungee jumping.[88] A decision not to prosecute was taken at an earlier stage, although civil proceedings are still in contemplation.

Signed notices in writing are certainly likely to be of more probative value than a set of conditions posted on the wall, so although 'signing a waiver' may be of no legal effect in exonerating from liability, it may be of evidential value in suggesting consent and the 'assumption of risk' by putting the potential claimant on notice of 'normal risks'. A waiver establishes a paper trail of evidence to show that a warning was given, but of course leaves open the question as to whether such a 'waiver' is effective; in contract law it never can be in a 'business transaction', and in tort law it has to be judged in the full circumstances of what might have been consented to. An 'accident' when a harness frees itself, as appears to have been the position with Mr Thomas, who hesitated and made three attempts before making his jump, might be one matter. By contrast a death caused

---

[84] Section 2(1) Unfair Contract Terms Act 1977. See also the Unfair Terms in Consumer Contracts Regulations 1999.

[85] 'Travellers on the danger list', *Sunday Times* (9 May 1993).

[86] *Canadian Business and Current Affairs* (23 November 1994).

[87] Toughen up on bungee rules, plead AMs', *Western Mail* (28 August 2002).

[88] '21-stone victim's death plunge', *South Wales Evening Post* (25 February 2005).

by too long a bungee cord or a failure to tie appropriate knots or a breach of the code of practice of the British Elastic Rope Sports Association would be entirely different.[89] For example, in a South Carolina case the bungee cage was being winched up and then jammed in the structure; this resulted in stress and the cable snapped, throwing participants down 160 feet. The parents sued for failure to employ a professional engineer and for a series of safety issues, and were awarded $12 million by a jury for the deaths.[90]

A sign needs to be judged in context: 'Trespassers will be prosecuted' is a common warning, but as the criminal law of trespass is very narrow, fairly recent and rarely fits the facts of trespass onto land, this notice has been called 'a wooden falsehood' and would rarely be more than a generalized attempt to warn off unwanted visitors. It is therefore probably not very effective, and a barrier is usually a much better deterrent. Signage can never be conclusive, particularly if it is in writing in Britain, with an estimated four million functionally illiterate inhabitants. The sign circumnavigated by ten Chinese cockle pickers who were drowned with an oncoming rip tide at Morecambe Bay in 2004 stated 'Danger. Beware. Fast Rising Tides. Quicksands. Hidden Channels' but even this listing of lethal dangers and verbal warnings by several local people did not deter those working for one pound a day for their gangmasters.[91] As with road signs, graphics might be more helpful than English language text, but at Morecambe Bay perhaps even that would have been ineffective, given the financial imperatives. After tragedies occur, then signs often go up. For example, after the Land's End deaths of four schoolchildren in 1985, and although at the inquest the owner of the adventure holiday centre said notices might encourage youngsters to climb down the cliffs, four notices went up immediately,[92] and then later a further six noticeboards went up stating 'The cliffs and sea are natural hazards and a potential danger. Please be careful'.[93] And after the series of rock/water deaths in the Neath Valley, a Waterfalls Safety Advisory Group was established in 2002, which put up extra warning signs and distributed leaflets to visitors explaining the potential dangers of the waterfalls.[94] Both locations subsequently had less of a problem with fatalities, injuries and 'near-misses'.

As contract waiver has the statutory veto of UCTA 1977 in 'business liability', the parameters in a non-contractual situation of signing a document purporting to waive rights are not exactly clear, nor indeed is the impact of a posted notice. In the medical context there is often a need to sign a 'consent form', which possibly gives some protection against a subsequent action for assault or battery as

---

[89] See for a case where the Court of Appeal determined there was no duty of care owed by HSE inspectors to the proprietor of a bungee jumping business, *Harris v Evans* [1998] 3 All ER 522.

[90] *Steinke v Beach Bungee Inc, U.S District Court*, D.S.C., No 4: 93-2679-2, 26 October 1995.

[91] 'Trapped by the tide and sinking sands in night of growing horror', *The Guardian* (7 February 2004).

[92] 'Cliff warning: Land's End', *The Times* (3 August 1985).

[93] 'Warning notices for Land's End', *The Times* (29 July 1985).

[94] 'Safety is stepped up at the falls', *South Wales Evening Post* (2 August 2004).

intentional torts, but could not waive the right to bring an action for negligence. The House of Lords have had to deal with issues of 'consent' and its extension to the 'doctrine of 'informed consent' in the medical context in the very important cases of *Chester v Afshar* and *Sidaway v Governors of Bethlem Royal Hospital*,[95] but so far there has not been a case on outdoor activities.

A pre-UCTA case on a non-contractual situation was *White v Blackmore* where the plaintiff's husband had entered in a charity 'jalopy race' for old cars in Gloucestershire. He paid admission fees for his wife and mother-in-law, but as a competitor he did not need to pay for himself. Both at the entrance and around the track notices were exhibited stating 'Warning to the Public. Motor Racing is Dangerous', and then indicating that the promoters were 'absolved of all liabilities'. Such a warning of danger was probably superfluous, a tautology, in that it added nothing to what participants already knew about their sport. However, when the racing started, a car's wheel became entangled with the safety rope about one-third of a mile away, and acting as a winch, pulled up all the stakes. The husband, standing with his family near the rope, was catapulted into the air and died. Lawton J found that the system of tying together all the safety ropes was negligent, but that the deceased had consented to such risks. On appeal, the Court of Appeal had to consider a defence of *volenti* and if this did not apply, then the exclusion of liability by notices in the programme and on the posted notices around the track. They held that *volenti* did not apply in this case, as the risk of injury did not arise from participation in the dangerous sport but from the 'organizer's failure to take reasonable precautions for the safety of visitors'. However, by a majority, the Court of Appeal held that the defendants had successfully excluded their liability for negligence, as they were entitled to do under section 2(1) of the Occupiers' Liability Act 1957, by the terms of the posted notices. The language of that section allows an occupier to 'extend, restrict, modify or exclude his duty to any visitor or visitors by agreement or otherwise'. However, Lord Denning MR in a powerful dissenting judgment noted that when the deceased signed in as a participant there was 'in small print the rules for jalopy races, and also some warning to the effect that competitors taking part in races did so at their own risk', but that this sheet of paper had been 'lost. So we do not know its exact terms'.[96] Lord Denning then vehemently stated that in his view the 'organizers of a sports meeting cannot get out of their responsibilities by putting up warning notices. It would be intolerable if they could do so'.[97] It may be that the Denning dissent is a more reliable indicator than the majority of any future analysis, as he alone seems to have considered the impact of section 2 (4) (a) of the Act on the critical matter that 'a warning is not to be treated without more as absolving the occupier from liability, unless in all the circumstances it was enough to enable the visitor to be reasonably safe', and this was surprisingly not referred to in argument, neither at trial nor at the appeal;

---

[95] *Chester v Afshar* [2004] 4 All ER 587 and *Sidaway v Governors of Bethlem Royal Hospital* [1985] 1 All ER 643.
[96] [1972] 3 All ER 158, at 162.
[97] At 166.

Lord Denning indicated he thought this section was 'decisive'.[98] There is an additional issue too with UCTA, as it only applies to 'business', a term that has no settled legal meaning. Section 14 of UCTA indicates that it includes a profession or the activities of any government department or local or public authority. It will include most outdoor activity centres where there is payment, but according to *Clerk & Lindsell* it leaves 'a wide area of doubt for future litigation'.[99] It may well be that the field used for charitable fundraising in *White v Blackmore*, and a series of other adventurous activities conducted by voluntary bodies, would not be covered, so this is a lacuna which should be rectified.

Turning a visitor into a trespasser by signage

The duty owed to a trespasser is of a lesser order, that of 'common humanity', so is it possible by notice to 'outlaw' a visitor down to the status of trespasser? Certainly there are cases where a visitor will 'outstay their welcome', and they can by formal written notice be requested to leave premises. However, in *Stone v. Taffe*,[100] involving a social event at the Gate Inn in Saltley after normal hours, one of the convivial participants plunged to his death down the unlit stairs. The Court of Appeal insisted that he had not become a trespasser to whom the brewery owed no duty of care at all. His last words to his wife were 'Hold on to the rail and you will be alright', but unfortunately he failed to take his own advice, and he was therefore adjudged to have been 50 per cent contributorily negligent. Where the court has to consider a written notice or a posted notice then they will look at the wording or graphics and apply some analysis. A quintessential case on what might be termed 'a defiant trespasser' is *Whyte v Redland Aggregates Ltd.*,[101] where the claimant had his action dismissed by both the trial judge and the Court of Appeal. He had sued the owners of a disused gravel pit, when he struck his head while diving, and was rendered paraplegic. The contention was that the owners had failed to give proper warning as to the danger; it was said that if they had erected 'No Swimming' signs, then he would not have gone in to the property. The defendants successfully countered, saying that their signs 'Danger, Keep Out' hardly needed any textual analysis and were sufficient warning. As Turner J held in another unreported quarry diving case, *Bartrum v Hepworth Minerals and Chemicals Ltd.*,[102] a sign warning 'No Swimming' is 'authoritative' in respect of trespassers who engage in swimming.

However, there are occasions when the meaning is unclear or inapposite. In *Harrison v Thanet District Council*,[103] a first instance decision of Daniel Brennan QC sitting as a deputy judge of the High Court, breach of a duty of care was

---

[98] Loc cit. para g.

[99] Clerk & Lindsell on *Torts* para 13-26.

[100] [1974] 3 All ER 1016.

[101] *The Times*, 27 November 1997. See also the mention in [1998] CL 485.

[102] QBD transcript (29 October 1999), noted by Ward LJ in *Tomlinson* (CA) [15].

[103] QBD transcript (22 September 1997).

proved because, despite a posted notice, the nature of the sign was held insufficient in the circumstances.[104] Edward Harrison had dived into the sea from the defendants' promenade, fracturing his neck and rendering himself tetraplegic. The defendants argued that such an accident was not foreseeable, but they were met by eye-witness evidence from local residents, supported by two videos taken by private investigators, which showed that swimming, jumping and diving regularly took place there. Once it was established that the lifeguards were aware of this practice, it was held that the defendant's failure properly to assess the risk or to erect suitably worded safety signs constituted a breach of duty under the 1957 Act. Note that this was a case of a 'lawful visitor' on premises, rather than a trespasser. However, the plaintiff was also found guilty of contributory negligence for diving into water of unknown depth, and was held two-thirds responsible for his own injuries. The proof of breach of a duty of care was through 'evidence of local residents in this case [which] is significant ... together with video evidence ... [which] is in my view of extreme importance in this case'. Mr Brennan followed this view with an analysis of 'ethos' and the Safety Signs Regulations 1980.[105] Whereas mention of the Royal Society for the Prevention of Accidents (RoSPA) seems to elicit libertarian fulminations,[106] in *Harrison* there is a careful discussion of Water Safety signs and their significance.[107] This is then applied to the location, with a finding of fact that it was foreseeable to contemplate 'jumping, swimming and even diving' from the ramp. The principal sign appears to have been one stating 'Thanet District Council. Attention: Designated Ski Area. No other water pursuits allowed' and there was another stating 'No bathing to the left of this sign', which was held to be inadequate because it did not have 'prohibitory significance ... either by words or image'. It followed that the signage was 'not enough to meet a danger or risk of which I find the defendants should have been aware'. Testimony as to the significance or otherwise of these signs ranged from 'an enthusiast for water safety' to 'an expert of the old school. As he rhetorically put it, are we in the sort of society where we are "nannying people" or where people should be taking

---

[104] 'Sign could have saved tragedy' *Belfast Telegraph* (16 September 1997). Mr Harrison was an Ulster carpenter from Limavady.

[105] 'The purport of such regulations was to ensure that by different grades of warning, such as prohibition down to advice, individuals would be able to take into account risks or dangers and take action to avoid them.'

[106] See also Lord Hoffmann in *Tomlinson v Congleton Borough Council* [2003] 3 All ER 1122, at 1153: 'It is of course understandable that organizations like the Royal Society for the Prevention of Accidents should favour policies which require people to be prevented from taking risks. Their function is to prevent accidents and that is one way of doing so. *But they do not have to consider the cost, not only in money but also in deprivation of liberty, which such restrictions entail*' [my italics].

[107] Water Safety Signs, using both drawings and words: prohibition; warning about a hazard; information signs; and mandatory signs. BS5499:2002 part 11 gives guidance on the standard international signs, which have been adopted by the National Water Safety Committee. See also http://www.rospa.com/cms/STORE/Water/signs_files/signs.htm

personal responsibility'.[108] This perhaps called to mind the famous dictum of Viscount Simmonds in *Smith v Austin Lifts*: 'I depreciate any tendency to treat the relation of employer and skilled workman as equivalent to that of a nurse and imbecile child'.[109] With respect, the judgment in *Harrison v Thanet District Council* is a textbook decision on risk assessment and signage which could well be emulated by appeal courts.

Harrison was not referred to in what must be taken to be the leading decision on signage, which is *Tomlinson v Congleton Borough Council*,[110] a case on occupiers' liability in a country park. A dim view too was taken of health and safety issues and risk assessments. John Tomlinson, aged 18, was paralysed from the neck down, after a plunge into a lake formed from a disused quarry. On a hot May Bank holiday weekend in 1995, he waded into the water up to his thighs, and then 'dived' from a standing position. This was clearly a catastrophe for him and his family, and a huge expense ahead, but was the local authority at fault? At first instance Jack J found against the claimant,[111] emphasizing that while angling, board-sailing, sub-aqua, canoeing and sailing model yachts were all permitted water activities at the disused sand extraction pit in Brereton Heath Park, notices had been posted reading 'Dangerous water: no swimming'. These notices had little or no effect in preventing occasional swimming, so the authorities had formulated a plan to design out the illicit swimming, by planting over the beaches to make access to the water much more difficult. But Jack J determined that the risk of danger was an obvious one, and Mr Tomlinson had willingly accepted it. In cross-examination Mr Tomlinson admitted he knew he should not dive in shallow water, and he had just 'assumed' that the depth was sufficient; 'In short, Mr Tomlinson took a risk'.

The Court of Appeal then took a different approach, and by a majority reversed that decision, finding that a breach of a duty of care had occurred, although holding the claimant two-thirds at fault. Ward LJ tracked the local authority paperwork trail from purchase in 1980 of land to be used for recreational amenity, through its conversion into a country park of some 80 acres with its centrepiece 'mere' of some 15 acres, right up to the injury itself in 1995.[112] As with other country parks, a management committee had been set up and in January 1983 they undertook a 'risk assessment'. This basic tool of guarding against hazards has had a lengthy history across many fields, in such varied areas as medicine, insurance and finance, but gathered impetus after the Health and Safety at Work etc Act 1974, when it entered common parlance. Although that Act principally concerns the workplace, the 'Five Steps' approach of the Health and Safety Executive has been widely adopted: 'A risk assessment

---

[108] *Harrison.*

[109] [1959] 1 WLR 100, at 105.

[110] [2003] 3 All ER 1122, [2004] 1 AC 46.

[111] Mr Tomlinson had been made an out of court settlement offer of £470,000, and was ordered to repay the interim award of £28,000; *Manchester Evening Post* (17 January 2002).

[112] See for a photograph of the lake and a description of the amenities, the Congleton Borough Council website page at http://www.congleton.gov.uk/default.asp?PageIndex=3300

is nothing more than a careful examination of what, in your work, could cause harm to people, so that you can weigh up whether you have taken enough precautions or should do more to prevent harm'.[113] As a legal requirement in any workplace, the aim of such an assessment is 'to make sure that no one gets hurt or becomes ill … Accidents and ill health can ruin lives'.[114] The local authority officers carried out their duties in an exemplary manner: they were mindful of the first listed hazard of 'slipping/tripping' (Step 1), and the requirement to 'pay particular attention to visitors' ('they may be vulnerable'), and in considering 'who might be harmed, and how – Don't forget: young workers … who may be a particular risk (Step 2)'.[115] Before the end of its first year, the minutes of 21 November 1983 recorded that: 'The risk of a fatality to swimmers was stressed and agreed by all.'

More discussions of the potential hazards led to a decision in May 1990 to plant over the beaches, and indeed this followed again part of the common-sense advice of the HSE to control risks by applying principles in the following order: 'try a less risky option; prevent access to the hazard (e.g. by guarding)…' (Step Three).[116] But in the labyrinthine financial processes of local government, Ward LJ noted that 'the budgetary bids for the relatively modest cost of doing this work had been repeatedly turned down'.[117] After the injury to Mr Tomlinson in May 1995 the planting was in fact fully carried out and proved to be an effective deterrent against swimming and 'diving'. But at the time, work had only just begun on this exercise. The Court of Appeal by a majority indicated that this delay of five years was a decisive factor in reversing the trial judge.

However, the Court of Appeal were in turn themselves reversed by the House of Lords. In a very significant judgement, Lord Hoffmann indicated that no liability arose under the Occupiers' Liability Act 1957 to 'visitors', as in disobeying the warning notices Mr Tomlinson had made himself into a 'trespasser'. But even if the 1957 Act had applied, he held that there would have been no requirement for the council 'to take any steps to prevent Mr Tomlinson from diving or warning him against dangers which were perfectly obvious.'[118] Turning to the law on trespassers in the OLA 1984, Lord Hoffmann concludes that 'plainly there can have been no duty under the 1984 Act.'[119] Ranging rather further than this, Lord Hoffman, under a somewhat Denningesque sub-heading of 'FREE WILL', also took the opportunity to state that 'it will be extremely rare for

---

[113] HSE, *Five Steps to Risk Assessment* (updated leaflet, 2004) 2. As with playgrounds, the regulatory authority for country parks is the HSE, by dint of section 3 of HSWA 1974, which contains provisions to protect people who may be affected by work activities even though they are not employees of the business or undertaking concerned. Crucially, this includes visitors to premises, including members of the public and their children.

[114] Loc cit.

[115] HSE, *Five Steps to Risk Assessment* 4 and 10.

[116] Ibid 5.

[117] *Tomlinson* (CA) 1125 [2].

[118] *Tomlinson* (HL) 1153 [50].

[119] Loc cit.

an occupier of land to be under a duty to prevent people from taking risks which are inherent in the activities they freely choose to undertake upon the land. If people want to climb mountains, go hang gliding or swim or dive in ponds or lakes, that is their affair.'[120] Lord Hobhouse of Woodborough follows this line of reasoning with his own warning that 'The pursuit of an unrestrained culture of blame and compensation has many evil consequences and one is certainly the interference with the liberty of the citizen'.[121]

Tomlinson raises some profound issues about the law on occupiers' liability, and whether that law is in need of updating in modern circumstances. *BRB v Herrington*[122] in 1972 was a radical break from the past in fashioning a duty of 'common sense and common humanity' towards trespassers, but there may again be a need to upgrade the law in the post-Health and Safety Act 1974 era. Lord Hobhouse indicates that 'the question remains what is reasonable to expect the occupier to do for unauthorized trespassers on his land.'[123] But this was a country park, specifically available to members of the public, and where better to go on a hot Bank Holiday weekend? The reality is that Mr Tomlinson was not a trespasser; he was a visitor to a public facility, and yet on touching water he was suddenly 'transmuted' into being an 'unauthorized trespasser' with few, if any, rights. He was also not 'swimming' or 'diving', but 'plunging'. Only Lord Scott of Foscote appears to pick up this really very fundamental point.[124] This leads to his conclusion, isolated from those of his judicial colleagues, that the notices prohibiting 'swimming' at Congleton did not transform Mr Tomlinson from being a 'visitor' to a 'trespasser'. However, Lord Scott then concludes that even the 1957 Act gives no assistance to a claim in these particular circumstances. His judgment deserves very serious attention: 'The park was open to the public and he was entitled to be there[125] ... All they were forbidden to do was to swim[126] ... [but] Mr Tomlinson did not suffer his tragic accident while swimming in the lake'.[127] That seems a much more analytically cogent perspective. However, subject to the issue of which Occupiers' Liability Act applies, Lord Scott is 'in complete agreement' with Lord Hoffmann, so presumably he finds that under the 1957 Act Mr Tomlinson was *volenti* to the risk, although he indicates that the claimant was 'not taking a pre-meditated risk', which others might judge to mean a high level of contributory fault rather than *volenti*, but that too is a matter of judgment. Lord Scott actually indicates some other situations of rather more 'obvious risk', such as swimming across the lake or diving from the branches of a tree.[128]

---

120 Ibid 1152 [45].
121 Ibid 1163 [81].
122 [1972] 1 All ER 749.
123 *Tomlinson* (HL) 1161 [73].
124 Ibid [94].
125 *Tomlinson* (HL) 1164 [87].
126 Ibid 1164 [88].
127 Ibid [89].
128 Loc cit.

Trespassers

The leading case on trespassers, *BRB v Herrington*,[129] in the House of Lords in 1972, had dealt with a boy aged six who strayed across a trodden-down chain link fence onto an electrified railway line, and is obviously a different case to *Tomlinson*, both as to the degree of danger and the age of the victim. The defendants had argued there that they were not liable to a 'trespasser', who had been a visitor at the adjacent National Trust property. But it was held that their failure to repair meant that they had fallen short of standards of 'common sense and common humanity'. In doing so, their Lordships had to over-rule the older approach in *Robert Addie & Sons (Collieries) Ltd. v Dumbreck*,[130] which Lord Reid said 'stood, disliked but essentially unshaken', where an occupier owed a duty only if they showed 'reckless disregard' to a trespasser. With five speeches in the *Herrington*, statute intervened to clarify the law in the Occupiers' Liability Act 1984.

The accidents of litigation produced another instance of serious folly by a 'diver' at nearly the same time as *Tomlinson*, but on this occasion the unofficial 'plunger' had serious diving credentials and clearly should have known better. This was the Court of Appeal decision in *Donoghue v Folkestone Properties Ltd*,[131] when there was a review of the Court of Appeal decision in *Tomlinson*, heard the year before, but with a separate bank of judges.[132] While the cases can helpfully be compared and contrasted, it is noticeable that the judges in *Donoghue* expend a great deal of energy in suggesting *Tomlinson* was incorrectly decided elsewhere in the Court of Appeal. John Donoghue, was a 31-year-old professional scuba diver, who had been fully trained in the Royal Navy to appreciate all the risks of diving into unknown waters. He continued on into civilian life to be a diving supervisor, with a responsibility to ascertain depths and ensure freedom from underwater obstructions before allowing a dive. And yet having consumed five pints in a public house on Boxing Day, he went to a slipway at midnight in Folkestone Harbour, removed all his clothes and dived into two feet of water, striking his head on a grid pile and rendering himself tetraplegic. This near-suicidal midwinter escapade by an experienced diver initially found favour with Judge Bowers, who held that the defendants should have taken further precautions by displaying 'at the top of the slipway a notice stating words to the effect "Danger; No Swimming, jumping or diving; Hidden objects; Shallow water" [which] would have dissuaded Mr Donoghue from diving off the slipway'.[133] Notices were posted, but at staircases rather than on the slipway, and these stated 'jumping into the harbour and swimming is prohibited'.

---

[129] [1972] 1 All ER 749.

[130] [1929] AC 358.

[131] [2003] 3 All ER 1101, [2003] 2 WLR 1138.

[132] The leapfrogging is noticeable: *Tomlinson* was heard on 16 January 2002, with judgment on 14 March 2002; *Donoghue* was heard on 11 February 2003, with judgment on 27 February 2003; and then *Tomlinson* in the House of Lords was heard on 22 and 24 June 2003, with speeches on 31 July 2003.

[133] *Donoghue* 1107 [22].

Children and the occasional adult swam in summer from the slipway, and sporadically security guards and the police would try to prevent this, but to no marked effect. The judge rejected Mr Donoghue's contention that he thought the harbour was a recognized place to swim and found that he 'realized perfectly well that swimming was probably unauthorized but difficult to prevent'.[134] Leaving aside for a moment the issue of notices and whether Mr Donoghue was a visitor or a trespasser, this was an 'open and obvious' danger to any experienced professional diver, and very strongly suggests that *volenti* would have been the appropriate way to deal with this reckless 'assumption of risk'. The issue of whether the 1957 or the 1984 Act applied was not an issue, since Bill Braithwaite QC, appearing for the claimant in *Donoghue* as he did in *Tomlinson* did not contest that Mr Donoghue was a trespasser and that the 1984 Act applied; indeed, given the circumstances of an experienced professional diver it would perhaps have been inconceivable. Lord Phillips helpfully sets out the duty to a trespasser owed by an occupier in succinct terms, in that where the state of the premises poses a danger, and that danger is one that 'poses a risk of causing injury to a trespasser', then there will be a requirement to safeguard the trespasser if 'in all the circumstances of the case it is reasonable to afford the trespasser some protection against the risk'.[135]

A good example of where there is a legal requirement to protect a trespasser occurred when a girl died on a school trip in 1947, *Buckland v Guildford Gas Co.*[136] This was well before the AALA and its research on school fatalities, and before *BRB v Herrington* and its later re-definition in the Occupiers' Liability Act 1984 Act; but the decision makes sense in the light of these later perspectives. Iris Buckland, aged 13, was at Sayers Croft, operated then by the London County Council. She climbed a large oak tree in a field near where her school was at camp. Owing to the density of the foliage, she failed to notice some 11,000 volt high tension wires passing over the tree and was electrocuted. Morris J had to consider if fault could be shown against the farmer, who had sadly discovered a 'motionless' body near the top of a tree and nearby 'the severed head of the girl lying on the ground'. The judge held that she was not a trespasser, as the tree was near a footpath and schools regularly visited the farm to see milking. However, he also considered that even if she was a trespasser, she was owed a duty to 'to take all reasonable steps to prevent the existence of a hidden peril' and the defendants 'could easily have taken various steps which would have avoided the grave risks of lurking, unseen danger'. He found breach established, pointing out that on

---

[134] Ibid 1104 [10].
[135] *Donoghue* 1109 [32]. The precise language of section 1(3) OLA 1984 is that: 'An occupier of premises owes a duty to another (not being his visitor) in respect of any such risk...
(a) he is aware of the danger or has reasonable grounds to believe that it exists;
(b) he knows or has reasonable grounds to believe that the other is in the vicinity of the danger...; and
(c) the risk is one which, in all the circumstances of the case, he may reasonably be expected to offer the other some protection.'
[136] [1949] 1 KB 410.

telegraph poles regulations stipulated anti-climb devices and warning notices, whereas here 'There was no notice on or near the tree conveying a warning that, concealed above the foliage, there were wires which would kill at a touch'.

Electrocution through contact with high-voltage wires generally occurs on construction sites, where the hazard is to be taken very seriously. In a recent Northern Ireland case where a motorway sub-contractor died, after an excavator touched overhead high-voltage electric cables as the men worked at night-time, Curran J imposed a fine of £100,000 on the defendant company. The judge added that 'the fine had to reflect the gravity of the incident and to send a clear message to the construction industry that health and safety regulations must be adhered to … A risk assessment should have been carried out and control measures identified'.[137] Following the death of a worker in Stoke in 2000, when a crane came within millimetres of an 11,000 volt power cable, his supervisor stood trial for manslaughter, but was acquitted after a jury at Stafford Crown Court deliberated for six hours; the defendant claimed that he 'did not realize he was risking' their lives.[138] Approximately two workers each year are killed by electrocution, but arcing across a gap is a significant hazard anywhere near power cables; Charlotte Miller, aged 19 and on a gap year in Ecuador, was apparently playing with a basketball on a beach near a damaged cable, although her mother, Baroness Miller of Chilthorne Domer, pointed out that there were many unanswered questions as to why this state of affairs was allowed on a public beach.[139] Although preventative measures would normally be possible to guard against this 'open and obvious' hazard of coming into contact with high-voltage cables, it may be that some outdoor activities such as ballooning carry a much higher probability; in 1997 a woman aged 75 and on a birthday trip died when the hot-air balloon she was travelling in with twelve others hit a 33,000 volt powerline on a farm near Hull. A spark ignited the gas cylinders, enveloping the gondola in flames.[140] An inquest jury later heard two weeks of evidence, including a report from the Civil Aviation Authority that a 'relatively inexperienced' pilot was 'at the limits of his ability' manoeuvring his craft in 'doubtful weather conditions' and that he had admitted a 'serious miscalculation' when he failed to add his own weight to that of the 12 passengers in assessing use of the burner to achieve lift-off.[141] Civil claims were then pursued, following a verdict of accidental death.[142] While trespassers arriving by balloon is not often foreseeable, in many circumstances of outdoor activities the necessity of taking precautions near high-voltage lines, many quite unobtrusive and not always marked, is vital.

---

[137] 'Construction firm to pay record fine', *Irish News* (19 November 2004).

[138] 'Driver Cleared', *Birmingham Post* (27 March 2003).

[139] 'Gap-year accident kills teenager', *The Times* (15 January 2001); 'Doubts on girl's death in Ecuador', *The Guardian* (3 August 2001); 'Just why did my daughter die?', *Evening Standard* (11 September 2002).

[140] 'Woman is killed on birthday balloon trip', *The Times* (21 July 1997).

[141] 'Balloon pilot "at limits of ability",' *Hull Daily Mail* (13 January 1999).

[142] 'Son tells of family trauma', *Hull Daily Mail* (15 January 1999).

Chapter 7

Defences

Although as we have seen in several cases, there is a complex inter-relationship between duty of care, breach, and the defences of *volenti* and contributory negligence, a separate analysis needs to be made of these defences. They are 'contentions with which a defendant repels a prima facie case which would otherwise attach liability'.[1] Broadly, any argument that there is an absence of a duty of care is a 'defence' to a claim. One possibility is that the claimant is the 'author of his own misfortune', and therefore 'causation' has not been demonstrated. Authority for this general principle is actually said by *Clerk & Lindsell* to be rather 'scanty' because it 'shades off into the topics of contributory negligence and remoteness'.[2] However, in *Vellino v Chief Constable of Greater Manchester*[3] the Court of Appeal in 2002 had to deal with a very unusual situation, where the claimant had a string of convictions for burglary, drugs and motoring offences, and who was about to be arrested for failing once again to turn up to court. When police came to arrest Carlo Vellino at his second floor flat he was in the habit of jumping out of his window. On this occasion he suffered severe brain damage and tetraplegia, and sued the police, claiming that they were 'under a duty not negligently to let him escape'.[4] Elias J at first instance held there was an entire absence of duty of care in these particular circumstances, and the majority of the Court of Appeal agreed. However, even if primary liability had been established, on the basis that officers 'stood by and let him do it when it was plain that he might injure himself', then Sedley LJ in the minority would have reduced damages by two-thirds for contributory negligence.[5] It can therefore be seen that, even once liability has been established – by the breach of a duty of care which caused damage to the victim – it will still be possible to plead specifically that these defences of *volenti* or contributory negligence will wholly or partially exonerate the perpetrator of injury. In the modern era it has to be said that courts tend generally to lean towards the use of contributory negligence, perhaps for 'policy' reasons; for example, Goddard LJ in *Bowater v Rowley Regis Corporation* in 1944 indicated that *volenti* would be applied only with 'extreme caution' in an employee case, where there would be some compulsion to obey orders and where the risks might not be fully known to the worker.[6] As the next year the proportionality defence of contributory negligence became available,

---

[1] Clerk & Lindsell on *Torts* para 1-133.
[2] Op cit para 1-135.
[3] [2002] 3 All ER 78.
[4] At 82.
[5] At 92.
[6] [1944] KB 476.

such a 'policy' view might also have thought that a complete bar would be unjust. A classic example of a contributory negligence defence occurred in a gymnastics case, *Fowles v Bedfordshire County Council*,[7] when the Court of Appeal in 1995 had to consider a participant, aged 21 and a University student, who failed to execute a forward somersault. His former gymnastics teacher described him as 'adventurous and fearless'. The allegation was that the spinal injury was due to a youth worker not having given sufficient warnings, and indeed not being qualified to teach at this level, particularly when such a difficult and potentially hazardous manoeuvre was being attempted. Ognall J at first instance found that the 'plaintiff put in an extra effort by way of acceleration and rotation in order to impress his audience and that it was this which caused him to go out of control on landing and to pitch forward into the wall', and that would lead to a reduction by two-thirds through contributory negligence. Otton LJ said in the Court of Appeal that this was 'an eminently reasonable and sensible (even generous) apportionment in all the circumstances of the case' and the award was upheld.

With such an interplay of possible options, it is often difficult in the cases to extrapolate quite what factors lead to a determination on primary liability or on the nature of the defences. One judge may adopt a merciful or 'generous' approach at first instance by adopting contributory negligence to bring about equity between claimant and defendant, while others on appeal will then hold the participant to be the 'author of their own misfortune' in denying the claim altogether, either on causation or because of the absolute defence of *volenti non fit injuria*. Rarely, but still possible, the appeal may go the other way, with the substitution of a finding of contributory negligence when, at first instance, there was a denial of liability.

Causation

Causation is a very multifaceted and difficult issue in some parts of the law, as for example when there are multi-causal possibilities in medical cases: in *Wilsher v Essex AHA* there were six possible causes of blindness in a premature baby, only one of which could be negligence, and the ultimate decision in the House of Lords was that the plaintiff had failed to prove causation.[8] An initial sieving on causation is carried out by the 'but for test', which is an inquiry to see if the damage would *not* have occurred *but for* a certain event; a classic example is *Barnett v Chelsea & Kensington Hospital Management Committee*[9] where a nightwatchman at a student hall of residence was taken ill after drinking tea on

---

[7] [1995] CLYB 3651, and *The Times* 22 May 1995.

[8] [1988] 1 All ER 871. See for a related area of scientific causation in chemical and drug exposures, Richard Goldberg, *Causation and Risk in the Law of Torts: Scientific Evidence and Medicinal Product Liability* (Oxford: Hart, 1999); and for a much more wide-ranging Australian study, Ian Freckleton and Danuta Mendelson, *Causation in Law and Medicine* (Aldershot: Ashgate, 2002).

[9] [1968] 3 All ER 1068.

New Year's Eve. A doctor at the nearby hospital refused to see him, and the staff at first considered the vomiting was caused by 'drinking to excess', although actually he and his colleagues had been poisoned by arsenic. When asked by a nurse to attend, Dr Banerjee, the casualty officer, said somewhat unsympathetically: 'Well, I'm vomiting myself and I have not been drinking. Tell them to go home and go to bed and call in their own doctors'. Nield J had no difficulty in finding the doctor to be in breach of his duty of care. But that was not an end to the matter, as the judge also found that even 'had all care been taken, the deceased might still have died' and therefore the widow had failed to establish causation. It could not be said that 'but for' the doctor's admitted refusal to see the deceased the patient would not have died; unfortunately medical assistance would not necessarily have saved him from arsenic poisoning.

Causation is also a very difficult concept in respect of industrial diseases such as dermatitis and mesothelioma, which still have many medical mysteries. Nevertheless, because they are 'caused' in general by straightforward breaches of statutory duties by employers, often with a component of strict or non-delegable liability, there has been some relaxation of stringent rules on causation. Lord Reid said in *McGhee v NCB* that 'in cases like this we must take a broader view of causation. The medical evidence is to the effect that the fact that the man had to cycle home caked with grime and sweat added materially to the risk that the disease [of dermatitis] might develop... it has often been said that the legal concept of causation is not based on logic or philosophy. It is based on the practical way in which the ordinary man's mind works in the everyday affairs of life'.[10] When *McGhee* was followed into the medical malpractice field at first instance by Peter Pain J in *Clark v MacLennan*,[11] and then in *Wilsher v Essex Area Health Authority*,[12] it was somewhat roughly received. *Clark* was expressly disapproved by Mustill LJ in *Wilsher* in the Court of Appeal[13] and ultimately too in the House of Lords.[14] Nourse LJ commenting in the Court of Appeal in a road traffic case said that *McGhee* is a 'benevolent principle which smiles on these factual uncertainties [of causation] and melts them all away'.[15] However, he pointed out that *McGhee* was a case where there was 'an imperfect state of medical knowledge' but where there were just two possible causes of dermatitis, whereas he was dealing with a case where medical experts were unable to say 'which of four impacts was more likely than any of the other three to have caused the plaintiff's tetraplegia'.[16] To some extent *McGhee* was rehabilitated in the mesothelioma decision of the House of Lords in *Fairchild v Glenhaven Funeral Services Ltd*[17] where it was 'explained and applied' to a very significant area of

---

[10] See *McGhee v National Coal Board* [1972] 3 All ER 1008 at 1011.
[11] [1983] 1 All ER 416.
[12] (1984) 135 NLJ 383.
[13] [1986] 3 All ER 801, at 815.
[14] [1988] 1 All ER 871.
[15] *Fitzgerald v Lane* [1987] 2 All ER 455 at 464.
[16] Loc cit.
[17] [2002] 3 All ER 305.

asbestos exposure; the issue there was that, although it was clear that the cause was asbestos exposure contrary to statutory regulations, there were two main employers and three possible defendants. Asbestos was thought at one stage to be a 'magic material' useful for its insulating and fire-resistant qualities, but now regarded as the cause of an 'epidemic' killing over 1,800 people in Britain each year.[18] Arthur Fairchild had worked for one employer building packing cases for industrial ovens lined with asbestos, and then for a builder, in whose employment he cut asbestos sheeting to repair roofs, including a factory for Waddingtons. He died from mesothelioma aged 60, and its only known cause is exposure to asbestos. However, his widow could not show on a balance of probabilities where the 'fatal fibre' came from, and it was accepted medically that just one 'guilty' fibre was needed. Curtis J and the Court of Appeal dismissed her claim against Waddingtons and the Leeds City Council against what was described by Lord Bingham of Cornhill as a 'rock of uncertainty'. But he then went on to state that 'The overall object of tort law is to define cases in which the law may justly hold one party liable to compensate another', and supported a view of Lord Hoffmann who 'has, on more than one occasion, discouraged a mechanical approach to the issue of causation'.[19] The unanimous view of their Lordships was that recovery could be against both defendants because it would be contrary to principle to apply a rule on a sole causative analysis which would 'yield unfair results'. Professor Jane Stapleton has noted that 'Certainly the decision is a bold one and admirably transparent on most issues', but *Fairchild* is also very controversial and may be confined to difficulties of dealing with causative problems on this lethal mineral.[20] Asbestos litigation has seen, world-wide, the most strenuous attempts to deny liability, utilizing all possible defensive devices available. In *Margereson v JW Roberts Ltd* those living near an asbestos factory in Leeds were exposed as children when playing 'snowballs' using dust in the nearby streets. Turner & Newalls argued unsuccessfully that mesotheliomas were contracted before the 'date of knowledge', which the defendants argued was a report in 1930 and a trigger for the Asbestos Industry Regulations 1931, but Russell LJ pointed out that there was an 'abundance of evidence' that asbestos was known to be deadly well before the deceased was born.[21] *Labour Research* has estimated that insurance companies are facing a bill of between £6 and £8 billion in the coming years on asbestos claims after the *Fairchild* decision, so this was a very significant result. So much so that a critic, Professor Tony Weir, has suggested that 'No longer does a claimant always have to prove that the defendant's misconduct actually contributed to the harm he is complaining of; it may be enough for him to prove that it probably contributed to the risk of the occurrence

---

[18] Professor Sir Julian Peto, *British Medical Journal* (31 January 2004), and Caroline White, 'Annual deaths from mesothelioma in Britain to reach 2000 by 2010', *BMJ* 2003, 326:1417 (28 June 2003).

[19] [2002] 3 All ER 305 at 314.

[20] Jane Stapleton, 'Lords a'leaping evidentiary gaps', 10 *Torts Law Journal* (2002) 276-305, at 305.

[21] *Margereson v JW Roberts Ltd* (*The Times*, 17 April 1996).

of that harm.'[22] However, these tort arenas are often discrete in their legal reasoning, and particularly in cases with unexplained or multi-causal medical issues, or with difficult questions on a 'surgeon's failure to warn the patient',[23] a highly contentious and complex debate is likely to run and run.[24]

On the whole, and by contrast, in outdoor activities cases the issue of causation is usually routine. There are few scientific mysteries on what has caused death when a climber falls off a mountain, a kayaker drowns in a whitewater rapid, or a skier skids off the piste into a tree. That is also true of most tort cases, as Lady Hale pointed out recently in the 'lost chance' case of an undiagnosed cancer, *Gregg v Scott*:[25] 'The Court of Appeal were divided about this case, as are we. We have found it very difficult. Yet the vast majority of personal injury cases are not difficult. The evidence may be complicated, witnesses may be confused or unreliable and the expert opinions may be contradictory or incomprehensible. But eventually the trial judge sorts it all out and makes findings of fact'. Rather more essential in the outdoor cases, and a very important question for the AALA and other experts on these cases, is not so much what happened, but *how* it was allowed to happen through poor supervision, preparation and organization, and whether appropriate preventative measures can be taken to stop its re-occurrence.

The impact of statute

If the duty of care has been created by statute, then the language of the statute may preclude the operation of defences or verge towards a strict liability perspective. This is often the position in health and safety matters. For example, in *Westwood v The Post Office*,[26] workers were in the habit of taking their breaks on a rooftop, by going through a lift motor room and climbing out of a window; the deceased trod on a trapdoor which gave way beneath him. A notice on the door indicated 'Only the authorized attendant is permitted to enter', and the door was routinely locked, although a key was available. O'Connor J held that this passage through the room was 'unauthorized but accepted' and that the deceased was 'not a trespasser' because 'a blind eye was turned to it'.[27] In rejecting that analysis, Lawton LJ stated bluntly that the findings indicated that 'This means that he was a trespasser there, and the trial judge should have so found.' He later

---

[22] See Tony Weir, 'Making it More Likely v. Making it Happen', 61 *Cambridge Law Journal* 519.
[23] Lord Steyn in the three to two majority decision in *Chester v Afshar* [2004] 4 All ER 587 at para 24.
[24] See Ian Freckleton and Danuta Mendelson, *Causation in Law and Medicine* (Ashgate Dartmouth: Aldershot, 2002).
[25] *The Times* (28 January 2005), at para 92 of the transcript.
[26] [1973] 1 All ER 283.
[27] Quoted by Lawton LJ at 286.

apologizes if this is an 'over-robust way' of dealing with the matter.[28] However, that was not the end of *Westwood*, as it was once more overturned on appeal in the House of Lords, who stated that being a trespasser made not the slightest difference, as the lift motor room was adjudged to be under the protection of the Offices Shops and Railways Premises Act 1963. The statutory language therefore overrode, and the fact that he was a trespasser there was considered irrelevant in the context of the legislation. Having established a primary duty under the safety legislation, a majority then went on to find no *volenti* or contributory negligence either. The Health and Safety At Work etc Act 1974 in the modern era often has a similarly all-encompassing ambit; another case on forbidden access and falling through trapdoors, is *R. v Gateway Foodmarkets Ltd*[29] where the Court of Appeal had to consider the death of a supermarket manager who, contrary to instructions, often went into a lift control room to rectify a fault manually; contractors had left open the trapdoor and, in the dark, he fell to his death. The appeal against conviction under section 2(1) of the 1974 Act was dismissed. That 'catch-all' provision relates to a 'duty of every employer to ensure, so far as is reasonably practicable, the health, safety and welfare at work of all his employees'. Section 3 of the Act then goes on to state that 'It shall be the duty of every employer to conduct his undertaking in such a way as to ensure, so far as is reasonably practicable, that *persons not in his employment* [my emphasis] who may be affected thereby are not exposed to risks to their health and safety.' This is a key provision, which provides the regulatory and criminal law framework applicable to outdoor activity centres and to many of their activities. Indeed it applied to the country park at Congleton in *Tomlinson*, where, as we have seen, a Bank Holiday weekend visitor who disobeyed 'No Swimming' notices was transformed into a 'trespasser'. It is noteworthy that there appears to be not one reference to the 1974 Act in the House of Lords; to the contrary, Lord Hoffmann avers that 'the fact that the council's safety officers thought that the work was necessary does not show that there was a legal duty to do it'.[30]

That case of *Tomlinson* illustrates the very important statutory area of occupiers' liability and the vital distinction between the Occupiers' Liability Acts of 1957 and 1984. The division between the 'sheep' and the 'goats' of visitors and trespassers has over time been a very stark divide, then it became blurred, and now it is perhaps rather distinct again. Lord Philips acknowledged the bizarre nature of someone suddenly turning into being a 'trespasser', and suggests a more neutral terminology for this category of being a 'non visitor', because the term 'trespasser' although 'it is convenient [is] not always accurate'.[31] Section 1 of the 1984 Act actually refers to 'person other than ... visitors'. The pre-1957 law was of course bedevilled by complicated categories, and it would probably not be helpful to start afresh with a new 'non-visitor' status by judicial formulation, but the practical difficulty remains if the lawful visitor to a country park is turned into

---

[28] At 289.
[29] [1997] 3 All ER 78.
[30] *Tomlinson* (HL) 1151 [43].
[31] *Donoghue v Folkestone Properties* [2003] 3 All ER 1101 at 1109.

an outlawed trespasser, as the majority found in *Tomlinson*. That pre-1957 common law had three categories for visitors: contractual entrants, invitees and licensees. Partly because of the restrictions from this tripartite classification, the courts tried to deal with issues on an 'activity' basis so as to accord with reality. Denning LJ indicated in *Slater v Clay Cross* some of the absurdity of these conceptual distinctions: 'If a landowner is driving his car down his private drive and meets someone lawfully walking on it, then he is under a duty to take reasonable care so as not to injure the walker; and his duty is the same no matter whether it is his gardener coming up with plants, a tradesman delivering goods, a friend coming to tea, or a flag seller seeking a charitable gift'.[32] Again with outdoor activity centres the vast majority of users are lawful visitors, often as paying customers, but nonetheless if ignoring a sign transforms such an individual into a trespasser with few legal rights, then there is the likelihood of a serious injustice.

'Horseplay'

One possibility for ignoring signs, or supervisory warnings, is to be engaged in 'horseplay'. Indeed, essentially this was what John Tomlinson was doing when he ignored the 'No Swimming' sign at Congleton. Many of the resultant injuries from 'plunging' occur in the outdoors in informal settings, where there is unlikely to be skilled diving supervision or lifeguard support, and where natural surroundings can increase hazard.[33] In indoor pools the risks of 'horseplay' have long been a feature of the aquatic literature. Pushing, shoving, chasing, tagging, running, dunking, bombing, somersaulting and diving into shallow water are all aspects of rough and tumble games that have been discouraged for many years in swimming pools because of the obvious 'trip and slip' hazards involved. Directly as a result of notices and leaflets displayed, and the frequent interventions of lifeguards, injuries have lessened. It is now rare to have a finding of negligence in such a well-ordered environment, although this did happen in *O'Shea v Royal Borough of Kingston Upon Thames*,[34] where the Court of Appeal affirmed a decision of Michael Davies J who found negligence. Diving had been prohibited at a municipal swimming pool, but the judge held that the authorities had failed to instruct the lifeguards to enforce such a prohibition. He also found 50 per cent contributory negligence, when the claimant, who was celebrating his 28th birthday at a Leisure Pool, 'dived' into the shallow water, keeping his arms to his sides, and became tetraplegic. With the level of signage, usually by graphics as well as by text, and the papertrail of instructions to lifeguards, backed up by verbal warnings, if someone is injured in this way, then it is likely that they

---

[32] [1956] 2 QB 264, 269.

[33] The evidence from the Royal Society for the Prevention of Accidents in *Darby v The National Trust* [2001] EWCA Civ 189 [10] was that approximately 450 people a year drown in the UK, 'the preponderance of these being young men swimming in open water.'

[34] CA transcript 4 November 1994.

would be held to be the 'author of their own misfortune'. This was the position when the Court of Appeal affirmed a judgment of Denis Henry QC, sitting as a deputy High Court Judge, in *McEwan v Eden's Saunasium*,[35] when a claim was dismissed on behalf of the deceased who had 'dived' into a four foot deep plunge pool at a sauna in Brighton. He had consumed 'between six and eight pints that day', and although advertisements outside showed pictorial representations of people diving into water, there was 'an adequate sign in position relating to the depth of the pool'.

The swimming pool environment has also seen the development of several common-sense rules to combat risk; for example, even until quite recently at the end of formal swimming competitions it had been traditional to throw in winners, losers, coaches, and even spectators. Most such participants were capable swimmers, but the risk was of injury from the 'boisterous' circumstances in slippery surroundings with hard surfaces. Poolside behaviour changed in Britain with the advent of widespread considerations of 'health and safety', the mantra introduced with the Health and Safety at Work etc Act 1974. As a result of such improvements, public swimming is now one of the safest possible sports for hours expended: 'The fact remains that public swimming pools are the safest places to swim ...Compared to a swimming pool, unsupervised open water presents many hazards'[36] It would appear that, from the last annual figures available, just nine people died in a swimming pool, out of 421 drownings; that is around two per cent of the total fatalities by drowning that year.[37] In the context of the numbers swimming in pools on a daily basis, this is a microscopic risk.

However, not all circumstances of 'horseplay' come about as a result of inadequate supervision. Even though children are often under 'control', particularly at school, there are circumstances where they might quite properly be 'let off the leash' and then engage voluntarily in 'horseplay', which is not necessarily anyone else's fault. A recent decision of the Court of Appeal, *Blake v Galloway*,[38] dealt with just this issue, at a field study centre in Devon. Ross Blake, aged 15, had been practising in a jazz quintet, but during the lunchtime break, went for a walk in the grounds. He and his friends engaged in what was described as 'high-spirited and good-natured horseplay' by throwing twigs and bark chippings at each other. The claimant did not engage in this at first, but then threw a piece of bark chipping at the defendant, hitting him on the lower part of the body. When it was thrown back it hit the claimant in the eye, causing a significant injury, with damages agreed at £23,5000. Judge Walker held that the injury was caused by negligence in this 'general messing around by all the participants' and he rejected *volenti* as a defence, although reducing damages by 50 per cent to reflect the claimant's contributory negligence. This case is a

---

[35] CA transcript, 23 October 1986.

[36] *Leisure Week* (23 October 1998) 21.

[37] The figures for drownings in the UK in 2001 by location were: rivers 41 per cent, coastal 18 per cent, canals 13 per cent, lakes 12 per cent, home baths seven per cent, docks three per cent, garden ponds two per cent, other two per cent; RoSPA website at http://www.rospa.com

[38] [2004] 3 All ER 315.

helpful analysis of the inter-relationship of these issues, and it is important to note that the Court of Appeal went right back to an analysis of breach and duty of care; Dyson LJ stated that 'This was an unfortunate accident, and no more. There was no breach of the duty to take reasonable care'.[39] There was therefore no need to consider the defences of *volenti* and contributory negligence, the Court of Appeal affirming a statement by Diplock LJ in *Wooldridge v Sumner* that the maxim *volenti non fit injuria* 'pre-supposes a tortious act by the defendant'.[40] *Blake v Galloway* also affirmed the principle that there is a higher duty of care in sports, which would require reckless conduct and not just negligence: 'A person attending a game or competition takes the risk of any damage caused to him by any act of a participant done in the course of and for the purposes of the game or competition, notwithstanding that such act may involve an error of judgment or lapse of skill, unless the participant's conduct is such as to evince a reckless disregard of the spectator's safety'.[41] Dyson LJ acknowledged that 'the horseplay in which the five youths were engaged was not a regulated sport or game played according to explicit rules, nor was it organized in any formal sense', but even with 'informal play' there were 'certain tacitly agreed understandings or conventions'. For example, the play would be limited to 'twigs, pieces of bark and other similar relatively harmless material that happened to be lying around on the ground' and these were to be 'thrown in the general direction of the participants in a somewhat random fashion, and not being aimed at any particular parts of their bodies; and they were being thrown in a good-natured way, without any intention of causing harm'.[42]

Somewhat oddly in *Blake v Galloway* Dyson LJ indicated that 'No authority has been cited to us dealing with negligence in relation to injury caused in the course of horseplay, as opposed to a formal sport or game'[43] and no mention is made of *Mullin v Richards*.[44] This was another case in the Court of Appeal, in 1997, where two 15-year-old schoolgirls were fencing with plastic rulers at the end of a class. A fragment of plastic from a snapped ruler caused Teresa Mullin to lose all useful sight in one eye as a result of what Hutchison LJ described as being 'engaged in playing around',[45] and which Judge Potter at first instance described as 'horseplay which, as they must both have appreciated became in its concluding stage dangerous because it involved rulers being used with some violence'.[46] The original decision was, as in *Blake v Galloway*, that injury was the foreseeable result of negligence, but that there should be a reduction by 50 per cent for contributory negligence. And again, on appeal, the claim was disallowed because there had been no breach of the appropriate duty of care. *Mullin* is

---

[39] At 322.
[40] [1962] 2 All ER 978 at 990.
[41] At 989-990.
[42] At 321.
[43] Loc cit.
[44] [1998] 1 All ER 920.
[45] At 921.
[46] At 923.

particularly interesting because it examines what should be the standard used for a teenager, which is not that of 'an ordinarily prudent and reasonable adult' but that of 'an ordinarily prudent and reasonable 15-year-old schoolgirl in the defendant's situation'.[47] The court cites with approval the Australian case of *McHale v Watson*,[48] where a boy aged 12 had acquired a piece of welding rod about six inches in length, and having sharpened the end, proceeded to throw it like a 'small harpoon' at a wooden post 'expecting it to stick in it'.[49] The rod bounced off and struck Susan McHale, aged nine, in her left eye, resulting in blindness. Owen J quoted approvingly from para 283 of the American *Restatement of the Law of Torts*: 'the standard by which his conduct is to be measured is not that to be expected of a reasonable adult but that reasonably to be expected of a child of the same age, intelligence and experience'.[50] Although there was a suggestion that the boy's father had given him the dart, and that the boy had thrown the implement deliberately at the girl, these contentions were not found proven, and the case was dismissed by Windeyer J on the basis of no duty of care owed; this was then upheld on appeal, along with a powerful analysis of the cases involving children, mostly on the defence of contributory negligence. For example, in a Canadian case, *Walmsley v Humenick*,[51] a child aged four had shot an arrow which blinded another child, and Clyne J indicated that 'what may be lack of reasonable care in an adult cannot be considered to be so in the case of a child having regard to its capacity to understand and appreciate the nature of its actions'. Butler-Sloss LJ in *Mullin v Richards* noted that Kitto J in *McHale v Watson* had stated that 'children, like everyone else, must accept as they go about in society the risks from which ordinary care on the part of others will not suffice to save them. One such risk is that boys of twelve may behave as boys of twelve', and she herself added that 'I would say that girls of 15 playing together may play as somewhat irresponsible girls of 15'.[52] A very important point in *Mullin v Richards* is that the teacher, whose Maths class was just coming to an end, was found 'not guilty of negligence' and therefore the case on 'lack of proper supervision in the classroom' against Birmingham City Council was dismissed early on.[53] However, Hutchison LJ points out that 'There was evidence which the judge does not say he rejects and which he may, since it was an admission against interest, be taken to have accepted, that ruler fencing was commonplace',[54] so this was a case somewhat near the line on a finding against the teacher and the local education authority. The Court of Appeal in *Kearn-Price v Kent County Council*,[55] the case of a football in the eye in the playground in 2002 which we

---

[47] At 924.
[48] (1966) 115 CLR 199.
[49] Per Windeyer J at first instance in *McHale v Watson* (1964) 111 CLR 384 at para 22.
[50] At 234 in *McHale*, and at 924 in *Mullins*.
[51] (1954) 2 DLR 232.
[52] *Mullins* at 928, quoting *McHale* at 216.
[53] At 921.
[54] At 926.
[55] [2002] All ER (D) 440.

have examined, clearly found that in the particular circumstances of that school, this line had been crossed, and there was a duty of care owed.

By contrast, David Berry, who was aged 16 and had a 'lifelong fear of water', was clearly beyond any supervisory responsibility of his school at the precise moment of his death. He was thrown from a bridge 'as a prank' by two classmates when celebrating the end of a GCSE French exam at a riverside picnic. The two culprits from Sturminster Newton High School were jointly charged with manslaughter at Bournemouth Crown Court. The prosecution claimed that the boys had been drinking since completing the exam, having stolen some lager from a shop, and flung their non-swimmer victim into the River Stour; the court was told that in police interviews the two boys said it had been a 'bit of horseplay'.[56] Mackinnon J was also told by one of the defendants at the trial that they had been 'mucking about', but when their victim had pleaded with them that he could not swim as he 'clung desperately to the railings of the bridge' they 'prised his fingers away and lifted him over the railings, chanting "Berry needs a swim".' One defendant pleaded guilty, and was given credit because of this with a sentence of eight months, while his co-defendant found guilty by the jury was sentenced to eighteen months.[57] Nevertheless the judge rejected claims of horseplay, saying the dangers were 'obvious' and that both defendants knew it was 'serious risk-taking with the life of an innocent 16-year-old which should never have happened'. After family allegations that the victim, who had special needs, was repeatedly bullied at school, the Headteacher denied that the victim, 'a quietly determined lad' had ever been subjected to this: 'We are confident that David did not experience bullying from other students'.[58]

Volenti or contributory negligence for 'self-evident' or 'obvious' risks

Where a visitor to premises knowingly exposes himself to a risk, an occupier may raise the defence of *volenti*, and this defence also applies more widely to those who have 'assumed a risk' in any activity. In *Simms v Leigh Rugby Football Club* Wrangham J had to deal with the broken leg of a teacher playing rugby league, who had just scored a try but was at the same time subjected to a tackle which threw him against a concrete wall; this barrier was a distance of seven foot three inches away, complying with the stipulation in the rules of rugby league for a distance of seven foot from the touchline. The judge noted that in rugby league 'violent tackling is legitimate and frequent' and held that the player was *volenti* to the risk of 'misadventure' in the tackle, which was a possible cause, or *volenti* to

---

[56] 'Pupil, 16, died when "thrown in river for a post-exam prank",' *The Times* (24 February 2005).
[57] 'Sentences for drowning son an insult, says father: teenagers get eight and 18 months for horseplay that ended in tragedy', *The Guardian* (12 March 2005).
[58] 'What message has the judge sent when the thugs who killed my son will be free in months?', *Daily Mail* (12 March 2005).

collision with the concrete barrier which may have been the alternative cause.[59] The maxim therefore applied because the participant knew the risks, but also willingly accepted them. Since 1945 when contributory negligence was changed from being an absolute defence to one of proportionality between the parties, it is considered by many commentators, as indicated in *Clerk and Lindsell*, that it is 'much more likely that the conduct of the visitor on premises will be dealt with as contributory negligence, resulting in a reduction of his damages, and not as a voluntary assumption of risk amounting to a complete answer to a claim'.[60] However, *Simms v Leigh Rugby Football Club* is a classic illustration of a voluntary assumption of known risks, and perhaps quite an unusual case; one can conjecture that the particular ferocity of rugby league was a factor, that the 'dual causality' might be another, but a major consideration was that even if the concrete barrier had been involved, it was indubitably beyond the stipulated seven feet range laid down by the sport. Given the 'licensed grievous bodily harm' aspect of rugby league it might also be thought that the maxim *de minimis non curat lex* (the law does not deal with trifles) might have been a consideration too.

More recently, the Court of Appeal in several cases has pioneered a concept of something that is 'self-evidently dangerous', when indicating that there is no duty to warn against a danger which is 'obvious'. This could apply in many outdoor activities when the courts might view warning notices as inappropriate or might judge them not to make any difference to the perception of hazards. Although safety notices, standard graphic signage and devices such as red flags are a feature of many such activities across the world, and would be readily understood by most people of any background, this concept of 'self-evidently dangerous' indicates that there are circumstances when such a notification would be superfluous, usually because the terrain is vast or because the context is so observably dangerous. The concept is a perhaps somewhat slippery term of art, and its parameters are not yet clear, but it relates to both *volenti* and contributory negligence. One illustration of its use was in *Cotton v Derbyshire Dales DC*,[61] in a classic area for hill walking, where a rambler fell over a cliff edge on an Easter Monday and was severely injured. There was nothing particular about this cliff, and the court held that the owner of the path was under no duty to put up a notice warning of the dangers, because these were 'obvious'. Owen J, who visited the location at High Tor, above Matlock, had found that the ground was 'very steep and dangerous', but that it was the claimant who had failed to exercise the 'great caution that was required', walking with a group of friends 'in boisterous spirits' after drinking four pints of beer. The weather that year was possibly the best in the decade.[62] Henry LJ in the Court of Appeal quoted with approval the dictum of Lord

---

[59] [1969] 2 All ER 923.
[60] Clerk & Lindsell on *Torts* para 13-27 commenting on the impact of the Law Reform (Contributory Negligence) Act 1945.
[61] *The Times* (20 June 1994).
[62] 'Easter it never rains but it pours' (*Daily Mail*, 10 April 1993): 'during the Easters of 1884 and 1987, we basked under blue skies and temperatures passed the 70F mark.'

Shaw of Dunfermline in *Glasgow Corporation v Taylor* that 'in grounds open to the public as of right, the duty ... of making them reasonably safe does not include an obligation of protection against dangers which are themselves obvious',[63] so that would appear to be the foundation of this concept. However, in the *Taylor* case the determining factors were that there was an 'allurement' of belladonna berries for a young child in the botanical gardens, and this 'deadly nightshade' was not properly fenced off or warned about in the circumstances of children. By contrast no such exceptional danger existed in *Cotton* for a 26-year-old rambler in the Dales, although the lack of a proper path, scree sliding away on a steep slope, and cliffs all around should instantly have alerted him to the need for 'exercising great caution'. A warning notice would therefore have been inessential to an assessment of risk by the rambler, and could also have been seen as obtrusive clutter in an area of outstanding natural beauty. Henry LJ concluded that 'Once it was appreciated that there was no path, the danger of proceeding down a steep gradient where the footing was insecure and unstable and where you could not see what was over the brow, would have been obvious'.[64]

May LJ makes a similar point too in *Darby v National Trust*, when the Court of Appeal overturned a large award to a widow, who had lost her husband in one of a set of lakes at Hardwick Hall. While swimming with his family, Kevin Darby, aged 44 and a swimmer there since childhood, 'got into trouble and drowned'.[65] The pond had no characteristics making it more dangerous than any other pond, but the National Trust was extremely concerned by the implications of a decision that it should have put up warning signs. The Trust is of course a charity, yet owns huge tracts of countryside, including thousands of ponds, lakes and other stretches of open water. In discussing swimming in such circumstances, May LJ found that there was no duty to warn against the dangers of drowning 'which were quite obvious to any adult', but also that 'It cannot be the duty of the owner of every stretch of coastline to have notices warning of the dangers of swimming in the sea. If it were so, the coast would have to be littered with notices in places other than those where there are known to be special dangers which are not obvious. The same would apply to all inland lakes and reservoirs.'[66] The Country Landowners' Association welcomed this 'logical' conclusion, stating that 'access to the countryside ...must [be] access at their own risk. Otherwise the countryside would be covered with signposts saying "Don't do this" and "Don't do that".'[67]

---

[63] [1922] 1 AC 44, 60.

[64] *Cotton v Derbyshire Dales District Council* (The Times, 20 June 1994).

[65] Per Swinton Thomas LJ at the application to appeal, *Darby v National Trust* (CA transcript 13 July 2000). Mrs Assistant Recorder Wilson in the Derby County Court gave judgment for the claimant in the sum of £114,194.

[66] [2001] EWCA Civ 189, [2001] PIQR P372 (29 January 2001) [27].

[67] 'Widow loses £114,000 award for pond death: husband should have known risk in swimming, say judges', *Daily Telegraph* (30 January 2001). Simon Wright, Mrs Darby's solicitor, said after the Court of Appeal hearing: 'this is a devastating blow to the widow. They are a working family who saw their father drown. This court has overturned the court of first

Darby v National Trust relied on another case in the Court of Appeal, where they had extended the 'obvious' analysis of *Cotton*. That was the case of *Staples v West Dorset District Council*,[68] where the claimant, aged 33, had fractured his left hip after slipping on algae at the Cobb, a stone sea wall at Lyme Regis. Auld J found that the Council was at fault, although he adjudged that the claimant was 40 per cent contributorily negligent. However, the Court of Appeal found that there was no warning needed for this 'obvious danger', although the Council had in fact placed a warning sign immediately after this incident. Described by the Court of Appeal as an 'experienced visitor' (he had previously done some sea fishing), Mr Staples was only doing what 'countless predecessors' had done and was 'well able to evaluate the danger'. Furthermore, 'even if a warning notice had been displayed the probability was that he would not have been affected by it.' With respect, that seems a conjecture too far, and unnecessary once the case had been decided on the basis that the claimant 'saw the algae and knew that it might well be slippery'; for instance Kennedy LJ indicated that 'to crouch down sideways on, and so close, to the edge to take photographs, without first checking the surface beneath him, was, in my view, negligent and a substantial co-operating cause of his fall'. But he also seems to view the notice posted by the Council after the accident as otiose; in that it warned users that the wall was slippery 'particularly when wet', and that this 'would not have told the plaintiff anything that he did not know'. But then many signs do that, and yet they could hardly be described as useless. Indeed, such signage may well confirm the common sense and good judgment of the visitor, and, if in 'boisterous company', may give them a helpful exit line when egged on to do something risky. The finding that the claimant 'was a visitor who needed no warning' appears to be a finding that he was certainly very particularly 'experienced', which is a robust view of an appellate court who did not see him in the witness box. This might also be to suppose that the Council was 'wrong' to put up a sign after the event, but surely that addition to the landscape was a helpful precaution to make sure that others, less experienced, did not follow on to disaster? May LJ used this line of reasoning in *Staples v West Dorset* to state in *Darby v National Trust* that 'One or more notices saying "Danger No Swimming" would have told Mr Darby no more than he already knew'. 'Obvious' has the connotation of 'realized at the first glance' (OED), and yet although Mr Darby was a frequent swimmer in the pond and Mr Cotton was allegedly an 'experienced visitor', both trial judges had found primary liability, so the dangers were not so 'obvious' to some members of the judiciary. It was the Court of Appeal on both occasions who then ruled that the dangers were so 'obvious' as to preclude liability, and that they were akin to the cliff edge in *Cotton v Derbyshire Dales*.

---

instance and expert evidence that the pond was wholly unsuitable for swimming. It will be very difficult for the children to understand what this court has decided today'; 'Widow loses £114,000 payout for husband's drowning', *The Times* (30 January 2001). See also 'Widow loses drowning damages' *Derby Evening Telegraph* (30 January 2001).

[68] *The Times* (28 April 1995), 93 LGR 536.

As well as the inherent difficulty of such a concept, it is clear that, in the past, when the term 'obvious danger' was used in employers' liability, that was not necessarily a reason to negate all liability. For example in *Jolliffe v Townsend Bros. Ferries*[69] Atkinson J held that 'obviously it would be a dangerous thing for anyone to try to descend that gangway until it had been made fast', but when the purser on just his eighth cross-channel voyage fell off the gangway when it had not been secured, even when admitting that he was 'in a tremendous hurry' to get to a bank before closing time and was 'extremely impatient', primary liability was found, but with a reduction of 60 per cent for contributory negligence. One firm indicator in the employers' liability cases is the bedrock of a 'common standard', often derived from statute, and in particular the Health and Safety at Work Act 1974. Such a view seems not yet welcome in the courts in other arenas, and indeed in the outdoor swimming cases, where one possibility in a case like *Darby* might be to look to advice from a national body such as the Royal Society for the Prevention of Accidents, there is actually a rather waspish comment. While the assistant recorder at first instance had accepted evidence from Rebecca Kirkwood, a Water and Leisure Safety Consultant for RoSPA, on appeal it was noted that 'it was for the court, not Miss Kirkwood... to determine whether there was a breach of the Occupiers' Liability Act duty in this case'.[70] RoSPA does not advocate automatic fencing of all deep water, suggesting that 'this would be impracticable, aesthetically damaging and ineffective in terms of denying access to determined swimmers. But as a minimum 'No Swimming' notices should be installed. Particular attention should be given to places where open water swimming is known to happen'.[71] That seems sensible and balanced advice, against the background of so many tragic open water drownings each year. Further cases will perhaps elucidate the full meaning of this concept of 'obvious danger', but open water must at present be considered in that category.

Volenti per se

It is not always possible from the law report or even the wider literature to unravel a strategic or tactical decision by the claimant's advisers. One such mystery was elucidated in a famous extra-judicial statement by Lord Asquith as to why he did not consider the defence of contributory negligence, rather than the *volenti* defence he rejected in *Dann v Hamilton*;[72] the answer was that the judge had tried unsuccessfully to persuade counsel to plead contributory negligence, but at the time this of course would have been a complete defence too.[73] In that case a

---

[69] [1965] 2 Lloyd's Reports 19.

[70] *Darby* para [26].

[71] At para [10].

[72] [1939] 1 All ER 59.

[73] *Law Quarterly Review* (1953) vol. 69, at 317, which dealt with criticisms, which 'were to the effect that even if the *volenti* doctrine did not apply, there was here a cast iron defence on the ground of contributory negligence. I have since had the pleadings and my notes exhumed,

passenger took a lift with the driver of a car who was obviously under the influence, to see the Coronation decorations in 1937; Asquith J held that the maxim *volenti non fit injuria* had no application to the case and he gave judgment in favour of the injured passenger. The position on travelling with a drunk driver has changed radically since then, as section 149 of the Road Traffic Act 1972[74] prevents the defence of *volenti* whatever the 'antecedent agreement' between passenger and driver. Although since 1945 it would appear that *volenti* has dwindled somewhat in significance in all areas, it is by no means dead. As a historical matter, Lord Denning indicated in *Nettleship v Weston* that

> In former times this defence was used almost as an alternative defence to contributory negligence. Either defence defeated the action. Now that contributory negligence is not a complete defence, but only a ground for reducing the damages, the defence of *volenti non fit injuria* has been closely considered, and, in consequence, it has been severely limited.[75]

Lord Denning also noted that the doctrine had been 'so severely curtailed that in the view of Diplock LJ 'the maxim, in the absence of express contract, has no application to negligence'.[76]

The translation of the full phrase *volenti non fit injuria* is 'No injury is done to one who consents', but this needs to be accompanied by the warning from *Clerk & Lindsell* that 'the maxim cannot be taken literally, and like other Latin maxims is apt to mislead. It represents the self-evident axiom that one who consents to injury cannot be heard to complain of it thereafter'.[77] The essence of the *volenti* defence is therefore that the claimant is fully aware of the risk and has willingly accepted it. The modern cases are of 'near-suicidal' behaviour. For example, in *Ratcliff v McConnell*,[78] a trespasser who intentionally crossed over barricades and locked gates must be taken to assume the full 'normal' risks. Lord Hoffmann indicates approval for *Ratcliff v McConnell* in *Tomlinson v Congleton BC*, although he makes an important distinction: Mr Tomlinson's 'dive' off the beach at Congleton was a 'relatively minor act of carelessness. It came nowhere near the stupidity of Luke Ratcliff'.[79] Luke Ratcliff, aged 19, was an agriculture student, who together with two friends climbed over a locked gate at night and dived into the shallow end of the College swimming pool. They had been drinking. The claimant suffered tetraplegia, and although at first instance he succeeded, subject to 40 per cent reduction for contributory negligence, the Court of Appeal came to a view that his admissions made it impossible for him to

---

and they very clearly confirm my recollection that contributory negligence was not pleaded. Not merely so, but my notes show that I encouraged counsel for the defence to ask for leave to amend by adding this plea, but he would not be drawn: why, I have no idea.'

[74] Now section 149 RTA 1988.

[75] *Nettleship v Weston* [1971] 3 All ER 581 at 587.

[76] Citing Diplock LJ in *Wooldridge v Sumner* [1962] 2 All ER 978 at 990.

[77] *Clerk & Lindsell Torts* (London: Sweet & Maxwell, 16th edition 1989) 1-159.

[78] [1999] 1 WLR 670.

[79] At 1140.

succeed. Stuart-Smith LJ noted that the claimant had intended to make a shallow dive, knowing that it was necessary to make sure that there was enough water available before diving, and he himself had indicated in the witness box that he must have dived deeper than he had intended; 'a risk of which any adult would be aware and which the plaintiff, as one would expect, admitted that he was aware'.[80] In any event Mr Ratcliff had ignored the prohibition on access and had crossed over barriers, which he knew would make him a trespasser. In those circumstances he was aware of the risk and had willingly accepted it.

There are many such 'student expedition' cases in the USA, and perhaps one of the most comprehensive demonstrations of an 'assumption of risk' is the Federal case of *Gard v US*,[81] where three Californian students, returning home from a trip to Nevada, saw the remains of an old mine approximately 200 yards from the highway. Descending a horizontal shaft with one flashlight between them on an illicit exploration, the claimant fell into a vertical shaft and became tetraplegic. There was of course no liability found for this suicidal excursion. Lord Phillips in *Donoghue v Folkestone Properties* also cites *Ratcliff v McConnell* with approval, along with an unreported Court of Appeal case of *White v The Council of the City and District of St Albans*, decided very shortly after the Occupiers' Liability Act 1984 came into force; at about midnight in November of that year, a short cut to the multi-storey car park on a rainy night caused John White to fall through a gap and over the edge. There was a perfectly satisfactory, and lawful route, for visitors and there was therefore no reason for him to trespass in this way, other than through a voluntary assumption of risk.[82]

Most *volenti* cases are of intentional and wilful conduct, but there is a related category of reckless behaviour in the cases, often related to intoxicants. For example, the Court of Appeal in *Whyte v Redland Aggregates Ltd*[83] had to deal with the paraplegia of Karl Whyte, aged 21, when he hit his head diving into a disused gravel pit in Basildon in 1988. Because of knowledge by the defendants that this 'swimhole' was regularly used, it was held by French J that there was an 'implied licence' to swim there, and therefore the claimant was to be judged as a visitor and not as a trespasser. However, Hirst LJ indicated that the claimant had made 'a racing dive from a standing position to a depth of three to four feet into the deep water and hit his head on an obstruction on the floor of the pit', which he alleged to be a concealed danger, but this was reckless in the circumstances, and the claimant had his action dismissed by both the trial judge and the Court of Appeal. A similar kind of case was *Bartrum v Hepworth Minerals and Chemicals Ltd*,[84] where again there was a semi-authorized access. Turner J found there was a history of prior injuries, and that Mr Bartrum, aged 36, who had been a regular 'visitor in the non technical sense' for 20 years, was well aware of the dangers. He had claimed that with a 'No Diving' sign 'he definitely would not have dived

---

[80] At 681.

[81] 420 F. Sup 300 (1976), affirmed 594 F. 2d 1230 (1979).

[82] *The Times* (12 March 1990).

[83] *The Times*, 27 November 1997. See also the mention in [1998] CL 485.

[84] (QBD transcript 29 October 1999), and noted by Ward LJ in *Tomlinson* (CA) [15].

in the area where the sign was located', but this was scarcely a serious argument. One factor in many of these 'reckless' cases is the presence of drink or drugs. Alcohol was a factor in *Donoghue v Folkestone Properties Ltd* (five pints), *Cotton v Derbyshire Dales DC* (four pints), *McEwan v Eden's Saunasium* ('between six and eight pints that day'), *Harrison v Thanet District Council* (sharing a bottle of beer with a friend, but rejected as amounting to contributory negligence), and a case referred to in *Tomlinson v Congleton BC* where another man had been 'swimming in lake, after drinking, and got into difficulty'. Mr Bartrum told Turner J that he was 'no longer affected by a small quantity of amphetamine which he had injected that morning. The effect had long since worn off'. Intoxication was also a factor in *Munro v Porthkerry Park Holiday Estates Ltd.*,[85] where Beldam J had to deal with two intoxicated 18 year olds ordered out of a cliff-top social club at a seaside leisure camp. Climbing over a chain-link fence, which was described as 'adequate to protect anyone from danger', they fell to their deaths. Beldam J described the claimant as 'merely merry, boisterous or devil-may-care', and not so drunk as to be 'incapable of taking care for his own safety'. These points again raise the complex inter-relationship on whether a duty of care is owed to someone who is so obviously 'the author of their own misfortune' or whether *volenti* is the appropriate defence when primary liability is established.

Some leading cases on *volenti* are perhaps illustrative of different judicial approaches: in *ICI v Shatwell*, when a shot-firer in a quarry was injured on a premature detonation, Elwes J found for him, considering that the defence of *volenti* was not available to defeat a claim founded on breach of statutory duty, but reduced the agreed damages by 50 per cent. However, Lord Reid in the House of Lords noted that, when asked why he did not wait ten minutes for further wire to be brought by an assistant, so that those involved could retreat the prescribed distance and get behind a shelter, George Shatwell said his 'only excuse was that he could not be bothered to wait'.[86] Their Lordships had no difficulty in deciding that, where the plaintiff had not only defied his employer's express instructions, but also contravened a statutory requirement on explosives, he was to be judged to have assumed the full risk and should be held *volenti*. This might be compared with another near-suicidal case, *O'Reilly v National Rail and Tramway Applicances*, where Mr O'Reilly's suggestion to a young apprentice was that he should 'have a go' with a sledgehammer when confronted with a live shell left over from the war. That case actually turned on the related issue of vicarious liability, with Nield J holding that the claimant was on a 'frolic of his own' outside the course of employment.[87] Another classic of stupidity was *Morris v Murray*[88] where the Court of Appeal had to deal with some roistering friends on a pub crawl, followed by a 'drunken escapade heavily fraught with danger' in a light aircraft, on a day when flying lessons had been cancelled because of poor

---

[85] *The Times* (9 March 1984).
[86] Per Lord Reid in *Imperial Chemical Industries Ltd v Shatwell* [1964] 2 All ER 999.
[87] [1966] 1 All ER 499.
[88] [1990] 3 All ER 801.

weather conditions. The flight was 'short and chaotic' and the inevitable disaster occurred. The judge at first instance, Judge Rice, adopted the merciful course of determining 50 per cent contributory negligence, but the Court of Appeal overturned that decision and said that the passenger was *volenti*; he had known that the pilot was drunk, and indeed Mr Murray had a blood alcohol content equivalent to 17 whiskies, three times the limit permitted for a car driver.[89]

Volenti is very often pleaded in personal injury claims, but rarely in the modern era has it been relied on in court decisions except in these menacingly hazardous circumstances of gross intoxication or explosives. Even when dangers are clear, or might be considered by some as 'obvious', a judge may feel that it is not appropriate as a defence when viewed in the context of safety measures and other considerations. For example, in *Wattleworth v Goodwood Road Racing Co*[90] Davis J had to deal with a driver who was killed on the racing circuit at Goodwood. He found that there was no breach of a duty of care, and that causation was not made out, but for the sake of completeness he also indicated that he would have rejected a *volenti* defence, in that a driver 'must be taken to have consented to the risks inherently involved in motor car racing, and I am sure that he did so. But that would have been on the basis that due steps would have been taken to see that the circuit (including the crash barriers) was reasonably safe'.

Very occasionally a case will go the other way on appeal, by imposing contributory negligence when at first instance it has been held there was no claim; in *Craven v Riches*[91] the claimant broke his neck while riding his motorcycle on the Knockhill Racing Circuit near Dunfermline at 125mph and was rendered quadriplegic. Both the judge at first instance and the Court of Appeal agreed that *volenti* was inappropriate as, in the words of Sedley LJ 'What the appellant volunteered to risk was not the kind of thing that happened', which was the 'poor arrangements' of mixing slower with faster riders: Judge Altman found that situation not to be a causative feature of the crash which occurred and held there was no liability, but the Court of Appeal found on the evidence that this factor was an operative cause, although they then reduced the damages by two-thirds 'to reflect the measure of his own responsibility for them'.

Contributory negligence

The Law Reform (Contributory Negligence) Act 1945 allowed a reduction of damages as the court thinks 'just and equitable' in the light of the victim's share of responsibility. As we have seen, until that Act contributory negligence had been an absolute defence. Even now, although perhaps only in theory, contribution can be assessed at 100 per cent;[92] indeed, that viewpoint has been

---

[89] At 803.
[90] [2004] EWHC 140.
[91] [2001] EWCA CIV 375.
[92] *Jayes v IMI (Kynoch) Limited* [1985] ICR 155.

doubted as 'jurisprudentially correct',[93] roundly criticized in the leading practitioners' manual *Munkman on Employers' Liability*,[94] and in the generality of tort cases it is unlikely as well as untenable. As Sedley LJ pointed out in *Anderson v Newham College of Further Education*,[95] 'If there is liability, contributory negligence can reduce its monetary quantification, but it cannot legally or logically nullify it' and concluded that the concept of 100 per cent contributory negligence in a case involving breach of statutory duty was misconceived. An employee had tripped over the frame of a whiteboard in a classroom, which had not been properly stored; at first instance Judge Rich found 90 per cent contributory negligence, which is of a very high order, and on appeal the defendants argued for 100 per cent, which led not only to Sedley LJ's remarks, but a finding that 'the only fair apportionment of liability by reason of contributory negligence was 50/50'. That is of course a very common view in the cases.

In one of the outdoor 'plunging' cases, *Donoghue v Folkestone Properties Ltd*, Judge Bowers at first instance found 75 per cent contributory negligence, although the Court of Appeal then determined that there was an absence of a duty of care altogether in the circumstances of a midnight escapade.[96] This illustrates neatly that very divergent judicial viewpoints are taken on the identical facts. Although the amount of reduction is always a matter for judicial discretion, it can be seen in several of the cases that a 50 per cent 'Solomon's judgment' is often utilized. In certain other areas the reduction has become routinized, as in the car seat belt decision of *Froom v Butcher*,[97] in 1975: Lord Denning indicated a 'tariff' of reductions, by 15 per cent when injuries might have been less severe if a seat belt had been worn; and by 25 per cent if 'damage would have been prevented altogether'. A similar reduction of 15 per cent applies on a failure to wear a motor-cycle helmet, following the case of *O'Connell v Jackson* in 1971.[98] Often however a court has simply to look at the circumstances of the individual case, and come to what must inevitably be a subjective view on the level of

---

[93] Per Sir Anthony Evans in *Billington v Maguire* (Transcript 9 February 2001); see also the view of the Home Office that 'a finding of 100 per cent contributory negligence could not be appropriate', per Mance LJ in *Home Office v Lowles* [2004] EWCA Civ 985 at para 17; '100 per cent contributory negligence is a contradiction in terms', per Evans-Lombe in *Barings plc (in liquidation) and another v Coopers & Lybrand* [2003] EWHC 1319 (Ch) at para 837; 'Nor do I find it necessary to decide whether in principle a finding of 100 per cent contributory negligence is possible, or whether such a finding could be made in this case', per Alan Boyle QC in *Manolakaki v Constantinides* [2003] EWHC 401 at para 82.

[94] (1990) 11th edition at 606: '*Jayes v IMI (Kynoch) Ltd* is an unfortunate decision which seems to have been made *per incuriam*'.

[95] [2002] EWCA Civ 505 at para 18.

[96] [2003] 3 All ER 1101.

[97] *Froom and others v Butcher* [1975] 3 All ER 520.

[98] [1972] 1 QB 270, [1971] 3 All ER 129, [1971] 3 WLR 463, 2 Lloyd's Rep 354, [1972] RTR 51. See on the inappropriate application of these standards to cycle helmets; Julian Fulbrook, 'Cycle Helmets and Contributory Negligence', *Journal of Personal Injury Law* (issue 3, September 2004) pp 171-191.

misbehaviour. In *Uddin v Associated Portland Cement Manufacturers, Ltd*[99] the Court of Appeal had to consider the actions of a worker who went into part of the premises forbidden to him. He had been stalking a pigeon, and the judge commented that 'Whatever were his designs … they were not actuated by benevolence'. In 'grabbing' the pigeon he had become 'inexorably involved' in the machinery, losing an arm. Lord Pearce sitting in the Court of Appeal considered that employers would be very fortunate 'only to employ persons who are never stupid, careless, unreasonable or disobedient, and who never have moments of clumsiness, forgetfulness or aberration. But a cross-section of humanity does not present that picture'.[100] The Court of Appeal then supported a finding of 80 per cent contributory negligence by McNair J, and indicated that although they might have assessed this at an even higher amount, they had to remind themselves that they had 'not had the advantage of seeing and hearing the witnesses called on either side'.[101] In *Slater v Clay Cross Co. Ltd*[102] the plaintiff, who was either an invitee or a licensee, was doing something that might also be classed under Lord Pearce's *dictum* as 'stupid, careless, and unreasonable'. She was taking a short cut through a tunnel and lost a leg when she was run over by a narrow gauge train. Nevertheless this tunnel was habitually used as a short cut, and although she took a risk, Denning LJ held that 'she did not take the risk of negligence by the driver' who did not blow the whistle and went too fast. Her knowledge of the danger was a factor in contributory negligence, but the level of 40 per cent contribution found by Ashworth J was upheld. As we have seen in *Ratcliff v McConnell*[103] an initial finding that a student who climbed over a locked gate at night and dived into the shallow end of the College swimming pool was subject to a similar 40 per cent reduction for contributory negligence, but in that case the initial finding was overturned by the Court of Appeal who found *volenti* as a complete defence.

Just as with an adjustable standard of care for children, based on their age and maturity, so too with contributory negligence the court must have regard to such mitigating factors. In *Gough v Thorne*[104] a girl aged thirteen was waiting to cross the road, going with her two brothers to a swimming pool in Chelsea. A lorry driver stopped and beckoned them across, but as Elizabeth Gough crossed, a 'bubble car' drove through a small gap and knocked her down. McKenna J found that the driver was negligent in going too fast and not keeping a proper lookout, but judged the plaintiff to have been one-thirds contributorily negligent. On appeal, Lord Denning took a paternalistic but merciful view, suggesting that 'a very young child cannot be guilty of contributory negligence' and that while due caution might be 'reasonably expected of a grown-up person with a fully developed road sense', this should not be demanded by a 'child of 13½'. In another case entirely,

[99] [1965] 2 All ER 213.
[100] Ibid.
[101] Per Willmer LJ.
[102] [1956] 2 All ER 625.
[103] [1999] 1 WLR 670.
[104] *Gough v Thorne* [1966] 3 All ER 398.

although with an identical surname, Matthew Gough, aged eight, had been severely injured when he slid down the banister at his school. Although Judge Grenfell determined that in the circumstances there was no liability, he indicated that if such had been found he would also have held that there should be 'a substantial percentage of contributory negligence, even against an 8-year-old, simply because clearly he knew there was serious danger involved in doing what he did'. And the judge indicated that if an adult had slid down the banister then he would 'undoubtedly have been the sole cause of his injury'.[105] The scale from zero reduction for a 'young child' up to full responsibility as an adult aged 18 is inevitably somewhat arbitrary, and will inevitably depend on the surrounding circumstances and the actual maturity of the individual.

Once there has been an assessment of the percentage for contributory negligence, it should be only in 'exceptional circumstances' that an appellate court will interfere. Lord Wright indicated that 'it would require a very strong case to justify any such review of or interference with this matter of apportionment where the same view is taken of the law and the facts',[106] but as we have seen, this review is not quite as rare as it might be assumed. Indeed, such a review of contributory negligence would also not of course prevent an appellate court taking an entirely contrary view on the primary issue of liability, which would then eradicate any contributory fault; in *Jolley v Sutton London Borough Council* the Court of Appeal reversed the trial judge's determination of 25 per cent contributory negligence, only themselves to be reversed by the House of Lords. Lord Steyn commented somewhat cuttingly that they would restore the original 'wise decision'.[107] Several other cases we have considered also failed completely on appeal by reason of an absence of liability, when initially a trial judge had indicated liability but with a reduction for contributory negligence; for example, *Donoghue v Folkestone Properties Ltd* (75 per cent);[108] *Tomlinson v Congleton Borough Council* (66 per cent in the Court of Appeal);[109] *ICI v Shatwell* (50 per cent);[110] *Morris v Murray* (50 per cent);[111] *Mullin v Richards* (50 per cent);[112] *Blake v Galloway* (50 per cent);[113] *Ratcliff v McConnell* (40 per cent);[114] and *Staples v West Dorset District Council* (40 per cent).[115]

A classic illustration when a defence of contributory negligence will fail is when it is raised against a child, particularly when an adult could straightforwardly foresee the possibility of harm. In the Privy Council case of

---

[105] *Gough v Upshire Primary School* [2002] ELR 169 at para 25.
[106] *British Fame (Owners) v Macgregor (Owners) (The Macgregor)* [1943] AC 197 at p 201.
[107] [2000] 3 All ER 409 at 417.
[108] [2003] 3 All ER 1101.
[109] [2003] 3 All ER 1122.
[110] [1964] 2 All ER 999.
[111] [1991] 2 QB 6, [1990] 3 All ER 801, [1990] 2 WLR 195.
[112] [1998] 1 All ER 920.
[113] [2004] 3 All ER 315.
[114] [1999] 1 WLR 670.
[115] *The Times* (28 April 1995), 93 LGR 536.

Yachuk v Oliver Blais Co. Ltd.[116] a boy aged nine, accompanied by his brother aged seven, bought petrol in Canada. His purpose was to re-enact 'a Red Indian scene' they had seen at the cinema. The company employee had doubts as to the propriety of the sale, and before the two children were beyond recall, he raised the matter with the assistant manager, but there was no response. At first instance it was held that there was liability against the company for the almost inevitable burns, but this should be scaled down as the boy was '75 per cent responsible' for his own injuries. That finding of contributory negligence was overturned on appeal in Ontario, and that view was upheld by the Privy Council. It was therefore held that having given an explosive substance to a boy who had limited knowledge of the likelihood of an explosion and its possible effect, and the boy having done that which a child of his age might be expected to do, the defendants could not avail themselves of the defence of contributory negligence. Lord Du Parcq indicated that the 'attempt to attribute the disaster which happened solely to the acts of the infant plaintiff must fail' as a boy of that age would have 'no knowledge of the peculiarly dangerous quality of gasoline', and any adult would know that. This case can perhaps be viewed as one where the 'magnitude of risk' was very high and preventative steps would be immediately required by any adult to prevent the clearly foreseeable calamity. When children are involved this is a distinct possibility, but the approach probably also applies to an adult in certain circumstances, although not necessarily with complete absolution; in *Brannan v Airtours PLC*,[117] the Court of Appeal had to deal with injuries sustained when, on a package holiday in Tunisia, Alan Brennan climbed on to a table and came into contact with a revolving fan. An attraction of the trip was a 'party night' with dinner, cabaret, discotheque and unlimited free wine. A previous incident of a partygoer cutting their hand on the fan led the compère to warn against climbing on the tables, but three hours after this warning, and according to Auld LJ, when the claimant was 'merry but not drunk', he tried to his leave seat to go to the conveniences. So as not to disturb other guests the claimant climbed over the table and came into contact with the fan. An assessment of 75 per cent contributory negligence was said to be 'outside the bounds of his proper margin of appreciation and was too high a proportion of responsibility and blameworthiness', and the Court of Appeal substituted 50 per cent. Auld LJ indicated that 'it was plainly foreseeable that party-goers might drink a bit too much and lose some of their normal inhibitions and close attention to their own safety'.

A final point to consider is when there is a combination of adverse factors. In *Tait v British Railways Board*,[118] a boy aged 16 was waving out of a railway carriage window as it left West Norwood station; the back of his head struck a bridge and he was very severely injured. Glidewell J reviewed in detail the standard railway clearances of 2 foot 4 inches specified, and found that out of ten accidents nationally in 1976, four occurred at this very location, so the defendants

---

[116] [1949] 2 All ER 150.
[117] *The Times*, 1 Feb 1999.
[118] QBD transcript 28 July 1982.

were on notice of the dangers caused by rebuilding the bridge. On the contention of a heavy reduction for contributory negligence he found that Christopher Tait was 'halfway between childhood and adulthood', but that he had special needs; this meant he could neither 'read the warning sign above the window so he was not blameworthy in that respect at all', but if he did hear his friend's warning shout 'his mental mechanism transmitted that message so slowly that by the time it had resulted in his muscles acting to pull himself back into the carriage it was too late'. Damages were therefore reduced by 25 per cent. In outdoor activities it is therefore important to take into account the 'attention deficit' of participants, particularly children and those with special needs.

In summary, the finding of a percentage reduction is very much in the personal discretion of the trial judge and therefore very much a matter of subjective assessment. As yet no obvious tariffs have developed in cases beyond seat belts and crash helmets, but it is also clear that, whatever the difficulties of reversing such a finding, many cases on appeal can produce a different perspective on both primary liability and what should be the appropriate percentage apportionment of blame.

PART III
PRACTICAL APPLICATIONS

Chapter 8

Risk and the Outdoors

Is *anything* risk free? The literature and the legal cases on outdoor activities demonstrate that injuries can occur in so many ways, sometimes even in a bizarre combination of freakish circumstances. But are there any common themes which could allow preventative steps to be taken? And in particular what should the 'reasonable person', or in many instances the reasonable teacher or reasonable expedition leader, do to avert harm? The answer is assuredly that there *are* appropriate steps to take, because lessons have been learned.

Perhaps the most obvious is that travelling to the activity is invariably much more dangerous than the organized activity itself. All forms of transport, and particularly the use of minibuses, can be considerably more hazardous than many outdoor activities. At the outset therefore of most outdoor activities, providers, schools and voluntary organizations will be judged on whether they are exhibiting 'reasonableness' on routine matters such as road fund tax, insurance, appropriate level of driver certification, seat restraints, roadworthiness, adequate rest for drivers and appropriate routes. We have seen in the cases the dire consequences of doing otherwise. These standard issues in transport liability are therefore a vital prerequisite. Indeed some of the lessons of the transport cases transfer across to motorized sport vehicles when used off-road, or on snow or on water. Following the death of a jet-skier in 2003, after a collision between two such specialist boats on a Club lake near Ripon (Jet Ski is a Kawasaki trade mark of a 'personal watercraft' capable of speeds up to 80mph), a coroner indicated that this had resulted in a 'blunt-force impact normally associated with road crash victims'.[1]

Risk assessment

Myths abound on the actual dangers to be encountered in outdoor activities, so it is important to unravel the cases and look in detail at their factual circumstances. The fundamental approach in the modern era has been to make a risk assessment. This is a process which can be very informal, or can be formalized, often in writing, and at some levels can become very technical, often unnecessarily so.[2] As a basic tool of guarding against hazards, risk assessment has had a lengthy history across many fields, in such varied areas as medicine, insurance and

---

[1] 'Jet-skier killed after accident on club's lake', *Northern Echo* (4 September 2003).

[2] See David Wright and John Copas, Chapter Two on 'Prediction Scores for Risk Assessment', in Robert Baldwin (ed) *Law and Uncertainty: Risks and Legal Processes* (London: Kluwer, 1997) 21-28.

finance, but gathered impetus after the Health and Safety at Work etc Act 1974, when it entered common parlance. Although that Act principally concerns the workplace, the 'Five Steps' approach of the Health and Safety Executive has been widely adopted in outdoor activities, as in so many other walks of life: 'a risk assessment is nothing more than a careful examination of what, in your work, could cause harm to people, so that you can weigh up whether you have taken enough precautions or should do more to prevent harm'.[3] Under section 3 of HSWA 1974, there are provisions to protect individuals who may be 'affected' by work activities, even though they are not employees of the business or undertaking concerned. Crucially, this encompasses visitors to premises, including members of the public and their children, but it also takes in under the principle of vicarious liability anyone affected by an employee's actions.[4]

As a legal requirement, the aim of a risk assessment is 'to make sure that no one gets hurt or becomes ill ... accidents and ill health can ruin lives'.[5] Step One is hazard identification. The HSE leaflet lists some common possibilities, starting with the ubiquitous 'slipping and tripping', and a requirement to 'pay particular attention to visitors' ('they may be vulnerable'). Step Two is to identify individuals at risk, and the HSE again notes that in considering 'who might be harmed, and how – Don't forget: young workers ... who may be a particular risk'.[6] Step Three is to consider the likelihood and severity of the risk, and whether precautions are adequate. In legal terms this third step is to engage with fundamental concepts such as 'foreseeability' and 'probability'. What more could 'reasonably' be done to reduce the risk? For example, when kayaking on the open sea, as at Lyme Bay, a straightforward assessment of the hazard of drowning (Step One) would indicate danger to all participants (Step Two), and the probability of it occurring in the prevailing conditions of March 1993, with so few precautions taken, as extremely high (Step Three). Step Four is to write down and itemize control measures. For example, the pre-eminent risk of drowning in novice kayaking is initially 'high risk', until itemizing the standard precautions to show the risk would be 'adequately controlled': a suitable location for first-timers on a pond, small lake or slow flowing river; supervision by appropriately qualified instructors; a standard swimming test well in advance of the activity to sort out any non-swimmers needing particular attention and to give some water confidence; and a mandatory wearing of an approved buoyancy aid. The risk of drowning then actually becomes very low. Such preventative measures long pre-date formal risk assessment, and can often be portrayed as 'common sense'. But these 'controls' are securely grounded in kayaking experience and are backed up by solid research. For example, in Canada, where canoeing and kayaking are national pastimes, about two-thirds of drowning victims were not wearing a 'personal flotation device', according to research from the Lifesaving Society of

---

[3] HSE, *Five Steps to Risk Assessment* (Sheffield: HSE Publications, latest version, 2004) 2.
[4] See generally DfES Guidance *Health And Safety: Responsibilities And Powers* (Organization & Management DfES/0803/2001, 2001).
[5] Loc cit.
[6] Ibid, 4 and 10.

Canada.[7] In the USA, around 750 people die each year in recreational boating incidents, and the US Coast Guard estimate that out of this total 86 per cent were not wearing personal flotation devices.[8] Research on canoe and kayak fatalities by the American Canoe Association shows that the key factors in paddler safety are 'wearing a properly fitted life jacket (personal flotation device), dressing suitably for the experience (critical when boating on cold water), avoiding alcohol, and selecting a waterway commensurate with one's experience'.[9] Apart from the alcohol, which in the USA was involved in at least a quarter of canoeing fatalities, all the other factors indicated in this detailed North American research were clearly present at Lyme Bay: inadequate buoyancy, paddling on the open sea in March in adverse conditions, without competent instructors, or indeed any support mechanisms. When factors such as 'operator inexperience' and 'hazardous water or weather conditions' are combined, then these account for 90 per cent of all kayaking fatalities in the USA.[10] Indeed, that study notes under 'Managing the Risks' that the 'basic way to improve paddler safety on the water is to respect the power of natural forces such as current, wind, waves, and weather'.[11] Any fleeting analysis of the hazards being faced at Lyme Bay, and the self-evidently inappropriate control measures would have shown that the risks were so gigantic that the proposed trip should have been cancelled forthwith.

Unfortunately, lessons are not always learned. An echo of Lyme Bay in March 1993 occurred in an Irish tragedy at Dunmore East in February 1995, when an adventure centre hired out six single kayaks and one double kayak to a group of young people ranging in age from 13 to 23. An instructor had allowed the group to go out without checking a weather forecast which had been broadcasting storm warnings all that day; the group were hit by a force 10 gale, with winds gusting at 60 to 70mph, and were swept out to sea. Rescue efforts were hampered by the conditions, and two young men, Ros Davies and Keith Crowley, died of hypothermia. Subsequently the parents of Ros Davies were awarded £90,000 in compensation in the Irish High Court against the Adventure Centre, who were also prosecuted and fined.[12] The final action is to review an activity (Step Five),

---

[7] Lifesaving Society of Canada, *National Drowning Report 2000* (Ottawa, 2000): 'About two-thirds of 1998 recreational powerboating (74%) and canoeing (61%) victims were not wearing a PFD when their fatal incident occurred, which usually involved capsizing, swamping or falling overboard ... Not surprisingly, drowning is identified by coroners and medical examiners as the primary cause of death in over 90% of preventable water-related deaths. Taking secondary contributing factors into consideration, coroners identify alcohol intoxication and not wearing a PFD as the next two most frequent contributing causes, followed by exposure to cold/hypothermia.'

[8] United States Coast Guard, *Boating Statistics – 2003* (2004) 7.

[9] Virgil Chambers, Foreword from the National Safe Boating Council in American Canoe Association, *Critical Judgment II: Understanding and Preventing Canoe and Kayak Fatalities 1996-2002* (Springfield, VA: ACA, 2004).

[10] Op cit, at 18.

[11] Op cit at 13.

[12] 'Justice for our son', *Daily Mirror*, (4 May 2000); 'His death was all so needless, so stupid', *Irish Examiner* (18 February 2005). Following a campaign by the parents, there were attempts

both 'ongoing' during the activity, but crucially after its completion. This is obviously a very sensible process to learn from personal experience, but also in learning from others by reading the literature and attending conferences. Hopefully the review process can learn from 'near-misses' and 'close calls' rather than catastrophe.

Although since the Health and Safety at Work Act 1974 the phrase 'risk assessment' has necessarily entered into every sphere of outdoor activity, it is essentially a traditional everyday method of looking for dangers and guarding against them. The Five Step procedure merely formalizes a methodical approach, and it has become the obvious yardstick for 'good practice'. Lady Hale of Richmond confirmed recently in the House of Lords that there is 'no civil liability for breach of the general obligation to assess risks' in the workplace,[13] but to demonstrate a complete lack of a risk assessment is a demonstration of incompetence, and a telling factor when considering breach of a duty of care, either under Common Law or by breach of the Health and Safety legislation or regulations. Inevitably the presence or absence of even a rudimentary risk assessment weighs very considerably in the balance of showing fault. As we have seen repeatedly in the cases, following 'good practice' significantly reduces potential legal liability. Recording risk assessments therefore helps immeasurably towards producing an evidential 'paper trail', which can be decisive in personal injury cases. However, what is important is the assessment rather than the paperwork. Lord Phillips of Worth Matravers, the Master of the Rolls, indicated extra-judicially that his daughter 'is a teacher and she tells me that before doing anything, even taking children across the road, they have to work out a risk analysis. This is all really disproportionate to the risk involved'.[14] No doubt this was meant semi-humorously, but the risks of crossing the road are a basic elementary point in 'Green Cross Code' education and are rather vital to learn for any child. It is suggested that it would be professionally improper *not* to make a risk assessment in such circumstances. However, if what Lord Phillips refers to as 'risk analysis' is not the assessment but voluminous paper, then this is a point about 'copious paper' which Marcus Bailie also makes with telling effect, using an analogy that 'No-one in their right mind would accept a risk assessment document for a proposed journey as an alternative to training the driver'.[15] Of course 'risk assessment is not a means of guaranteeing that accidents will not

---

in Ireland to pass an Activity Centres (Young Persons' Water Safety) Bill in 1999, *Parliamentary Debates (Dáil and Seanad)* 30 March 1999, and an Adventure Activities Standards Authority Bill in 2000, Parliamentary Debates (Dáil and Seanad) 16 May 2001; the latter passed into statute in 2001.

[13] Dissenting in *Fytche v Wincanton Logistics plc* [2004] 4 All ER 221 at 236.

[14] 'Judge Risk-it dares you to live on the edge', *Sunday Times* (15 August 2004).

[15] 'Competent People versus Copious Paper', *Horizons* (forthcoming summer 2005).

happen on expeditions', as Clive Barrow, a leading overseas expedition expert has pointed out, but it does provide a technique for thoughtful analysis.[16]

One winnowing method of looking for Step One hazards is to take into account previous legal cases and to consider the research, but also to consider insurance practice. On all these points it is necessary to separate out myth from reality. For example, even the AALA in an article on their website suggest that 'the number of opportunistic, frivolous, and downright malicious claims goes up and up',[17] which is very difficult to square with the reality of legal claims going persistently down in both the UK and the USA.[18] Similarly the research demonstrates, perhaps counter-intuitively, but after analysis making considerable sense, that the inexperienced person taking a canoe out on a placid lake or a gentle river is often at much greater risk than 'the experienced and skilled adventurer' on whitewater. This is because 'the prudent paddler can recognize hazards, assess risk, knows his or her limits, and exercises good judgment', particularly on what this American research shows to be six critical factors of paddling safety: wearing buoyancy;[19] not drinking alcohol;[20] understanding the limitations of the craft; planning ahead on aspects such as weather and equipment; knowing how to swim; and never paddling alone.[21] Although it is very difficult to obtain precise information on insurance claims, because of the sensitive commercial nature of their profit and loss risk assessment, inevitably the insurance industry is not averse to individuals and organizations taking out premiums against a 'perception' of increased risk. In recent years the insurance companies have been hard hit by legal claims on asbestos and environmental pollution, so it has been useful to recoup in other areas. Suggesting a need to protect against a wider and higher range of risks is no doubt a helpful way to boost premiums even further, but may not always accord with the reality of risk.

The yardsticks of 'good practice'

One of the most significant documents produced by the AALA is their *Self Assessment and Guidance for Providers of Adventure Activities*[22] which is a structured approach by questionnaire 'to the management of safety issues in outdoor adventurous activities'. The aim is to 'unearth safety issues' centred on

---

[16] Field Director for Operation Raleigh 1985-89, Operations Director for World Challenge Expeditions, 1989-96, speaking at 'Expeditions and Fieldwork: Safeguarding opportunities for young people', Proceedings of a conference held at the Royal Geographical Society in 1999.

[17] 'Insurance of the Adventure Activities Sector', article posted on the AALA website, 24 September 2002.

[18] See for a recent analysis, Richard Lewis, 'Insurers and Personal Injury Litigation', *Journal of Personal Injury Law* (2005) 1/105 1 *et seq.*

[19] Linda Quan et al, 'Are life vests worn?', *Injury Prevention* vol 4 (1998) 203-205.

[20] Peter Cummings and Linda Quan, 'Trends in unintentional drowning: the role of alcohol and medical care', *Journal of the American Medical Association* (1999) 2198-202.

[21] ACA, op cit at 14.

[22] Reprinted First Edition (Cardiff, 2001), downloadable from the AALA website.

three key areas: '(a) people, (b) procedures, and (c) activities, facilities and equipment'.[23] This is a practical guide to carrying out a written risk assessment which contains a wealth of useful information. It deserves very wide recognition. First issued in March 1998, this paper incorporates the collective wisdom of the AALA inspectorate and is based on their licensing and personal experience. It is therefore an invaluable self-assessment procedure for all involved in outdoor activities. That should include not just those providers within the AALA remit, but all those, such as schools and voluntary organizations, who are generally outside. Indeed, those involved with activities outside the licensing arrangements altogether, but whose arrangements have obvious comparabilities, for example rock climbing on indoor climbing walls or bungee jumping, would benefit by a close analysis. Appendix One deals with 'Risk Assessments for new providers of adventure activities' and gives a clear outline of considerations; for example, it sensibly indicates that 'you can not guarantee to prevent every accident. The best that you can do is to make judgments about the likelihood of an accident happening, the likely consequences or seriousness of that accident, and then to take appropriate preventative measures'.[24] Many of the themes are a synthesis of world-wide research and experience on outdoor activities, but there is a helpful sprinkling of new ideas and theories, along with the well-worn pathways to achieving standards of safety.[25]

Another key document is 'HASPEV', which is the acronym for *Health and Safety of Pupils on Educational Visits: A Good Practice Guide*, and which was first published in 1998. A further document, *Health and Safety: Responsibilities and Powers*, was sent by the Department for Education and Skills to all schools and local education authorities in December 2001. HASPEV now comes with several supplements, introduced from 2002 onwards: *Standards for adventure*, dealing with supervision, risk assessments and staff-pupil ratios for adventurous activities; *Standards for LEAs in overseeing educational visits*, which clarifies the responsibilities of the Outdoor Education Adviser in a local education authority, along with the Educational Visits Co-ordinator (EVC) for each school, and the role of governing bodies and headteachers; and the very helpful Part Three Supplement which is a *Handbook for Group Leaders*, issued in 2003.[26] Although the *Handbook* states that 'No guidance should be taken as an authoritative interpretation of the law. That is for the courts' it has an abundance of well-

[23] At vi.

[24] At A1.

[25] For comparable approaches see British Association of Advisers and Lecturers in Physical Education (BAALPE), *Safe Practice in Physical Education and Sport* (2004); for Australian Government policies on 'Outdoor Adventures' for their schools and colleges, see literature at http://www.decs.act.gov.au/policies/pdf/outdoor_adventures.pdf; and for the USA, see Neil J. Dougherty, IV (ed), *Outdoor Recreation Safety Book* (Champaign, IL: Human Kinetics Publishers, 1998).

[26] These and other documents on school visits and trips are all available for downloading from http://www.teachernet.gov.uk/visits

informed and sensible advice which would be a useful benchmark for any leader in a school or voluntary organization.

Actual risks in the outdoors

Perhaps unexpectedly, deaths while engaged in the pastime of angling are marginally just short of fatalities in mountaineering and air sports. Indeed, fishing has three times the number of fatalities of sports considered 'dangerous', such as rugby and football. Professor David Ball, who compiled a UK survey from a ten-year study of all sports injuries, viewed this finding at first with some disbelief, but 'when I think back to when I was younger and regularly fished on the River Thames, I remember the crazy things we did and I'm not surprised.'[27] Fatalities have of course to be considered alongside injuries, and on that score fishing is fairly safe, with an occasional hook piercing the thumb, whereas rugby players are often carrying minor injuries in what is a jarring contact sport. Andy Ripley, a former British Lion, compared his summer sport of running track, where athletes are 'highly tuned', to a rugby player 'who usually trains in the cold and wet, suffering from tonsillitis, a broken hand and a divorce ...A dressing room before a game is often like a casualty ward as players strap themselves up'.[28] The clue on the fishing deaths is contained in the information that 'swimming' is the riskiest activity, claiming 191 lives in four years, so that many fishermen are actually drowning through 'unofficial' swimming, perhaps falling from boats or slipping from the riverbank, sometimes while inebriated and usually without the protective assistance of a buoyancy aid,[29] or they are electrocuted when arcing takes place from high voltage cables on to fishing rods.[30] Risk analysis therefore has to be activity specific, although experience from one area can often be cross-fertilized to another activity. For example, another activity prone to electrocution is sailing, with a reminder in 2003 by the AALA about powerlines in an *Infolog*,

---

[27] 'Fishing is more likely to kill you than rugby', *Daily Mirror* (15 September 1998). Care has to be taken with the statistical context; RoSPA point out that 'Daredevil sport such as mountain climbing and alpine skiing cause fewer injuries in a year than more everyday activities such as football', but this needs to be seen in the light of the numbers involved and angling is of course the largest participant recreation in Britain, 'How to play sports safely', *Daily Record* (8 April 1998).

[28] Andy Ripley and Liz Ferris, *Forty Plus: Use it or lose it, the ultimate fitness guide* (London; Stanley Paul 1991)15.

[29] The American Canoe Association publication *Critical Judgment II: Understanding and Preventing Canoe and Kayak Fatalities 1996-2002* (2004) reports that many fatalities in canoeing are 'casual paddlers using a canoe while fishing', that 'among fatalities who had been paddling canoes at the time of death, 83 per cent were not wearing a personal floatation device', and that 'approximately 50 per cent of victims categorized as canoeing and kayaking fatalities were fishing when the accident occurred', at 25.

[30] 'Anglers must remain vigilant over disease', *Lincolnshire Echo* (6 January 2005), which mentions the twin dangers of drowning and contact by poles on powerlines, but also indicates several cases of leptospirosis from contact with contaminated water.

that 'as is often the case, the oldest lessons remain the best'.[31] Despite such warnings there were several more yachting electrocution cases in 2004: Peter Holt, moving a catamaran when it hit an 11,000 volt powercable in Devon;[32] Chris Smith's mast hitting a powercable in a Pembrokeshire boatyard – his sailing companion told the inquest 'I had not noticed that the power cables were there', and someone at the yard agreed that 'I'd forgotten the power cables were there because they were there all the time';[33] and a near miss in County Down when a yachtsman escaped from a burning boat after its metal mast hit an overhead power line.[34] Indeed, the highest award paid out by the Ministry of Defence relates to the electrocution of an unnamed Lance Corporal, who was loading vehicles onto a train in Germany and was ordered to retrieve a petrol can from the top of a tank; the contact with an overhead power cable resulted in his being paralysed with the loss of a leg, and his award was £3.62 million.[35]

Professor Ball's study showed that in the UK there are about 160 sport-related deaths each year, with approximately half a million individuals needing hospital treatment. Definitions are important here; although mountaineering is at the top of the risk list, the North Wales coroner Dewi Pritchard Jones has pointed out that in recent years 'Walkers have replaced climbers as the most likely to die, partly because of improvements in climbing equipment and techniques'. Mountaineering and hillwalking are seasonally affected, and annual statistics vary with weather extremities; again Dewi Pritchard Jones points out that the risks are 'greatest in spring, when ice lingers in shady places although the sunshine may feel quite warm'.[36] Nevertheless it would appear that, in spite of an increase in participation, the number of fatal accidents on British hills and mountains has actually remained 'broadly the same' over several decades with an average of 24 a year; a peak in 1993 was said to be 'the worst year on record', when there were 62 fatalities, and in the winter of 1995 in Scotland there were 37 deaths alone, of which 23 involved snow or ice.[37] Risks with mountaineering are 'self-evidently' high, although perhaps this is not always appreciated with hillwalking, thought often to be 'low risk', even though they are on a par. A tragic instance of a hillwalking death from 'trip and slip' was that in 1996 when Frazer Ross, aged 17 and climbing with his family, fell just seconds after conquering his 82nd Munro on the Cuillins in Skye. It was thought by Mountain Rescue that he had perhaps 'lost his footing on loose rock or slipped on ice', falling on to a snow ledge 250 feet below, and then when that collapsed, killed with a further fall into a 'snow-

---

[31] AALA, 'Overhead Electric Cables', *Infolog* Entry No. 28 (Aug 2003).

[32] 'Sailor shock', *Western Daily Press* (29 October 2004).

[33] 'Sailor Dad electrocuted as he raised dinghy mast', *Western Mail* (27 August 2004).

[34] 'Sailor's electric shocker', *Daily Mirror* (8 June 2004).

[35] 'MoD to cap Armed Forces injury payouts', *Sunday Telegraph* (16 September 2001). A similar sort of case occurred the following year in Kosovo; 'Soldier In Power Cable Death', *Birmingham Evening Mail* (4 September 2002).

[36] 'Warning: leisure can cause death', *Western Mail* (8 February 2003).

[37] 'MP renews call for climbers to have insurance', *The Independent* (6 April 1996).; 'Leave mountain rescue service alone', *The Guardian* (23 April 1996).

filled boulder field'.[38] Top of the league table for injury is soccer, which accounts for more than 25 per cent of all sports injuries, but it is of course a mass participation activity and the world's leading sport. By contrast the risk of a substantive injury in rugby is three times that of soccer.[39] Indeed, rugby is the worst sport for injuries, with 440 in 100,000 players going to hospital; an earlier study by Sheffield University showed that rugby players run four times the risk of death and at least three times the risk of serious injury compared with players of other team games such as soccer, cricket and hockey.[40] The football accident rate is less than half that of rugby, with 200 injuries for every 100,000 taking part. Indoor sports are perhaps the safest, with billiards and snooker almost risk-free, with just one injury for every 500,000 players and no recorded deaths.

Although risk analysis is important in considering suitable activities, and particularly in taking account of preventative measures, it is vital not to lose sight of the 'benefit' in any serious cost-benefit analysis. And the benefit of outdoor activities, particularly in providing education and in expanding the horizons of young people, is immense. Marcus Bailie has suggested that there has been a 'moral panic' about the risks of outdoor education and adventurous activities.[41] He contrasts starkly the figures on these activities with some other indices of disease. For example, when considering school visits up to June 2002, he showed that in the previous 17 years there had been just 42 pupil deaths and four adult deaths, which, broken down further, revealed 16 as road traffic related, 19 drownings and one murder.[42] His informed estimate is that in all adventurous activities there are a total of between 130 to 180 deaths per year, although he points out that some national governing bodies are not forthcoming with more accurate figures. He then makes the bleak comparison with other major causes of death in society: annually 100,000 for smoking-related illnesses; 30,000 for obesity and unfitness; 20,000 alcohol-related; 10,000 for a total casualty figure for 'accidental deaths'; 6,000 suicides; 4,000 accidents in the home; 4,000 for asthma; 3,500 road traffic fatalities; 600 through drowning, of which 200 drown in lakes and open water; 500 young people between the ages of 5 to 14 falling down stairs; 400 through ecstasy use; and 350 through accidents at work.

No-one can doubt that there are some serious hazards in some outdoor activities, and even though they probably pale in medical comparison with the

---

[38] 'Schoolboy in summit death fall', *Daily Mirror* (3 April 1996).

[39] J.P Nicholl, P. Coleman and B.T. Williams, 'The epidemiology of sports and exercise related injury in the United Kingdom', *British Journal of Sports Medicine*, vol 29, Issue 4, 232-238.

[40] Medical Care Research Unit at the University of Sheffield, 'Doctors cry foul on rugby death toll', *The Times* (12 July 1994).

[41] Marcus Bailie, 'Smoke without fire: moral panics revisited', *Expeditions and Fieldwork: Safeguarding opportunities for young people*, Proceedings of a conference held at the Royal Geographical Society, London (29 May 2002).

[42] See generally the AALA's working document for inspectors *Good Practice in Adventure Activities within the Education Sector* (Version Two 10 June 2002) Appendix 2: Summary and analysis of School Trip Fatal Accident Records between May 1985 and November 2001.

long-term risks of a sedentary lifestyle,[43] it is important to consider 'control measures' where possible. While there has been a huge expenditure of effort on health and safety in the workplace and on road transport safety, by comparison there has not yet been the same body of research on sports and outdoor activities. However, issues and possible solutions are being thrown up, not just in wide-scale studies like that of Professor Ball, but in the medical literature too. For example, the cost-effectiveness of some endeavours to raise donations can be questioned; a study in Scotland showed that parachutists who jump to raise money are costing the National Health Service almost £14 for every £1 they gain in sponsorship, because of injuries. The orthopaedic surgeon who conducted the five-year study said he 'would rather pay them not to jump ...the cost of treating the 11 per cent who are injured is far more than any money raised by the rest'. However, instead of calling for an outright ban he urged preventative measures such as more stringent selection procedures and better training, pointing out that 94 per cent of those hospitalized were injured during their first charity jump.[44] Assessing the actual risks for outdoor activities is difficult, even for an 'air sport' such as parachuting where it might be thought there would be a register of incidents, because of so many unofficial and semi-official jumps. The British Parachute Association reports an average of fewer than three cases of death or permanent disability a year, but about 250 cases for 'lesser' injuries, which would seem to suggest it is a relatively safe sport, although these figures might be a considerable underestimate on injuries.[45] The parachuting variation known as 'base jumping' – from the acronym for 'building, aerial, span and earth' – is rather more risky; Gary Connery, whose stunts include riding off Beachy Head on a mountain bike, jumping 'for Tibet' off Nelson's Column, and plunging from the Eiffel Tower, spent seven days in hospital in Paris after the latter exploit.[46] A related 'air sport' is 'skysurfing', the pastime of a psychology teacher Chris Gauge, which involves parachuting with a specially-designed snowboard strapped to his feet; in 1990 he surfed into a 158,000 volt power line, spending a week on a life support unit and unable to 'do anything much for about a year... At that point I did seriously consider giving it up'.[47] Lembit Opik MP, a qualified paraglider, was hospitalized with fractures after a fall in 1998;[48] the injuries probably uniquely qualify him to speak in Parliament against a ban on that sport when he initiated a private members' debate on health and safety in the outdoor pursuits

---

[43] Theodore Ganley and Carl Sherman, 'Exercise and children's health', *The Physician And Sportsmedicine*, vol 28, No. 2 (2000).
[44] C.T. Lee, P. Williams, W.A. Hadden, 'Parachuting for charity: is it worth the money? A 5-year audit of parachute injuries in Tayside and the cost to the NHS', *Injury*, 1999 vol 30(4), 283-7.
[45] 'When facing danger, run for cover', *Mail on Sunday*, (6 June 1999).
[46] 'Wish you were fear; why more of us crave daredevil hols', *Daily Mirror* (29 July 1999).
[47] 'Daredevils who dice with death', *Daily Mirror* (27 June 1998).
[48] 'Paraglider MP injured in 40ft fall', *The Times* (15 April 1998).

industry in 2005.[49] It is therefore perhaps not surprising to find that when insurance companies use a six category analysis to assess the level of risk involved in outdoor activities and sports, category 6 includes bungee jumping and mountaineering over 4,500 metres, powerboat racing, overland expeditions in Africa, Asia or South America, and base jumping. That top category also includes 'any professional sport', but this is because the categorization is not only to do with the nature of the hazard, but also the possible levels of compensation required for some highly paid individuals with considerable potential earning power. Mr Opik's paragliding is in category 5, along with other forms of parachuting, hang gliding, pot holing, rock climbing, mountaineering up to 4,500 metres, off-piste skiing, and ice hockey.[50]

Research carried out for the European Union on 'potentially dangerous sports and leisure activities' had its focus on skiing, climbing, swimming, diving and other water sports, along with leisure activities in amusement parks such as slides and shooting ranges. This study by the Consumer Safety Institute in the Netherlands estimated in 2003 that there were half a million casualty treatments, 18,000 hospitalizations and 200 fatalities related to such activities in the European Community each year. However, having investigated skiing injuries in particular their view was that this is 'an underestimation of the size of the problem' and they made recommendations to improve injury surveillance systems. The study set skiing injuries in the context that there are over 26 million people skiing each year in Europe.[51] As we have seen there have been just a handful of British school ski trip deaths, so 'control measures' are on the whole very effective in this activity. Inevitably there is a very subjective debate underway in most sporting disciplines, and particularly in skiing, about what further can be done to improve safety. Dr Michael Turner, chief medical adviser to the British Ski and Snowboard Federation, was of the view that 'you are as likely to be injured playing table tennis as you are on the piste' and claimed that golf was twice as dangerous as skiing.[52] That is a contested viewpoint, and subject to statistical juggling, as the context of his statement in 1998 was that in Austria alone 81,000 skiers had been involved in 'accidents' that year – 25 of them fatal. The comparison with France was that there were more than 100,000 skiing 'accidents'. Such carnage seems a little unlikely on the golf course. In Italy in 2003, following a collision with a snowboarder which left a skier dead in

---

[49] 'Outdoor activities in legal firing line', *Western Mail* (23 February 2005). See for a case which decided that a trainee paraglider who was injured was not on an 'aircraft' under Carriage of Air Acts regulations, but could claim in tort; *Disley v Levine* [2001] PIQR 159.

[50] Category Four includes scuba diving and wintersports generally; category three hot air ballooning, micro-lighting, skateboarding and white water rafting; category two physical contact amateur sports such as rugby and soccer; and category one non-contact amateur sports such as abseiling and sailing inside territorial waters; 'Daredevils who dice with death', *Daily Mirror* (27 June 1998).

[51] C. van der Sman, A. van Marle, J. Eckhardt, D. van Aken, 'Risks of certain sports and recreational activities in the EU', (Amsterdam: Consumer Safety Institute, 2003).

[52] 'What if they had worn ski helmets?', *Mail on Sunday* (11 January 1998).

Cortina, the Italian Government proposed to make helmets compulsory for children under 14 and to have separate pistes for skiers and snowboarders.[53] The helmet law for children has come into effect in 2005, although as in many disciplines there is contradictory scientific evidence on the effectiveness of head protection.[54] Separate pistes are still under review, although other measures were enacted in Italy to allow breathalysing, speed cameras and on-the-spot fines for offences such as dangerous skiing, failing to give way to skiers from the right and skiing while drunk; the first year's figures showed some fall in the level of injuries, although this may be due to other factors.[55] The Italian insurance company, SAI, indicated that the 'accident figures on the slopes in 2004 year had been like the casualty figures from a small war', with 13,252 injuries – 1,800 more than the year before – and 17 deaths.[56] Helmets have been compulsory for child skiers in Norway since 1991, are near universal for them in the USA, and are becoming very common in Europe. Again there is a heated debate: Dr Turner, who also advises the Jockey Club where in amateur equestrianism there is a similar helmet debate, points out that 'About half of all skiing fatalities occur in avalanches, where a helmet would not save you, and the other deaths occur from collisions with trees and pylons, usually off-piste. The sort of macho men – and they are usually men – who indulge in reckless off-piste skiing are just the sort of people who would refuse to wear helmets in any case'.[57] Despite high profile deaths in 1998 of Congressman Bono and Michael Kennedy, son of the late Senator Robert Kennedy, who both skied into trees in the USA, a nine year study in America concluded that the average holiday skier, skiing one week per year, would have to ski for 55 years before suffering any injury.[58]

The input from insurance

Important knowledge about hazard and risk is provided by the insurance world, but often through the prism of business considerations. Nevertheless some very interesting information can be derived from this perspective. For example, at the time of the *Van Oppen* rugby case in 1988, Brown Shipley (Schools) Ltd, which insured about 350,000 children attending one thousand private schools, reported that since the introduction of an annual comprehensive accident scheme in 1980,

---

[53] 'Deadly slopes', *The Guardian* (16 January 2003).

[54] See for a related debate in cycling; Julian Fulbrook, 'Cycle helmets and contributory negligence', *Journal of Personal Injury Law* (September 2004) pp 171-191.

[55] 'Call for crash helmets after collisions on the ski slopes', *The Times* (14 January 2005). In 2002-03, there were 13,252 injuries in Italy, whereas in 2003-04, after new safety regulations, there were 11,926 injuries.

[56] 'Drunk Britons face speed fines on piste', *The Times* (10 March 2004).

[57] 'How dangerous is skiing?', *Sunday Times* (11 January 1998).

[58] 'How common sense can save lives', *The Times* (10 January 1998). The survey, published in the *Western Journal of Medicine* in April 1996, also found that knee injuries accounted for one-third of all accidents, whereas head injuries accounted for less than nine per cent of skiing injuries.

it had a total of just 680 claims, most of them for road injuries. Of the other claims, 278 related to recreational activities, largely in playgrounds, with climbing frames and unorganized games prominent factors. Only ten injuries were in formal sport: four in rugby, two in football, one in hockey, one in athletics, one in climbing and one in diving.[59] The contextual framework is very important. Municipal Mutual, now part of the Zurich Group, insure 90 per cent of all local authorities and their schools, including around 99 per cent of all school trips. With such a huge pool the premiums are in fact very cost-effective, even for activities such as skiing where injuries such as a broken leg will require hospitalization abroad and special repatriation arrangements. However, this is on the basis that schools will invariably insist on a 'standard appropriate to the insured's experience and training as judged by qualified instructors' and indeed premiums for children 'tend to be half or even a quarter of the adult rate because the risk is lower at their nursery slope skiing level, because they are usually part of a block policy involving lower administrative costs and because most of the trips are planned, booked and insured a year or more before they take place'.[60] A study five years later by the Royal Society for the Prevention of Accidents, based partly on insurance claims analysis, estimated that there were more than three million injuries in Britain involving children up to the age of 19, and around 20 per cent required hospital treatment. They noted that 'summer is a high-risk period', and that the 'odds favouring mishaps are shortened by factors such as unsupervised leisure and public misbehaviour'; the latter they suggested was the main cause of park and fairground injuries.[61] The euphemism 'public misbehaviour' was illustrated by RoSPA pointing out that in 1991 there had been 723 people injured by fireworks in the month leading up to Guy Fawkes night on the fifth of November, and 460 of these were children.[62] Despite annual safety warnings and preventative measures this figure, according to RoSPA was 1,136 in 2003. Increased regulation to prevent those under 18 buying or, from 2003, even possessing fireworks, has not as yet reduced the casualty rate, and incidents connected with 'firework-throwing yobs' has led to a National Campaign for Firework Reform to call for a complete ban on sales.[63]

Although the insurance industry is therefore a key arena for research on risks, care has to be taken in interpreting their perspectives, even if they release information; first because many individuals are uninsured, particularly when in outside organized activities in schools and voluntary organizations, and secondly because insurance is a business which inevitably has to take a market view in a very competitive field. As well as 'loss leader' areas and 'balancing', which are inevitable to sell insurance policies at attractive rates, it is also clear that the

---

[59] 'Former pupil loses rugby injury claim against his school', *The Times* (23 July 1988).

[60] 'When insurance can turn out to be child's play on the nursery slopes', *The Times* (2 December 1989).

[61] 'Running for cover in high summer toll of children's accidents', *The Guardian* (28 August 1993).

[62] 'Policies to play safe, rather than sorry', *The Times*(31 October 1992).

[63] 'Is it time to put these out?; firework ban plea', *Daily Mirror* (5 November 2003).

insurance industry has been under very considerable pressure in recent years, particularly from heavy losses on asbestos and environmental pollution. The Scout Association adroitly dealt with some of the pressure on premiums for personal accident and liability insurance by shifting 'offshore' to the Channel Islands. In 2001 they had been given six months' notice by Norwich Union that it would no longer provide insurance for the standard Scout activities of walking, caving and climbing. The September 11th disaster in the USA then happened in that period and it was only with difficulty that the Association secured a new insurer, but with a premium doubled to £1.2 million per annum. It would have been even higher if there had not been primary cover from Scout Insurance (Guernsey) Ltd set up in 1991 and the Association's insurance manager, John Grantham, indicated that with rising premiums 'in the future, people are going to have to find more innovative ways of facing these risks'.[64] Other activity organizations do not have the financial clout or adaptability of the Scouts, so many have been in very serious difficulty; for example the Welsh Rugby Union's policy failed completely when Dewi Coates broke his neck playing for the Welsh Schools in an international against New Zealand in 1995. Mr Coates was forced to sue the WRU and its insurers, ITT London and Edinburgh, taken over by Norwich Union in 1998. A judge at Swansea County Court gave judgment in his favour and criticized what he called the 'ambiguous' wording of the WRU's two insurance policies which cover individual players and clubs.[65] This case also saw some very unsavoury tactics when an undercover agent posing as a former Neath College student putting together a handbook on sport tricked his way into Mr Coates' home to film his movements with a hidden camera, with the intention of discrediting a medical report; responding to an accusation that this was 'sly' and 'underhand', a spokesman for Norwich Union indicated that 'from time to time we do use investigators to validate claims'.[66] The WRU had already been very badly hit when it faced the collapse of Independent Insurance, which went into liquidation in 2001, and when considering an appeal to the House of Lords in *Vowles v Evans* it was estimated that the WRU were £66 million in debt, with £49 million to pay on the Millennium Stadium in Cardiff, and all of this on a turnover of £38 million a year.[67]

Water activities

As we have seen in the legal cases, perhaps the most serious risk in the outdoors is a water-associated death – 19 out of 46, the highest category in Marcus Bailie's

---

[64] 'Charity finance: Insurance: Be prepared', *The Guardian* (9 July 2003).

[65] 'Recent high-profile civil actions by injured rugby players', *Western Mail* (11 November 2004). See also for a similar claim against the WRU and Norwich Union for non-payment to Paul O'Keefe, 'Injured rugby player sues WRU', *Western Mail* (11 November 2004).

[66] 'Injured rugby star was secretly filmed', *South Wales Evening Post* (7 February 2000).

[67] 'Welsh rugby clubs face threat of £5m legal bill', *The Times* (29 April 2003).

analysis of school trip deaths.[68] These fatalities are associated particularly with 'plunging' and the 'rock/water interface'. Boisterous behaviour by young men sadly leads to many water-related injuries around the world, so much so that a 'syndrome' has been identified: macho male diving syndrome. An American expert, Professor Clements, states that 'head first shallow water entry injuries are believed to represent the single largest group of severe injuries, not involving deaths, in all aspects of sport'.[69] Such injuries very rarely occur in any activity that could properly be called 'diving'.[70] For example, a survey in the USA in 1988, in a country where swimming is second only to walking as a means of exercise, found that 'no record exists of a fatality or catastrophic injury connected with a supervised training session or competition in competitive diving.'[71] Subsequently there has been a case in California in 2003, which involved a diver undergoing training, who landed on a synchronized swimmer also using the pool, leading to the diver's tetraplegia.[72] This illustrates the potential risks but also the obvious safeguards taken in most pools to avoid such injury. As we have seen in the leading British case of *Tomlinson v Congleton BC*, although the judgments through the courts repeatedly refer to 'diving', Lord Scott of Foscote describes that approach as 'unreal' and 'misdescribed.'[73] Lord Scott preferred instead the terminology 'forward plunge',[74] although as with many such cases, it is not entirely clear what happened: Jack J found the claimant 'waded' and 'then threw himself forward in a dive or plunge';[75] Lord Hoffmann conjectures that he 'ran out into the water and dived';[76] whereas Lord Scott of Foscote indicates that he was 'not diving nor swimming... He simply ran into the water and when he could not run any further, because the water was above his knees and the galloping action that we all adopt when running into water on a shelving beach had become

---

[68] Appendix 2: Summary and analysis of School trip fatal accident records between May 1985 and November 2001, in Marcus Bailie, 'Good Practice in Adventure Activities within the Education Sector', Version Two 10 June 2002.

[69] Annie Clements, *Legal Responsibility in Aquatics* (Aurora, Ohio: Sport and Law Press, 1997) 69.

[70] Note too that this expression can cover scuba diving, which has special risks such as decompression sickness, know as 'the bends'; 'Deadly wreck claims life of another diver', *Aberdeen Press and Journal* (24 August 1998).

[71] J. L. Gabriel, *Diving Safely* (1988), quoted in Clements, loc cit. In the USA approximately 43,000 people are injured and 650 people drown in and around swimming pools each year, but 'Most pool fatalities occur in backyard pools rather than public facilities protected by lifeguards', Western Insurance Information Service quoted in *Business Wire* (22 July 1997).

[72] *Shropshire v City of Walnut Creek*, Cal., Contra Costa County Super. Ct., No. 01-02541, 5 May 2003. A jury awarded $27.75 million, finding a violation of a local law prohibiting joint use of the swimming pool, and apportioned liability on the basis of 60 per cent against the City, 20 per cent against the synchronized swimmer, and 10 per cent each against the synchronized swimming club and the diving coach.

[73] *Tomlinson v Congleton Borough Council* [2003] 3 All ER 1122, at 1165 [93].

[74] Ibid [94].

[75] Quoted by Ward LJ at *Tomlinson* (CA) 1126 [6].

[76] Ibid [3].

too difficult, he plunged forward. This is something that happens on every beach in every country in the world, temperature and conditions permitting.'[77] It is perhaps inevitable that the precise facts are often hotly disputed by the opposing parties in such a legal case, and therefore they are not readily discernible, even after, as in this case, three levels of court examination. What is clear is that many of the resultant injuries from 'plunging' occur in the outdoors in informal settings, where there is unlikely to be skilled diving supervision or lifeguard support, and where natural surroundings can increase hazard.[78] A critical factor in injury prevention is therefore this aspect of supervision, particularly if there is any likelihood of 'boisterous' behaviour.

A different problem, and one that perhaps only emerged after Stainforth Beck in 2000, is the 'walking in water' syndrome; the power of moving water was perhaps not fully realized by many, although it is clear that less than two feet of water can float a car. In 1995 a pair of gamekeepers were in a car crossing a ford in the Yorkshire Dales near Hawes when they were washed more than 400 yards downriver – one reported that 'the car floated along like a boat, as we crashed into rocks and went over rapids: it was all a bit exciting'.[79] Lack of appreciation of one of the fastest flowing rivers in the country, the Swale, perhaps due to having 'drunk more than three times the drink-drive limit for alcohol' led to the death of Ben Clarke in 1996; an off-duty soldier, he waded across the river with his father, as a short cut home from a pub. The father survived, and the coroner indicated that with such a high reading for alcohol 'one is bound to wonder how that did affect his and your judgement and indeed his performance in the cold water'.[80] Skidding on slippery surfaces at the side of the river, just as much as walking in it and being swept away, can lead to death by drowning or head injury or to entrapment. On the same day as the gamekeepers' escapade in Yorkshire a man in Chichester was frantically looking for his son aged four, who had slipped into a river but had been pulled out by his older brothers, when he himself slipped and fell in upstream of a tunnel carrying flood water and drowned while trapped there.[81] Entrapment is a very well-recognized hazard in kayaking and canoeing, either from snaring the boat in 'strainers' such as fallen trees or undercut rocks, but also in trapping legs when wading. Modern hazards for 'pinning', wrapping or entrapment include shopping trolleys, barbed wire fences, bridge struts and abutments, old cars and washing machines, and a huge variety of discarded household and building waste, and can all be added to the list of natural debris in rivers.[82]

---

[77] Ibid [94].

[78] The evidence from the Royal Society for the Prevention of Accidents in *Darby v The National Trust* [2001] EWCA Civ 189 [10] was that approximately 450 people a year drown in the UK, 'the preponderance of these being young men swimming in open water'.

[79] 'Gamekeepers escape after car rides rapids', *Glasgow Herald* (13 February 1995).

[80] 'Tragic misjudgement' led to river drowning', *Northern Echo* (8 February 1996).

[81] 'Man drowns in river as he searches for son', *Glasgow Herald* (13 February 1995).

[82] See for an analysis of hazards, Matt Berry, 'Reading White Water', in Franco Ferrero (ed) *BCU Canoe and Kayak Handbook* (Bangor: Pesda, 2002) 290.

Slipping on wet rocks near the coast is another hazard, as we have seen in the 'coasteering' cases. Most such fatalities are not during organized outdoor pursuits, but are simply a classic 'slip and trip' in hazardous terrain; for example the Pembrokeshire coroner in 2002 recorded a verdict of accidental death on Stephen Gutteridge, who despite 'wearing extremely good footwear' appeared to have 'slipped on a rock' while on the coastal footpath, had fallen and broken ribs, and was then discovered dead from drowning in a cave which became flooded at high tide.[83] Another drowning that year in a flooded coastal cave, this time in Cornwall, seemed to have been the result of an 'impromptu party' near Newquay, which led to the presumed death of Stephen Park, the owner of a backpackers' hostel; 'presumed' because his body was never found after surf washed through the cave.[84] Spontaneous exploring will often have potential for disaster; in 2001 Martin Shaw, aged 13, slipped and fell 40 feet when exploring 'old quarries and caves' near Brixham. A group of teenagers had 'clambered over rain-soaked rocks' before he fell to his death on a cliff face; the coastguard who abseiled down to try and resuscitate him indicated that he himself 'would never have attempted to climb down unaided'.[85]

Hills and mountains

Another classic instance of risk in the outdoors is slipping while hillwalking. An Australian case, *Nicholas v Osborne*, pointed out that although there might be a 'perceived' increase of risk in the outdoors, in law it is essentially the same legal duty of care for teachers and activity leaders whether in the school playground or on trips and expeditions, but just applied to different circumstances.[86] And these surrounding circumstances are of course critical, particularly when considering preventative measures to safeguard against harm, often because outside school premises and particularly in 'wild country' there is likely to be a delay in obtaining medical assistance. Felicity Nicholas, aged 14, was on a field trip for an elective called 'Bushcraft and Camping' when she slipped and suffered minor injuries. Then another student slipped and sustained serious head injuries. A teacher remained with them, while two teachers returned with the bulk of the students to arrange rescue. During the night the seriously injured student died. Lazarus J was highly critical of the manner in which the activity had been carried out; he held that the pupil-teacher ratio was totally inadequate in view of the weather, which was cold and wet, and the nature of the terrain; the information sent home as a parental briefing had been 'inadequate'; and deviating from the original route notified to the Education Department to take 'a route higher up' was held to be negligent. A legal commentary on the case by Dr Stewart suggests that its significance for Australian schools is not to ban such trips from the

---

[83] 'Drowning riddle of Mr Sensible', *Liverpool Echo* (31 May 2002).
[84] 'Cave party death', *The Times* (18 September 2002).
[85] 'Cliff climb alert after boy's death', *Torquay Herald Express* (19 January 2001).
[86] *Nicholas v Osborne* (Unreported Victoria County Court, November 1985.)

curriculum, but 'to improve school legal risk management policies and practices'.[87]

The issue of ratios discussed in that leading Australian decision can actually be rather baffling, as there are so many variations. For example the British Government's adult to child ratios in *Sure Start* apply only to those under the age of eight, and state as mandatory the minimum standards for all 'childcare' situations. These are 1:3 for children under two years of age, 1:4 for children aged two; and 1:8 for children aged three to seven years of age. Further stipulations are that there will always be 'a minimum of two adults on duty' and that there are 'adequate staff to ensure the security of any group of children which is constantly changing'.[88] HASPEV indicates the same 1:8 ratio for children in the three to seven age group.[89] However, different institutions have their own standards; for example, the Welsh Assembly childminding regulations have now gone to 1:6 for under eights; each Local Education Authority can also have its own regulations, so for example Flintshire LEA says that for 'Environmental Education visits ... we need a ratio of 1:5 adults to children for all of our programmes offered',[90] and the Scottish Commission for the Regulation of Care, which enforces national care standards, goes in the other direction by stipulating that after-school clubs for primary pupils have 1:10 if the club is running for no more than four hours, although they also require two members of staff to be present at all times.[91] When looking at the particular hazards relating to water activities or hillwalking, then necessarily a tighter ratio may be appropriate. For example, a recent survey of the 33 London boroughs showed that some swimming pools and some boroughs demanded that each child under the age of four was supervised by one adult, whereas some pools stated that an adult could look after three under eights, while others say the limit is two. One council, Hounslow, had different rules for different swimming pools.[92] Professor Frank Furedi, a sociologist at the University of Kent, finds it puzzling that his son, under eight years of age, was turned away when going to a swimming pool on his own, and suggests that 'instead of trying to protect children from life, parents need to throw their children into it'.[93] Parenting standards obviously differ hugely, and significantly

---

[87] See Doug Stewart, 'Judicial Influence On Educational Policy And Practice' (Australian Association for Research in Education Conference, 1991), and see generally Doug Stewart and Andrew Knott, *Schools, Courts and the Law* (Melbourne: Pearson International, 2002).

[88] Para 6.4 of *Sure Start*, 'National standards for under 8s day care and childminding', developed from the Day Care and Childminding (National Standards) (England) Regulations 2003 No.1996, under the Children Act 1989.

[89] *Handbook For Group Leaders, HASPEV Supplement 3, Health and Safety of Pupils on Educational Visits: A Good Practice Guide* (2003).

[90] Flintshire County Council, *Environmental Education Service* leaflet.

[91] Set up under the Regulation of Care (Scotland) Act 2001.

[92] 'Compensation culture kills off the great family swimming trip', *Evening Standard* (26 January 2005).

[93] 'Is it safe to send our children on school trips?', *Sunday Express* (8 July 2001). See also his *Paranoid Parenting: Why Ignoring the Experts May Be Best for Your Child* (Chicago: updated version, Chicago Review Press, 2002).

by geographical location, but the Institute of Sport and Recreation Management recommends that children under five be supervised individually near water and those under eight at a ratio of two per adult. They also recommend that Councils can take into account factors such as the size of their pools and the experience of their staff.[94]

Similarly bewildering divergences occur in the voluntary organizations in relation to hillwalking. The Scout Association has settled on a maximum party number of seven in the hills, although this can exceptionally be increased to eight when there is a second authorized leader; their recent *Review* proposes a number of changes but states that 'Group sizes are an important element of safety management and will remain as they stand'.[95] At the other end of the spectrum is the recommendation in the Highland Council's *Outdoor Education Safety Document* for schools and voluntary organizations coming to the hills in Scotland, which gives some very wise advice, but suggests group sizes of up to fifteen in the Scottish hills, although indicating that size must always allow 'the leader to remain in total control and in effective contact with all members of the group'.[96]

Review

This is Step Five of the HSE risk management procedure, and under the Management of Health and Safety at Work Regulations 1999, employers have a legal duty to assess the risks to health and safety of anyone who might be affected by their operations. But even where organizations may not have an employer's duty to comply, it is equally important for them to conduct an evaluation and debriefing after every activity. This gives the opportunity to calculate any risks of the activity with a view to minimizing them in the future, and of course provides an important evidential 'papertrail'. These written records provide not just an essential history of any incidents, and hopefully they will be a near-contemporaneous account, but they will be critical in any subsequent litigation. Good record keeping is therefore helpful as demonstrating competence, but will be vital in resisting any negligence claim. A chronicle of 'near misses' or 'close calls', and remedial action for the future, actually suggests a serious organization, because it is based in the realism that no-one is immune from danger. Learning can also of course be from other comparable organizations, and as we have seen,

---

[94] ISRM, 'Swimming pool child admission policy for unprogrammed swimming' Policy Statement (Loughborough University) 2005.

[95] *Review of the Scout Association's Authorization Scheme for Adventurous Activities (Phase Two)* (October 2004) 8. See also *Policy Organization and Rules* rule 9.32 and 9.32d; 'Adventurous Activities Abroad', *Fact Sheet* 120085 (October 2003); 'Mountaineering with Scouts – The Vital Culture', *Fact Sheet* 120415 (March 2001).

[96] The 'optimum size' indicated for a hillwalking party is 10, dropping to six for High Hills in Winter, with a 'maximum total group size' of 15, dropping to 12 for 'Remote Areas Winter' and 'High Hills Summer', and down to 10 for 'High Hills Winter'; ibid 24.

legal cases and incidents can also provide an impetus for reviewing procedures. When in 1991 a boy aged thirteen was airlifted from an island on Loch Leven after setting fire to himself while refilling a methylated spirit stove during a school canoeing trip there was inevitably a review of safety procedures for such stoves.[97] Subsequently a series of 'safety tips' and leaflets have been produced for the correct use of 'trangias', culminating after another incident in 1999 with an AALA *Infolog* warning of dangers, particularly on re-fuelling when the stove appears to be extinguished.[98] It was reported in 2004 that the majority of first aid incidents at the Glastonbury Festival were 'the result of people falling over tent pegs, particularly in the dark, and burns from camp stoves', so training on stoves probably needs to be more extensive amongst young people in Britain.[99]

Preventative measures and a cost-benefit analysis

Tort law does not guarantee safety, and an important element in considering the appropriate balance in cases is to estimate the cost of remedial or preventative measures. An American judge, Learned Hand, produced an opinion in *United States v Carroll Towing Co.*, which has been said to be 'canonized' in the law and economics literature. In dealing with a vessel breaking loose from her moorings he indicated that the owner's duty was to be considered in the light of three variables: the 'probability' that she would break away; the 'gravity' of the resulting injury, if she does; and the 'burden of adequate precautions'.[100] Many tort cases show that preventative measures can be inexpensive; for example the simple and perhaps elementary precaution of the latched gate to protect children in *Carmarthenshire CC v Lewis*. A recent example of a failure to provide such a necessary precaution in Florida led to a jury award of $100 million, the largest personal injury award in the state, and without any element of punitive damages, in the case of *Hinton v 2331 Adams Street Corporation*.[101] A toddler aged two suffered permanent brain damage after nearly drowning in an apartment swimming pool, and the court found that this was insufficiently protected, because the gate was not lockable. The plaintiff's attorney noted that 'every Home Depot sells a self-latching

---

[97] 'Fearful toll on roads, hills and at sea', *The Scotsman* (8 March 1994).

[98] AALA, 'Trangia Stove', *Infolog* Entry No 3, 1999. See also the Trangia 'Directions for use and recipes' 21: 'Warning: Never attempt to pour spirits into the burner unless the flame is extinguished'.

[99] 'Festival founder fumes over event's exploitation', *The Independent* (26 June 2004).

[100] 159 F.2d 169 (2d Cir. 1947). See Allan M. Feldman and Jeonghyun Kim, 'The Hand Rule And *United States v Carroll Towing Co.* Reconsidered', Brown University Department of Economics Working Paper No. 2002-27 (October 2002) 1.

[101] *Lawyers Weekly USA*, 17 February 2003. A previous Florida case had reduced an award by 90 per cent for the mother's negligence in allowing her child to wander off, but there was still an award of $966,800 in *Collyar v Harley*, Florida, Hillsborough County Circuit Court, No. 92-7369, 21 September 1995 when a child aged four wandered through the neighbour's home and opened a non-childproof gate leading to the swimming pool, installed by a building contractor.

gate that closes on itself and hooks into place for $36'. Several witnesses testified that numerous complaints had been made to the management about the broken pool gate, so there was an evidential trail to show breach of the duty of care. The US courts have certainly been quite fierce about control measures. In *Hoyem v Manhattan Beach City School District*,[102] a pupil aged ten slipped away from school and was run over by a motorcyclist four blocks away; the school district was held liable, even though successful prevention of unofficial absences from schools through 'bunking off' has taxed the ingenuity of school authorities throughout the world. And in a Federal case, *Bryant v United States*,[103] involving three Native American Indian boys, aged seven, eight and ten, who had run away from a boarding school and were trapped in a snowstorm, the supervisory system was held to be inadequate. This was despite nine head counts each day, that their absence was discovered within 20 minutes of their departure, and that a full search was begun immediately. The three boys were found four days later, suffering extreme frostbite, which necessitated a double-leg amputation for each of them. It would appear that the 'likelihood' of their running away to make their way home through the mountains to a Navajo Indian Reservation was very high, and the 'foreseeability' of hazards in winter and in this terrain was very high too.

Risk analysis is obviously the key here, when scrutinizing the balance of cost and benefit, and indeed there may in fact be no financial outlay but merely a re-ordering of arrangements and perhaps layout. The courts have consistently stressed a 'common sense approach' to the duty of care, but as Mitchell J pointed out in *Morrell v Owen*, just 'relying on the common sense of the participants is a singularly unimpressive approach to the discharge of that duty'.[104] This is a useful case on preventative measures, as there were special circumstances with the participants, who needed greater care even though they were adults. Wendy Morrell was a disabled archer, who was struck on the head by a discus thrown in a sports hall in Birmingham when both activities were being pursued at the same time. The archery team was to compete in the disabled world championships that year in Holland, so the level of expertise was high and there were coaches and officials present. However, the claimant had not long taken up the sport and this was her first such event. In her personal life she was a teacher and the suggestion was that she was well able to appreciate a danger when a discus was thrown and caused a safety net to billow some three to six feet into the archery section; she agreed that it 'was plain common sense to keep out of the way of the bulges' but had additional difficulties with her wheelchair, and was waiting for an archer to shoot before crossing the line of fire when she was hit by the discus. A coach somewhat predictably enunciated that 'safety was of the utmost importance at all times' – but when asked about any arrangements concluded between the coaches of the two events, admitted that there had been none. The judge found on the evidence that there was 'insufficient regard for the difficulties of the wheelchair archers' and liability resulted. The Learned Hand formula is a useful analytical

---

[102] 585 P. 2d 851 (California 1978).
[103] 565 F. 2d 650 (10th Circuit, 1977).
[104] *The Times* (14 December 1993) and QBD transcript 1 December 1993.

tool in such situations. Although there are actually few injuries caused by throwing a discus, as the supervision is usually very tight, and the 'probability' of an injury is therefore fairly low, it is 'foreseeable' that if an injury resulted it could be very serious, so the 'magnitude of risk' is high. The potential for such 'gravity of injury', particularly when there are 'informal' circumstances, was shown in 2003 when a schoolboy, Stephen Comney, aged 14, died after being hit between the shoulder blades by a discus. He and his friend, keen to start an after-school athletics session, took practice throws in breach of the rules. The coroner surmised that the shock caused a brain haemorrhage in conjunction with a latent defect. Their teacher had shouted a warning, but 'it all happened in a couple of seconds'.[105] Considering factors such as probability and gravity does not of itself guarantee that no injuries will result, and even when fully supervised by an experienced coach who had attended a refresher training course on using projectile sports equipment just a month before, there is still inevitably still some risk with athletic missiles. Jon Desborough, an experienced teacher and athlete in Merseyside, died in what was described as a 'freak accident' in 1999. He was demonstrating throwing a javelin to a class, lost his footing and slipped while going to retrieve the javelin, and the blunt end pierced his eye. His widow understandably called for a complete ban; 'The javelin is an outdated field event and I would like to see it banned in schools altogether'.[106] Although the Learned Hand 'burden' is generally taken to mean a financial equation, it is clear that the human costs and the social costs have to be weighed; in athletic events such as these it is suggested that giving appropriate education in risk management to children on items such as javelins, which clearly could prove dangerous if not used properly, is a very considerable social benefit.

There has been much litigation on that other sporting missile of the outdoors, the golf ball, but this is rarely a game played by children and even less likely to be under supervision, although it raises points of etiquette and inevitably a cost-benefit analysis on preventative measures such as fencing and layout of the course. According to a report by the Safety in Leisure Research Unit at the Swansea Institute of Higher Education, golf is significantly more dangerous than climbing, sailing or canoeing.[107] In the Court of Appeal case of *Pearson v Lightning* a golf ball bounced off a tree and hit another player on an adjoining fairway in the eye, with such force that he was never able to play again. Simon Brown LJ, a keen golfer himself, emphasized the view that golfing etiquette required Mr Lightning to warn a fellow golfer before attempting to strike the ball: 'the defendant shouted "fore", the golfer's time-honoured cry of warning [but] the plaintiff, however, as so often happens, did not hear it'. He noted also the rules which state 'Prior to playing a stroke the player should ensure that no one is in a position to be hit by the ball.' The cry of 'fore' as the ball was sailing towards the victim was therefore too little too late, and although the risk of injury was small, it

---

[105] 'Tragedy of boy hit by friend's discus', *Daily Mail* (19 December 2003).

[106] *The Times* (4 September 1999). See also 'Widow urges school javelin ban after freak death of games master', *Birmingham Post* (2 May 2000).

[107] 'How safe are activity centres?', *The Times* (12 February 1994).

was sufficient to render the defendant liable.[108] A similar kind of case occurred in New Jersey, when a golfer was hit in the face by a golf ball, breaking bones that required surgery to repair. A trial judge in *Schick v Ferolito* found no liability because these were not 'wilful, wanton or intentional acts' in line with the reckless standard of care applied to sports in that state.[109] A factual dispute was never entirely resolved as to whether this was a drive off the tee with golfing partners or a quick 'reload'. On appeal to the Superior Court it was held that the recklessness standard was appropriate only in 'rough and tumble' sports; in such sports it was said 'anticipated risks are an inherent or integral part of the game', whereas in golf the heightened standard would be appropriate only for anticipated risks of the game, such as an errant ball as a result of a 'slice', 'hook', or 'shank'. Here there had been an 'unanticipated risk', which was 'an unannounced and unexpected second tee shot, or mulligan'.[110] Predictably this case set off a storm of controversy, with predictions of a doomsday scenario for golf in the USA,[111] before the Supreme Court of New Jersey held that recklessness was still the appropriate standard, and remanded the case to resolve factually what precisely the technical nature of this shot was.[112] As in the British school skiing case of *Woodbridge School v Chittock*[113] in 2002, it appears to be the interim decision of the lower court that lingers in the collective memory and not the final result.

The fundamental preventative aid in a whole range of water activities such as kayaking, canoeing, sailing, windsurfing and dragonboating, is to wear a buoyancy aid. This 'personal flotation device' has become axiomatic in kayaking and nearly so in most other water sports. It is of course a relatively inexpensive but proven aid to safety, necessary even for strong swimmers when coping with the shock of sudden immersion, particularly in cold water. An incident in 2000 at the National Water Sports Centre at Holme Pierrepont was yet another reminder. Wayne Smith, by occupation a paramedic with the East Midlands Ambulance Service, drowned when his dragonboat capsized. Six of the other 18 crew members were treated for hypothermia. None were wearing buoyancy aids, but even worse, Mr Smith had training weights on his wrists.[114] Exacerbating the situation were a series of other difficulties. Although following the death in 1991 of a kayaker at Holme Pierrepont, Trevor Bailey, also not wearing a buoyancy aid, the centre had been ordered to install CCTV and telephones along the course, these were not working on the day the dragonboaters capsized in 2000. As a result it took fifteen minutes for the centre's rescue boat to arrive. Recording a verdict of accidental death, the coroner stated that 'This was a tragic accident but when we look at it this was an accident waiting to happen', and he ordered both

---

[108] *Pearson v Lightning, The Times* (30 April 1998), 142 SJ LB 143.

[109] 136 N.J. 494, 643 A.2d 600 (1994).

[110] 327 N.J. Super. 530 A-1315-98T5 (2000).

[111] See for example David Owen, 'Could this be the end of golf?', *Golf Digest* (May 2000), and 'Better not forget to yell "fore",' *Golf Magazine* (7 July 2000).

[112] *Schick v Ferolito* (A-108-99), decided 12 March 2001.

[113] [2002] EWCA Civ 915, [2002] ELR 735.

[114] 'Paramedic drowns in dragon boat accident', *The Independent* (28 February 2000).

Sport England and the British Dragonboat Association to tighten up procedures, for example by insisting on buoyancy aids and banning weights. The family sued for compensation, and their solicitor stated that 'the family is looking for changes regarding safety in the sport'.[115] Holme Pierrepont was opened in 1973 and is used by more than 50,000 people every year, having been a venue for the 1990 Dragonboat World Championships. This sport began in China more than 2000 years ago, commemorating the death of the Chinese poet Qu Yuan, who drowned himself in the Mi Lo River in 295BC in protest at the corrupt government of the time, and it is reputedly the UK's fastest growing 'corporate activity'.[116] The AALA quickly indicated that although the British Dragon Boating Association concentrates primarily on competition where buoyancy aids 'have not been seen as compulsory for many competitors', it would be very unlikely that one of their recreational providers would be licensed for dragonboating with those under 18 without this obvious control measure. A straightforward piece of advice in an *Infolog* states that 'Sudden immersion, unexpectedly, in cold water whilst hot, excited and possibly exhausted has taken the lives of many recreational water users, even those who were good swimmers, because they weren't wearing buoyancy aids'.[117] Unfortunately, even when rescue procedures are in place, buoyancy is worn and there is extensive safety cover, there can still be deaths in kayaking; Iain Hickson, aged 19, was taking part in the annual Welsh University slalom competition at Llandysul in 2001, and an inquest accepted the investigation of Mike Devlin from the BCU that 'with the best of motives, he probably hung on to his canoe for too long', although he was being urged by safety assistants to let it go and save himself.[118]

One issue that is often seen in the cases is the 'improvised' nature of activities which leads to hazard. Risk assessment always has to be 'ongoing', but inevitably it has to be weighed against not just 'stifling' creativity, but also sometimes the very considerable costs of preventative measures. In *Gordon v Los Angeles Unified School District*,[119] the claimant was aged seven and was playing indoor 'floor hockey' in a youth club. The organizer made a makeshift hockey puck by crushing a drink can and wrapping it in tape, but this was unfortunately hit into the plaintiff's right eye, blinding him. His attorneys urged that eye protection equipment should have been used, and the court discussed cost factors and the lack of prior injuries. Before the court resolved the matter, the parties settled for $1.38 million. The test, as we have seen, would have been whether 'reasonable' precautions had been taken, and while these circumstances were not ideal it appeared that the tape was sufficient to mask any cutting propensities, and that this may just have been a very unfortunate and random hit.

---

[115] 'Safety dispute after dragonboat tragedy', *Nottingham Evening Post* (3 November 2000).

[116] 'Dragon Boat Race, Hong Kong', *Daily Telegraph* (29 May 2004).

[117][117] See AALA, *Collective Interpretation 6.09*, 'Dragon Boating with Young People', and 'A dragon boat capsized during a race training session: one man was drowned', *Infolog Entry* No. 9, (Feb 2000).

[118] 'Canoeist died trying to save kit', *Western Mail* (4 May 2001).

[119] California, Los Angeles County Superior Court, No. LC036226, 8 July 1998.

Marcus Bailie has tried to sum up the essentials of a risk assessment for outdoor activities, and claims that 'the basic problem is that for several years people have not understood what they have been trying to do when writing Risk Assessments and Safety Statements', and have approached it as 'busy work' documenting everything under the misapprehension that this papertrail will reduce risk, rather than examining key issues.[120] He suggests 'the Idiot's Guide approach to things... there are only three things which will cause death or disabling injury during an activity session: drowning, impact with something solid (which either falls onto you or onto which you fall); and hypothermia'.[121] Rob Hogan adds to this list from the Australian context: heat stroke, severe burns from stoves and tent fires, electrocution from lightning strikes, poisonous bites from snakes and spiders – all of which could be vital considerations on overseas trips from Britain – and pre-existing medical conditions such as asthma, diabetes, cardiac irregularity and extreme allergies.[122] Grant Davidson from New Zealand in an analysis of 'predictors of potential for serious injury' indicates what four factors may produce serious injury: activities 'led by inexperienced staff; limited or no supervision; containing high energy sources such as height, speed, changes in weather, moving water, fire or other heat; and carried out in a water environment'.[123] This sounds like a topic for a good debate around a campfire. American commentators such as Drew Leeman and Scott Erikson, who have investigated dozens of incidents, would characterize the Bailie threesome as 'environmental', focusing on 'the powerful unforgiving forces of the natural world, such as weather, gravity or strong currents', but would then go on to deal with two very 'people-oriented' matters: the desire to seek outdoor challenges which places individuals in 'risky situations', and the 'decision-making process' of participants.[124] A Canadian canoeing perspective from Bill Mason would challenge the wisdom 'in all circumstances' of staying with an 'overturned or

---

[120] Marcus Bailie, 'Risk Assessments, Safety Statements and all that Guff', *Far Out – Practical and Informative Adventure Education*, vol. 1, No. 3 (1996) pp 6-7. See also his 'Competent People versus Copious Paper', *Horizons* (forthcoming summer 2005).

[121] Loc cit.

[122] Rob Hogan, 'The Crux Of Risk Management In Outdoor Programs – Minimising The Possibility Of Death And Disabling Injury', *Australian Journal of Outdoor Education*, vol 6, No. 2 (2002) 71-79. See for some suggestions on avoiding lightning strikes in the outdoors, Michael Cherington, 'Lightning Injuries in Sports: Situations to Avoid', *Sports Medicine* vol 31, No. 4 (2001) 301-308.

[123] Grant Davidson, 'Exploring the Myths: Analysis of incidents and accidents in professional outdoor education in New Zealand 1996-2000', *Journal of Adventure Education and Outdoor Learning*, vol 4, No. 1 (2004). One of the 'most obvious' lessons he draws from his study is a need for a national incident database. See the excellent New Zealand Recreational Canoeing Association incident database at www.rivers.org.nz, although this is of course limited to kayaking and canoeing.

[124] Drew Leeman and Scott Erikson, 'How Accidents Happen' in Deborah Ajango (ed), *Lessons Learned: A Guide to Accident Prevention and Crisis Response* (Anchorage: University of Alaska, 2004) 5-32.

swamped craft',[125] with differing interpretations on kayaking and canoeing safety from an abundance of perspectives in the USA and Europe.[126] Pick any other outdoor activity and you would have a similar galaxy of viewpoints. Nevertheless, what is abundantly clear from a full overview of risk and the outdoors is that, in spite of particular hazards that need to be scrutinized and then guarded against, there is an overwhelming benefit to participants in such activities. It should be the purpose of the law to buttress that perspective, by retaining clear guidelines as to acceptable behaviour.

---

[125] Bill Mason (ed Paul Mason), *Path of the Paddle* (Toronto; Key Porter, 1984, 1995) 175-177 on 'Wilderness Safety; Avoiding Tragedy', and the famous sequence in his film *Waterwalker*.

[126] See for example Les Bechdel and Slim Ray, *River Rescue: A Manual for Whitewater Safety* (Boston; AMC, 1985, 1997); Charlie Walbridge and Wayne Sundmacher, *Whitewater Rescue Manual: New Techniques for Canoeists, Kayakers and Rafters* (Camden, ME: Ragged Mountain, 1995); Franco Ferrero, *Whitewater Safety and Rescue* (Bangor: Pesda, 1998); Peter Reithmaier, *Sicherheit im Wildwasser* (Wien: Naturfreunde Oesterreich, 1994); C.E.S. Franks, *The Canoe and White Water; from essential to sport* (Toronto: University of Toronto Press, 1977); and the 'bible' of the BCU, Franco Ferrero, *BCU Canoe and Kayak Handbook*, (Bangor: Pesda, 2002) Chapter 26.

Chapter 9

Planning and People

There is no complete checklist on what safety precautions need to be taken on outdoor activities, but there are common themes that can be extrapolated from the legal cases and from 'good practice' around the world. A number of organizations have been analyzing these matters for many years, and there are some well-trodden pathways. For example, Becky Kirkwood, the leisure adviser at the Royal Society for the Prevention of Accidents, in giving advice to parents about school trips in the aftermath of Lyme Bay, indicated in 1994 that they should 'ask to see written evidence of instructor qualifications, the emergency action plan and affiliation to any sports with governing memberships, [ask] Is there a doctor on call or a resident nurse? What are the staff pupil ratios? And is there a special "parent line" to ring in emergencies?'[1] Marcus Brown of the Association of Mountaineering Instructors indicated in 1998 that 'accident reporting by mountain rescue teams shows that only too often what needs to be taught is actually common sense: choice of equipment, clothing and footwear; choice of route; sensible appreciation of personal fitness; attention to the weather'.[2] The AALA in its *Sample Risk Management Summary* for licensed providers gives a template for wider use which covers key issues such as staff competence and qualifications (usually those of national governing bodies), child protection, supervision when not on activities, risk assessment, insurance, fire protection, transport arrangements, equipment and security.[3] As an *Infolog* from the AALA notes 'If you think safety is expensive, try having an accident!'[4]

No complete itemization is possible across all endeavours in the outdoors, but what follows is an analysis of some key areas. The division between 'people issues' relating to planning and staffing dealt with in this chapter, and the 'physical issues' relating to facilities and equipment in the next chapter, is of course fairly arbitrary. The two are so often inter-related. However, any analysis shows that the quality of the individuals involved in the leadership and supervision of outdoor activities is paramount. An apt summary of both the legal requirements and the safety issues at stake is the statement by Marcus Bailie from the AALA, that 'Accidents are best prevented by having competent people in charge of the activity'.[5]

---

[1] 'How safe are activity centres?', *The Times* (12 February 1994).

[2] Letter to *The Independent* (4 July 1998).

[3] AALA, Ref.: 11.08.03 C/Int 50v02. See for the usage of such a framework on the Dorset coast, the representative brochure of the Allnatt Centre in Swanage at http://www.allnatt.co.uk/RiskMan/riskman.htm

[4] AALA, 'Quotable quote', *Infolog* Entry No. 10 (Feb 2000).

[5] See his 'Competent People versus Copious Paper', *Horizons* (summer 2005).

Planning

Preparation for the activity shows essential appreciation of the potential hazards involved. The *ad hoc* 'arrangements' in some of the disastrous cases we have considered shows an absence of planning. The classic instance is Glenridding Beck in 2002, where the death on a school trip of Max Palmer, aged ten, led to a plea of guilty to manslaughter by his geography teacher. The HSE report by Dr Stephen Garsed in 2005 bluntly states that this death while 'plunge pooling' during an activity weekend was due to a combination of factors: 'The weather was poor. The stream was in spate. The water was very cold. And, most of all, there were serious deficiencies by the party leader in planning and leading the activity'.[6] The jumping was from a height of four metres, which is very considerable, considering that the International Maritime Order for 'Personal Survival Techniques', a course mandatory for those going to sea, requires an upper limit of 4.5 metres for practice jumps with a buoyancy aid for adults.[7] The investigation on Glenridding Beck showed that 'the chain of events leading to it began long before the fateful weekend': for example, the teacher claimed in his job application to have mountain leadership qualifications, but although he had attended a course he had not qualified, and this false claim was never double-checked by the school; no medical forms were sent out; no parental briefing was held; no educational objective was considered other than 'for them to enjoy themselves'; the ratio of novice to 'experienced' on this trip was 17:1; there was a failure to take local weather or river conditions advice; a stark refusal to heed a warning of dangerous conditions from another school party who had assessed the risks; a complete failure to have available an appropriate throwbag or an emergency procedure when trying to make what was essentially a whitewater rescue; and at trial this was a leader who 'said in mitigation that it had never occurred to him that anything could go wrong'. Dr Garsed comments that 'These very chilling words are often heard following serious incidents. They explain much about the underlying causes of this tragedy'.[8]

Although it is not a completely tested hypothesis, it would seem intuitive that the inexperience of leaders causes undue risk; interestingly it is clear also that there are serious problems with the opposite end of the spectrum, in that some experienced leaders display a 'sense of invincibility', possibly where 'familiarity breeding contempt', or where instructors 'bored with the "easy and familiar" routes ... take clients to more challenging venues simply for personal pleasure'.[9] The Scout Association, following their disaster with Jonathan Attwell falling to

---

[6] HSE, *Glenridding Beck – Investigation Report* (7 March 2005). See 'Parents urged to scrutinize trips', *The Times* (10 March 2005).

[7] The National Sea Training Centre in Gravesend runs the British courses; Regulation VI/1 of the Annex to the International Convention on Standards of Training, Certification and Watchkeeping for Seafarers, 1978.

[8] See generally HSE, loc cit.

[9] Deborah Ajango, 'Learning from Ptarmigan Peak', in her *Lessons Learned, A Guide to Accident Prevention and Crisis Response* (Anchorage : University of Alaska Press, 2000) 83.

his death from Snowdon in 1999, noted that 'it is probably true to say that a safe, interesting and enjoyable day in the mountains for the young people, will be described as "boring" by the leaders but that is better than having to live with the outcome of a young person dying because a leader wanted to complete his ego trip'.[10] However, the novice background of a teacher was the problem in the Australian case of *Beck v State of New South Wales*,[11] where the defendants were held to be negligent by Studdert J for injuries caused to and by a trainee teacher on a school trip to the snow, and for failure to plan adequately and inquire about the relevant activity. Damages were reduced by 20 per cent for contributory negligence because the plaintiff should also have appreciated the risks involved even with very limited snowfield experience. Key aspects in such a 'novice' case will have been the need for 'apprenticing' with someone more experienced; the requirement for an induction process, and this is important too even for experienced instructors and teachers when they move to a new location or activity; and the need for nationally validated training, updates and monitoring.[12] The law can perhaps appear harsh, in setting just one standard for a 'learner', but there are important policy reasons for doing this, as was made clear by the Court of Appeal in the novice driver case of *Nettleship v Weston*: Megaw LJ in particular made clear the rationale for setting just one 'common standard', when comparing a refusal to take account of any defence on the basis of a 'young surgeon' when an operation goes wrong or a suggestion that 'the young, newly-qualified, solicitor owes a lower standard of skill and care'.[13]

Planning will usually involve a reconnaissance to the activity site for an assessment of risks by someone appropriately qualified. Such a visit may be impracticable in overseas expeditions, but that leads on immediately to the critical necessity of taking local advice. Reading the guidebook is no substitute and sometimes even local advice may be deficient if it is not from experts; in 2002 a gap year student, Amy Nichols, went swimming while on a camping trip near the Tsavo West National Park shortly after she had arrived in Kenya to work on a conservation scheme organized by Africa & Asia Venture. The guidebook, *Rough Guide to Kenya*, stated that Lake Challa was 'a pleasant place to swim' and the group only went swimming after local hotel staff assured them that it was safe. Her dismembered body was later recovered from the lake, and experts warned that the number of local people killed by crocodiles throughout the country was increasing and 'no lake could be guaranteed safe'.[14] Another such death occurred to Laura Campbell-Preston, while on a World Challenge Expeditions gap year in Tanzania; she was swimming in a waterhole in 1996 'known locally as being perfectly safe although we are talking about a country infested with crocodiles'.[15] In a further animal encounter on a gap year David

---

[10] 'Mountaineering with Scouts – The Vital Culture', *Fact Sheet* 120415 (March 2001) 2.

[11] [2001] NSWSC 278.

[12] Marcus Bailie, loc cit.

[13] [1971] 3 All ER 581 at 594.

[14] 'Armless body of student found in crocodile lake', *The Independent* (12 March 2002).

[15] 'Scot killed by crocodile in Tanzania', *The Scotsman* (8 May 1996).

Pleydell-Bouverie was mauled to death by lions while on safari in Zimbabwe, but an inquest was informed that he had broken one of the 'key' rules of the safari and slept with his tent door open.[16] Gap years for many probably exhibit an absence of 'planning', but prior thought about arrangements can ward off hazards. Sadly there have been several murders of those on gap years, usually associated with robbery, one of the most recent being that of a backpacker, Caroline Stuttle, who was thrown off a bridge in Australia in 2002; her mother has set up a charity to equip gap year travellers with personal alarm bracelets and has arranged for the wide distribution of a backpacking safety video to sixthformers, along the lines of the work done in Britain by the Suzy Lamplugh Trust after another senseless murder.[17] However, it is probably correct to surmise that 'more Britons have been murdered during a foreign holiday than have died participating in adventure activities abroad',[18] so such cases need to be put in perspective, although any death is a tragedy and more dissemination of potential hazards and preventative measures would be useful.

Risks can often be very much higher in certain locations in the world. UCAS estimate from the University admissions process that something like 26,000 students travel abroad on a gap year before commencing University studies, and although many will be holidaying for most or part of the time there are very significant numbers engaged in voluntary work. Even reputable organizations suffer loss, usually on the roads, as happened in 2001 to three gap year volunteers with Africa & Asia Venture, who were teaching at a mission school in Malawi. They died when the pick-up they were travelling in, having hitched a ride, skidded into a ditch and overturned.[19] The owner of the company indicated that it was the 'first such tragic accident that we have suffered during seven years of operation in Africa',[20] but hitch-hiking with an unknown driver will inevitably increase risk anywhere; the driver was subsequently charged with murder.[21] Less common but still following familiar patterns were the deaths on gap years in 2004 of two students intending to study at Edinburgh University: Eleanor Rutter, a member of the Great Britain Junior Ladies Kayak team and from Yorkshire, intending to read medicine, was trapped under a rock on the Crooked River in New Zealand,[22] while Jack Salt, from Kent and planning to read psychology, fell to his death 'while on a mountaineering exercise' with the school he was teaching at in Ecuador.[23] These overseas cases again illustrate some classic hazards of the outdoors – transport, entrapment, and falling from a height – all carrying a risk and not always completely preventable. As a control measure the Scout

---

[16] 'Sheriff's son killed by lions "broke key safari rule",' *The Guardian* (16 December 1999).

[17] 'Drive for safer gap years', *The Guardian* (23 October 2004).

[18] 'Travellers on the danger list', *Sunday Times* (9 May 1993).

[19] 'Triple tragedy of dream holiday friends', *Western Daily Press* (5 April 2001), 'Crash Driver's On Murder Rap', *News of the World* (18 March 2001).

[20] 'Travel boss's anguish as girls die in crash', *This is Wiltshire* (28 March 2001).

[21] 'Murder charge facing gap-year deaths driver', *Birmingham Post* (19 March 2001).

[22] 'Top kayaker from Yorkshire killed in river tragedy', *Yorkshire Post* (31 March 2004).

[23] 'School stunned by double tragedy', *Sevenoaks Chronicle* (28 October 2004).

Association took a lead among voluntary organizations in banning 'hitch hiking',[24] but the toll of road deaths cannot be entirely eliminated, and particularly not in sometimes very hazardous circumstances overseas. During the very same weekend that Jack Salt fell to his death in Ecuador, a former classmate at Sevenoaks School, Natalie Skilbeck, died when the car she was driving collided head-on with a lorry on the French-speaking island of La Réunion, where she was a gap year volunteer.[25]

Policies and guidelines

Adherence to external guidance may not absolve from liability for providers, schools and voluntary organizations, but this goes a long way to display a conformity to an agreed 'common standard' in the activity. It is noteworthy that the Scout Association does not appear to have had a single fatality to a Scout when Leaders were obeying their organization's activity rules. A case we have examined which might appear to be an exception is where four Scout Leaders died in an avalanche in 1998, but they were on an external training course, and their instructor, Roger Wild, was of course fully exonerated of any negligence in the subsequent public inquiry.[26] A policy document will necessarily deal with such standard legal and procedural issues as child protection, medical support, the pastoral care and welfare of participants, insurance, the experience and competence of instructors, the adequacy of supervision, and above all, staff-student ratios for each excursion, taking into account age, health, fitness and maturity. It will be very difficult to defend a legal action when an organization fails to follow recommendations in its own guidelines, and, unless the organization has higher standards, very difficult too when it breaches generally accepted national standards. A brief scrutiny of a brochure or literature produced by an organization can be a telling analysis of its competence; for example, a phrase such as 'PGL complies with all relevant safety regulations', followed by an extensive listing of these,[27] is a likely precursor to reliable standards, and indeed PGL is not only the largest UK provider of adventurous activities, but has developed into Europe's largest provider of children's activities and travel.[28]

---

[24] Rule 9.74, *Policy, Organization and Rules*, one of only very few bans in Scouting; the others include activities such as bungee jumping and paintballing.

[25] 'School stunned by double tragedy', loc cit.

[26] 'Climbing guide cleared of blame', *Glasgow Herald* (15 December 2000).

[27] PGL indicates its adherence to a comprehensive list of 'The Health and Safety at Work Act 1974, the Health and Safety (First Aid) Regulations 1981, the Activity Centres (Young Persons Safety) Act 1995, the Reporting of Injuries, Diseases and Dangerous Occurrences Regulations 1995 and the Management of Health and Safety at Work Regulations 1999; see generally http://www.pgl.co.uk

[28] It is a myth that PGL stands for 'Parents Get Lost'; the acronym was based on the initials of Peter Gordon Lawrence, who founded the company in 1957 by running canoe trips on the River Wye, and who died in 2004; 'Pioneer of adventure holidays dies at 69', *The Gloucester Citizen* (24 August 2004).

Some guidelines will be mandatory, such as child protection procedures instituted in the Protection of Children Act 1999 to guard against abusive relationships, and which requires a list to be kept of individuals considered unsuitable to work with children, with repeated checks against that list of anyone coming into unsupervised contact with children. There are of course criminal and civil sanctions in most jurisdictions against child abuse, but the aim of the 1999 Act in Britain was to prevent this. When abuse occurs then penalties can be high and the subsequent furore of public interest can severely damage an organization; in a recent criminal case in the Boston Archdiocese a defrocked priest who has allegedly been the centre of widespread abuse, Paul Shanley, aged 74, was imprisoned for a minimum of 12 years when he was convicted of child rape, indecent assault and battery. Documents before the court showed that church officials knew of numerous sexual abuse allegations against him and that the priest had publicly advocated sex between men and boys. Despite this, Father Shanley was shuttled from parish to parish, and eventually transferred to California with a letter of recommendation from one of Archbishop Cardinal Law's deputies; the judge said 'It is difficult to imagine a more egregious misuse of trust and authority', but resisted the prosecution's demand for a life sentence.[29] However, it is the civil compensation against churches, schools and voluntary associations in the USA which has attracted most comment. In a typical Californian case in 1999, *William S. v Bonita Unified School District*,[30] a boy was sexually abused by his soccer coach, who was also an elementary school teacher. The perpetrator was sent to prison, and in the resultant civil action the allegation was that the School District had been negligent after an earlier incident when they knew he had taken photographs of a boy and because they had also received a letter accusing him of molesting boys. The District countered that after these warnings they had 'watched him carefully' and saw no inappropriate behaviour, but a jury awarded $10.8 million in damages, 55 per cent against the culprit and 45 per cent against the District for vicarious liability. In recent years the level of damages has mounted exponentially; the Archdiocese of Boston paid $85 million in a settlement on abuse by priests and lay employees in 2004,[31] followed by an unprecedented Californian settlement in the Archdiocese of Los Angeles which set a 'going rate' of $3 million per plaintiff and may amount to payments of more than $1.5 billion from the Catholic authorities in California.[32] Litigation is still underway in many other parts of the USA.

The legal and political climate has changed in Britain too on this central issue of child protection, and following the report of Sir Ronald Waterhouse, which uncovered widespread abuse in children's homes in North Wales, a new criminal charge of 'abuse of a position of trust' was created under the Sexual Offences Act 2000. This offence was widened in sections 16 to 24 of the Sexual Offences Act

---

[29] 'Shanley gets 12 to 15 years; defrocked priest's accuser hailed as hero', *Boston Globe* (16 February 2005).

[30] California, Los Angeles County Superior Court, No. KC024405, 29 March 1999.

[31] 'Diocese settles abuse cases for record amount', *New York Times* (3 December 2004).

[32] 'Damage claims may top $1.5 billion in Los Angeles', *Miami Herald* (30 August 2004).

2003. All such changes were vehemently opposed by the main teaching unions, with Chris Keates of the NASUWT pointing out that those found guilty faced not just imprisonment but being barred from their profession for life and being placed on List 99, the sexual offenders list held by the Department for Education and Skills. That union was particularly concerned at the number of malicious allegations against teachers, with a claim that 97 per cent of cases collapsed.[33] However, some have succeeded. In 2004 Justine Rowe, a teacher in Berkshire who had commenced a lesbian affair with a student in activities such as an overnight 'Readathon' and on a school trip to Manchester, was imprisoned for 12 months for what was described as a 'gross breach of trust'.[34] By contrast Adrian Bull, a drama teacher in Bristol was sentenced to a three year community order when Bristol Crown Court accepted that there was no 'evidence of coercion, manipulation, corruption, grooming or taking advantage of the pupil', and indeed, conversely, a female pupil aged 15 had deliberately set out to seduce her teacher.[35] As a benchmark of changing conditions, Chris Woodhead, the former Chief Inspector of Schools, infamously commented at the time of the legislative change that relationships with teachers could be 'experiential and educative'. He was himself promptly engulfed in accusations that he had started an affair with one of his pupils when he was a teacher, later leading the National Association of Head Teachers to refer the case to the Director of Public Prosecutions for perjury. The allegations came not just from Mr Woodhead's ex-wife, a former Vice-President of the British Mountaineering Council and not necessarily fitting the portrayal of a 'woman scorned', but from several teaching colleagues from that era, and corroborated by a solicitor's contemporaneous note in 1976 which recorded, in something of a legal understatement, that Mr Woodhead did not want the co-respondent's name disclosed as 'she was a sixth-former when the adultery started and it was understood the teaching profession were averse to teachers committing adultery with sixth-form pupils'.[36]

Currently this new legislation does not apply to voluntary organizations, even though in his report on safeguards for children living away from home in 1997, the first Chief Inspector of Social Sevices Sir William Utting concluded that child abusers were 'frequently in a position of responsibility, authority and trust'.[37] A number of campaigners, such as Baroness Blatch, have consistently argued for the criminal charge of 'abuse of a position of trust' to include youth

---

[33] 'She undressed. I was way out of my depth', *The Times* (4 March 2004).

[34] 'Teacher who had lesbian affair with pupil is jailed', *The Times* (10 December 2004).

[35] 'At 15, I was a stalker and Sir was my prey', *Mail on Sunday* (27 April 2003).

[36] 'Woodhead begged wife not to expose his lies', *The Observer* (11 April 1999). See also 'Woodhead lied under oath on affair', *Observer* (25 April 1999) and 'Exclusive: The ex-wife of schools chief Chris Woodhead reveals how he lied over his affair with a schoolgirl and how he tried to make all three live together in a bizarre ménage-à-trois', *Mail On Sunday* (7 March 1999).

[37] Department of Health and Welsh Office, *People like Us, The Report of the Review of the Safeguards for Children Living Away from Home*, HMSO 1997, Summary Report, 7.

organizations.[38] In an extraordinary Illinois case in 1999, *Doe v Goff*,[39] the Court of Appeals held that the Boy Scouts of America owed no duty of care to a member who was allegedly molested by a camp volunteer because 'sexual assault of a Boy Scout by an adult Boy Scout volunteer was not foreseeable' (sic).[40] The alleged molestation had been in 1987 or 1988, and the claim was that the BSA had failed to investigate the moral fitness of their volunteer, and allowed him to participate in scouting activities knowing that he was a paedophile, but the defendants said they were unaware until 1992 of any such crimes, and the culprit was a paediatrician who had no criminal record and no known propensity to be a child molestor. The Illinois court indicated that there were over a million Scout volunteers each year in the USA and it would be difficult to obtain a serious check on them. However, the case saw a vigorous dissent by Breslin J, and it would seem unlikely to be followed elsewhere, and particularly not now in the USA. Civil litigation is additional to criminal charges such as indecent assault, of which unfortunately there are several instances in voluntary organizations despite all the internal checks, as well as now in Britain the Criminal Records Bureau procedure. Consultation has just closed on whether sports coaches should be brought into the scope of offences under the Sexual Offences Act 2003. At least two national governing bodies expect their coaches to take a role that a 'reasonable and prudent parent would expect from a teacher in a school environment' or that of a 'responsible parent', so the concept of coach is closely aligned already to that of a teacher *in loco parentis*.[41]

Given the many hundreds of thousands of volunteers in British organizations, and the 'honey pot' nature of these organizations for paedophiles, it is perhaps unsurprising that the occasional abuser slips through the net, although it is noticeable that in more recent times they are often described as 'former' members of such groups: recent examples include 'a former Sea Scout leader who set up his own activity group for young boys';[42] a primary school teacher who was a Childline counsellor and who 'was a Scout Leader';[43] a police officer who had engaged in assaults while a scout leader;[44] a teacher convicted of indecently assaulting pupils who had managed to get work at four Staffordshire schools despite facing similar allegations in previous posts, despite having been suspended from a school and despite having been dismissed as a Cub Scout Leader in a different part of the country;[45] and an offender 'who was once a scout

---

[38] House of Lords *Hansard* (1 April 2003) col 1288.

[39] 716 N.E.2d 323 (Illinois Appeals Court 1999).

[40] At 324.

[41] These formulations related to the Karate Union for Great Britain and the Amateur Swimming Association; see generally Yvonne Williams, 'Playing it safe'. *New Law Journal* (18 February 2005).

[42] Part of a headline in the *Eastern Daily Press* (26 February 2005) on a 'pillar of society' who had obtained lottery funding to purchase canoeing equipment.

[43] 'Childline worker abused young boys', *Birmingham Post* (15 January 2005).

[44] 'Police officer assaulted boys while scout leader', *This is Local London* (10 December 2004).

[45] 'Pervert's victims failed by system', *Stoke Sentinel* (13 November 2004).

leader'.[46] Anyone who is remotely complacent about these issues should perhaps study the case in 2004 of William Goad, a millionaire market trader in Plymouth, who was thought by police to be the country's 'most prolific paedophile' and who was sentenced by Judge Taylor to life imprisonment. He had raped and sexually abused thousands of young boys over the past 40 years, driving two to suicide, and was described by the prosecution at Plymouth Crown Court as 'voracious, calculating, predatory and violent', having employed children in shops and on market stalls, owning two houses overlooking school playgrounds, having set up play centres, and having run a private camping club.[47]

Legally it is now much more difficult to claim that an errant employee was acting on a 'frolic of their own' in perpetrating criminal acts.[48] Perhaps in time a similar standard of vicarious liability will apply even for errant volunteers, although there does not yet appear to be a decided case on this volunteer aspect in Britain. In the leading employee case of *Lister v Hesley Hall*,[49] the House of Lords had to consider liability in respect of the warden of a boy's boarding school in Doncaster for those who had emotional and behavioural difficulties. Lord Steyn said that the sexual abuse was 'inextricably interwoven' with the carrying out of his duties, 'committed in the time and on the premises of employers'.[50] Lord Millett pointed out that 'vicarious liability is a species of strict liability. It is not premised on any culpable act or omission on the part of the employer; an employer who is not personally at fault is made legally answerable for the fault of his employee. It is best understood as a loss-distribution device.'[51] While as yet there does not appear to have been a case in Britain on the vicarious liability of voluntary organizations in this area of child protection, there has of course been *Vowles v Evans* on vicarious liability for a volunteer rugby referee engaged in negligent conduct, and it is suggested that the same principles would apply.[52] The Charity Commission indicates that trustees may be liable for 'the wrongful actions or omissions of employees, volunteers or others which they have sanctioned' and 'occasionally they will even be liable for the acts or omissions of

---

[46] 'We help cage this pervert; ex-Scout Chief gets 3½ Years', *Birmingham Evening Mail* (20 April 2004).

[47] 'Paedophile gets life sentence', *The Guardian* (5 October 2004). A reference by Lord Goldsmith, the Attorney-General, to increase the minimum tariff for when parole might be considered was turned down by the Court of Appeal, but they made it clear that the full circumstances would be considered at an appropriate time; *R v Goad, Attorney General's Reference (No 131 of 2004)* [2005] All ER (D), 30 January 2005.

[48] See the review of expanding liability by Ewan McKendrick, 'Vicarious Liability and Independent Contractors – A Re-examination', 53 *Modern Law Review* (1990) 770.

[49] [2001] 2 All ER 769.

[50] At 778. See also two other very important recent cases on vicarious liability: *Dubai Aluminium v Salaam* [2003] 1 All ER 97 and *Mattis v Pollock (trading as Flamingos Nightclub)* [2004] 4 All ER 85.

[51] At 793.

[52] See J. Michael Martinez, 'Liability and volunteer organizations: A survey of the law', *Nonprofit Managementand Leadership* vol 14, No, 2 (2003) 151-169.

employees and volunteers which they have *not* expressly sanctioned'.[53] The Supreme Court of Canada has specifically rejected a contention that non-profit organizations should be the subject of a judicial exemption from vicarious liability, and coupled with litigation on Common Law principles in the USA it would seem very likely that Britain would follow suit.[54]

However, there are perimeters to liability. A grim case which is a reminder of possible dangers in the most unlikely circumstances, but also of matters that are likely to be out of the control of party organizers, is the Pennsylvania case of *Fay v Thiel College*.[55] Amy Fay was participating in a College course, involving a trip to Peru, when she became ill and was admitted to a medical clinic. The trip organizers arranged for an American woman missionary to act as her translator, and this chaperone asked if she could be present when surgery was advised for an appendicitis. That request was refused, and in the absence of the missionary, the student was sexually assaulted by both doctors while undergoing allegedly unnecessary surgery. An appeal in the USA turned on whether a release signed by the student was entered into voluntarily, and this was considered in Pennsylvania to be a 'take it or leave it adhesion contract and therefore unenforceable', so the case was sent for jury trial to determine whether there had been negligence on the part of the College; the case seems to have been settled, although it would appear very unlikely that the missionary could have insisted on 'crossing a line' in an operating theatre, because of the hygiene implications, and very unlikely that she or anyone else could 'reasonably foresee' sexual assault by surgeons.

There has been a complete change too in the climate in Britain and elsewhere on checking references, with potential negligence liability under *Spring v Guardian Assurance*,[56] particularly in respect of former employees. In 1994, in the wake of the Lyme Bay disaster, a TV researcher applied for a job to twenty outdoor activity centres; none of them bothered to check his qualifications, which were bogus, and six offered him a job without an interview.[57] In the USA there has also been a finding on third party liability, in that a school trying to 'pass the

---

[53] See generally Charity Commission for England and Wales, 'Vicarious Liability of a Charity or its Trustees', *Guidance for Charities on Good Practice*.

[54] See *Bazley v Curry* [1999] 2 S.C.R. 534 and *Jacobi v Griffiths* [1999] 2 S.C.R. 570. The first case was a employee in a non-profit residential care facility for the treatment of emotionally troubled children who turned out to be a paedophile, and liability was found. By contrast, in the second cases, on the facts, a Boys' and Girls' Club was held not vicariously liable for sexual assaults committed on two children by a volunteer who pursued his own 'agenda of personal gratification'. Inevitably much depends on the facts; see Peter Cane, 'Vicarious Liability for Sexual Abuse' 116 *Law Quarterly Review* (2000) 21, at pp. 24-25. See also Elizabeth Grace and Susan Vella, *Civil Liability for Sexual Abuse and Violence in Canada* (Toronto: Butterworths, 2000), and for a comparative law perspective, Duncan Fairgrieve and Sarah Green (eds), *Child Abuse Tort Claims Against Public Bodies* (Aldershot: Ashgate, 2004).

[55] 2001 Pa. D & C, Lexis 235 (December 2001).

[56] [1994] 3 All ER 129.

[57] Working on BBC2's *On The Line*; 'How safe are activity centres?', *The Times* (12 February 1994).

buck' by giving a good reference to an employee suspected of inappropriate conduct with students, a classic way of disposing of suspicious circumstances, may be liable for subsequent abuse; the Californian Appeals Court held in *Randi W. v Livingston Union School District*[58] that school authorities who favourably recommend a former employee for employment at another school may be liable for their former employee's subsequent molestations at the hiring school on the basis of fraud, negligent misrepresentation and negligence *per se*. In Britain, a key change in the practice here was the setting up by the Home Office of the Criminal Records Bureau, established under the Police Act 1997, and undertaking detailed background checks in England and Wales, with a Disclosure Bureau under the Scottish Criminal Record Office north of the border working along similar lines.

As well as these legislative rules on the paramount issue of child safety, an adherence to AALA or DfES guidelines generally, while not mandatory for all, is certainly sensible in avoiding legal problems. For example, the *Handbook for Group Leaders* under the heading 'supervision' deals with such straightforward issues as 'responsibility, head counts, the buddy system, remote supervision and whether this is appropriate in the circumstances, rearranging groups and down time'.[59] Such an analysis should obviously be routine on a school trip, and measured against, for example, the disappearance of Bunmi Shagaya, who drowned on a school trip to France, it is understandable why very serious questions needed to be asked in that case about how she could have gone unaccounted for and why 'no head count was carried out when the school party left the lake to walk to a nearby slide adventure ride'.[60] Sadly the conclusion drawn from that case by the NASUWT seems to have been that 'parental demands for 100 per cent safety were impossible to meet',[61] although a more objective analysis of that school trip abroad would suggest that certain elementary rules of supervision seem to have been disregarded. Such rules are near-universally observed in other primary schools, and although the 'crocodile' of walking in pairs may seem rather old-fashioned, its more modern counterpart of a 'buddy system', or the variant described in the *HASPEV Handbook for Group Leaders* of a 'circle buddy' system, is not just common sense to ensure that pupils cannot 'vanish' but is legally essential for anyone *in loco parentis*.[62]

---

[58] 48 Cal. Rptr. 2d 378 (Ct Appeals. 1995).

[59] *Handbook for Group Leaders*, HASPEV Supplement 3, *Health and Safety of Pupils on Educational Visits: A Good Practice Guide* (2003).

[60] 'Bunmi teachers could face charges', *Daily Mail* (13 July 2001).

[61] Chris Keates quoted in 'School trips threatened by a teachers' boycott', *Daily Mail* (27 July 2001). See for other commentaries by the NASUWT in the light of Bunmi Shagaya's death, 'We'll axe the school trips; teachers fear legal action over accidents', *Daily Mirror* (7 August 2002), 'Teachers warned: don't accept job of running school trips', *The Independent* (7 August 2002), 'End of school trips; teachers tell MPs: we're so frightened of being sued that we dare not take children out of class', *Daily Express* (1 November 2004).

[62] See the paragraphs in *Handbook for Group Leaders*, HASPEV Supplement 3, *Health and Safety of Pupils on Educational Visits: A Good Practice Guide* (2003).

Information and briefings

As we have seen, giving participants, and in many cases their parents, adequate information about activities, the risks involved and the levels of supervision enables them to take an informed view. Contact information, personal kitlists and a programme of activities reinforces confidence in a well-ordered itinerary. One useful point mentioned by the AALA is that a medical emergency or complication to a teacher or other accompanying adult can be just as threatening as to a young person, and yet many providers only request medical forms from youth participants; in 1998 Oliver Basham, aged 11, saved the life of a field studies instructor on the Isle of Wight, when she suffered an epileptic fit while measuring on a beach and fell face down into the sea.[63] Although the issue of 'consent forms' is unacceptable in Britain if attempting to exempt liability, some signature on a document is useful evidence of an acceptance of the information given out and the circumstances of the activities; the purpose of such a form in Britain is therefore not to provide indemnity or exclusion through a 'contract of adhesion', but to indicate a necessary standard of care in preparing for the activity. As we have seen in many cases, probably the most important issue in water activities is whether a participant is a non-swimmer, where special safeguards will be vital. Similarly, details of special needs, medication, allergies and dietary restrictions need to be taken, the latter potentially life-threatening with anaphylactic shock. In a Californian case in 1995 a woman dining at a Spago restaurant informed the waitress that she was 'deathly allergic' to nut products and ordered a dessert only after the waitress reassured her it did not contain nuts. Within 15 minutes the victim had a violent allergic reaction, suffered a stroke, and was left with permanent brain damage, leading to a settlement of the case for $1 million.[64] Where a participant comes from a non-English speaking background, then there is a heightened duty to make them and their family fully aware of the necessity to provide information on the appropriate forms; this may be an issue in the continuing Herve Bola case where it is alleged that he was a known non-swimmer from a form filled in prior to the trip.

Staffing

This is probably the prime consideration in the outdoor cases where supervision is so often an issue. An appropriate level of technical expertise in the relevant activities is vital for an instructor. The chief qualification after that is adequate first aid proficiency. This competence is a critical component of the overall structure of safety in all organizations dealing with the outdoors. Prompt

---

[63] AALA, 'Medical Information on accompanying adults', *Infolog* Entry No. 12 (May 2000); 'Brave Oliver to the rescue', *Western Daily Press* (17 July 1998).

[64] *Doe v Trattoria Spago*, California, Los Angeles County Superior Court, No BC105476, 15 September 1995. See also a similar case on allergic reaction to peanut butter contained in a saltwater taffy: *Link v Dolles Candyland Inc*, settled before filing Kansas, 21 July 1995.

intervention, even at a lowly level of expertise, saves thousands of lives each year; for example, with asthma affecting approximately one-third of the school-age population and deaths running at 4,000 or so a year in Britain it is inevitable that most trips and expeditions will include someone who needs their inhaler and might need prompt attention. In *Hippolyte v Bexley London Borough*[65] the Court of Appeal upheld a decision by French J that Elizabeth Hippolyte, aged 16, who suffered brain damage as a result of an asthma attack at school in Erith was not negligently dealt with. She had been hospitalized on three occasions in the last seven months as a result of frequent attacks, and her family sued on the basis that the school had not acted with due diligence. However, the facts did not support this contention; an experienced teacher supervised her use of an inhaler and three times suggested the schoolgirl should go home, and then summoned assistance and called for an ambulance. On the facts there could be no doubting the teacher's professionalism. By contrast, in a New York school case, *Garcia v City of New York*,[66] a girl aged 13 was permitted to bring food to her class after lunch but began choking on a piece of hot dog; she stood up, said she had to leave for the toilets and rushed out. A moment later she came out, gestured frantically, spun around, threw herself against a wall and collapsed. A teacher trained in first aid, 'including the Heimlich manoeuvre' the court noted, was brought in from a nearby classroom, but seems merely to have checked the pulse of the victim. The school guidelines required the blowing of a whistle in emergencies, which would have summoned a teacher trained in cardio-pulmonary resuscitation techniques, but this was not done and a jury awarded $1 million for the subsequent injuries. A similar sort of decision was reached by a Californian jury in *Kinney v Grossman-Cuyamaca Community College*[67] where a mature student collapsed and the professor allegedly told fellow students he was having a narcoleptic fit and they should leave him alone, only relenting when breathing had stopped. Following a jury direction that an individual may not 'unreasonably prevent third parties from giving aid to prevent physical harm, the widow was awarded $2.08 million. The Heimlich Manoeuvre mentioned in the *Garcia* case has been credited with saving very many lives, probably more than 100,000 since it was invented in 1974 by Dr Henry Heimlich, a Cincinnati thoracic surgeon. Indeed, the Heimlich Institute he established suggests that 'he has saved the lives of more human beings than any other person living today,' and the numbers increased considerably after Dr Heimlich's procedure was immortalized in the film *Mrs Doubtfire*, which produced a mass audience for an obscure first aid technique.[68] British Government figures show that about 16,000 people end up in hospital each year after choking on food, and of these over 200 die each year. However, as with any manoeuvre it needs to be correctly applied; in 2002 a woman in Lancashire was

---

[65] CA transcript 23 November 1994.

[66] New York, King's County Superior Court, No. 26134/91, 24 October 1995.

[67] Cal., San Diego County Superior Court. No. GIE018319, 10 March 2004.

[68] 'I saw Robin Williams do it in the film and knew exactly what to do', a teaching assistant Susan Atkinson commented after saving the life of a boy who was choking on a 50p coin, 'Movie's a life-saver', *Sun* (1 May 2004).

wrongly assumed to be choking 'when a piece of the scampi she was eating went down the wrong way', and a 'rescuer' using the Heimlich technique proceeded to break her ribs and land her in a hospital rather than on the holiday she was just about to take – the victim's comment was that 'I am sure the man who did this to me was acting with the best of intentions but he really did not know what he was doing'.[69]

On many outdoor activities the overwhelmingly important issue is hypothermia, where the core body temperature drops to a dangerous level. Wind chill factors in air and particularly immersion in cold water can exacerbate the temperature loss. As water conducts body heat away up to 26 times faster than air of the same temperature, 'cold water near drowning' is also a serious hazard associated with all water activities.[70] If signs of 'incipient hypothermia' are spotted by a competent person, then steps can immediately be taken to avert disaster. Somewhat surprisingly the 'entry level' First Response course taken by many teachers and outdoor activity leaders, and which was a course 'designed specifically for adult leaders in The Scout Association and Girlguiding UK based on the situations and issues that occur within those roles', did not at first include any instruction about hypothermia. This has been revised,[71] but the syllabus for several other courses, such as the 'Appointed Person' certificate under the Health & Safety (First Aid) Regulations 1981 still does not include the hypothermia issue. The longer eight hour courses by the leading organizations such as the Red Cross and St. John's Ambulance Brigade, and the various ancillary courses run by bodies such as the BCU, RYA and the Mountain Rescue Council all do contain this critical point and it is arguable that these specialist courses are in any event a rather more appropriate qualification for the outdoors.

In the USA an absence of skill in cardiopulmonary resuscitation (CPR) is an immediate indication of a lack of training; for example, in the Florida case of *Johnson v City of Hallendale*, a child aged five in a city day camp drowned, and neither the camp workers nor the lifeguards could perform CPR. A jury awarded $17.5 million. In Florida there is a damages 'cap' of $100,000 in claims against municipalities, so there was a petition to the state legislature to give permission to award damages above that ceiling, and in this interregnum the case was settled for an undisclosed amount.[72] In another case in that state involving a fairground, *Ingram v Busch Entertainment Corporation*, a girl aged 13 with a heart abnormality was found not to be breathing at the end of a rollercoaster ride. The attendants turned away a nurse who offered to assist, a rescue unit was delayed waiting for a security escort outside, and then the escort led them in the wrong direction. The mother sued when her child died, alleging inadequate attendant

---

[69] 'Life-saving move hospitalizes woman who just needed a sip of water', *The Times* (18 December 2002).

[70] See generally Chapter Eight in Rick Curtis, *The Backpacker's Field Manual : A Comprehensive Guide to Mastering Backcountry Skills* (New York: Three Rivers Press, 1998).

[71] Scout Association 'First Response: Definition and Equivalents', *Fact Sheet* FS310547 (Edition No, 4, March 2004).

[72] Florida, Broward County Circuit Court, No. 96-2465 (14), 25 July 1997.

training and an inadequate emergency response plan. It was admitted there had never been an emergency drill, the first attendant was untrained in emergency aid, and although the second had CPR training he did not use it. The counter-claim was that the mother should never have allowed her daughter on a rollercoaster ride when a sign warned that it was not recommended for people who had heart problems. The jury awarded $500,000, but reduced this by 30 per cent for the mother's 'comparative' negligence.[73]

With the wide availability of first aid courses it would be wholly remiss not to have an appropriately trained first aider somewhere close in most outdoor activities. But what is the level of expertise required? Most first aid is of the 'band aid' variety, and self-administered; minor cuts, grazes and blisters go with the territory. An adequate first aid kit is usually all that is required. Next up the continuum is the tilting of a head to clear airways or the 'recovery' position to assist someone in breathing while fluids are draining; this is an elementary matter which even young children can grasp and which can save many lives. For example, the syndrome of 'swallowing the tongue' on experiencing a shock, in reality the tongue falling back and obstructing the small aperture of the windpipe, is a common feature of road accidents and sports injuries after an impact. The advice of organizations such as the BBC Sports Academy is to 'remove a mouth guard if they have one to help breathing and check they haven't swallowed their tongue,'[74] whereas the American Red Cross suggests that 'swallowing the tongue is an urban legend'.[75] Asphyxiation led to the important case of *Barrett v Ministry of Defence*,[76] where we have seen that a failure to place an unconscious naval airmen into the recovery position after heavy drinking, and then a failure to maintain a constant watch, led him to choke on his vomit – sadly a fairly common occurrence in drunk individuals, and by no means rare in the armed forces over the centuries. This was a rare finding both on liability for an 'omission' and also in a successful case against the MoD. Drinking in one of three bars on this isolated base at Barduffos in northern Norway was described as 'one of the main recreations', and the deceased drank in excess of seven cans of cider and eleven double Bacardis. Following a collapse, he was taken by stretcher to his bunk and placed in the recovery position, and the evidence was that he was 'in a coma but tossing and turning', so there was a serious risk of death, which was why Queen's Regulations provided not only that commanding officers should 'discourage

---

[73] Florida, Hillsborough County Circuit Court, No. 95-5183, 14 June 1996.

[74] BBC Sport Academy Parent, a website aimed at parents involving their children in sport; http://news.bbc.co.uk/sportacademy/parent/hi/default.stm

[75] Greg Stockton, American Red Cross. The other 'household truths' he cites as 'common errors include pounding on the back of someone choking, using tweezers to remove stingers after a bee sting and putting butter on a burn to soothe the pain. The first rule of responding is to cause no further harm'; Mason Booth, 'Lifesaving Lessons for Everyday Emergencies', http://www.redcross.org. The National Health Service still recommends placing someone in the recovery position, because this ensures that 'the tongue cannot be swallowed'; http://www.nhsdirect.nhs.uk

[76] [1995] 3 All ER 87.

drunkenness' but also were required to 'take appropriate action to prevent ... possible injury or fatality, including medical assistance if it is available'.[77]

Another leading case on the lack of quality first aid which brought a finding of negligence we have examined is *Watson v British Boxing Board of Control* in 1999. While brain damage in 1991 was foreseeable when Mr Watson was knocked down in a boxing match, and he was clearly assuming a risk every time he entered the ring, the level of medical attention available was considered insufficient.[78]

Beyond first aid there is an increasing view in the literature of the requirement for 'effective leadership'.[79] What this means precisely is a subject of considerable debate. Even the 'hard skills', preferably at the level of a recognized national governing body level, taper off into the 'soft skills' needed for those who are to organize, supervise and lead activities. For example, the Royal Yachting Association criteria to be a Powerboat Instructor includes the requirement to have 'a friendly, supportive manner towards students' along with 'good boat control at all times'.[80] Hard skills are generally matters such as technical competence in the activity, safety expertise, and perhaps even environmental skills in the modern era to prevent harm to natural surroundings by encouraging minimum-impact travel and 'leave-no-trace camping'. Soft skills are about organizational ability, instructional skills, and facilitating teamwork particularly where there is to be 'remote supervision' of a group. Professor Simon Priest in Canada has also pioneered the concept of 'higher-order meta skills', which he characterizes as a 'glue' to integrate hard and soft skills through a flexible leadership style which has 'experience-based judgment' and teaches problem-solving and decision-making skills.[81]

What competent staffing is generally about is that critical word 'supervision', which we have seen repeatedly in the cases. Sometimes there will be a divergence of opinion and the facts will not always be clear. For example, when the instructor Graham Lipp died in the Porth yr Ogof caves in 1992, he was hailed by some as having 'sacrificed his life to save a teenager drowning in an underground lake', as he had 'dived into the icy water and managed to drag the unconscious schoolboy to the side, before he, too, was swept underwater by strong currents and became entangled in tree roots'. Despite the gratitude of 14-year-old Wayne Brown's parents – 'It was a tremendous act of unselfishness to put Wayne first' – even they had to point out that warning signs indicated no-one should enter without 'wet gear and breathing apparatus'. Wayne's Headteacher at Y Pant

---

[77] At 96 per Beldam LJ.

[78] *The Times*, 12 October 1999). A report in the *Daily Telegraph* (9 October 2001) deals with the subsequent settlement by agreement in the High Court.

[79] See generally Simon Priest and Michael A. Gass, *Effective Leadership in Adventure Programming* (Champaign, Il: Human Kinetics Publishers, 1997).

[80] RYA, *Powerboat Instructors Handbook* (1997 G19/97) 7.

[81] See additionally Simon Priest, 'Effective Outdoor Leadership' in Deborah Ajango (ed), *Lessons Learned: A Guide to Accident Prevention and Crisis Response* (Anchorage: University of Alaska, 2004) 33-64.

comprehensive school in Llantrisant also added his thanks that 'We are all very grateful for Mr Lipp's heroism and unselfish act and we are relieved that the tragedy did not take the lad as well'.[82] The Cave Rescue team leader Huw Thomas also praised Mr Lipp's courage, saying 'He undoubtedly saved the boy's life' on the basis that he 'waded into a treacherous underground lake when he heard screams from the party of youngsters'.[83]

The heroism theme was somewhat difficult to maintain at the subsequent inquest when Mr Lipp was criticized for taking the children into the resurgence pool as a method of 'taking a more adventurous way out', knowing that they were 'wearing wellington boots, waterproof coveralls, jumpers, and jeans unsuitable for swimming'. When Jody Parry pointed out the sign saying 'Danger. Deep pool ahead,' the instructor allegedly said 'As you can see, caving is very dangerous if you are not qualified. A lot of deaths have occurred in these caves,' swam to the centre of the ten foot deep pool and shouted for the children to link hands to walk into the pool. Wayne Brown was actually dragged clear by his classmates who administered mouth to mouth resuscitation, and were commended by the coroner 'for your marvellous bravery'. A solicitor representing Mid Glamorgan County Council, which ran the outdoor pursuits centre at Dolygaer employing Mr Lipp, told the inquest that 'it does appear Mr Lipp did something he was not authorized to do. In fact, he had been specifically directed not to go in this pool'. The jury returned a verdict of accidental death, with the coroner stating that 'there is evidence that there was a breach of his duty to care for the pupils by Mr Lipp' and that the only explanation was that 'it must have been a rush of blood to his head to make him do this' in taking first-time cavers into a pool which has claimed so many lives.[84] Gary Evans, of the West Brecon Cave Rescue Team, indicated in 2002 about this particular location that 'in the past 30 years, there have been 11 deaths in the caves, 10 of which have involved the resurgence pool'.[85]

Failure to supervise was also an issue in a Californian case where there was a church-sponsored camping trip; a boy aged 14 had abseiled down a cliff and was told to take a trail back to the top, but he attempted to climb up the face of the mountain rather than take the approved route, fell, and as a result was unlikely ever to live independently or be gainfully employed. The allegation was not just the failure to supervise, but also that the camp counsellors running the abseiling did not have sufficient experience to lead such a high-risk activity. The case settled for $4.4 million.[86] A European case involved criminal proceedings brought in Italy against a German teacher, Volker Sonntag, who was prosecuted

---

[82] 'Cave hero's sacrifice; instructor drowns after diving into underground torrent to save teenager', *Daily Mail* (16 October 1992).

[83] 'Instructor died saving teenage potholer in cave', *Glasgow Herald* (16 October 1992).

[84] 'Instructor "died trying to save boy from cave pool",' *Glasgow Herald* (28 November 1992).

[85] 'Teenage soldier dies on Army exercise', *Derby Evening Telegraph* (24 July 2002).

[86] *Dunn v Southern California Seventh Day Adventists*, California, San Bernadino County Superior Court, No. SCV31030, 18 January 1998.

for manslaughter in Bolzano for causing the death of a pupil who had died on a school trip there. The parents and brother of Hans Waidmann, the deceased, joined the criminal proceedings as civil parties, seeking an order against Mr Sonntag for compensation. The teacher was found guilty on the criminal charges and was also ordered to pay 20 million lira in damages and to bear the legal costs. The family then enforced this judgment in the German courts. On procedural points the case went on appeal to the European Court of Justice, but the essential issue was that the teacher had failed in his supervisory duties.[87]

However, on every occasion the issue is raised, adequate supervision has to be judged in the circumstances. In an Australian case an intellectually disabled boy aged thirteen suffered severe head injuries in a game called 'Rob the Nest' at his school, when he struck the knee of a classmate. The game was supervised by the class teacher as well as a physical education teacher, and the Supreme Court dismissed the case because the risk of injury caused by bodies manoeuvring at low speed was small and supervision was adequate. It was not reasonable to ban the game as it fulfilled an appropriate purpose of developing skills and team spirit.[88]

Supervision is not easily disentangled from 'chaperonage'. The distinction is probably that a 'chaperon', from the circumstances of a mature woman in charge of a young woman on social occasions, has the connotation of 'one to one' supervision, which may be required in the circumstances of age, ability or high risk. In *Drummond v Tandy Corp*[89] a boy aged seven on a trip to an ice-skating rink with a day care centre in Texas was knocked unconscious, suffered a coma for two days, and then was found to have a permanent learning disability. The allegation was improper supervision, with 'no chaperon present', but there was also a case brought against the rink for not providing helmets. The evidence was that there had been more than 100 head injuries at the rink in the previous four years; the case was settled on undisclosed terms. Another case on ice-skating, this time in Florida, *Trotter v Magic City Ice, Inc*[90] was brought solely against the rink, for negligent maintenance of the surface but also for inadequate supervision by 'skate guards' who were employed to maintain good order. However, the claimant, who broke a leg when executing a 'hockey stop' to avoid a collision, was aged 44 and hardly in need of 'chaperonage'. Nevertheless, liability was established on inadequate maintenance and the case was settled for $52,000. The opposite end of the supervision spectrum from being chaperoned 'one to one' is the concept of 'remote supervision', which is the term used to describe an

---

[87] *Sonntag v Waidmann* C-172/91 [1993] ECR I-1963. See the ECJ report at 'Compensation order claim is civil', *The Times* (18 May 1993).

[88] *Kretschmar v State of Queensland* [1989] 180-272. See also the 'reasonable teacher' standard in *Geyer v Downs* (1977) 138 CLR 91, indicating that the notion that a school teacher is *in loco parentis* does not fully state the legal responsibility of a school, which in many respects goes beyond that of a parent. See Peter Williams, 'Sport in schools: some legal liability issues', *Sports Administration* vol 3 (2001).

[89] Texas, Dallas County 192d Judicial District Court., No. 92-9531, February 1, 1995.

[90] Florida, Orange County Circuit Court., No. CI 94-4311, 27 June 1995.

occasional visit to check an independent team. A classic instance is on a Duke of Edinburgh's Award expedition, where the requirement for a supervisor is to visit a team 'once a day, or as often as safety demands', with the emphasis on the participants gaining maturity and self-confidence through 'unaccompanied and self-reliant expeditioning'.[91]

Emergency management

Grim as the prospect seems, there is no provider, school or voluntary organization that can escape the possibility of injury. In 1997, in a very famous American case, a group of novice mountaineering students at the University of Alaska fell nearly a thousand feet down a snow gully on Ptarmigan Peak. Two students died and others were seriously injured. A very thorough investigation by the University indicated that mistakes had been made: the group should have chosen a more easily accessible, non-technical route; the descent technique was inappropriate for the snow conditions; and there were several contributory factors such as the steepness of the terrain, the abilities of the students, fatigue, inadequate footwear and the lack of a safe run-out. Being a University there was an immense analysis culminating in a book, a significant lesson of which is the 'imperative' need for organizations to have a 'media response plan in place, up to date, and readily available'.[92] Establishing such a 'doomsday scenario' is of course hopefully informative in establishing clear procedures to avoid catastrophe for any organization, rather than dealing with one. In the same way as fire drills and evacuation procedures are essential, so too is a consideration of how to respond to the potential for injury. Contingency planning is also needed at a somewhat lower level of risk, for matters such as adverse weather conditions, vehicle breakdown, loss of equipment or breakdown in communication. Often termed 'Plan B arrangements', although even in a modest excursion alternatives can range through the alphabet, it is important to show prior thought. Andrew Dismore MP indicated in a Parliamentary debate that cancelling an activity outright in the interests of safety can sometimes be difficult in the light of parental protest; as a Sea Scout aged 17 he had abandoned a sailing expedition because of the weather. This led to an outburst from a parent who had 'played hell with me', and when Mr Dismore indicated that 'there was a force 9 gale blowing' the parent's further response was 'What's that got to do with it?'[93]

In 2004 the Greater Manchester Fire Authority was prosecuted following the death of a part-time firefighter, Paul Metcalf, who had drowned in 1999. He had been called to search for Reyaz Ali, aged 15, a New Zealand schoolboy boarding at the Darul Uloom Islamic College in Bury, who had fallen into a lake from a rope swing near the school. Although the boy had been underwater for a

---

[91] Wally Keay, chapter 6.2 on 'Supervising qualifying ventures', *DofE Expedition Guide* (HMSO, 4th edition, 2000) 413 *et seq*.

[92] Deborah Ajango (ed), op cit at 145.

[93] House of Commons *Hansard* (16 July 2004), col 1712.

considerable length of time by the time the fire service arrived, a helicopter reported bubbles and the fire-fighters attempted a rescue in scenes which were described at the inquest as 'chaotic', and at a later criminal trial as 'uncoordinated' and 'out of control'. Mr Metcalf waded in with a rope tied around his waist, which was critically not floating line, and in trying to recover the boy the rope passed under a tree branch and he was pulled underwater. An inquest in 2000 recorded an open verdict on the fire-fighter and one of misadventure on the boy. Subsequently the fire-fighter's family indicated they would not sue for the death, but they pursued the possibility of a prosecution.[94] Since this double drowning, buoyancy aids and floating rescue lines have been issued to crews in Greater Manchester. After the trial at Bolton Crown Court alleging a 'catalogue of failures' by the fire brigade, a jury acquitted the defendants on charges under the Health and Safety at Work Act 1974. Mr Metcalf's twin brother claimed that there had been concerns about water rescues dating back to 1994 when there was a memo from a fireman requesting the provision of buoyancy aids, and in 1998 a risk assessment of water rescues had been carried out, but this had not been implemented.[95] The circumstances of this case suggest a close call for the defendants on the 'state of knowledge' they had, and it is very likely that such a basic error as the provision of non-floating line for a river rescue would lead to legal disaster for any other fire authority who did not take serious notice of the lessons from this tragedy. Serious training and adequate equipment is obviously essential in such rescues.

Group management

The final item on planning and people issues is to tie together all the related areas in effective management of the party or group. This involves an understanding of the nature and rules of the activity, and certainly the risks involved. Detailed and clear instructions need to be given to participants as to boundaries, safety rules, dangers and behaviour requirements. Beyond the initial briefing there must then be practical enforcement of these matters, with a range of suitable warnings and a level of appropriate vigilance by staff. One response to these requirements, particularly from the 'too much red tape' libertarian perspective, is to attempt to be 'leader free', with the suggestion that a group of acquaintances paddle together with no leadership and the hope that no individual has any responsibility for anyone else. While an emphasis on personal safety and the acquired competence to be a 'self rescuer' is desirable, there are limits when combining in any group or team. For example, 'peer group paddling' is a vogue which stresses self-reliance, and makes the sensible suggestion that in whitewater 'the limiting factor of what you will personally run should be your own intuition of what consequences you

---

[94] 'Tragic fireman's family won't sue', *Manchester Evening News* (17 January 2002).
[95] 'Twin's anger over fireman's lodge death', *This is Lancashire* (29 October 2004).

will be able to deal with on your own'.[96] In extreme conditions there is no prospect of a rescue other than a self-rescue, whether you are in a group or not; the kayaker Doug Gordon, 'first among equals' on a number of Himalayan expeditions had written the year before his own death in the Tsangpo Gorges of Tibet of 'the increasing number of river deaths' and that paddling Class VI whitewater was 'risky business', where hazards should be recognized, minimized if possible and learned from.[97] Similarly, in mountaineering there are the much-debated issues of 'cutting the rope', such as the famous occasion for Joe Simpson and Simon Yates in the Peruvian Andes.[98] When solo, then personal responsibility is clear, as when Aron Ralston, having been pinned for five days under a boulder in Utah, sawed off his arm with a penknife to save himself.[99] While it is logical that personal accountability is the test for solo trips, and in small teams in extreme conditions, once there is a group then other considerations apply. If the attempt is made, as it often is, to suggest a legal stratagem to get around vicarious liability by propounding 'peer group' activities where 'friends' or 'acquaintances' get together informally, then it is doomed to failure. This might be viewed as a harmless ruse to avoid paying minimal dues to the appropriate national governing body for third party liability, but it will never waive any legal requirements for joint and several liability in tort for a group or a team. Furthermore, what it may do is deny an innocent victim a claim against insurers when the rest of the party turn out to be 'persons of straw' in legal terms, who could not support a financial claim. And such a ploy would certainly never avoid a criminal charge where personal liability for actions, whether in a joint enterprise or not, is always the hallmark. Such 'organization' of an event so that there was an attempt not to have an 'organizer' therefore looks doomed to fail if it is an effort to avoid legal liability.

In the more normal way of groups there will of course be an obvious organizer, and hopefully third party cover if things were ever to go wrong. As we have seen, the principal method to avoid difficulties is by appropriate risk assessment on behalf of the group. Such risk management can often be divided into three parts: 'generic' relating to an activity as a whole; then 'specific' to the group or location; and then 'ongoing' risk assessment during the activity. The HASPEV *Handbook for Group Leaders* suggests that there should always be 'ongoing risk management', as 'risk assessment does not end when the visit begins', and then gives a practical checklist as to issues such as changes to the itinerary, the all-important weather forecast, suggests the good practice of 'briefings each night to take stock', seeking local knowledge of potential hazards,

---

[96] Paul Mason and Mark Scriver, *The Thrill of the Paddle: an Illustrated Guide to Extreme Canoeing* (Toronto: Key Porter, 1999) 185.

[97] Douglas Gordon, 'They don't come any better', *American Whitewater* (September/October 1997). See generally Wickcliffe W. Walker, *Courting the Diamond Sow: A Whitewater Expedition on Tibet's Forbidden River* (Washington: National Geographic Society, 2000).

[98] Joe Simpson, *Touching the void; the true story of one man's miraculous survival* (New York: Harper & Row, 1990).

[99] Aron Ralston, *Between a rock and a hard place* (New York: Atria, 2004).

the classic alternative of a 'Plan B' (or a few other drop out and emergency options), behaviour issues, illness or injury, emergency planning and a wealth of advice on specific activities. For example, *HASPEV* indicates that 'many of the incidents affecting pupils have occurred by or in the sea'[100] so the *Handbook for Group Leaders* gives guidance on 'coastal visits' such as assessing risks from 'tides, rip tides and sandbanks', group awareness of 'warning signs and flags' and that 'the local coastguard, harbour master, lifeguard or tourist information office can provide information and advice on the nature and location of hazards'. Again it is easy to see that tragedies such as Lyme Bay itself in 1993, Land's End in 1985, the drowning of Laura Zielinski at Shell Island 1997, Gemma Carter at Le Touquet in 1999, and the 'near miss' school outing in 2003 at Druridge Bay, would have had very different outcomes if these guidelines had been followed. In particular the point in *HASPEV* about 'swimming and paddling or otherwise entering the waters of river, canal, sea or lake should never be allowed as an impromptu activity' has a resonance in many of the drowning cases which form the majority of the school fatalities.[101] Unsupervised and 'spontaneous' play is of course a major factor in open water drownings each year; in 2004 a teenager playing on a makeshift raft with three friends on the River Ebbw was drowned, on a weekend when there was a flash flood, the river was described as 'a torrent' and winds gusting up to 74 miles were recorded.[102] Sadly no parent seemed available to 'supervise' what was a very hazardous enterprise when such weather was forecast.[103] If such an activity had been allowed to occur on a trip organized by a school or a voluntary organization then clearly this would have been negligent in the circumstances.

---

[100] Paragraphs 181-2.

[101] See generally *Handbook for Group Leaders*, HASPEV Supplement 3, *Health and Safety of Pupils on Educational Visits: A Good Practice Guide* (2003).

[102] 'Raft boy dies in "torrent" as storms cause chaos', *Daily Mail* (2 February 2004).

[103] See the excellent RoSPA pack *RUA Dummy 2?: Water Safety and Risk Perception for Young People* (2004), produced in conjunction with the Environment Agency and aimed at 12 to 16 year olds to encourage a consideration of risks posed by inland waters.

Chapter 10

Facilities, Equipment and Clothing

Professor Thomas Lambert, for many years the editor of the Association of Trial Lawyers of American *Law Reporter*, gave a succinct description of the social policy of deterrence that underlies the tort of negligence: 'a fence at the top of a cliff is better than an ambulance in the valley below'.[1] When dealing with the physical backdrop to activities there are again many instructive points that can be taken from prior experience, and many now rather more sophisticated than a simple barrier. But as with 'driver error' on the roads, the 'people' aspects are usually very much more important than the 'property' aspects. However, much depends on the nature of the activity; for example, with an airsport such as paragliding or a mountaineering specialism such as waterfall ice-climbing, the correct selection of terrain and equipment is literally life-defining. Even away from such extreme sports the correct use of 'low tech' gear can be essential, particularly the issue of clothing, so these are never considerations that should be overlooked.

Facilities

The surrounding physical milieu is obviously an essential backdrop to safety. We have seen that location is a vital consideration, both for overnight accommodation and in the particular circumstances where the activity is to take place. Risk assessment often requires a balancing of sometimes competing considerations. For example, the murder in 1996 of Caroline Dickinson in a youth hostel on a school trip to Brittany was possible because doors were required to be left unlocked due to the need for a quick exit in case of fire. Risk assessment of such considerations in residential accommodation is difficult enough, but many outdoor activities combine with camping, and here there are special considerations. Induction, briefings and ongoing assessment as to hazards will be even more important. In 1995 an outdoor company Mountain Ventures Ltd was prosecuted and fined £8,000 following serious injury to Lyndsey Henderson, aged 12 and part of a school group. They were bivouacking overnight in Snowdonia, and she got up in the night and stepped over a low wall, not realising a cliff face was on the other side, falling thirty feet into a quarry and suffering a punctured lung, a ruptured spleen and broken ribs. No-one in the school group had been made aware of the potential dangers of this campsite, which was a salutary reminder of risk assessment of the surroundings and a briefing to

---

[1] Quote in his obituary, *ATLA Law Reporter* vol 43 (2000) 4.

participants.[2] Despite this disaster, that company has continued with an excellent safety record to provide adventurous activities for schools and other groups, regularly inspected by the AALA. In 2000 the AALA also pointed out a 'near miss' on a campsite, when outside the activity centre the driver of a passing car lost control and drove through the hedge, stopping just short of a tent full of children. The AALA suggestion of a 'prudent' response was 'to give this possibility some thought when choosing a site to pitch tents'.[3]

Probably the most risky scenario of most campsites is when they are 'excrementally challenged', and this is also a risk on farm visits too. This hazard became more widely known following the case brought by the parents of Tom Dowling, aged four and from Edgware Infants School, who brought an action against Bowmans Farm, near St Albans, and Barnet Council, the LEA. That was the third time E.coli 157 had been contracted at the farm in six weeks but his parents were not told of the potential risk. Until the visit Tom Dowling was described as 'a bright, lively nursery class pupil', but following a twelve day coma at Great Ormond Street Hospital for Sick Children, a 'brain scan revealed he would probably never see, hear, walk, talk or feed himself again'. The infection was traced to a goat in the 'touching pen', which was later destroyed, although no-one saw the boy contact an animal. However, E.coli 157 bacteria are found in the faeces of infected animals and on anything it touches, and are therefore easily transmitted from hand to mouth, particularly when children may not be able to wash with anti-bacterial soap for the recommended four minutes. The Dowlings' solicitor indicated that 'those children went to that farm like lambs to the slaughter. It is vital people realize the risk when they visit farms, particularly with small children'. A representative of the National Association of Farms for Schools stated that E.coli 157 was 'a constant risk which could be minimized by awareness. Bowmans is a model farm that was extremely unlucky'.[4] Subsequently the *HASPEV Handbook for Group Leaders* in 2003 quotes the Chief Medical Officer's statement in 2000 that 'there is a link between farm visits and infection in young children' and indicates the precautions that should be taken.[5]

---

[2] 'Schools: Perils down a legal loophole', *The Guardian* (17 March 1998). See the correction of some factual inaccuracies in the original article by a subsequent letter from Bob Llewellyn of Mountain Ventures in *The Guardian* (14 April 1998).

[3] AALA, 'Car through a hedge', *Infolog* Entry No. 13 (May 2000). Three Italian Scouts, one girl aged 13 and the other two aged 12, left their tents in 1999 to sleep outdoors near an Alpine stream, and were then swept away to their deaths when the water rose because of a sudden storm, so location of a campsite is very important; 'International News', *Newcastle Journal* (9 August 1999).

[4] 'School farm trip left us with only the shell of our lovely son', *Evening Standard* (1 June 1998).

[5] 'Farm Visits' and the advice on E.coli 157 infection in *Handbook for Group Leaders*, HASPEV Supplement 3, *Health and Safety of Pupils on Educational Visits: A Good Practice Guide* (2003). See also 'Chief Medical Officer Advice on Farm Visits: A Department of Health Press Notice', 12 April 2000.

It may be that these precautions need to be observed in other environments too. Following the death in 1999 by kidney failure of Heather Preen, aged eight, and on holiday in Devon, her mother set up a Trust to campaign for new guidelines on reducing the risks for children from E.coli 157. Two other children were taken ill, with the source thought to be a contaminated beach. An environmental group, Surfers Against Sewage, suggested that there had been three discharges of raw sewage on to the beach at Dawlish, but South West Water described these allegations as 'scaremongering', although this was unfortunately also their response to complaints at the time of the Camelford case, when the company were convicted of a public nuisance at Exeter Crown Court because 180 victims suffered ill effects from drinking contaminated water when twenty tonnes of aluminium sulphate was negligently dumped into the water supply.[6] In the subsequent civil action, *AB v South West Water Services,*[7] when the company admitted liability for both public nuisance and statutory breach, they were also accused of compounding the problem by acting in a 'arrogant and high-handed manner in ignoring' complaints by customers, and stating repeatedly that their water was fit to drink, although a claim for exemplary damages was struck out by the Court of Appeal. Various theories were put forward as to the contamination at Dawlish which led to Heather Preen's death, including dog faeces, but on examination of the facts an inquest jury found death through misadventure and the coroner called for the sewage treatment works to be 'cleaned up'.[8]

However, most infections seem to occur on farms, and Professor Hugh Pennington has called for an end to farm visits for children aged under five.[9] He was the leading scientific expert who, in 1996, investigated the outbreak of E.coli 157 in Lanarkshire which claimed 21 lives, and he also gave evidence at the inquest on Heather Preen; his view is that E.coli 157 is a 'virulent if relatively new organism', surfacing only in the 1980s.[10] The cause of the Lanarkshire outbreak was a church lunch of steak pie with a contaminated gravy served to pensioners, but most instances connect directly to animals; an E.coli 157 outbreak in 2000 on a Scout camp in Aberdeenshire was linked to sheep droppings on the field where they pitched their tents,[11] to cattle in 2003 after another outbreak affecting Scouts, this time in Fifeshire,[12] and to a contaminated water supply on a farm when thirteen Guides and their Leader became ill after a camp in Inverclyde in 2001.[13] Professor Pennington repeats his warning that 'good personal hygiene, specifically hand washing, is the best defence against possible infection,'[14]

---

[6] 'Health group slams beach claim over E.coli death', *Birmingham Post* (20 August 1999).
[7] [1993] 1 All ER 609.
[8] 'Coroner orders death beach clean-up', *The Times* (12 February 2000).
[9] 'New code to beat bug', *Exeter Express & Echo* (29 June 2000).
[10] 'Interview: no flies on me', *The Observer* (13 February 2005).
[11] 'Sheep blamed for Scouts' E coli illness', *The Guardian* (10 June 2000).
[12] 'Third child suffering E-coli after visit to Scout camp', *Glasgow Herald* (27 August 2003).
[13] 'Tap water is blamed for E-coli outbreak at Girl Guide campsite', *Glasgow Herald* (16 June 2001).
[14] 'Scots scientists close to developing E coli vaccine', *The Scotsman* (27 February 2003).

although a vaccine is being developed. This issue may then join the lengthy list of such matters as diphtheria, polio and tetanus where immunisations are routine, and advised by all reputable voluntary organizations, and the even longer list of advisable precautions in different parts of the world. However, as the AALA pointed out after several youngsters were hospitalized in 2000, their problems were not caused by contaminated food or being on grazing land, but 'poor basic camp hygiene – Don't forget the basics'.[15]

Facilities need a straightforward inspection, which is why a reconnaissance visit is so important for off-site trips. Even a cursory examination will often reveal obvious dangers that need to be guarded against, and a failure to inspect can be disastrous. For example, 'fencing' is not just a vital consideration in factory premises, where it has been mandatory in Britain since 1834, and at times was of such a strict liability that in *Summer v Frost* the House of Lords indicated 'great sympathy' with the defendants' argument that if they had increased the guard on a grinding wheel anymore it would have become unusable, but nonetheless the law required a verdict in the plaintiff's favour.[16] In a more recent case involving an indoor amusement park in Massachusetts, *Foti v Bonkers 19, Inc.*,[17] a girl aged eight was riding on the 'Mini-Himalaya', a roller coaster for young children. The motor was behind the seat and her hair slid back through a gap between the seating and a cover, ripping her scalp away. The mother who was present with her daughter, and her father who subsequently saw her in the 'immediate aftermath' at the hospital, both suffered psychiatric damage. They sued for a failure to inspect, which would have revealed the gap, and the case was settled for $1.69 million. The AALA warned of a similar sort of problem when an adult accompanying a school group on a High Ropes Course and Assault Course opted to participate. The group were told to remove rings and other jewellery, and the instructors checked that the children had, but unfortunately the adult did not, and during the session she caught her ring, and stripped the flesh, subsequently needing the finger to be amputated. The AALA suggest a similar warning, and perhaps policy, 'on virtually all activities' and a possible extension to 'those with body piercings'.[18]

Equipment

Of principal importance here is a suitable first aid kit for the activity. Equipment checklists thereafter vary immensely with the nature of the excursion, particularly if there is a need for specialist gear. We currently know a great deal more about expeditioning needs than when the renowned polar explorer Fridtjof Nansen 'embarked on a pioneering ski tour' in 1883, in an uninhabited mountain range in Western Norway. Setting off 'in moonlight' and accompanied by his dog, Flink,

---

[15] AALA, 'Camp Hygiene', *Infolog* Entry No. 15 (Dec 2000).

[16] [1955] AC 74.

[17] Massachusetts, Norfolk County Superior Court, No. 96-02188, 2 July 1998.

[18] AALA, 'Ring Injuries', *Infolog* Entry No. 29 (Aug 2003).

Nansen was equipped with 'a piece of cheese and some home-made crispbread', along with some matches, but had 'neither map nor compass... neither tent nor sleeping bag', and found shelter for the night 'between a boulder and a snow hummock [where] he lay down having put on a woollen sweater, his only extra clothing'. Skiing in terrain never skied before, 'gripped by a raging thirst' and falling on ice with 'nothing worse than a few grazes', Nansen records in his diaries that 'the dog, poor devil, had a bad time'.[19] Over a century later the legendary explorer would be certifiable for such a venture.

Sadly, not all the lessons of the ensuing years have been learned. In July 2004, in a classic case of its genre, a group of 39 London schoolgirls accompanied by just one teacher from Beth Jacob Seminary for Girls had to be rescued from near the summit of Meall a'Bhuachaille, a 2,500 foot peak in the Cairngorms. They were found wearing school uniform skirts, trainers and bin liners. The group tackling the mountain initially numbered 60 pupils and two teachers, but some turned back when high winds, rain and mist swept over them. Mountain Rescue were 'flabbergasted' when asked by the teacher on a mobile telephone borrowed from a pupil if their driver could manoeuvre his coach to the summit to pick them up or whether 'the group could be airlifted off the peak by helicopter'. When rescuers arrived the school group was described as 'a rain shower away from death'.[20] The rescue team leader, John Allen, said 'it was possibly the worst case of a group being ill-prepared that he had seen in 25 years of rescue work' with the schoolgirls 'strung out for about a kilometre down the track', 'wearing skirts, tights and trainers', and that the rescuers had been 'totally amazed and astounded' at the scenario they found; the staff-pupil ratio had been 'quite unbelievable'; and 'it was quite horrendous – the whole situation'.[21] Such an internal school expedition is of course outside the AALA jurisdiction, and as a private school, outside LEA guidelines too. Nevertheless it could serve as an object lesson in how to court disaster, starting with an alleged refusal to take local advice and a failure to obtain a weather forecast which would have shown worsening conditions through the day. Problems like this are not of course confined to school groups. A decade earlier, this time in January 1994 the Kintail Mountain Rescue team found three 'holidaymakers' from Manchester 'wearing jeans and trainers' after spending 12 hours in the snow up Carn Loch na Eun, and without route plan, equipment or clue as to where they were. The rescue leader, Ron Porter, commented 'I don't like criticising hill-walkers but they weren't hill-walkers. They were just people out for a walk'.[22]

---

[19] Roland Huntford, *Nansen: The Explorer as Hero* (London: Abacus, 2001) Chapter Six 'A Foolhardy Trip' 43-49.

[20] 'Drive coach to mountain top, rescuers told', *Aberdeen Press and Journal* (2 July 2004), 'Cairngormless; teacher takes girls up mountain with no map or compass wearing bin liners', *Daily Mirror*, (2 July 2004).

[21] 'School party lost on peak "broke every safety rule",' *The Times* (2 July 2004), 'Ill-equipped for mountain venture', *Western Morning News* (23 August 2004).

[22] 'Rescue teams warn of the hazards as the unwary risk their lives on winter hills', *Glasgow Herald* (29 December 1994).

Weather is of course the key issue in determining what sort of equipment is needed, particularly in the hills. As many experienced observers have commented, the nature of the climate in the British Isles can quickly produce some of the most adverse conditions in the world. In 2004 a party of 34 teenagers with just one teacher from Drogheda in the Republic of Ireland were rescued from the Mourne Mountains in Northern Ireland, with four suffering from hypothermia and another dozen treated in hospital. A Mountain Rescue team happened to be training in the area when the alarm was raised, and their leader stated 'they were very, very badly equipped ... We were expecting – according to weather forecasts – gales and storms. Fortunately it didn't materialize, otherwise we would have been talking in terms of deaths'.[23] Accurate weather advice is also needed by many other activities. The AALA have a salutary warning of a kayaking instructor who failed to check the precise date of the weather forecast on the harbour office noticeboard, leading to a multiple capsize, which was fortunately 'well handled'.[24] Even below ground in caving there is a need to keep a wary eye on the weather above; in 2001 two potholers had spent hours below in the Pennines and were making their way out when the weather deteriorated, with 'icy rain water and melting snow [turning] a steep pitch close to the cave entrance into a torrential waterfall. It is thought they died trying to climb through the raging torrent'. The coroner recorded deaths of misadventure on Julian Carroll and Ray Lea.[25] This is why so many Alpine caving expeditions take place in winter, because with freezing conditions there is 'no risk of being caught by a flash flood', but nevertheless a wary eye needs to be maintained on sudden melt above.[26] One old-fashioned myth frequently expressed in activities such as inland sailing and canoeing is that 'weather forecasts are unimportant' if you have the right oilskins or waterproofs, but this is of course nonsense with just a momentary consideration of severe storms, gales or indeed lightning. Lyme Bay is necessarily the catastrophe to remember in Britain, but there are many such cases around the world. When considering the drowning of two adult Scout Leaders and two Venture Scouts, struck by gale force winds when kayaking across Lake Alexandrina in South Australia, the coroner found that not only had the party leader ignored weather forecasts, but he had removed buoyancy from the kayaks and paddled across open water on the lake in the interests of taking a short cut.[27]

The worst-ever school trip canoeing disaster in Canada justifiably deserves the book-length analysis given to it by Professor James Raffan in *Deep Waters: Courage, Character and the Lake Timiskaming Canoeing Tragedy*. He catalogues the fundamental errors that led to the death of a teacher and twelve schoolboys in

---

[23] 'Lucky to be alive', *Belfast Telegraph* (4 October 2004).

[24] AALA, 'Right forecast, wrong date', *Infolog* Entry No. 14 (Sep 2000).

[25] 'Horror deaths in icy torrent – cavers were near safety when hit by floods as weather broke', *Newcastle Evening Chronicle* (18 May 2001).

[26] 'Truly, madly, deeply; the Everest of all caverns', *Glasgow Herald* (24 July 2004).

[27] Rob Hogan, 'The Crux Of Risk Management In Outdoor Programs – Minimising The Possibility Of Death And Disabling Injury', *Australian Journal of Outdoor Education*, vol 6, No. 2 (2002) 71-79.

Lake Timiskaming in 1978: an overnight journey by road to the put in; a lake notorious for cold water; wind funnelling through the hills to produce gusts; several 'near misses' and worse with hypothermia in a manic school programme designed to 'toughen up' the boys; newly purchased 'war canoes' modified overnight by raising seats so that food boxes would fit underneath; and a haughty refusal to take account of local knowledge with warnings of a freshening tailwind – 'no condition more difficult in which to steer a canoe'.[28] Professor Raffan is one of Canada's leading canoeists and 'experiential education' authorities, as well as the author of the masterly *Fire in the Bones: Bill Mason and the Canadian Canoeing Tradition*,[29] so his is an overwhelmingly damning critique of foolhardiness that imperilled lives. Not too many lessons seemed to have been learned from Timiskaming when cold water was again a major factor in the deaths of two Canadian Girl Guides from hypothermia in May 2003 at Camp McDougall on Lake Huron. The coroner examining that case in 2004 issued a series of forty recommendations, eight of which were directed specifically to the Girl Guides of Canada on the classic themes of risk assessment, routes, floatplans and route plans, canoeing expertise, swimming ability, supervision, maps and nautical charts, briefings for parents and participants, and the canoeing qualifications of the instructors and supervisors.[30] It is estimated that Canada has three times the canoe and kayak deaths per exposure hours compared to the USA, predominantly because of colder waters, and in a famous rescuer case, *Horsley v MacLaren*,[31] when a pleasure cruiser on Lake Ontario, *The Ogopogo*, lost someone overboard, and a passenger then dived in to attempt a rescue, both 'died by shock due to the low temperature of the water'. Even in summertime when wearing a PFD, as the Canadian Girl Guides had done on Lake Huron, such insulation will not be sufficient to ward off immersion hypothermia. 'Near misses' are not always quite so newsworthy as fatalities, but just a few miles east of Camp McDougall, at the St. John's Island YMCA, a chance encounter with a large powerboat saw the timely rescue of an entire primary school class of 25 children from Elliott Lake in Ontario afloat in canoes in June 1998; the powerboat was able to radio ahead and have three ambulances standing by to treat for hypothermia.[32] All such instances record what the AALA noted in a British case was the 'startlingly short length of time' it takes before hypothermia sets in with cold water immersion; a 20 stone man had fallen overboard from a keelboat and although the accompanying rescue boat arrived within seconds the man

---

[28] James Raffan, *Deep Waters: Courage, Character and the Lake Timiskaming Canoeing Tragedy* (Toronto: Harper Collins, 2002) 145.

[29] (Toronto: HarperCollins, 1997).

[30] Girl Guides of Canada, 'Coroners' Inquest Recommendations', 2004. See also Girl Guides of Canada-Guides du Canada, *Guider Responsibilities and Personal Liability* (30 November 2004).

[31] Canadian Supreme Court [1971] 2 Lloyd's Rep 410.

[32] Tim Ingram, 'Ontario Level Flotation Law for Canoes and Kayaks'; see generally his *Canoe and Kayak Scam kills 1000 Americans* (Toronto: Lightning Source, 2003).

quickly lost the ability to assist his rescuers and he died in the water.[33] It is therefore imperative to recover victims of capsize as quickly as possible. Indeed, sometimes the very shock of capsizing into cold water can cause a 'vagal cardiac inhibition', as happened with Andrew Read, a student whose raft capsized on a whitewater course at Holme Pierrepont in 1998, when an inquest found that there was no evidence of drowning, but rather an unknown 'susceptibility'.[34]

Because of these considerations it is essential that appropriate equipment and an appropriate rescue plan is available to make a speedy recovery following immersion. In a recent and very important High Court case, *Davis v Stena Line Ltd*,[35] the family of Michael Davies were able to prove 'negligent rescue' and recovered £250,000 in damages.[36] Mr Davies had fallen from a Stena Line ferry crossing from Rosslare to Fishguard in very poor weather in October 2000. The alarm was raised in moments and Mr Davies, who was a strong swimmer, was spotted 'still very much alive' after fifty minutes in the water, but then six minutes later was found to have died before rescue could be completed. Forbes J held that the likelihood was that the victim had 'lost his footing' and had fallen over the safety rails or through a gap where an access gate had been left open, but the key negligence was there was 'no clear and carefully prepared plan of rescue'. The judge referred to the 1994 *MS Estonia* disaster in the Baltic, in which 852 people died, and the knowledge subsequently that it was 'near impossible for high-sided vessels to rescue a man overboard'. However, 'neither the captain nor his crew had received any guidance or training on what to do in such circumstances'. A nearby container ship had on board a 'fast rescue boat, which could be launched in adverse conditions and which was crewed by skilled ex-fishermen [and] was obviously the best option for a rescue', but the ferry captain did not request the launch of that boat, and instead 'proceeded with his plan to manoeuvre his ferry close to Mr Davis in order to try and retrieve him through the vessel's bunker door', which Forbes J considered to be an 'ad hoc, ill prepared and not well thought out' plan, such as to be 'so hopeless and so risky' that the captain should not have proceeded with it unless there was no other option. In a noteworthy judgment, Forbes J indicated that 'if Stena had properly taken into account the lessons of the *Estonia* – and also of the report into the sinking of the *Marchioness* pleasure cruiser – it would have provided Captain Williams and his officers with appropriate advice and training... Its palpable failure to do so was plainly negligent'.[37] In his closing submissions, Simon Kverndal QC for Mrs

---

[33] AALA, 'Failure to recover man-overboard', *Infolog* Entry No. 2 (May 1999).

[34] 'Cold Water Shock Killed Raft Student', *Birmingham Post* (5 February 1998).

[35] [2005] All ER (D) 276.

[36] 'Rescue blunder doomed father in ferry plunge', *Daily Mail* (18 March 2005).

[37] 'Rescue "So hopeless and so risky",' *Western Mail* (18 March 2005). 51 people died when the pleasure boat *Marchioness* sank in the River Thames in August 1989, after it collided with the dredger *Bowbelle*. The dredger's captain and second mate were arrested for failure to keep a proper lookout, but were acquitted in 1991. In April 1995 an inquest jury returned verdicts of unlawful killings. See generally Hazel J. Hartley, *Exploring Sport and Leisure Disasters: a socio-legal perspective* (London: Cavendish, 2001). An official Swedish investigation into the

Davis, alleged that Stena Line had shown 'antipathy' towards risk assessment and failed to 'think through the risks and problems' they would face in a man overboard situation in rough seas.[38] The case is currently on appeal.

Footwear is essential equipment in many outdoor environments, because of the pre-eminent danger of 'trip and slip', so the absence of appropriate footwear is a continual theme in the hillwalking and mountaineering death and injury cases. As well as the wholly inadequate 'jeans and trainers' cases which are so frequently described by mountain rescue teams, there is a need to upgrade equipment well beyond basic climbing boots in snow and ice. For example, when three climbers from the Mayo family died in the Cairngorms in 1993, it appeared that their deaths had been 'avoidable', as inadequate footwear was the main factor. Only the team leader was wearing crampons, footwear considered essential for the conditions which were described as 'steep and unsafe slopes covered in snow and ice'. In addition, the team were not roped, nor had they left details of their proposed route, and with two members wearing 'bendy boots' they did not have the hard edges and rigid soles considered necessary by Mountain Rescue to be out in the conditions.[39]

The actual 'failure' of modern equipment is a rarity, but it is always of course important to have correct usage. This seems to have been a factor in several bungee deaths; for example, the 2005 inquest into the death in 2002 of Christopher Thomas, which we have examined, recorded a verdict of accidental death 'because he was too heavy for his harness'[40] A previous bungee death in 1986 occurred when a member of the public rehearsing a TV stunt for the Noel Edmonds' 'Late Late Breakfast Show' plunged 160 feet to his death after the equipment failed; the BBC was fined the maximum of £2,000 in a magistrates' court for failing to make a risk assessment and to take adequate safety precautions.[41] A few months before the death of Mr Thomas in 2002 there had been a double bungee death at Polino in Italy, when a paratrooper Alberto Galletti and his fiancée Tiziania Accora fell to their deaths when both snap hooks holding the equipment to a bridge appeared to give way.[42] A similar equipment problem with a safety harness seems to have caused the death of Tanya Bocking, an instructor at Blackland Farm, the activity centre owned by Girlguiding UK. She became entangled in her harness in 2003 while she was preparing an aerial runway for a lesson with someone who suffered from cerebral palsy. A spokeswoman for West Sussex Fire and Rescue said that she was testing out the

---

sinking of the *MS Estonia* in the Baltic Sea found the accident had been a combination of mistakes by the crew and design faults in the ferry's loading-bay door.
[38] 'Widow suing ferry faces wait', *Western Mail* (4 December 2004).
[39] 'Rescuer blames climbing deaths on footwear', *Glasgow Herald* (22 February 1993). John Allen, the team leader, indicated that without a route plan this had been a 'search the Cairngorms job', with more than 120 people involved.
[40] 'Bungee death', The Times (25 February 2005).
[41] 'Maximum fine for the BBC over TV death plunge stunt', *The Times* (17 April 1987).
[42] 'Bungee jump couple fall to deaths', *Daily Telegraph* (3 May 2002).

wire 'when her harness came undone'.[43] Ms Bocking's brother called for better safety measures at outdoor centres after the East Sussex Coroner recorded a verdict of death by misadventure.[44] The activity session was being run by an external organization, Adventure Unlimited, who run camps for many disadvantaged youngsters every year, and it was clear that Ms Bocking was 'very experienced and well qualified to give instruction on the zip wire'.[45]

In several cases we have seen perhaps an overly ambitious utilization of terrain for the standard of equipment, particularly in respect of footwear; this happens especially when 'hillwalking' turns into 'scrambling' or even 'climbing'. The army officer leading the 'trekking' expedition in Vietnam, where Amy Ransom died on a school trip with World Challenge Expeditions, admitted at the inquest that it was his first time on Mount Fansipan and that they 'had been ill-equipped for such a difficult climb'.[46] However, as with road accidents investigation, it is more often 'operator error' rather than the equipment to blame; in 2004 Les Gorham had just fulfilled his ambition to scale 'the country's highest vertical cliff face', the 305 metre St John's Head in Orkney, and then the next day fell while abseiling. The Orkney police suggested that 'it was the end of the day and perhaps Mr Gorham was a bit tired and in a hurry to get home', as it appeared he had 'clipped one of the ropes instead of two and fell right through the loop'.[47] A not entirely resolved mystery, which led to protracted court proceedings, centred on climbing equipment and perhaps the 'suppression' of evidence at an inquest; Jeremy Turner, an experienced abseiling instructor in Wales died in 1989, and the coroner returned a verdict of misadventure on the basis that he appeared to have disengaged himself from a safety line. That ruling was quashed after an appeal to the High Court by Mr Turner's father. At a new inquest Alun Jones QC, representing the family, suggested that 'evidence was suppressed that might have indicated the cause of death was due to faulty equipment', because the initial coroner, Peter Brunton, represented the outdoor activities company, Celmi.[48] That coroner had opened the inquest, adjourned it, and then later on handed over the case to a colleague; he then was present in his capacity as a solicitor with a 'watching brief' at the reconvened inquest, and then represented the company at the second inquest; Mr Brunton was ultimately admonished by the Lord Chancellor for conduct falling 'below the standard of diligence that I expect from the holders of judicial office', after being reprimanded by the Solicitors' Disciplinary Tribunal for 'acting in conflict of interest and for bringing

---

[43] 'Woman dies at camp site', *Kent and Sussex Courier* (12 December 2003).
[44] 'Slide tragedy', *The Times* (25 February 2005), *East Grinstead Courier* (2 January 2004), 30 December 2003).
[45] 'Obituary: harness tragedy of instructor, 41', *East Grinstead Courier* (18 December 2003).
[46] 'Girl died on "poorly equipped" expedition', *The Times* (11 December 2001).
[47] 'Climber Les killed after fulfilling his life's dream', *Manchester Evening News* (5 August 2004).
[48] 'Coroner "suppressed fall evidence",' *The Independent* (9 January 1992).

himself and the profession into disrepute'.[49] The coroner at the second inquest recorded an open verdict, saying 'I am quite satisfied that insufficient inquiries were made at the time'; Mr Turner's father had discovered witnesses, who had not been called to give evidence at the first inquest, who had seen a safety-line trailing from his son as he fell, indicating that the equipment might have failed.[50]

Communications equipment is playing a more important part in rescue work, and in safety generally. With increasing range and coverage mobile telephones in particular have been responsible for saving several lives in the outdoors; for example, Darren Alcock walking on his own in the Stirling Range in Australia lost his way in fog in 2001 and telephoned his father 9,000 miles away in Great Yarmouth for 'advice'. The father used directory inquiries to telephone the police in Western Australia, and the rescue services found his son just minutes before they were about to call off their search; Mr Alcock commented that 'I will check the weather forecast more carefully in future before embarking on any other expedition'.[51] Stephen O'Brien was sea kayaking off the Skerries lighthouse in Anglesey, when 'freak waves' turned the canoe over; 'I was on my own, which was a mistake', but he was able to telephone the coastguard before being 'knocked over by another huge wave' and lost his telephone and flares overboard – he was picked up two and a half hours later just before dark.[52] In the USA in 2005, two kayakers died on a school trip off the coast of Florida when adverse weather set in, and 'the choppiness of the water and the inexperience of the kayakers led some boats to get separated from the group'; the rest of the party were rescued when an adult was able to paddle for four hours to a location where he 'was finally able to use his cell phone' to call his wife in Georgia, who then called the coastguard.[53] Nevertheless, even when a party is equipped with a mobile, it is a necessity to have it attached by lanyard and in a waterproof case; in 2005 eight shipping executives on a training course at the Brenscombe Outdoor Centre in Dorset, all in just two open canoes, started to swamp, and in the process of getting on board their instructors' safety motorboat, capsized that too. In the ensuing mêlée the sole means of communication, an instructor's mobile telephone, dropped to the bottom of Poole Harbour. The ten participants were picked up by a BP supply vessel, the *MS Furzey Squirrel*, and then transferred by an RNLI lifeboat and ambulances for medical treatment for asthma and hypothermia. Coastguards commented adversely on the lack of a radio or flares,

[49] 'Courts warned off jury "professionals",' *The Guardian* (5 April 1996), '"Compromised" coroner faces loss of his post', *The Guardian* (16 December 1994).

[50] 'Inquiry into conduct of coroners is reopened', *The Independent* (11 March 1993).

[51] 'What do you do if you're cold, wet and lost in one of Australia's remotest parks? Phone your dad for help... in Norfolk', *Daily Mirror* (16 August 2001).

[52] 'How my mobile saved my life', *The Guardian* (11 November 2002).

[53] 'Bodies of teen kayakers found', *St Petersburg Times* (28 February 2005).

and indicated that 'if it was not for the fact that the *Furzey Squirrel* was in the area at the right time the people would have been in a lot more trouble'.[54]

Another lone sea kayaker, Dr Mark Ashton-Smith, then of the Department of Experimental Psychology at Cambridge but now describing himself on his website as an 'independent adventurer',[55] telephoned his father in Dubai 4,000 miles away in search of a rescuer when he capsized off the Isle of Wight in 2001. After a series of family telephone calls to Cambridgeshire, Derbyshire, the Thames coastguard, the Swansea coastguard, a search was finally put underway from the Solent coastguard less than a mile away. Following his being winched to safety by helicopter from alongside his capsized kayak in a force six gale, which he seemed incapable of re-entering, Dr Ashton-Smith was given a safety lecture and commented 'I have learnt that I can get hold of the coastguard by dialling 999. I'll be better prepared next time'. The coastguard watch manager, Bob Terry, said that his team had been 'bewildered', and indicated that anyone preparing to go to sea should take a course in marine emergency communications, carry a portable marine radio, and check weather conditions.[56]

Arguably the worst case in Britain on both inadequate supervision and the absence of equipment was the death we have already examined of Hayley Hadfield, the schoolgirl who died after falling at the Manor Adventure Centre in 1992, before Lyme Bay and the licensing regime. The details are not edifying, and the stipendiary magistrate indicated that, if he had been 'allowed to impose imprisonment' he would have found it 'hard to avoid'. The evidence showed that the owner himself had failed to act in an emergency: 'quite despicably you took no action to deal with the problem yourself when you were told about it', and both he and the adventure centre were fined £15,000 each. The court had been told that the schoolgirl had fallen into a tree 'while scrambling down a steep bank during a night hike supervised by an unqualified instructor' who was taking a short cut; that emergency procedures 'were nothing less than lamentable', in that it took 'one and a quarter hours before an ambulance was called'; that it had been 'left to two 11-year-old boys to administer first aid'; that an instructor tried to drive to the location in the firm's minibus, which was known to have a defective starter motor and which duly stalled on a track and then became stuck in deep ruts; and that the centre's equipment did not include a stretcher or torches and just one first aid kit. An investigation found that 'company failures could have meant the difference between life and death'.[57]

Equipment is almost certainly subject to the concept of 'state of knowledge'. The magnetic compass appears to have been invented by Luan Te around 83AD, and was used by Chinese sailors from the third century in the form of a lodestone

[54] 'Shipping firm's high fliers sink in harbour', *Bournemouth Echo* (13 April 2005); The Maritime & Coastguard Agency, 'Ten people pulled from water in Poole Harbour', *Press Release* (6 April 2005).

[55] http://www.exploreclimbing.com/mark.htm

[56] 'Adrift in the Solent, lecturer sends SOS to Dubai', *The Times* (10 September 2001).

[57] 'Outdoor centre fined over death of girl, 11; emergency system "lamentable" after accident in night hike', *The Independent* (9 November 1993).

floating in a bowl of water or hanging from a line; its application as a navigational instrument was possibly transported to the west by Marco Polo, where its first recorded use was in 1190 to 'navigate the seas in cloudy weather'.[58] A cursory glance at the bewildering array of binnacles, barometers, anemometers, hygrometers, electronic chartplotters, radar and autopilot steering gear systems which makes up modern yachting suggests that marine navigational accessories have developed rather considerably since. Maps of a rudimentary sort are of an even earlier vintage than compasses, with charts producing a number of breakthrough developments such as contour lines. King George II commissioned a military survey of the Scottish highlands in 1746, and the Ordnance Survey was duly implemented right across Britain by 1790. Since then 'topographical' maps have become ubiquitous in the outdoors, with many specialized varieties. With the development by an Aberdeen company in 1994 of 'a pocket satellite receiver which helps lost climbers by telling them their exact position, day or night, in any weather', the additional navigational aid of the global positioning system (GPS) was made available for hillwalkers, and this is rapidly becoming a near-essential item in wild country, just as it has been for some time in air and marine navigation.[59] However, as with all such matters, there needs to be a cautionary word about the malfunction, or more prosaically, the loss of any such equipment; reliance on the sun, the stars, or the growth of lichen on trees is probably only of curiosity interest for most individuals in the outdoors, but it still may be vital for survival for some – and makes for good television.

Clothing

Adequate clothing for most outdoor activities is essential, particularly in wintertime, and although this could be considered just another piece of equipment, it is so important as to merit separate consideration. The usual problem is in keeping warm to prevent incipient hypothermia or even frostbite to the extremities.[60] The fundamental principle is layering to trap air which is warmed by the body. This layering starts with modern thermal synthetics, or perhaps at a higher price with merino wool, silk or cashmere next to the skin, so as to wick away moisture from perspiration. Then come successive insulating

---

[58] Shen Kua, a Chinese mathematician, wrote about the device in *Torrent of Dreams*, published in 1086; the writings of an Augustinian monk, Alexander Neckam in 1190; see Ingeborg H.M. van Oorschot, *Chemical distinction between lithogenic and pedogenic oxides in environmental magnetism* (unpublished PhD thesis, University of Utrecht 2001).

[59] 'Pocket receiver comes to the rescue', *Glasgow Herald* (3 March 1994).

[60] See the esoteric discussions of 'Arctic Willy' in the *British Medical Journal* (1989) 299 (6715)1573-4, and (1990) 300 (6719) 263, and the work of Dr Howard Oakley, the Head of Survival and Thermal Medicine at the 'world's only cold injury clinic' at the Portsmouth Institute, who trains marines for arctic conditions by locking them in a special cold room with temperatures of 30 degrees below; 'Marines prepare for freezing walk', *Scunthorpe Evening Telegraph* (18 February 2000).

layers until an outer defence, which is waterproof but breathable; such systems have become axiomatic in outdoor activities. Hypothermia is when the vital core of the human body is cooled to danger levels, and this is the essential hazard to guard against; if this cooling is not checked then it leads to classic warning signs such as uncontrollable shivering, but ultimately to unconsciousness, respiratory and cardiac failure, and death. The aim with adequate clothing is to keep a constant temperature of 37°C in the 'inner core' of head and abdomen, but the quickest method of cooling is to immerse in water, which is why in water activities this topic is even more important. The *Titanic* disaster showed survival in arctic waters to be a matter of minutes, although the Inuit live comfortably in a similarly hostile environment because they are trained, dress well, and are experienced in avoidance techniques. As well as immersion hypothermia there is also a wind-chill factor to consider. This is the combination of air temperature and wind speed which is a particular characteristic of the outdoors, and in amalgamation with the loss of insulating efficiency when clothing is wet, it is easy to understand the advanced hypothermia suffered by the Lyme Bay kayakers in 1993. Developments in clothing are made constantly; for kayakers synthetic piles and drysuits have almost replaced the traditional wool and neoprene wet suit which would have been required at Lyme Bay. In the Irish case at Dunmore East Adventure Centre in 1995, Barry Hogan spent nine hours in February seawater holding on to two kayaks containing his sons, which he had rafted up; but as he was wearing a dry suit, this was 'believed to have been a key factor in his survival'.[61]

Outer waterproofs are an important consideration in most activities in the British climate, but problems with perspiration need to be overcome with vents or breathable material such as Goretex, as dampness can lead to a vicious circle when stationary. In inclement weather the absence of hat, adequate footwear or even gloves can be disastrous, and combined with factors such as exhaustion, physique, lack of training and conditioning, dehydration, illness or low morale, then this is a potent elixir for disaster. Younger children also have additional physical concerns due to size, weight and their ability to withstand poor conditions, even in summertime. In 1989 Helen Mallinson, aged eight and from Göttingen, on holiday with her German family in August, died from hypothermia on a twenty mile walk. The family had often climbed far higher in Europe, but the notorious Scottish weather changed, and when the father went to seek help, his daughter died, 'lying against a boulder'.[62] As Professor Curtis points out, 'Medical research on hypothermia and cold injuries is always changing knowledge and treatment'.[63] Certainly training, the right clothing and the right

---

[61] 'His death was all so needless, so stupid', *Irish Examiner* (18 February 2005).

[62] 'Mountain death', *The Independent* (16 August 1989).

[63] Rick Curtis, 'Outdoor Action Guide to Hypothermia and Cold Weather Injuries', Outdoor Action Program, Princeton University (1995). See generally William Forgey, *Hypothermia: Death by Exposure* (ICS, 1985), *The Basic Essentials of Hypothermia* (ICS, 1991), *Basic Essentials of Hypothermia (Winter Sports)* (2nd edit, Globe Pequot Press, 1999) and the classic *Wilderness Medicine: Beyond First Aid* (5th edition: Globe Pequot Press, 1999).

attitude can make a great difference. In a controversial case involving Jacqueline Greaves in 1994, a school secretary from Warrington on a climbing trip in the Cairgorms fell through an overhang of snow and became separated from her friends, who went to find help. She was found by Mountain Rescue 71 hours later, having dug herself out and then surviving two nights of winds of 60mph and temperatures down to -27°C, in one of the coldest parts of Britain. Her previous training in the use of bivvy bag and snowholes, and her levels of fitness and equipment, were certainly major factors in her survival. However, when she sold her story to a national newspaper for £20,000 and appeared to give nothing towards her rescue, with costs of an estimated £100,000, as well as the risks to over 70 volunteers, there was dismay that the 'considerable donation to the mountain rescue teams' she promised never materialized.[64]

The opposite risk of hyperthermia or overheating is also a possibility, perhaps more associated with overseas trips, but again the use of a sun hat, appropriate clothing and in particular liquid intake, is essential to ward off heat exhaustion and ultimately death by heatstroke. A classic instance of disaster was Tom Simpson's death on the 13th stage of the Tour de France in 1967, when there was a fatal combination of circumstances: diarrhoea and illness over several days, lack of bidons to drink from when dehydration was not fully understood, amphetamine use when it was still legitimate in cycling, and even alcohol intake from an impromptu stop at a hostelry at the start of the climb up the unforgiving treeless limestone mountain of Mont Ventoux in baking heat.[65] We now know that internal body temperature can be readily affected by infection, which was an allegation made in the unsuccessful attempt of an army boxer claiming in the Court of Appeal that he did not recover from a head injury sustained in the ring; however, this claim in *Fox v Ministry of Defence* was dismissed, following cogent evidence of a careful examination in advance by a doctor.[66]

Charles Rigby of World Challenge, the largest of the British Third World expedition organizers, indicated at a symposium on the fifth anniversary of the Lyme Bay disaster that he knew 'of a teacher who, without any local knowledge, plans to take a group into a desert where the temperature range will be sub-zero at night to plus 34C'.[67] What is legally clear about any injuries resulting from that absurdity is derived, as we have seen, from the classic statement of the legal duty of care relating to doctors (or outdoors leaders or anyone else who should have professional expertise) in *Bolam v Friern Barnet Hospital Management Committee*: 'A man need not possess the highest expert skill; it is well established

---

[64] 'Rescue turned sour', *Aberdeen Evening Express* (17 December 2003); their annual football match has a cup for the runners-up named the 'Jacqueline Greaves Perpetually Lost' trophy, 'We're game for laugh at Rescue Gran', *Sun* (12 January 2001); 'Rescue: height of exploitation', *Scotland on Sunday* (20 February 1994) on the ensuing media frenzy to gain an exclusive story.

[65] See for a full analysis, William Fotheringham, *Put Me Back On My Bike* (London: Yellow Jersey Press, 2002).

[66] [2002] EWCA Civ 435.

[67] 'Schools: perils down a legal loophole', *The Guardian* (17 March 1998).

law that it is sufficient if he exercises the ordinary skill of an ordinary competent man exercising that particular art'.[68] Despite the viewpoints of some of the teachers' unions this is not by any means an insuperable legal hurdle; but it does require some preparation, some guidance, and what for teachers should be automatically considered necessary – some instruction. Along with the many training courses run by the national governing bodies, the Royal Society for the Prevention of Accidents launched in 2004 its own specialist course for teachers undertaking school trips; Juliet Barratt, RoSPA's head of safety education and a geography teacher for six years, indicated that she had developed the course because she herself had received absolutely no health and safety training before leading school trips, and added that 'having the knowledge to carry out a risk assessment properly is an essential tool with which all teachers should be equipped'.[69]

---

[68] [1957] 2 All ER 118, at 121 per McNair J.
[69] 'Schools urged to curb their fears of the great outdoors', *The Times* (28 September 2004).

Chapter 11

Conclusion

As we have seen, repeatedly after death or injury in outdoor activities, a suggestion has been made that this was merely an 'accident'. Unfortunately, rather closer analysis shows that these are very rarely events without a cause. Almost invariably there will have been multiple reasons for such a catastrophe, and just as in road 'accidents' the principal causes will usually be human error. The tort of negligence has never demanded absolute liability on perpetrators of harm, but in personal injury cases the courts insist that individuals do not behave 'negligently'. There are various euphemisms for what this means in practice – such as 'fault' or 'carelessness' or 'blameworthiness' – but the critical standard to bring a legal action is that conduct must be shown to have breached a duty of care.

There is now a growing list of legal precedents to demonstrate what this means in relation to outdoor activities in Britain and in comparable common law jurisdictions. In addition to these legal cases, the essential principles on breach of a duty of care are well established in related fields. Contrary to mythology, they are also relatively straightforward. Tort law may be a 'forensic lottery',[1] but that has more to do with procedure, the vagaries of legal assistance, and with esoteric points of causation in medical cases, rather than with the substantive law in a relatively straightforward area linked to well-established tort topics such as roads, premises and workplace liability. The essential requirement of the law on outdoor activities can be summarized as the requirement to be a 'reasonably prudent' teacher, volunteer or leader of trips and expeditions. This does not mean becoming a paragon of virtue who is faultless on every occasion, but it does mean observing 'common standards'. Such standards will inevitably change with research and experience which develop knowledge and understanding of safety issues, and the 'reasonable person' will always want to update their skills by training, reading the literature, and practice.

The essential tool to show 'reasonableness' is the concept of risk assessment. It probably always was the major consideration, although such an attitude was often referred to as 'just plain common sense'. In an informal process this type of analysis is a natural development of an unconscious search for safety by considering hazards, risks, and preventative measures to combat harm. In a bowdlerized and pejorative form, this essential theme has become 'risk assessment paperwork', in mountainous form, where it can get out of all proportion to the activity involved. No doubt to some hard-pressed teachers, chafing at the amount of other paperwork they need to deal with, risk assessment

---

[1] Terence Ison, *The Forensic Lottery: a critique on tort liability as a system of personal injury compensation* (London: Staples Press, 1967).

can seem an insuperable obstacle to any and all trips and outings. Fortunately a great deal of excellent information is now readily available to teachers, and also to providers and voluntary leaders, so this seemingly Herculean task can be more easily surmounted by looking at the documents provided by the DfES, by voluntary organizations, and notably by the AALA. Increasingly too these very sensible guidelines are freely available for downloading.

However, the important legal point to note is that although the courts will always prefer an evidential 'papertrail' which documents a 'reasonably prudent' approach to an outdoor activity, the critical requirement is the right approach and not the right paperwork. The documentation is important because of centuries of experience in trial courts of the sometimes great difficulty with witnesses who in oral testimony may have trouble remembering quite what they thought before, during or immediately after an occurrence. The supremacy of a written document over hazy recollection, sometimes many months or years after an event, therefore leads inevitably to Step Four of the HSE Five Steps procedure, which is to write down preventative measures against perceived hazards. This is in pursuit of the lawyer's principal maxim 'Get it in writing'. Not only is such documentation a useful defence in resisting any legal claims, but it acts as a vital prophylactic checklist to prevent injuries arising in the first place. Where safety considerations are paramount, as with the pre-flight procedure of air pilots in the cockpit, then such a procedure is an ordered method of accomplishing an important task. A similar process of planning ought to become 'common practice' in outdoor activities too.

Just as with any driver on the road, there is the remote possibility of criminal culpability for teachers, providers and volunteers. Indeed, on the road, liability commences at the standard of negligence, with the charge of 'driving without due care and attention'. With outdoor activities it commences at the higher level of 'recklessness' or 'gross negligence' for the manslaughter charge, about which there seems to exist currently an almost unreasoning terror among some teachers, volunteers and leaders. In the overall context of millions of school visits and outdoor activities led by volunteers and providers this charge of manslaughter is exceedingly unlikely, as the negligence displayed must be shown to be 'gross'. As we have seen, such a criminal charge is uncommon and exceptional, and in any event needs proof at the higher evidential level in criminal trials, where the burden on the prosecution is to demonstrate their allegations 'beyond a reasonable doubt'. Manslaughter therefore requires irresponsible conduct well above the ordinary standards of negligence. A cursory glance at these rare criminal cases shows that only extreme culpability will produce a successful prosecution: the multiple-layered irresponsibility with young lives of Lyme Bay in 1993 which Ognall J described as a 'complete failure to heed ... [the warning] given in chillingly clear terms of the risk you were running' or as at Glenridding Beck in 2002 which Morland J described as a party leader who was 'unbelievably foolhardy'. None of the most elementary precautions were taken in these cases, and on a series of 'checklist issues' established by experience over the years on items such as planning, leadership and equipment there was self-evident recklessness. The cases serve as grim warnings of what can go wrong.

In other cases where there have been manslaughter charges, merciful juries, perhaps mindful of the extreme difficulty in finding the volunteers who provide the backbone of most outdoor activity organizations in Britain, have acquitted defendants who had clearly been negligent, but whose incompetence or disobedience of their organizations' own rules had perhaps not quite attained 'gross negligence'. The classic example in a voluntary organization is the acquittal of Peter Finlay, who by his own admission had 'done no planning for the trip' and was in breach of Scout mountain rules when Jonathan Attwell fell to his death from Snowdon in 1999. If the Scout Association in their subsequent inquiry characterized some of their leaders and instructors as displaying a 'cavalier' attitude to safety in the outdoors, then a comparable description of some of the Army training of young people appears on occasions to exhibit the very worst 'gung ho' attitude possible. As we have seen, crown immunity draws a discreet veil across some of these worst excesses, although the 2004 manslaughter charges against Matthew Doubtfire lifted the veil sufficiently to show that there had been 16 such drownings in the past seven years. Mr Doubtfire was of course acquitted when a jury failed to agree, but the Army had to admit that Kevin Sharman was a 'known non-swimmer' who was taken into perhaps the most dangerous resurgence pool in the country. That case is particularly noteworthy because the HSE had also gained the very unusual Crown Censure against the Army following a special private hearing relating to Kevin Sharman's death, and although details are very difficult to obtain of this procedure, censures were also issued against the Army after the deaths of teenagers Clare Shore in 1998 and Wayne Richards in 2005.

The concept known to lawyers as 'accidents of litigation' has to be assessed too; undoubtedly the worst Scouting case was the death of Lee Craddock falling 360 feet to his death in the dark in the caving systems near Gaping Ghyll. The simple reason for manslaughter charges not being preferred in that case was that the party leader died shortly afterwards; certainly the evidence in the later civil case against the Scout Association appeared to show levels of recklessness and 'loss of control' by him which would have clearly supported such a charge, although the facts on which this would have been based were vigorously disputed and might not have held up in a criminal trial. In respect of Army training, were it not for the fact of immunity, then there are clearly several cases at this level of culpability, as demonstrated in the Crown Censure cases and other matters which were very close to being put through that cumbersome and secretive process. Indeed, proposals in some sort of 'Promotion of Volunteering' Bill to give the same sort of blanket immunity from prosecution to all volunteers, and similar suggestions for teachers, would seem very questionable in the light of this Army record, and would certainly prove counter-productive if it engendered any feeling of teachers and volunteers being above the law.

Opinions are necessarily going to vary on disputed facts, and the Crown Prosecution Service will very properly take a wide view of the circumstances of every fatality or injury: theirs is a discretion to exercise and they may decide not to bring a prosecution for manslaughter or to prefer lesser charges for health and safety issues, as at Stainforth Beck in 2000. Factors influencing that decision would have been that knowledge of the rock/water interface was still developing and the party leader had fallen ill, leading other teachers to take over in difficult circumstances, but this was of course a very controversial decision and the level of the fine against Leeds City Council at £30,000 was a significant sum.

However, all of these criminal cases are exceptional. Although it is always important to analyse the 'worst case scenarios', because that is where significant lessons can be learned for all outdoor activities, it is clear that the vast majority of legal cases will not be criminal prosecutions but will be civil claims for compensation on the basis of the negligence standard. However, here too it seems that paranoia may be setting in amongst teachers, volunteers and leaders. Such an attitude is possibly enhanced by the irrational perspectives of some of the teaching unions and commentators. For example, Eamonn O'Kane, then the general secretary of the NASUWT, in reiterating that union's boycott of school trips in 2004, made the dubious statement that 'in an increasingly litigious society which no longer appears to accept the concept of a genuine accident, our first responsibility must be to protect our members' interests'. While understandable that a union would inevitably be expected to represent its members, it is debatable that the proposition of 'an increasingly litigious society' can be maintained when tort claims are falling, and the concept of 'a genuine accident' in the light of the legal cases and outdoors experience generally is not in accord with reality. Sadly, as we have seen, in the vast majority of these matters there are invariably the same patterns, and these are causative features, often of human error, which are not random 'accidents'. It would also seem unfortunate that the NASUWT lose sight of the principal aim of educating children, as that objective is certainly damaged by this union's stance. Mr O'Kane went on to indicate that 'in recent high-profile cases teachers have been heavily penalized. Some have lost their jobs as a result of alleged misjudgments'.[2] While it is of concern if anyone suffers an injustice, it would certainly appear from some of these 'high-profile' legal cases where NASUWT members have been sued as parties in tort cases, that negligence was very clearly established. The first NASUWT case appears to go back to Land's End in 1985, where an inquiry found that the Headteacher 'failed to plan the trip adequately, failed to organize sufficient supervision and failed to act when he saw the children in danger'. Recent NASUWT cases complained about involved the deaths of Gemma Carter, Max Palmer and Bunmi Shagaya. All three fatalities led to a consideration of criminal charges: a successful appeal in France against conviction on negligent homicide by Mark Duckworth, a guilty plea to manslaughter by Paul Ellis, and criminal investigations still pending against four teachers in the last matter. It would legally be rather difficult to argue on the facts in those cases that at the lower standard of simple negligence there was not a *prima facie* case on tort liability in each of these matters: the most basic supervisory rule of them all, head counts, was adjudged to be a factor in the deaths of Gemma Carter and Bunmi Shagaya, and Max Palmer's death was

---

[2] Press release 18 February 2004, indicated as the current policy on the NASUWT website.

described by a High Court judge as 'inexcusable' and indeed led to a guilty plea by the accused.

In a tort action it is of course routinely a school or local education authority which will be held vicariously liable for the actions of teachers, although there might well be consequences for that teacher in their employment. However, a serious assessment of the legal cases, just a tiny handful in an ocean of successful school trips, can hardly justify the sort of comment by an NASUWT health and safety expert, writing in a personal capacity, who suggests that:

> the fact of the matter is that when something like this happens there has to be a scapegoat and in ALL cases it is ALWAYS the teacher who takes the blame. No matter how careful you are it is impossible to make a risk assessment of every factor. When something goes pear shaped, and with the benefit of hindsight, it becomes very easy to point the finger. My personal advice to all members is to completely BOYCOTT ALL SCHOOL TRIPS – and I'm not just referring here to fancy high wire expeditions, I mean outings to the churchyard in pursuit of local history, to the park, farm visits etc.[3]

That perspective is in stark contrast to the views of the largest teaching union, the National Union of Teachers, which indicates that it 'was at the forefront of guidance on school visits with its publication of *Beyond the Classroom* in the 1980s' and which supports the DfES policy on outdoors education outlined in HASPEV and its supplements. Lord Slynn pointed out in *Phelps v Hillingdon Borough Council* in the House of Lords that 'the professionalism, dedication and standards of those engaged in the provision of educational services are such that cases of liability for negligence will be exceptional', and in his view 'claims should not be encouraged and the courts should not find negligence too readily' in cases involving schools, but nevertheless 'valid claims' in the law of tort should not be excluded.[4] For most commentators that would seem a reasonable approach when considering the risks involved in safeguarding the lives of children, and the NASUWT viewpoint would appear somewhat out of proportion.

A balance of fun and safety

To be educational and motivational, outdoor activities certainly need the 'fun' factor. Several commentators suggest that with increasing safety awareness this enjoyment objective has been displaced and indeed there is a danger of societal paralysis in the face of what Professor Huber and his 'anti-torts' lobby term 'phantom risks'.[5] While these may be spectral dangers to guard against, it is very

---

[3] 'School Trips', North West NASUWT *Health and Safety News* (September 2002).
[4] [2000] 3 WLR 776, 792.
[5] See generally the writings of Peter Huber, *Liability: The Legal Revolution and its Consequences* (New York: Basic Books, 1988), and Kenneth R. Foster, David E. Bernstein and Peter W. Huber (ed) *Phantom Risk: Scientific Inference and the Law* (Cambridge, Mass: The MIT Press, 1993).

clear that for the overwhelming majority of outdoor activities in Britain there is a great deal of pleasure, underpinned by a proper assessment of real risks. Indeed, there is questionable 'fun' in landing up at the top of a mountain clothed in a bin liner against the elements, no pleasure at all in a 'near miss' cold water drowning, and a total and cataclysmic devastation for a family or a school or a voluntary organization when a child does not return home safely after an adventurous activity.

Because coming home alive is so desperately important, and because there has been so much good experience and research in outdoor activities around the world, we have the benefit of knowing a great deal more about what actually is dangerous. We also have the means to guard against many of the risks of injury and death. For example, any analysis of accidents sustained by schools and voluntary organizations carries the very clear message that travel to and from the outdoors is usually very much more risky than any outdoor pursuit. Carnage on the roads is therefore very much the predominant hazard to guard against. Fortunately in recent years, and particularly since the school minibus disaster on the M40 in 1993, which alone accounted for a quarter of all school fatalities in Britain, this issue has been taken very much more seriously. The excellent initiative of the Community Transport Association in setting up a Minibus Driver Awareness Scheme (MiDAS) in 1996 has meant that those accredited drivers are not just aware of their legal responsibilities, but have serious guidance in matters such as defensive driving and passenger safety. The majority of minibuses are of course driven by volunteers or teachers, and unfortunately, as the Institute of Advanced Motorists point out, they 'almost all have one thing in common, they have had no proper driving instruction in the vehicle they are driving'.[6] The Scout Association in 2001 started to recommend in their pre-activity checklist for adventurous activities that the minibus driver should perhaps not be someone involved in the activities but should focus on the vital task of driving, and this is sensible advice.[7]

On the broader issues of safety in the outdoors, one essential question is whether participants are safer since the passage of the Activity Centres (Safety of Young Persons) Act 1995 and the subsequent Adventure Activities Licensing Regulations 1996. The answer is definitively in the affirmative, not necessarily because of the licensing regime itself, which as we have seen applies only to a fraction of outdoor activities, but because of the spin-off from the publications of the AALA. Their work, allied to the research world-wide on these issues, means that we know a great deal more about hazards in the outdoors, the probability of risks occurring, and the appropriate preventative measures required. Serious attention to this literature by national governing bodies and the wider outdoors community has led to cross-fertilisation of ideas, an increased sophistication of risk assessment beyond the self-defeating 'copious paper' overload, and a general raising of standards. Daphne Metland revisited six residential camps in 2003, a decade after investigating them, and reported that 'safety standards have

---

[6] *Minibus Driving: Your Skill – Their Care*, The IAM Minibus Driver's Guide (1995).
[7] 'Activities: Risk Assessment', *Scout Association Fact Sheet* FS120000 (January 2001) 6.

improved noticeably'; on the first occasion she had reported on issues such as unlocked and unsupervised swimming pools, along with a 'general slackness about wearing safety equipment'.[8] And the original Consumer Association report in 1986 on children's activity holidays, which led to the foundation of the British Activity Holiday Association a month later, contained a disturbing list of lack of supervision, missing equipment and poor standards which would be unthinkable today. This change of ethos has been propelled by the AALA in such publications as their extremely helpful working documents such as *Good Practice in Adventure Activities within the Education Sector* and *Self Assessment and Guidance for Providers of Adventure Activities*. The spin-off from the AALA also includes the excellent DfES HASPEV, and its supplements such as the *Handbook for Group Leaders*, which are basic tools for teachers and very useful for providers and voluntary organizations too. And the voluntary sector has now also developed a whole range of procedures, training and publications which have continued to raise awareness of safety issues and assist in a practical way.

The question remains as to whether the AALA remit needs to be expanded to include schools and voluntary organizations. On the fifth anniversary of the Lyme Bay disaster, Marcus Bailie was definitely of the view that 'schools need to be brought into the licensing framework', and that was a perspective shared by the National Union of Teachers. The AALA head of inspection warned starkly that 'Current guidance is not read, not understood, not acted on'.[9] With the further passage of time, such an extension may not be appropriate. First, because the AALA guidance is more likely to be heeded; secondly because of the legal 'overkill' of having all adventurous activities placed on a licensing par with the nuclear or explosives industry when there is clearly not the same level of risk; but thirdly because the AALA has had an immense advisory influence in the last decade and to extend the remit of the AALA to cover schools or voluntary organizations or to expand overseas or to envelop all adventurous activities for any participant of any age would be financially and logistically very onerous. Inspection fees for the sort of expertise that the AALA can offer are not cheap, and this could be a very significant burden on schools and voluntary organizations who do not have 'customers' to pass costs on to. As well as even more 'paperwork' there would also be the possibility that the AALA would start to lose focus if its investigative and inspection work was more widely spread on a mandatory basis.

There are still many critics of the AALA, mostly on the 'paperwork overload'. For example, the Royal Yachting Association in 2003 suggested that for their sailing instructors: 'the additional regulatory burden over the past few years has been immense... the RYA is pressing for outdoor recreation standards to be set and monitored by governing bodies alone, without the costly wasteful duplication of controls.'[10] They claimed that RYA Training Centres have 'to steer through an increasing tangle of red tape', and that one area of 'duplication is the Activities

---

[8] 'Are summer camps up to scratch for both safety and fun?', *The Times* (14 June 2003).
[9] 'Schools: perils down a legal loophole', *The Guardian* (17 March 1998).
[10] The Royal Yachting Association, *RYA Instructor's Newsletter* (July 2003).

Centres Regulations, introduced by the Government following the Lyme Bay canoeing tragedy in 1994'. Their protests are perhaps from a general 'libertarian' perspective, as they also indict 'other areas of control, all intended to improve our quality of life' including what one might think are unimpeachable matters such as child protection.[11] However, such views have their echoes too in mountaineering, where Sir Chris Bonington, who chairs the risk management committee of the Outward Bound Trust, has 'railed against the effects of a culture of safety at all costs'; in an interview he pointed out that 'after every crisis there are screams to make things safer, but at what cost to education?'[12] Although mountaineering is inevitably hazardous and has led, as we have seen, to fatalities for young people, it would appear that many lessons have been learned by providers, schools and voluntary organizations. Research by the Mountaineering Council of Scotland to identify those groups of people most 'at risk' in the Scottish mountains significantly does not find those under 18 to be particularly at danger. The study, partly funded by the Leverhulme Trust, was based on an examination of over a thousand incidents. An important finding was that the majority of incidents involve hillwalking, pointing up that mountaineering is actually becoming safer with higher skills, better technique and enhanced equipment. The detail also shows that slips and stumbles remain the prime causes of incidents; that older, experienced hillwalkers (especially women) are especially prone to slips; that many slips result from poor concentration (especially men); and that almost half take place walking uphill or on the flat.[13] An interesting point in this survey is that just 5.6 per cent of the incidents related to 'guided' groups which included 'Scouts, Boy's Brigade, DofE, school groups, or led by guides, instructors and leaders', which suggests that on the whole schools and the voluntary sector are actually rather well taken care of.[14] The comparable figures for caving rescues for Scouts, who are one of the only voluntary groups participating in that activity, were also about 5 per cent of the total.[15] When such figures are set in the context of about 10,000 local Scout Groups in Britain, many engaged in the most adventurous activities, then this is a very significant argument, suggesting that cases such as Jonathan Attwell and Lee Craddock are thankfully exceptions rather than the general rule in Scouting. It would therefore seem to suggest that, even before their subsequent reform of Scouting authorizations, a serious attempt has been made by this largest of youth organizations to make 'the change in safety culture required'.[16] That might be a useful precedent for the Army in reviewing

---

[11] The RYA full list includes 'Health and Safety at Work Regulations, the Working Time Directive, Minimum Wage Regulations, Food Safety Regulations, Maritime Coastguard Agency Codes, Port Safety Code, Risk Assessment for safety in harbours, and child protection procedures'; ibid.

[12] Phil Revell, 'Education: lest we forget', *The Guardian* (17 October 2000).

[13][13] Bob Sharp, *Strategies for Improving Mountain Safety*, Analysis of Scottish Mountain Incidents 1996/99 (University of Strathclyde, 2001).

[14] At 12.

[15] See British Cave Rescue Council, *An Analysis of Cave Rescues* 1989-1998 (1999).

[16] John Bevan's signed Annual Report 2000-2001 of the Scout Association, 6.

their 'protocols', particularly in respect of non-swimmers engaged in 'wading' or the use of live ammunition or poorly-driven vehicles on training exercises. If, as we have seen, there has been public alarm about fatalities in schools and Scouting, then there should continue to be the most rigorous investigation of safety in Army training, and indeed it is suggested that Crown immunity should be lifted for all 'leisure' outdoor activities in that sector.

No doubt there will continue to be a spirited debate on the right balance in the outdoors between safety consciousness and the demands of spontaneity, between what Lord Scott of Foscote in the House of Lords in the leading case of *Tomlinson v Congleton Borough Council* suggested were the contrasts of 'some risk of accidents arising out of the *joie de vivre* of the young' and the straitjacket of 'imposing a grey and dull safety regime on everyone'.[17] Lord Hoffman's strident perspective in a sub-heading in that case, 'FREE WILL' (his capitals),[18] led to those *obiter* remarks being duly translated by the *Sunday Telegraph* as 'Britain's most senior judges have demanded an end to "the culture of blame and compensation" in a landmark ruling which decrees that individuals must take responsibility for their own actions'.[19] The *Daily Mail* followed suit with a diatribe against 'ambulance-chasing' law firms, stating with enthusiasm in a headline that the law lords in *Tomlinson* 'brand compensation culture as a crippling "evil",' and quoting a representative of the law firm representing the Borough Council saying 'this decision effectively means that people can enjoy themselves as much as before'.[20] While some might quibble that 'enjoyment' can include breaking your neck, a more reasoned review of that case might see a difficult balance on 'cost-benefit analysis', with the majority in the Court of Appeal tilting one way and the House of Lords tilting in the opposite direction. The old aphorism that 'hard cases make bad law' suggests that this might be a 'fact sensitive' judgment, rather than a clarion call for the overthrow of tort law.

What cannot be doubted in a survey of all the cases and literature on the outdoors is that these activities are progressively becoming safer, as we gain knowledge and experience. Expeditions are certainly rather less dangerous than Henry Stanley's second trans-Africa journey, where over two-thirds of his party did not return; the hazards were rather different in the Congo in the 19th century, as a third of his party were eaten by cannibals and another third died of opium abuse.[21] But can danger ever be reduced to 'zero risk'? The answer is that this is philosophically improbable, but even if the attempt is made then there is a serious economic as well as a societal cost. Frances Cairncross, the Rector of Exeter College, Oxford, has pointed out that although 'it is difficult to define what is an acceptable level of risk', and 'zero risk' is rarely attainable, as an economist it is

---

[17] *Tomlinson v Congleton Borough Council* [2003] 3 All ER 1122 at 1166.

[18] Sub-heading at 1152.

[19] 'End this compensation nightmare, say judges', *Sunday Telegraph* (3 August 2003): 'Law lords rule that Britain's growing culture of liability is an "evil" that interferes with civil liberties and freedom of will'.

[20] *Daily Mail* (4 August 2003).

[21] 'Explorer: prepare for emergencies', *The Independent* (13 November 2004).

necessary for her to point out that 'the elimination of risk comes only in exchange for costs that rise ever faster, the nearer "zero" approaches'.[22] Nevertheless as the legal analysis of outdoor activity cases in Britain and elsewhere makes clear, there have been very considerable gains made in safety at relatively low cost. Some of the 'near misses' and 'close calls', as well as the calamities, a few rather too recent for comfort, suggest that there are still plenty of inexpensive advances yet to be made. So long as 'common sense' remains an integral part of risk assessment, then the lessons learned will continue to be of considerable benefit to participants in the outdoors. And although standards will necessarily develop in new circumstances of improved skills, new activities, and upgraded equipment, the lessons will be important in forming the prior decision-making of teachers, volunteers and leaders – and when needed, of the subsequent decisions of the courts.

---

[22] 'Messing about on the water', *Risk & Regulation* No. 8 Winter 2004, 4.

Table of Cases

Collyar v Harley, Florida, Hillsborough County Circuit Court, No. 92-7369, 21 September 1995.

Condon v Basi [1985] 2 All ER 453.

Cooke v Great Western Railway of Ireland [1909] AC 229.

Cotton v Derbyshire Dales DC The Times (20 June 1994).

Cotton v Trafford Borough Council (Manchester County Court, unreported).

Craven v Riches [2001] EWCA CIV 375.

Crawn v Campo 643 A.2d. 600, 601 (New Jersey 1994).

Dann v Hamilton [1939] 1 All ER 59.

Davis v Stena Line Ltd [2005] All ER (D) 276.

Darby v The National Trust [2001] EWCA Civ 189.

Doe v Athletic Alliance Risk Purchasing Group, Nassau County Superior Court, No. 29967/99, 11 March 2003.

Doe v Goff 716 N.E.2d 323 (Illinois Appeals Court 1999).

Doe v Trattoria Spago, California, Los Angeles County Superior Court, No BC105476, 15 September 1995.

Donoghue v Folkestone Properties Ltd [2003] 3 All ER 1101.

Donoghue v Stevenson [1932] All ER Rep 1.

Dotzler v Tuttle, 449 N.W.2d 774, 779 (Neb. 1990).

Drummond v Tandy Corp, Texas, Dallas County 192d Judicial District Court., No. 92-9531, 1 February 1995.

Dubai Aluminium v Salaam [2003] 1 All ER 97.

Dunn v Southern California Seventh Day Adventists, California, San Bernadino County Superior Court, No. SCV31030, 18 January 1998.

Dutton v Bognor Regis UDC [1972] 1 QB 373 at 397.

East Suffolk Rivers Catchment Board v Kent [1940] 4 All ER 527.

Evans v Vowles [2003] EWCA Civ 318, [2003] PIQR P544.

Fairchild v Glenhaven Funeral Services Ltd [2002] 3 All ER 305.

Fay v Thiel College 2001 Pa. D & C, Lexis 235 (December 2001).

Fitzgerald v Lane [1987] 2 All ER 455.

Foti v Bonkers 19, Inc., Massachusetts, Norfolk County Superior Court, No. 96-02188, 2 July 1998.

Fowles v Bedfordshire County Council [1995] CLYB 3651, *The Times* 22 May 1995.

Fox v Ministry of Defence [2002] EWCA Civ 435.

Froom and others v Butcher [1975] 3 All ER 520.

Fytche v Wincanton Logistics plc [2004] 4 All ER 221.

Garcia v City of New York, New York, King's County Superior Court, No. 26134/91, 24 October 1995.

Gard v US 420 F. Sup 300 (1976), affirmed 594 F. 2d 1230 (1979).

Gauvin v Clark, 537 N.E.2d 94, 96 (Mass. 1989).

Geyer v Downs (1977) 138 CLR 91.

Glasgow Corporation v Taylor [1922] 1 AC 44.

Gordon v Los Angeles Unified School District, California, Los Angeles County Superior Court, No. LC036226, 8 July 1998.

Gough v Thorne [1966] 3 All ER 398.

Gough v Upshire Primary School [2002] ELR 169.

Leonard v Behrens No. 180 / 97-2191 (13 October 1999).

Lilya v The Greater Gulf State Fair 855 So. 2d 1049 (Ala. Sup. Ct., February 2003).

Link v Dolles Candyland Inc, settled before filing Kansas, 21 July 1995.

Lister v Hesley Hall [2001] 2 All ER 769.

Manolakaki v Constantinides [2003] EWHC 401.

Marchetti v Kalish 559 N.E.2d 699, 703 (Ohio 1990).

Margereson v JW Roberts Ltd (*The Times*, 17 April 1996).

Mark v Moser No. 29A02-0010-CV-623.

Martin v Middlesbrough Corporation (1965) 63 LGR 385.

Mattis v Pollock (trading as Flamingos Nightclub) [2004] 4 All ER 85.

Maynard v West Midlands Regional Health Authority [1985] 1 All ER 635.

McDermid v Nash Dredging and Reclamation Co. Ltd. [1987] 2 All ER 878.

McEwan v Eden's Saunasium, CA transcript 23 October 1986.

McGhee v National Coal Board [1972] 3 All ER 1008.

McHale v Watson (1966) 115 CLR 199.

Miller v Jackson [1977] 3 All ER 338.

Morrell v Owen, *The Times* (14 December 1993) and QBD transcript 1 December 1993.

Morris v Murray [1990] 3 All ER 801.

Mullin v Richards [1998] 1 All ER 920.

`*Munro v Porthkerry Park Holiday Estates Ltd*, *The Times* (9 March 1984).

Nettleship v Weston [1971] 3 All ER 581.

Nicholas v Osborne (Unreported, Victoria County Court, Australia, November 1985).

Novak v Lamar Insurance Co., 488 So.2d 739 (Louisiana 1986).

Novak v Virene 586 N.E.2d 578, 579 (Ill. App. Ct. 1991).

O'Connell v Jackson [1971] 3 All ER 129.

OLL Ltd v Secretary of State for Transport [1997] 3 All ER 897.

O'Reilly v National Rail and Tramway Applicances [1966] 1 All ER 499.

O'Shea v Royal Borough of Kingston Upon Thames, CA transcript 4 November 1994.

Osterlind v Hill 1928, 263 Mass. 73, 160 NE 301.

P & O European Ferries (Dover) Ltd (1991) 93 Cr App R 72.

Paris v Stepney Borough Council [1951] 1 All ER 42.

Pearson v Lightning, *The Times* (30 April 1998), 142 SJ LB 143.

Pfister v Shusta 657 N.E.2d 1013. (Illinois App. Ct. 1995).

Phelps v London Borough of Hillingdon, Anderton v Clwyd CC, Jarvis v Hampshire CC [2000] 4 All ER 504 at 519.

Phipps v Rochester Corporation [1955] 1 All ER 129.

Picou v Hartford Ins. Co., 558 So. 2d 787, 790 (La. Ct. App. 1990).

Pitcher v Huddersfield Town Football Club, QBD transcript 17 July 2001.

R v Adomako [1994] 3 All ER 79.

R v Barnes [2005] 2 All ER 113.

R v Gateway Foodmarkets Ltd [1997] 3 All ER 78.

R v Goad, Attorney General's Reference (No 131 of 2004) [2005] All ER (D).

R v Jackson Transport (Ossett) Ltd., unreported September 1996.

R v Kite [1996] 2 Cr. App. R. (S.) 295.

Tomlinson v Congleton Borough Council [2003] 3 All ER 1122.
Trotter v Magic City Ice, Inc, Florida, Orange County Circuit Court., No. CI 94-
      4311, 27 June 1995.
Turcotte v Fell 502 N.E.2d 964, 968 (New York 1986).
Uddin v Associated Portland Cement Manufacturers, Ltd [1965] 2 All ER 213.
Van Oppen v Clerk to the Bedford Charity Trustees [1989] 1 All ER 273.
Vellino v Chief Constable of Greater Manchester [2002] 3 All ER 78.
Watson v British Boxing Board of Control (*The Times,* 12 October 1999).
Wainwright v Home Office [2003] 4 All ER 969.
Walmsley v Humenick (1954) 2 DLR 232.
Ward v Hertfordshire CC [1970] 1 All ER 535.
Watson v British Boxing Board of Control, The Times, 12 October 1999.
Wattleworth v Goodwood Road Racing Co [2004] EWHC 140.
Westwood v The Post Office [1973] 1 All ER 283.
White v Blackmore [1972] 3 All ER 158.
White v The Council of the City and District of St Albans, The Times (12 March
      1990).
Whyte v Redland Aggregates Ltd, The Times, 27 November 1997, [1998] CL 485.
Wilkinson v Downton [1895-99] All ER Rep 267.
William S. v Bonita Unified School District, California, Los Angeles County Superior
      Court, No. KC024405, 29 March 1999.
Wilsher v Essex AHA [1988] 1 All ER 871.
Woodbridge School v Chittock [2002] EWCA Civ 915, [2002] ELR 735.
Woodroffe-Hedley v Cuthbertson, QBD transcript 20 June 1997.
Wooldridge v Sumner [1962] 2 All ER 978.
Wright v Mt. Mansfield Lift, Inc., 96 F.Supp. 786 (D. Vt. 1951).
X (Minors) v Bedfordshire County Council [1995] 2 AC 633.
Yachuk v Oliver Blais Co. Ltd. [1949] 2 All ER 150.
Zelenko v Gimbel Bros 287 N.Y.S. 134 (1935).

Select Bibliography

Adventure Activities Licensing Authority, *Self Assessment and Guidance for Providers of Adventure Activities* (Reprinted First Edition, Cardiff: AALA, 2001).

Ajango, Deborah, (ed), *Lessons Learned: A Guide to Accident Prevention and Crisis Response* (Anchorage: University of Alaska, 2004).

American Canoe Association, *Critical Judgment II: Understanding and Preventing Canoe and Kayak Fatalities 1996-2002* (Springfield VA: ACA, 2004).

Anderson, Sarah, and Johnson, Christopher, 'Expedition health and safety: a risk assessment', *Journal of the Royal Society of Medicine* vol 93 (2000) 557-561.

Atiyah, P.S., *The Damages Lottery* (Oxford: Hart, 1997).

Atiyah, P.S., *Vicarious Liability in the Law of Torts* (London: Sweet & Maxwell, 1967).

Bailie, Marcus, 'Lessons learned from Stainforth Beck?', *Institute for Outdoor Learning* (20 August 2003).

Bailie, Marcus, 'Risk Assessments, Safety Statements and all that Guff', *The Journal of Adventure Education and Outdoor Leadership and Far Out* Vol. 13, No. 3 (Autumn 1996).

Bechdel, Les, and Ray, Slim, *River Rescue: A Manual for Whitewater Safety* (Boston; AMC, 1985, 1997).

Beloff, Michael J., Kerr, Tim, and Demetriou, Marie, *Sports Law* (Oxford: Hart, 1999).

Buckinghamshire County Council, *School Visit to Cornwall by Stoke Poges County Middle School* (Bucks CC, 1985).

Buckley, R.A., *The Modern Law of Negligence* (London: Butterworths, 1993).

Buckley, R.A., *Salmond and Heuston on the Law of Torts* (21st edition, London: Sweet & Maxwell, 1996).

Calabresi, Guido, *The Cost of Accidents: A Legal and Economic Analysis* (Hartford CT: Yale, 1970).

Cane, Peter, *Atiyah's Accidents, Compensation and the Law* (6th edition, London: Butterworths, 1999).

Cane, Peter, 'Vicarious Liability for Sexual Abuse', 116 *Law Quarterly Review* (2000) 21 et seq.

Clements, Annie, *Legal Responsibility in Aquatics* (Aurora, OH: Sport and Law Press, 1997).

Conaghan, Joanne, and Mansell, Wade, *The Wrongs of Tort* (2nd edition, London: Pluto Press, 1999).

Curtis, Rick, *Outdoor Action Guide to Outdoor Safety Management* (Princeton, 1995).

Curtis, Rick, *The Backpacker's Field Manual* (New York: Three Rivers Press, 1998).

Davidson, Grant, 'Exploring the Myths: Analysis of incidents and accidents in professional outdoor education in New Zealand 1996-2000', *Journal of Adventure Education and Outdoor Learning*, vol 4, No. 1 (2004).

Deakin, Simon, Johnston, Angus, and Markesinis, Basil, *Tort Law* (5th edition, Oxford: OUP, 2003).

DfES, *Health and Safety of Pupils on Educational Visits* (HASPEV), first published in 1998, and supplements: *Standards for LEAs in Overseeing Educational Visits*, *Standards for Adventure*, *A Handbook for Group Leaders* and *Group Safety at Water Margins*.

DfES, *Every Child Matters: Working with voluntary and community organisations to deliver change for children and young people* (DfES/1123/2004).

DfES Guidance, *Health And Safety: Responsibilities And Powers* (Organisation & Management DfES/0803/2001, 2001).

Department for Education and Science, *Safety in Outdoor Education* (HMSO, 1989).

Dewees, Donald N, et al, *Exploring the Domain of Accident Law: Taking the Facts Seriously* (Oxford: OUP, 1996).

Dougherty, Neil J. IV (ed), *Outdoor Recreation Safety Book* (Champaign, IL: Human Kinetics Publishers, 1998).

Dugdale, Tony (ed), *Clerk & Lindsell on Torts* (18th edition, London: Sweet & Maxwell, 2001).

Fairgrieve, Duncan, and Green Sarah (eds), *Child Abuse Tort Claims Against Public Bodies* (Aldershot: Ashgate, 2004).

Ferrero, Franco, (ed) *BCU Canoe and Kayak Handbook* (Bangor: Pesda, 2002).

Ferrero, Franco, *Whitewater Safety and Rescue* (Bangor: Pesda, 1998).

Fleming, John G., *The Law of Torts* (8th edition, London: Sweet & Maxwell, 1992).

Fleming, John G., *The American Tort Process* (Oxford: OUP, 1988).

Forgey, William, *Basic Essentials of Hypothermia (Winter Sports)* (2nd edition, Globe Pequot Press, 1999), *Wilderness Medicine: Beyond First Aid* (5th edition: Globe Pequot Press, 1999).

Fotheringham, William, *Put Me Back On My Bike* (London: Yellow Jersey Press, 2002).

Fulbrook, Julian, 'Cycle helmets and contributory negligence', *Journal of Personal Injury Law* (issue 3, September 2004) 171 et seq.

Fyffe, Allen, and Peter, Iain, *The Handbook of Climbing* (London: Pelham, 1998).

Gardiner, Simon, et al, *Sports Law* (2nd edition, London: Cavendish, 2001).

Genn, Hazel, *Hard Bargaining: Out of Court Settlement in Personal Injury Actions* (Oxford: OUP, 1987).

Grace, Elizabeth, and Vella, Susan, *Civil Liability for Sexual Abuse and Violence in Canada* (Toronto: Butterworths, 2000).

Grayson, Edward, *Sport and the Law* (London: Lexis, 1988).

Hanna, Glenda, *Outdoor Pursuits Programming: Legal Liability and Risk management* (Edmonton: The University of Alberta Press, 1991).

Harlow, Carol, *State Liability: Tort Law and Beyond* (Oxford: OUP, 2004).

Hartley, Hazel J., *Exploring Sport and Leisure Disasters: a socio-legal perspective* (London: Cavendish, 2001).

HSC, *Guidance to the Licensing Authority on The Adventure Activities Licensing Regulations 1996* (HMSO: HSE Books, 1996).

HSE, *Five Steps to Risk Assessment* (HMSO: HSE Publications, 1994, 2004).

Hogan, Rob, 'The Crux Of Risk Management In Outdoor Programs – Minimising The Possibility Of Death And Disabling Injury', *Australian Journal of Outdoor Education*, vol 6, No. 2 (2002) 71-79.

Huber, Peter W., *Liability: The Legal Revolution and its Consequences* (New York: Basic Books, 1988).

Hunt, Lord Hunt of Llanfair Waterdine (ed), *In Search of Adventure, a study of opportunities for adventure and challenge for young people* (London: Talbot Adair Press, HMSO and the Royal Geographical Society, 1989).

Ison, Terence, *The Forensic Lottery: a critique on tort liability as a system of personal injury compensation* (London: Staples Press, 1967).

Jones, Michael A., *Torts* (8th edition, Oxford: OUP, 2002).

Kaiser, Ronald A., *Liability and Law in Recreation, Parks and Sports* (New York: Prentice-Hall, 1986).

Keay, Wally, *Duke of Edinburgh's Award Expedition Guide* (4th edition, HMSO, 2000).

Kevan, Tim, Adamson, Dominic, and Cottrell, Stephen, *Sports Personal Injury: Law and Practice* (London: Sweet & Maxwell, 2002).

Langmuir, Eric, *Mountaincraft and Leadership* (British Mountaineering Council, 1984).

Lewis, Adam, and Taylor, Jonathan, *Sport: Law and Practice* (London: LexisNexis, 2004).

Lewis, Richard, 'Insurers and Personal Injury Litigation', *Journal of Personal Injuries Law* [2005] 1/05 1 et seq.

Martinez, J. Michael, 'Liability and volunteer organizations: a survey of the law', *Nonprofit Management and Leadership* vol 14, No. 2, (2003) 151 et seq.

McKendrick, Ewan, 'Vicarious Liability and Independent Contractors – A Re-examination', 53 *Modern Law Review* (1990) 770.

Mortlock, Colin, *Adventure Education and Outdoor Pursuits* (self-published, 1973).

Ofsted report, *Outdoor Education: Aspects of Good Practice*, (September 2004, Office for Standards in Education, HMI 2151).

Pearson Royal Commission, *Report of the Royal Commission on Civil Liability and Compensation for Personal Injury* (1978) Cmnd. 7054.

Priest, Simon, and Gass, Michael A., *Effective Leadership in Adventure Programming* (Champaign, IL; Human Kinetics Publishers, 1997).

Prosser, William, and Keaton, W. Page, *The Law of Torts* (New York: West, 1984).

Raffan, James, *Deep Waters: Courage, Character and the Lake Timiskaming* (Toronto: Harper Collins, 2002).

Riffer, Jeffrey K., *Sports and Recreational Injuries* (New York: McGraw-Hill, 1985).

Rogers, W.H.V., *Winfield and Jolowicz on Tort* (16th edition, London: Sweet & Maxwell, 2002).

Royal County of Berkshire, *Report of the Altwood School Inquiry Panel* (Berks CC, 1989).

Slapper, Gary, *Blood in the Bank: social and legal aspects of death at work* (Aldershot: Ashgate Dartmouth, 1999).

Stewart, Doug, and Knott, Andrew, *Schools, Courts and the Law* (Melbourne: Pearson International, 2002).

Van der Smissen, Betty, *Legal Liability and Risk Management for Public and Private Entities* (Concinnati OH: Anderson, 1990).

Walbridge, Charlie. and Sundmacher, Wayne, *Whitewater Rescue Manual: New Techniques for Canoeists, Kayakers and Rafters* (Camden, ME: Ragged Mountain, 1995).

Walbridge, Charlie, and Tinsley, Jody, *River Safety Anthology* (Birmingham, AL: Menasha Ridge, 1996).

Weir, Tony, *Tort Law* (Oxford: OUP, 2002).

Wells, Celia, *Negotiating Tragedy: Law and Disasters* (London: Sweet & Maxwell, 1995).

Wells, Celia, *Corporations and Criminal Responsibility* (2nd edition, Oxford: OUP, 2001).

White, G. Edward, *Tort Law in America: an Intellectual History* (New York: OUP, 2003).

Williams, Glanville, and Hepple, Bob, *Foundations of the Law of Tort* (London: Butterworth, second edition 1984)

Index